Nov/03   29.95

INSPIRING WOMEN

INSPIRING WOMEN

A CELEBRATION OF HERSTORY

MONA HOLMLUND & GAIL YOUNGBERG

FOREWORD BY MARGARET ATWOOD

COTEAU BOOKS
WWW.COTEAUBOOKS.COM

Edited by Mona Holmlund and Gail Youngberg.

Cover and book design by Duncan Campbell.
Cover painting by Marie la France, mixed media © 2003 by the artist.
Printed and bound in Canada at Houghton Boston Lithographers, Saskatoon.

National Library of Canada Cataloguing in Publication Data

Inspiring women : a celebration of Herstory /
[edited by] Mona Holmlund & Gail Youngberg ; foreword by Margaret Atwood.

Compiled by the Saskatoon Women's Calendar Collective.
Includes bibliographical references and index.
ISBN 1-55050-204-2

1. Women—Canada—History. 2. Women—Canada—Biography.
I. Holmlund, Mona II. Youngberg, Gail III. Saskatoon Women's Calendar Collective.

HQ1453.I57 2003   305.4'0971   C2003-905094-7

1 2 3 4 5 6 7 8 9 10

401-2206 Dewdney Ave.
Regina, Saskatchewan
Canada   S4R 1H3

Available in the US and Canada from:
Fitzhenry & Whiteside
195 Allstate Parkway
Markham, Ontario
Canada   L3R 4T8

The publisher gratefully acknowledges the financial assistance of the Saskatchewan Arts Board, the Canada Council for the Arts, the Government of Canada through the Book Publishing Industry Development Program (BPIDP), the Government of Saskatchewan, through the Cultural Industries Development Fund, and the City of Regina Arts Commission, for its publishing program.

Since time began women have struggled
against tremendous odds to build houses,
not only clean them;
to create books as well as type them;
to serve communion as well as coffee;
to stand behind podia as well as pillars
and to utilize scalpels as well as scissors.
This is a long heroic story.
—Gail Corbett, 1975

Gail Ann Youngberg,
16 July 1939 - 18 December 2000

This book is dedicated to the memory of colleague, friend, and mentor
Gail Youngberg. Gail died before our project of many years was completed.
Her wit, wisdom, and intelligence are greatly missed. Her spirit infuses this book
and it is my hope that through its pages you will discover women who fascinate,
inspire, and encourage—women like Gail. —MONA HOLMLUND

TABLE OF CONTENTS

foreword

INSPIRING WOMEN

MARGARET ATWOOD

Nobody comes from nowhere. We all had grandmothers.

My own grandmother was born in the nineteenth century and died in the twentieth. During her lifetime of almost a hundred years, the possibilities open to women changed more dramatically than they'd changed in the thousand years before that. But "women" almost always means "some women," and although things changed for others, myself among them, they did not change much for her. For most of her life she lived on a small farm, made her own butter, kept chickens and a kitchen garden, cooked three meals daily on a wood stove, and slept under quilts she'd made herself. She raised five children, whom she taught to read by the light of a kerosene lamp. She worked a twelve-hour day, for which she was never paid a cent. Net worth in cash was not how she valued herself. Without her, I myself, in my present form—university graduate, writer, and so forth—would not have been possible. It was she who educated my father at home and encouraged him to go away to school—far away, both in space and in intellectual distance, because, like countless Canadian women of her kind and of her generation, she was left behind in many ways.

My other grandmother had a somewhat different trajectory—as a country doctor's wife in a more accessible area, she had "help," and got electricity earlier, and a telephone—but her story contained the same number of children, and the same long hours of unpaid work. She did have a paying job, once—as a young unmarried woman she worked as a secretary in Toronto, and had her purse stolen while standing on a street corner there. This story about her functioned as a kind of emblem: why pay women much, when what they were paid could so easily vanish? And when they themselves could so easily vanish from the workforce into marriage; for as one of my aunts said to me, "Marriage was what you did then." Not everyone did it, of course; and many did both it and something else. But achievement in the outside world, for women, was attained uphill, against the current. Its emotional costs were large.

For that generation, the relationship with money was custodial: they were not to earn it, but they were to manage it, and to save it. Having lived through the First War and the depression following it, then through the Great Depression of the 'thirties, then through the Second World War, these women were ruthless scrimpers. Everything was saved, and turned into something else. Nothing was wasted. And this was where I grew up, in the mental landscape of the turned collar and the casserole made from leftovers.

Words were saved, too. You didn't expend them, or strew them about carelessly. My grandmothers were frugal with their speech, one because she was shy, the other because she was tactful to the point of opacity. When she was in her eighties, I published my first novel, and a neighbour duly arrived at my grand-mother's house to complain about its scandalous nature. My grandmother smiled, and talked about the weather.

How far the more recent and more vocal generations of women have travelled on the credit earned for them by the silent and often desperate lives of others; lives lived still by many women, worldwide but also here. How little we know really about what goes on behind "the scene"—behind, that is, what we think we can see.

Herstory has been a long and lovingly prepared celebration of women's lives, Canadian women's lives, all sorts of them. These lives were lived sometimes in the full public glare of the political spotlight, with attendant ridicule and aggravation, and sometimes off to the side. All of these lives are noteworthy, all are courageous, all are different. Some would be unbelievable as fiction: you couldn't make them up. Read on, and be surprised.

THE HISTORY OF *HERSTORY*

Herstory began in 1972 in Saskatoon, Saskatchewan.

Five women—June Bantjes, Beth Foster, Gwen Morrison-Gray, Colleen Pollreis, and Erin Shoemaker—were students at the University of Saskatchewan. Several of them were single mothers who had returned to school later in life, juggling study, work, and family. Like many of their generation, these women were the inheritors of a decade of protest, a revolution touching every aspect of their lives. Women were re-examining their personal histories, rewriting themselves, so to speak, from a new perspective. "The personal is political" became both a slogan and a guiding principle. How did nice girls like us find ourselves in a place like this, they asked. Where we earn an average 67 cents on the dollar compared to what men earn? Where we are as scarce as hens' teeth in senior management levels everywhere we look? Where we are not safe in our own homes? When they turned to history for the answers, they found none.

In 1972, history, as defined by academic historians, was about white, male elites. Women were literally footnotes, mentioned only if they played some supporting role, or were "the wives of" prime ministers and governors general. There was little analysis of women's contribution or experience and almost nothing about "ordinary women." Women's lives were not seen as producing anything of historical interest. Women did not sign treaties, win elections, or fight battles. They left behind only traces of daily life in their letters, diaries, and drawings. And the vast majority of women would have had neither the education nor the leisure to produce even these meager artifacts.

It was in this environment that those first five women decided to do something. They formed the Saskatoon Women's Calendar Collective to create a Canadian women's calendar. They had never attempted commercial writing or publishing. They had no experience in doing historical research and they knew almost nothing about the history of Canadian women. But they pursued women's stories. Since there was little in the way of published material, they looked instead for books written by female authors, they interviewed local pioneers and sought out interesting women in the community and beyond.

They discovered local history rooms and archives and found a treasure trove in the papers of Violet McNaughton. They were encouraged by the tremendous excitement of discovering what so many Canadian women of the past had said and done. With little experience in research, with almost no material available, and working against the received notion of history, they created *Herstory: The Canadian Women's Calendar.*

In 1974, when the first Calendar appeared, many thought a publication written by a community-based cooperative with transient membership could not last; the fact that this Collective wrote about women made it only more unlikely. There have been some 50 women involved with *Herstory* since 1972. Twenty-nine editions have gone to press and onto bookshelves across the country. When the first volume of *Herstory* appeared, women's history was beneath notice; today it is a staple in most Canadian universities. As early as 1976 the Collective noted: "In its own small way the survival of *Herstory* reinforces what our research has taught us and what we have tried to share through this book: a growing respect for the hardihood and vigour of womankind."

Herstory has always been a labour of love. Work on the calendar has been organized around other priorities—studies, mothering, working at jobs—sometimes all of these at once. Some of *Herstory's* creators have worked on a single edition, others on many. Even in 1983 and 1984 when the publisher's failure and a lengthy search for a new one made publication impossible, the Collective remained strong. Their dedication to the project is exemplified by one 1979 member from northern Saskatchewan, who routinely travelled hours by bus in the middle of the night to attend meetings in Saskatoon. The Collective today is still committed to telling the story of women in Canada from a non-elite, non-academic point of view, using the best primary sources available.

Inspiring Women is a celebration of Canadian women sampled from the pages

Herstory HAS ALWAYS BEEN A LABOUR OF LOVE. WORK ON THE CALENDAR HAS BEEN ORGANIZED AROUND OTHER PRIORITIES—STUDIES, MOTHERING, WORKING AT JOBS—SOMETIMES ALL OF THESE AT ONCE.

of *Herstory* 1974-2000. It reflects the preoccupations and passions of the many women who have written these stories over 30 years. Like the calendars, this eclectic collection is national in scope, committed to representing the regional and cultural diversity of Canadian women, and reflecting the variety of endeavours, associations and issues in which women have been involved. It records not only outstanding achievements but also characteristic lives. It contains brief biographies of interesting women, quick takes on burning issues, historic photos, and comment on women's organizations. It reflects the idiosyncrasies of the members over the years and the wonderful variety of directions that research into Canadian women's history can take.

Women's history is a work in progress. We invite you to browse through these pages, making connections across time and theme—to see yourselves and the women around you in a new light. In doing so you will witness the development of *Herstory* as well as of the women it chronicles. *Herstory* is a record of growing consciousness. Vocabulary and interests fall in and out of fashion revealing cultural trends. You can see when women working on the *Herstory* project first used the terms "Ms" and "feminist" or took up specific causes. Varying styles highlight the fact that *Herstory* has been the work of dozens of authors since its inception. We have preserved the original *Herstory* profiles as much as possible to capture the breadth and depth of *Herstory's* investigations into Canadian women's stories before it became popular to do so. Many of those featured over the years are still achieving and accomplishing things of note, so stories have been updated to mark important changes or corrected as more information has come to light. A few subjects were revisited in our 25th Anniversary edition in 2000, and we have combined both profiles here. The original date of publication follows each entry so you can see when stories were uncovered and which contemporary caught the Collective's eye in 1975, or '85 or '95.

Herstory often celebrated important women before they came to national attention. You can see, for example, why *Herstory* was proud of Roberta Bondar even before she became Canada's first woman in space, or why we were reading Carol Shields' novels before she won the Pulitzer Prize.

As you read through these pages, we ask you to consider what it means for women to be "extraordinary." Do they do more than meet the expectations of their world? Do they prepare the way for others in addition to making their own? There is an inherent problem in trying to pour women into the moulds of traditional history—women tend not to be "just" doctors or physicists or reformers, as if, being a woman you can never be just one thing. Nellie McClung, for example, was a writer, a lecturer, a reformer, a politician, and a mother all at the same time. What that means for the organizer of an anthology on Canadian women's history is that whatever structure is chosen will be insufficient: the subjects, the issues and themes will insistently spill over into other categories, or sink below the surface to bob up and reappear elsewhere.

As we read through past editions of *Herstory: the Canadian Women's Calendar* a story emerged. We found that *Herstory* had been chronicling women's increasing participation in ever more complex levels of society. Women in Canada started out struggling to feed and clothe their families and have ended up writing the great Canadian novel. In this anthology we chart women's course from subsistence to cultural production. As we trace the building of a nation through individual lives, it is not a straightforward story of progress. The image to remember throughout the following chapters is one of waves that surge and recede. Women's history is also women's present. We were continually struck with how old some of the "new" topics are. The phrase "equal pay for work of equal value" figures in a National Council of Women's platform in 1920. In many instances, what women had already attained in status and influence would be revoked, only to be won again through hard-fought struggle. Women's history is fluid. As you glance through these pages you will follow its ebb and flow, and be carried along by the tide of impressive, courageous, and inspiring Canadian women.

In Chapter One—In the Beginning—we look at how women in Canada created a young nation in an old land. From the Aboriginal and Scandinavian women of prehistory to the European settlers, women have provided the basic stuff of life. For thousands of years women have been making this country by hand.

Chapter Two—A Great Race of Women—chronicles women's struggle to gain a voice in their new country. Once the nation was established, women found they now had political and legal battles to fight to regain the impact they had once had as a matter of course.

In Chapter Three—My Sister's Keeper—we see how women have always been on the vanguard of reform. Whether in their homes, their communities or globally, the women featured here have tried to make the world a better place.

Chapter Four—The Door Steadily Opens—celebrates the women who overcame tremendous obstacles to participate fully in the world. Many "firsts" are recorded here as homage to barriers broken and doors now open to all of us.

In Chapter Five—The Long Distance Race—we see what women can accomplish when they have seized the chance. Here we applaud women who have not only entered new professions—they have excelled at them.

Finally, in Chapter Six—Voices and Visions—we look at what women have to say for themselves. *Herstory* seems to have a soft spot for writers and artists—perhaps because, like the Collective, they speak of their experience and communicate it to the world. The freedom to do this is a far cry from the subsistence struggle of the first women in Canada. And in view of the plight of our sisters in parts of the world today, it is still a right to be cherished.

In 1972, five Saskatoon women decided that we all needed to know more about our foremothers. They imagined themselves laying the groundwork for others who would take up the challenge of discovering the stories of Canadian women. But did they dream that 2003 would see *Herstory* still thriving?

We wonder if they realized how strong would be their voice and how compelling their example. We are sure they knew well, as have all the Collective's women, how powerful it is to discover and commemorate together the great things women have done, and are doing—and can do. *Inspiring Women: A Celebration of* Herstory is answer to that clarion call and the courageous ambitions of the founding five. We hope it will inspire you, as it has us, to learn more, and do more, to create women's history. *Herstory* looks forward to another century of writing the lives of Canadian women, reclaiming them from the past, and celebrating them as they change the course of our future.

A STORY OF CREATION

In the beginning there was nothing but the wide, wide sea and the animals that live in and on the water. Then out of the sky world fell a woman—a divine person.

As she fell, two loons flew beneath her and, joining together, carried her safely upon their backs. They cried to the other animals for help, and soon the other creatures had gathered together.

Then Great Turtle emerged from the council and told the others to place the divine woman upon his broad back. The council discussed what could be done to save the woman, and soon they decided she must have earth to live on. So Great Turtle sent the many creatures down to the bottom of the sea to bring up some earth. Many dived below, but came back with nothing. At last Toad descended into the waters, and when he finally returned, Great Turtle found some earth in his mouth. This he gave to the woman.

Taking the earth, she carefully moulded it and placed it all around the edge of Great Turtle's shell. On all sides this earth grew and spread, until it formed a great land where trees and plants could grow. So the earth was created, and to this day Great Turtle carries the earth on his broad back.

In time, the woman gave birth to twins. These twins were very different from one another, and fought even before they were born. One said he was willing to be born in the usual manner, but the other said he was not. He broke through his mother's side and killed her.

So she was buried in the earth which she had formed, and from her body grew the plants which would feed the human beings yet to be created. From her head grew the pumpkin vine; from her breasts the corn; and from her limbs grew beans.

The twins, who were known as Evil Brother and Good Brother, continued to prepare the earth for the people who would live there, and often struggled with one another. And though the woman had died, Good Brother continued to be aided by her powerful spirit.

This story is told by the Hurons and the Six Nations of the Iroquois Confederacy.
[HS-1982]

CHAPTER I

IN THE BEGINNING

History is made of the stories we choose to tell about ourselves. Canada is a country with many peoples, and many different traditions about our beginnings. We are a small nation that has many nations within it. We are a huge country, with room for an immensely varied and complex geography of both land and peoples, and we seem determined to take full advantage of our opportunities. Here is a selection of some of the stories told in *Herstory* of the origins of Canada, and the part women played in those beginnings.

We know very little about the lives of women in Canada prior to European contact, the Native women on whose shoulders much of the material culture of the original inhabitants rested. These are the women who shared the hardships of early exploration and settlement, who were instrumental in bridging the old and new societies, and who founded a new nation. In trying to reclaim a story that has been lost, we acknowledge we can't tell it fully. The records of later settlers may help us to surmise what life was like for the Aboriginal women who lived here for thousands of years before western history began its chronicles.

This is the story behind the story of Canada's development. By reconstructing women's experiences of nation building, we realize the enormous scope of their contribution. What follows is an account of their tremendous, but often unsung, role in the creation of the social order in Canada—a tale of making a country by hand. We celebrate here the pioneer spirit of our foremothers—the women who gathered berries, snared rabbits, cleaned fish, planted seeds, preserved food, tanned leather, plowed fields, milked cows, churned butter, baked bread, made, washed and mended clothes, cut sod, bore children, tended the sick, endured privation and isolation and survived to become our grandmothers and heroes.

opposite: Alice Hagar with baby Rosie (left) and Mary Hagar with baby Bella (right) at Mayo, Yukon, 1937

WOMEN OF THE BLACKFOOT

"The women of our camp were continually at work, gathering wild berries and firewood, cooking, dressing skins, and making clothes...They enjoyed their work, smoking, gossiping, and feasting. The lodge covers were so large that one woman could not handle them alone. It was the custom for a number of women to cooperate, making it a social affair with light refreshments. When the women finished at one lodge, they moved on to another...a Mother trained her daughter from childhood in tanning skins and making them into clothes and shelter; also in the knowledge of herbs and wild vegetables, which were used for eating and healing. Women considered this their special vocation, and allowed no interference from the men, who were unfitted for the work." —*Blackfoot tribe, as observed by Walter McClintok, ca 1896*

THE HOLY WOMEN

Among the people of the Blackfoot Nation, the legend of the medicine lodge says that the Sun is the main representative of the Creator, and that long ago people were taken up to the Sun to bring blessings back to the people on earth. Much of the religion of the Blackfoot centres around the legends and ceremonies brought back from the Sun. The ancient Sun Dance, or medicine lodge ceremonies, comprise their most sacred religious events.

Women played an important part in these sacred ceremonies, for it was the holy women who always acted as sponsors of the Sun Dance, women who had led upstanding and virtuous lives, above reproach. Each holy woman who sponsored a Sun Dance represented one of the legendary messengers of the Sun. They were known as Sun Women, and the lodges they sponsored were known as Sun Lodges.

All the bands of the tribe gathered together in the summer to build these lodges; in the old days this was often the only time of year when all the bands congregated. It was a great spiritual event. For four days pre-

ceding the building of the medicine lodge, the holy women fasted and did ceremonial work. Most of these ceremonies were performed in private, but toward the close of the rites, the teepee of the holy woman was opened so that all could view the Natoas, the sacred headdress, being fastened on her head.

In the old days, four or more women would often vow to build the Sun Dance for the same year, and all

above: Blind Blackfoot woman with travois

I think it would help the present world situation if we all learned to value and respect the way of the grandmothers—our own as well as everybody else's.
—Beverly Hungry Wolf, 1980

right: Snake People Woman, of the Blood Nation, wears the ceremonial headdress of a member of the secret women's Motokikis Society

of them went through the entire ceremony together. Inside the Sun Lodge, everyone could go before the holy woman and receive some of the blessings sent down from the Sun.

This revered position reflected and led to special standing in the tribe for women. Although the Sun Dance is no longer held every year as it once was, the elder holy women among the Blackfoot continue to initiate their younger successors into carrying on this sacred tradition. [HS-1982]

WOMAN OF NOOTKA SOUND

In the mild, damp climate of the Pacific coast, clothing made of vegetable fibres was far more practical—largely water and mildew proof—than leather. This woman's cloak (above) is woven of shredded inner cedar bark. The band of fur at the neck is for both decoration and protection against the coarse bark. Her hat is woven of split spruce roots, decorated with killer whales and canoes.

T he first of the exploring European nations to come to this part of the world were the Norse, some of whom had left the Scandinavian peninsula that was their homeland and moved westward across the Atlantic to establish colonies first in Iceland, then in Greenland. According to oral traditions, preserved in their song-stories or sagas, some of the more adventurous of them eventually reached what they called Vinland, and what we know as Newfoundland. Among them was Gudrid.

GUDRID

Born in 980 AD, Gudrid spent her childhood and youth in the west of Iceland, later moving to the newly colonized Greenland with her first husband. Although Thorer died before the winter was out, Gudrid remained in Greenland. Several years later she married Thornstein, a son of Erik the Red. The couple attempted an exploratory trip to Vinland but were thwarted by a severe storm. At the end of that winter Thornstein died, and Gudrid made her home with Leif the Lucky.

In 1006 the twice-widowed woman married Karlsefni, a wealthy merchant trader. She and others persuaded him to send an expedition to Vinland, and so a party of 160 people, including five women, set off to form a colony. The new party settled in Leif's empty houses [from a previous expedition] on the south shore of the Strait of Belle Isle. That first autumn, in 1007, Gudrid gave birth to her first child [a son, Snorri] and became the first mother in the colony.

During the third winter in Vinland, discontent, jealousy, and distrust rumbled through the colony. A council was held, and it was decided that they would return to Greenland. Gudrid lived with her husband in Greenland until his death. When her son had grown, she travelled to Rome, then returned to Iceland to enter a monastery and live a life of seclusion.

The sagas tell us that Gudrid was a beautiful woman "distinguished in everything she did," that she was a bold explorer, and that she was one of the first colonizers of Canada. [HS-1978]

right: Gudrid, as imagined by Patricia Wilson Johnston

left: "Woman of Nootka Sound," drawn in 1778 by J. Webber, artist with the Cook expedition

...les qualités que l'on refusait la femme, telles que la rigueur intellectuelle, ou la capacité d'administrer ou de diriger, furent celles qu'elle mit en relief avec éclat au sein des communautés religieuses. —Michèle Jean

right: Marie Guyart de L'Incarnation

This chapter reveals women's staggering resourcefulness in the face of seemingly endless want—and opportunity. These "Mothers of Confederation" were, as always, just doing what needed to be done. In Canada's early days it was often the women who established the first schools, hospitals, and businesses.

MARIE GUYART DE L'INCARNATION

In 1639, after a three-month voyage over pirate-infested seas, Sister Marie de l'Incarnation arrived at the site of the tiny Iroquois settlement of Stadacona, that was to grow into the city of Quebec during her lifetime. There, in an unheated borrowed shack that she called her "Louvre," Marie founded the first Ursuline convent school in New France devoted to teaching Indian and French girls.

Born in 1599 in Tours, France, Marie wanted to become a nun from an early age, but was married off at 17. Widowed two years later, with an infant son to care for, she refused to remarry and went to live with her sister and brother-in-law, who were in charge of a large transportation company. Marie had a genius for business and before long managed the whole enterprise. She continued to do so for ten years, until she became an Ursuline nun in spite of fierce opposition from her family, including her young son.

Commanded by a vision to become a missionary in Canada, Marie built a convent in Quebec in 1642. Eight years later the building burned to the ground while the nuns chanted a *Te Deum* barefoot in the snow. The convent was rebuilt against immense financial odds, thanks to Marie's talent as business administrator.

Marie de l'Incarnation became the friend of governors, intendants, and other notables, who regularly consulted her on political and economic matters. She learned the Algonkin and Iroquois languages and composed dictionaries and grammars for them. In 1654 she published *Relation*, a spiritual autobiography that ranks her among the greatest mystics of the Roman Catholic Church. Her correspondence, numbering over 12,000 letters, is an irreplaceable document of colonial history. [HS-1978]

below: "Micmac Woman," 1865, probably Christianne Paul Morris, ca 1804-1886, of Nova Scotia, who was renowned for her great skills in all the Native crafts

JEANNE MANCE

Jeanne Mance was one of Canada's greatest woman colonists. A superb administrator, she combined practicality and vision instrumental to the survival of one of Canada's earliest European settlements—that of Ville-Marie [which the Iroquois called Hochelaga], now known as Montreal.

Her family, of French bourgeois stock, was horrified when she announced her intention to work in France's new colony. It was a highly unusual choice for a young woman of her class, but she was not to be dissuaded.

She offered her services as a nurse, but her natural ability in organization and administration, coupled with the impracticality of those financing the colony, meant that she was gradually required to play a more important role.

She left France for Quebec City in 1641, and in the following year, with a band of 40 men and women, travelled up the St Lawrence to the settlement. There they pitched their tents, put up a palisade of pickets as protection against hostile Indians, and began their mission-colony.

Jeanne's duties were to take charge of Ville-Marie's hospital, to supervise supplies for the colony, to organize their communal household, and to care for the sick and wounded. There were years when the fort was almost constantly under siege, and at one time, close to half of the colonists had been killed, captured, or disabled by the Iroquois. As a consequence, she also cared for a number of orphaned children.

But her greatest contribution was to solidify the colonization company's shaky financial foundations. Even before she first left for New France, she devised a promotion scheme that put the company on a firm financial footing. In the years that followed, there were other financial crises: Jeanne was required to return to France three times to help reorganize the company's affairs. She died in 1673. [HS-1978]

MARGUERITE BOURGEOYS

Marguerite Bourgeoys came to New France in 1653, a member of La Congrégation Notre Dame. She was to be a teacher for the children of the French settlers. However, when she arrived in Montreal, she found that few of the infants born in the colony had survived. Marguerite went to work helping Jeanne Mance care for the sick at the Hôtel Dieu and visited the settlers' homes, teaching mothers how to care for their children and their homes. Five years later she opened the doors of her school—a

left: "Ojibway Woman and Child," engraved from a photograph taken in 1858 by H.L. Hime, photographer to the Assiniboine and Saskatchewan exploring expedition led by Henry Hind

remodelled stone stable—to nine pupils. In following years she made successive trips to France to recruit more sisters; in 1670, she founded a teaching order on Canadian soil.

Marguerite's leadership proved vital in setting up many social organizations in New France. In Quebec and Montreal, she founded institutions known as La Providence, in which girls were taught arts and crafts to enable them to earn their living. Under her direction several schools were opened, including a boarding school in 1673, and a school for the Iroquois in 1676. Thirteen years later, she opened a general hospital in Montreal, where the sick and indigent could be taught a trade.

At the time of Marguerite's death in 1700, her small order of nuns had grown to include 39 women, though the road was not always easy. While the order had been authorized by Louis XIV in 1671, it was not approved by Bishop Laval of New France until 1676. And it was not until 1698 that 24 nuns took their first vows. Bishop Laval and his successor were not favourably disposed towards the new order's independence. Marguerite and her sisters had to withstand constant pressures from all sides wanting them to become a cloistered order. Fortunately for New France, these dedicated sisters realized the needs of the colony, and maintained their active involvement in the community. [HS-1977]

left: Marguerite Bourgeoys

History that includes women will be the history of family relationships and ordinary life. The feminist enterprise is nothing less than restructuring society, a rebuilding perhaps best undertaken from the ground up. Knowing our foremothers' lives tells us where we have come from, what we have to build on. It is essential information. —Herstory 2000

Even in this relatively enlightened century, the human condition continues to be considered as something quite apart from the female condition.—Maxine Nunes and Deanna White, 1972

SARA KIRKE

The records of early European settlement in Newfoundland hold some tantalizing traces of women who exercised considerable social and economic power in the tiny colony, but whose personal stories have never been recorded.

One of these is Sara Kirke, who appears in the census of 1676 as "The Lady Kerke," and in 1677 as "Lady Sara Kirke." She was married to David Kirke, adventurer and conqueror of Quebec (1629) and first governor of the island (1636-52). The son of a merchant, Kirke was knighted in 1633 by Charles 1 of England.

By the time Lady Kirke appears in the census records she had been a widow for 20 years and had herself assumed the role of a "planter," managing the family's lands and fishing facilities at Ferryland in the Avalon Peninsula. In the late 1670s she is recorded as having from 16 to 25 servants (many of whom would have worked in the fishery); four or five boats; one "stage" (a tidewater structure for handling fish); and four "rooms"—a shore-side property. A map of 1663 shows "Lady Kirk" in possession of the "plantation," as the shore-based settlements were called, on the south side of the harbour at Ferryland.

Altogether, Lady Kirke appears to have been in charge of the family fortunes for approximately 30 years. She had accompanied her husband when he was

recalled to England as a Royalist after the Cromwellian Revolution. She was allowed to return to Newfoundland to superintend his business, while he remained in prison, where he died in 1654.

Sara Kirke was not the only woman managing a "plantation" in Newfoundland at the time. "Lady Hopkins" appears in the census as well, apparently employing 15 men and possessing 15 head of cattle. Another woman, with 20 men and four boats, appears simply as "Wm Roberts Wife." Were it not for these few records, we would have no idea what a significant role women played in 17th-century Newfoundland. [HS-1990]

By decree of Louis XIV, the law in New France was essentially the same as the Custom of Paris. Under this custom, marriage created a community of property between the spouses. By contrast, English law decreed that a married woman's property belonged outright to her husband. Furthermore, the Custom of Paris did not dissolve the marital community of property on the death of one spouse. In other words, a widow continued to own the property she and her husband had owned during their marriage. Again, English law permitted widows only a small portion.

These provisions of the customary law helped to make it possible for enterprising French women to own property and establish businesses [see p. 42].

[see p. 42]

The law is a reflection of public sentiment, and when people begin to realize that women are human and have human needs and ambitions and desires, the law will protect a woman's interest.
—Nellie McClung, 1915

Map: Kirke lands at Ferryland on the Avalon Peninsula, Newfoundland ca 1663

MADAME DE REPENTIGNY

Early in 1705 news arrived in the small colony of New France that the *Seine,* the ship bringing the year's supplies for the colony, had been wrecked. Among the supplies which would be most sorely missed were bolts of fabric for clothing. To avert the potential crisis, Agathe de Saint-Père, Mme de Repentigny, stepped in and set up a native cloth manufactory.

Since the age of fifteen, when she had taken over the raising of her orphaned brothers and sisters, Agathe de Saint-Père had been managing people and money. Her easy-going husband left her free to manage the family fortunes. She bought and sold land, signed contracts and made loans in her own name, made a profit in the fur trade, and settled her husband's and brothers-in-law's debts.

When the potential clothing crisis struck the colony, Agathe was well prepared to cope. She had already experimented with fibres derived from nettles, bark, cottonweed, and buffalo hair. Agathe ransomed nine English weavers from captivity with the Indians, and set them to work at looms in her own home. With an eye to the future, she assigned French apprentices to learn the trade, and, using the single loom she had for a pattern, had twenty others built and established around Montreal. Once her workers were in production, Agathe's factories turned out some 120 ells of coarse cloth and canvas per day.

Agathe continued with her experiments, discovering new native dyes and new processes for fixing the colours in her fabrics. She also devised new processes for dyeing deerskins, the other major clothing material. By the time her English weavers were ransomed again, by colonists in Boston, Agathe's French apprentices were well enough trained to take over the looms and keep the industry going.

By 1713 the native industry was well-established, and the clothing crisis in the colony was over. The King had granted Agathe an annuity of 200 *livres* for her services to the colony. Little is known of Agathe's activities after she sold her cloth business, but she must have continued to manage her fortunes well. When she died, in 1747 or 1748, at the age of 90, she left a substantial legacy to the convent where she had spent her last years. [HS-1986]

MARIE-ANNE BARBEL

A good example of a widow carrying on the family business is Marie-Anne Barbel, Mme Fornel. Marie-Anne Barbel married Louis Fornel in 1723. The couple had 14 children, whose care must have absorbed most of Marie-Anne's time during her marriage. However, Louis died in 1745, and Marie-Anne took over the administration of the family business. The Fornel business interests were far-ranging and complex, including sealing at Hamilton Inlet on the Labrador coast, fur trading at Tadoussac, and real estate in Quebec City.

Marie-Anne expanded the business interests that Louis had established, and embarked on new ventures. During the late 1740s, the war with England interrupted the shipping of earthenware from France, so Marie-Anne established a pottery business in a building she owned in Quebec's Lower Town. Her products, well-made and well finished, were immediately successful, and she continued in the business until at least 1752. [HS-1987]

LES HABITANTES

"The Habitans have almost every resource within their own families. They cultivate flax, which they manufacture into linen; and their sheep supply them with wool, of which their garments are formed. They tan the hides of their cattle, and make them into moccasins and boots. From woollen yarn they knit their own stockings and bonnets rouge, and from straw they make their summer hats and bonnets. Besides articles of wearing apparel, they make their own bread, butter, and cheese; their soap, candles, and sugar; all of which are supplied from the productions of their farm."— From John Lambert's *Travels Through Lower Canada...in the Years 1806, 1807, 1808* [HS-1992]

right: Habitante in her summer dress, 1810

War, whether waged between national armies, or at the level of local raids, was a fact of life and death for women in early Canada, whether European or Native. They endured, occasionally participated, and sometimes triumphed.

MOLLY BRANT—KONWATSI'TSAIÉNNI

Molly Brant [Konwatsi'tsaiénni] was a Mohawk who served as a spy for the British in the 18th century. Molly was born around 1736. She spoke English fluently and was a skillful writer. As a member of the Iroquois, she grew up in an environment which treated women with great respect. It was believed that family honours passed to men from their mothers, and that women possessed the wisdom to guide important decisions.

Molly became the wife of William Johnson in 1753, according to Mohawk rites. Mother of eight children, she was also adviser to Sir William in his dealings with the great Mohawk nation. Following his death in 1774, Molly carried on the work, providing information to the British about troop movements in the rebel American camps. When the revolutionary forces discovered her activity, she was forced to flee to Niagara with her children. There her home became a gathering place, where leaders of the Six Nations conferred about developments on the other side of the border.

Molly's brother, the great chief Joseph Brant, [Thayendanegea], for whom Brantford was named, consulted her regularly for advice.

Her dedication and bravery were a result of the great sense of loyalty she felt for two cultures. When she died in 1796, there was little recognition of the contribution she had made to Canadian history. [HS-1980]

[In recent years, as more information has come to light, *Herstory* has made an effort to recover the stories of Aboriginal women. Molly Brant's real name was Konwatsi'tsaiénni. She was born at Cayahoga (near Akron, Ohio, in the modern United States), in the Mohawk nation. Her husband, a British landowner and militia officer in the Mohawk Valley, was the first superintendent of northern Indian affairs for the British Crown. She advised him regarding the Iroquois or Six Nations League, and in turn encouraged them to keep their alliance with the Crown. She also managed the family estate during her husband's frequent absences, and became the head of the women's society within the League. She and her brother Thayendanegea had hoped to unite the Indian nations to block the expansion of the American colonies westward. Thayendanegea was a war chief during the Seven Years' War and again during the hostilities against the American revolutionaries. He was commissioned a captain by the British in 1780. Their dream of security for Indian nations was prevented, however, by factions among the Indians, opposition by the Americans, and betrayal by the British. After the war, in 1784, Thayendanegea and his people settled on a tract of land on the Grand River in Upper Canada (now Ontario) granted by the Crown in compensation for their losses. Konwatsi'tsaiénni continued to be an influential advisor on all matters of importance on both sides of the border. She retired to Cataraqui (Kingston, Ontario), where she died. Her role in the protection of "British North America"—largely neglected by the settlers who were her beneficiaries—made her one of the most important women of her time. Eds.]

At the same time Konwatsi'tsaiénni was struggling to find security for her people amid the upheavals created by conflicts among newcomers to North America, Samuel Hearne, an English explorer working for the Hudson's Bay Company north of 60°, recorded the story of a Dene woman captured by enemies.

THE SURVIVOR

"On the eleventh of January...my companions...discovered a young woman....She proved to be one of the Western Dogribbed Indians...taken prisoner by the Athapuscow Indians....[She] had eloped from them, with an intent to return to her own country; but the distance being so great, and having...been carried in a canoe the whole way, the turnings and windings of the

Our identity is our culture, our language, and our land, and we watch helplessly as we see a part slipping away.
—Jella Alikatuktuk,
Inuit woman from
Broughton Island

below: "O-ma-ma-ma, Earth Mother of the Cree," as imagined by unknown artist

rivers and lakes were so numerous, that she forgot the track; so she built the hut in which we found her, to protect her from the weather during the Winter, and here she had resided from the first setting in of the fall....

"She had been near seven months without seeing a human face...she had supported herself very well by snaring partridges, rabbits, and squirrels...beaver and some porcupines....She did not seem to have been in want...as she had a small stock of provisions by her when she was discovered; and was in good health and condition.

"It is scarcely possible to conceive that a person in her forlorn situation could be so composed as to be capable of contriving or executing any thing that was not absolutely necessary to her existence; but there were sufficient proofs that she had extended her care much farther, as all her clothing, besides being calculated for real service, shewed great taste, and exhibited no little variety or ornament....

"Her leisure hours...had been employed in twisting the inner rind or bark of willows into small lines...of which she had some hundred fathoms by her; with this she intended to make a fishing net...

"Five or six inches of an iron hoop, made into a knife, and the shank of an arrow-head of iron...were all the metals this poor woman had with her when she eloped; and with these implements she had made herself complete snow-shoes, and several other useful articles.

"Her method of making a fire was...two hard sulphurous stones. These, by long friction and hard knocking, produced a few sparks...she did not suffer her fire to go out all the Winter....

"When the Athapuscow Indians took [her]...they killed every soul in the tent, except herself and three other young women....Her young child...she concealed in a bundle of clothing, and took it with her; but...one of the [Athapuscow] women took it from her, and killed it....

"This...gave her such a disgust...that she rather chose to expose herself to misery and want, than live in ease and affluence among persons who had...murdered her infant....

"This woman told us...that she had never seen metal, till she was taken prisoner."—*January 1772, south side of Athapuscow [Great Slave] Lake* [HS-1989]

LAURA INGERSOLL SECORD

Laura Secord is, to most Canadians, a silhouette on a chocolate box. The real woman is not so well known. Born in Massachusetts in 1775, she moved to Canada when she was 20, where, in 1797, she married James Secord. When the war of 1812 broke out, James, the son of a Loyalist officer, joined the militia. When he was wounded at Queenston Heights, Laura found him on the battlefield and helped him home.

He was still an invalid some months later, when Laura overheard some American officers planning to ambush a British outpost at Beaver Dams. Unable to find a man to take a warning, she went herself. Laura walked for the whole of a hot summer day over rough country, avoiding the roads and afraid of encounter-

above: Laura Secord delivers her message, as imagined by C.W. Jefferys

I am now advanced in years and when I look back I wonder how I could have gone through so much fatigue, with the fortitude to accomplish it.—Laura Ingersoll Secord, 1853

ing enemy soldiers. She reached Beaver Dams in time, and the American plan failed.

After the war, Laura and her husband claimed financial reward for their services to the Crown. James eventually acquired a patronage post, which helped the family until he died in 1841, but Laura's contribution was dismissed as insignificant. Laura stubbornly con-

tinued to push her claim. In 1860, when she was 85, she insisted on being included among the veterans of the War of 1812 who presented an address to the Prince of Wales during his tour of Canada. The Prince was impressed by her case and sent her £100.

From then on, and especially after her death in 1868, Laura's legend grew. In 1913, the centennial of her walk, a new candy company adopted her name for its products. By the 1920s, the story was so embellished that serious historians began to dismiss it as near-fiction. Perhaps Laura Secord's true importance lies in what her story tells us about how history treats women. The stubborn old lady who only wanted her fair share of the patronage rewards was too real and too much like a man. She had to be turned into a noble heroine, not very real, but sweet enough for a candy box. [HS-1996]

[Monuments to Laura Secord's exploit stand in Lundy's Lane, Niagara Falls, and on Queenston Heights, Ontario. Eds.]

MIKAK

A young Inuk named Mikak was one of fashionable London's sensations for the "season" of 1768-69. Mikak and a group of her people had been taken prisoner after a skirmish with the soldiers of Fort York, Labrador. She had learned English during the year she was a prisoner in the fort. In the fall of 1768, the Governor of Newfoundland ordered Mikak and two boys taken to England, where they could be impressed with the power of the English and the wisdom of co-operating with them.

Eighteenth-century European intellectuals were fascinated by the idea of "noble savages," and London society received Mikak with considerable interest. The Princess of Wales gave her a dress trimmed with gold lace.

left: "An Eskimo Woman," by Angelica Kauffman, ca 1770. The woman's parka of seal fur with a wide boot to carry her child was a typical garment of the Labrador Inuit of the 18th century

Mikak used her familiarity with the English nobility to urge the cause of the Moravian Brethren, who wished to set up a mission in Labrador. She had met these missionaries some years earlier, and was impressed both by their preaching and by the trouble they had taken to learn the Inuit language. Before her return to Labrador Mikak learned that the Moravians had received a charter for their mission. Several years later, when the Moravians arrived on the Labrador coast, Mikak met them wearing her European gown and accompanied by her new husband, an influential shaman. Mikak and her husband helped the missionaries to select a site and establish their mission.

Her forceful personality and intelligence, her knowledge of faraway places, and her impressive appearance in the golden gown combined to make Mikak an important person among her people. She influenced their decision to allow the Moravians to establish a mission, and helped to draw more of the Inuit to listen to the missionaries. She remained her own woman, however, and did not convert until the end of her life. After some years, during which the missionaries saw little of her, Mikak returned to their post in 1795. There she finally accepted Christianity and, shortly afterwards, died. [HS-1986]

F ew events in Canadian history are more tragic than the extermination of the Beothuk tribe of what is now Newfoundland. Shawnadithit was the last of her people.

SHAWNADITHIT

The Beothuks had adapted to coastal life in Newfoundland, but, as the Dorset Eskimos began moving southward [in about 500 BC], the Beothuks retreated inland in deference to these skilful invaders. The arrival of Europeans later forced them to move yet again, this time in a northerly direction. Here they were placed in direct conflict with a group of immi-

grants, many of whom were fugitives from the law in their homeland. The frontier spirit prevailed, and the slaughter of the Beothuks, often in a brutal and unmerciful fashion, occurred with disturbing frequency. According to some historians, many also died at the hands of the Micmac Indians, armed by the Europeans. As well, the tribe had no immunity to tuberculosis, and hundreds died from the disease. Many succumbed to the starvation which resulted from increased demand upon local sources of food.

By 1820, only 20 Beothuks remained alive. Three years later, Shawnadithit, her mother, and sister were captured by Sir John Peyton and taken to St John's. Some concerned individuals who realized the impending fate of the tribe felt it best to safeguard the lives of the three survivors. However, their protectors seemed uncertain as to the best course of action, and the three women were returned to Red Indian Lake. Historical accounts differ on the exact time of the deaths of the mother and sister, but agree that tuberculosis took their lives. Unsuccessful in her search for other survivors, Shawnadithit returned to St John's, where she served as a domestic in Peyton's home. During this time, attempts were made on her life, as one local inhabitant sought to reach the 100 mark in the number of Beothuks he had killed.

While in Peyton's employ, Shawnadithit was approached by William Cormack, a scholar, who had established the Beothuk Institute for the protection of the tribe in 1827. She supplied him with drawings and verbal descriptions which represent the most reliable source of information on the culture and lifestyle of her people. Without her careful record and detailed sketches, we would have nothing to remind us of these early inhabitants of the east coast. Shawnadithit, the last surviving Beothuk, died in June 1829 of tuberculosis. [HS-1982]

A portrait of Shawnadithit's fellow captive, Demasduit, survives in the Public Archives of Canada, painted by Henrietta, Lady Hamilton, ca 1819. Lady Hamilton refers to her subject as "Mary March, a female Native Indian of the Red Indians who inhabit Newfoundland..." so named, she records, because she was always "merry" and was "found" in March. [HS-1985]

above: Portrait of Demasduit, "Mary March" ca 1796-1820

The experience of all oppressed groups is that it is not in the interest of the oppressor to give up the power.
—Shirley Finson, ca 1982

above: *Marie Marguerite d'Youville*

Women's capacity to make the necessities of life with the work of their hands, and for simply making do, provided essential service to individuals, families, and the nation in the early centuries. The fabric of Canadian society was woven by their energy, their determination and their deeds.

THE GREY NUNS/SISTERS OF CHARITY AND MARIE MARGUERITE D'YOUVILLE

The pioneering spirit and dedicated work of the Sisters of Charity, the Grey Nuns, exemplify the important contributions of women in building this country. Founded in Canada, by a Canadian, on little more than physical energy, determination, and the will to be of service, the Order continues from generation to generation its proud heritage of service to those in need. The Order had its beginning in 1737, when a poor Montreal widow, Marie Marguerite d'Youville, and three others dedicated their lives to the needy. Women were not allowed in the city's hostel for the poor; Mme d'Youville took them into her home. In 1747 the small group took over operation of Montreal's Hôpital Général, complete with derelict building and large debt; soon after, they took in their first "patients."

Their grey robes occasioned some insults, since "gris(e)" also means "tipsy" in French and the women were known to work with alcoholics. The fine reputation of "les Soeurs grises" grew, however, with their hard work and courage under abject conditions. "Go to the Grey Nuns; they will help you," became a catch-phrase.

In 1844 Bishop Provencher arrived from the Red River settlement, needing Sisters to run his girls' school. No fewer than 17 volunteered for the difficult journey of over 2,000 km by canoe. One can scarcely imagine the thoughts of the four chosen pioneers, leaving family and friends, setting out for the unknown.

Within 20 years the order had moved into what is now northern Saskatchewan and Alberta. By the 1930s, a hospital was operating in Chesterfield Inlet, NWT. At the end of this century their work goes on from New England to the remote North, and in missions in South America.

The Nuns undertook to educate, not only the Red River children and others, but also Aboriginal populations. They helped adults learn life skills and home crafts. They shared music and creative talents. They cared for the sick, the elderly, the abandoned. They founded hospitals in all the present-day large Prairie cities, and became the West's first nursing order.

For over two centuries, they have given help and hope, responding in traditional and innovative ways to the emerging needs of society. [HS-1976, 2000]

By their work of bearing numerous children and of maintaining life and home, women made possible the survival both of the people themselves and the colony [New France].
—The Corrective Collective, in *Never Done*, 1974

...in America, of all countries in the world, prosperity depends on female industry.
—Emily Shaw Beavan, 1845

ÉLISABETH BRUYÈRE

In 1845, Bytown (now Ottawa) was a rugged lumber town of 6,000, without adequate schools, hospitals or support for the poor. The Sisters of Charity (Grey Nuns) of Montreal accepted the Roman Catholic Bishop of Kingston's request to establish an order there; four nuns traveled to Bytown in February 1845. Twenty-six-year-old Élisabeth Bruyère was elected superior.

Élisabeth's father had died when she was four; her mother supported her seven children by working as a housekeeper. Élisabeth attended Notre Dame School until her mother's cousin, a priest, supervised her education, in a time when few young women were educated. She joined the Grey Nuns in 1839.

The day after arriving in Bytown, the Sisters began visiting the sick and destitute. In March, they opened the first school for girls; in May, the first "hospital and home." Twenty days later, presented with an abandoned child, they established an orphanage. By the end of 1845 they had 238 students, fourteen patients, fourteen orphans, and were nursing 250 patients at home.

Because the Kingston diocese offered little financial assistance, the Sisters regularly sewed and laundered clothing in order to earn money. In addition to poverty and exhaustion, they coped with religious and cultural tensions. In 1847, immigrants brought typhus to Bytown. During the epidemic, Élisabeth contracted with the Immigration Office to nurse the sick in a lazaretto built on their land. Seventeen of her 21 sisters were afflicted but survived. In spite of obstacles, they continued to serve everyone in need.

Under Mother Bruyère's direction, schools multiplied in Ottawa, Ontario, Quebec, and New York State. Construction began on the Ottawa General Hospital in 1860 (now the Élisabeth Bruyère Health Centre); substantial shelters for single women, the orphaned, the destitute, and the elderly were built; and the religious community expanded.

Élisabeth died in 1876, aged fifty-eight. [HS-1991]

opposite: Grey Nuns visiting harvesters, Manitoba

LIFE IN THE BACKWOODS OF NEW BRUNSWICK

Emily Shaw was the daughter of an Irish sea captain, who brought her to New Brunswick around 1836. In 1838 Emily married Frederick Beavan, and the couple lived on a homestead at English Settlement near Long Creek. In 1843, she returned to Ireland, and two years later, published a vivid description of the lives of pioneer women.

Sketches and Tales Illustrative of Life in the Backwoods of New Brunswick is both Emily's reminiscences of her former neighbours and a handbook for prospective settlers. She is particularly good when describing the lives of the women of the settlement. She gives a wonderful portrait of the log cabin home of Sybel and Melanchthon Grey, a pair of young United Empire Loyalists. Sybel is justly proud of her skill and industry in making a home for her husband and two young children.

Most of the furniture in the Greys' little cabin is made from wood cut on their own land. Sybel is skilled in identifying herbs for medicines, for cooking, dyeing, and for keeping her woollens scented and moth-free. She is an accomplished weaver who has furnished her one-room home with piles of snowy woollen blankets, and woven and sewn her family's clothes, displayed on hooks around the walls. Her pride and joy is the beautiful coverlet on the bed. This is a symbol of the young couple's prosperity; they keep enough sheep to provide wool for this luxury item as well as for the family's necessities, and Sybel has the time and skill to make something beautiful. [HS-1992]

above: Élisabeth Bruyère.

below: "The Seignory of Beauharnois." The House is very prettily situated on a sloping bank, close to the river, which is so broad that it looks more like a large lake. It is called Lac St. Louis. The Ottawa and St. Lawrence join here and both are splendid rivers. I am quite pleased with the place this morning.—Water-colour and diary entry by Katherine Jane Ellice, 1838

above: portrait of Thanadelthur

Indian women performed a variety of important tasks vital to the functioning of the fur trade besides fulfilling the role of wife and mother.
—Sylvia Van Kirk, 1975

Whether they were helping to make domestic life possible in a harsh environment, or negotiating trade and peace treaties, women worked with men exploring the continent and establishing peaceful relations among its many and varied inhabitants. The records of the first Europeans to travel in the continent reveal their dependence on the Native women who were already at home here.

In the early years of the fur trade, it was common for European men to marry First Nations women. Such marriages were termed "marriage à la façon du pays" or "country marriages." The Hudson's Bay Company had gone so far as to introduce a marriage contract which emphasized a husband's economic obligations to his country wife. While these First Nations women were an important liaison between cultures and, as such, the backbone of the fur trade, the status of country marriages and the fate of the women who entered into them shifted constantly throughout the 19th century.

SALLY ROSS—A "COUNTRY" WIFE

"The manners of the Oakinackens are agreeable, easy, and unassuming, and their dispositions mild. They are at times, subject to gusts of passion, but it soon blows over; and, on the whole, they are a steady, sincere, shrewd and brave people....

"[The women] have in general an engaging sweetness, are good housewives, modest in their demeanour, affectionate and chaste, and strongly attached to their husbands and children. Each family is ruled by the joint will or authority of the husband and wife, but more particularly by the latter."

Alexander Ross, the author of this commentary, had good reason to write so familiarly and fondly of the Okanagans. In 1849, when this account was published, he had been married to an Okanagan woman for many years. Sally and Alexander Ross were married around 1812, when he was a fur trader in the Oregon territory. In 1825 the Hudson's Bay Company transferred him to the Red River Settlement. Although he

wrote later of his anguish at leaving Sally and most of their children behind, Alexander took their oldest son and went ahead to prepare a home for the family. Sally and the four younger children followed later. They travelled with a company brigade, wintering over in the Rockies, and crossing the Great Plains on horseback. By the time of her death in 1884, at about age ninety, she was known and loved in Red River as "Granny Ross." [HS-1986]

THANADELTHUR

In the spring of 1713, Thanadelthur, a young Chipewyan woman, was taken captive during a Cree raid. She and a countrywoman escaped from their captors in the fall of 1714. Subsisting on the meagre catches from their snares, the two women were soon overcome with hunger and cold. Thanadelthur's companion perished. Days later Thanadelthur came across tracks leading to the camp of some Hudson's Bay Company geese hunters. Starved nearly to death, she was taken to York Factory.

Upon recovering, Thanadelthur began to play an important role in establishing trade relations between the Hudson's Bay Company and her people. To do this, peace had to be established between the warring Chipewyans and Cree. Fearing their enemies, the Chipewyans would not travel to Bayside. In June 1715, a peace party one hundred and fifty strong, consisting of several Cree bands, William Stuart of the HBC, and Thanadelthur, set out to approach the Chipewyans. Thanadelthur was to fill the vital role of interpreter.

Sickness and starvation plagued the expedition and many of the bands turned back. The party's mission seemed doomed when they discovered nine Chipewyans who had been killed by one of the other Cree bands. Certain the Chipewyans would seek revenge, the group was anxious to turn back. It was then Thanadelthur boldly volunteered to find her people and bring them back to the Cree party. Alone, she journeyed across the Barren Grounds to the Chipewyan camp. And alone, she convinced them that the Crees' intentions were truly peaceful. When at last the two tribes met, Thanadelthur played an active and forceful part in the negotiations, even scolding those who remained doubtful of a settlement.

On 7 May 1716, the successful peace party returned to York Factory. Thanadelthur remained influential in the Factory's affairs until her death on 5 February 1717. She was mourned by many who would not forget her great spirit and courage. [HS-1977]

NATAWISTA

Natawista, or Medicine Snake woman, was born somewhere in southern Alberta about 1824. She was born into an important family of the Blood tribe of the Blackfoot, just as her people were becoming involved with the affairs of whites. About 1840, while still very young, she married Alexander Culbertson of the American Fur Company. As they roamed the West she came to see herself as a negotiator between her husband's people and her own. She caught the interest of several of the white travellers she met. Through their diaries she has become one of the few Native women of her generation whom we can know as an individual.

The picture of Natawista is filtered through the eyes of Victorian white men. They had difficulty matching their stereotype of a savage, sullen, but docile Indian woman to the strong-minded and independent Natawista. John James Audubon, the naturalist, watched her leading a wolf hunt across the prairie. She was "a wonderful rider," he said, "possessed of both strength and grace in marked degree." Although she was "handsome and really courteous and refined in many ways," he said, "I cannot reconcile to myself the fact that she partakes of raw animal food with such evidence of relish."

Another traveller noted she "has much presence, grace and animation for a *full blooded Indian.*" His account goes on to say that the Indians "required of the female sex...no social qualities; the gentle sex, therefore, exercised no refining influence on the strong." His description was far from true of Natawista. In 1854 she insisted on acting as intermediary between her people and the American government, smoothing the way to a peaceful treaty.

For 10 years she lived with Culbertson in the settlement of Peoria, Illinois. Living most of the time as a white woman, she still spent part of the year in a teepee on her lawn. About 1870, when her children were all grown and established in the white world, she returned to her own country. She took another white husband for a time but spent most of her last years with her relatives. She died in 1893 on the Blood Reserve at Stand Off, Alberta. [HS-1995]

JOSETTE LEGACÉ WORK

Josette Legacé was born about 1809 near Kettle Falls on the Columbia River, now in Washington state. Her father was a fur trader, her mother a Spokan, and Josette likely grew up around the trading posts. When she was about 16 she married John Work, a Scots trader in the service of the Hudson's Bay Company. Although this was a "country marriage," the Works formed a partnership which lasted until John's death.

Since the beginnings of the fur trade, Europeans had found Native wives invaluable. Their skills in trapping, collecting, and processing food, and producing such items as moccasins, snowshoes, and canoes were essential to wilderness survival. The women also served as guides, interpreters, and mediators between White and Native men.

Like many country wives, Josette accompanied her husband both at postings to various forts, and on trading expeditions which took them as far east as present-day Idaho, and as far south as northern California. Several of their 11 children were born during these journeys.

During the late 1830s and 1840s, Work was in charge of Fort Simpson, near the mouth of the Nass River. Here Josette introduced elements of European housekeeping to the Tsimshian women, and both Works concerned themselves with trying to moderate the practice of slavery among the Tsimshian.

above: Natawista

I am afraid that they and the Whites will not understand each other...but if I go, I may be able to explain things to them and soothe them if they should be irritated. I know there is great danger.—Natawista, 1854

above: Josette Legacé Work with children Suzette and David, ca 1875

Nous disions donc qu'à part les lois (dont on se plaint beaucoup), il n'y a guère de bienfaits nationaux auxquels la femme n'a pas contribué chez nous.—Joséphine Dandurand, 1901

In 1849 Work retired from the HBC and took his family to Victoria. In November 1849 their long-standing partnership was formalized by a Christian marriage ceremony. Work bought a substantial parcel of land and built a mansion to house their large family.

Josette spent the last years of her long life as a proper Victorian matron. She was particularly known for her kindness and hospitality to new immigrant women.

John Work died in 1861, but Josette survived until 1896. When she died, at the age of 87, she was recognized as one of the oldest residents of British Columbia, and was given a special tribute in the provincial legislature for her "usefulness in pioneer work and many good deeds." [HS-1999]

The lives of women in the West during the 19th century spanned tremendous changes in economic circumstances and social frameworks. The buffalo were gone and the world of the fur trade gave way to the surveyor and the agriculturist. Women who had been leaders in the old structures became pioneers in the new ones, or lost their place.

MARGARET TAYLOR

Margaret Taylor was the child of a country marriage. Her father was George Taylor, one-time sloop master at York. Her mother's name was not preserved by European historians. When Margaret became involved with George Simpson, Governor of Rupert's Land, in 1826, country marriages were generally accepted in fur trade society.

Simpson himself had shown considerable intolerance for country marriages, and a cavalier attitude toward the First Nations women he took up with. He referred to his partners as "my article," or "the commodity." But Margaret Taylor appeared to have stolen his heart. She had two sons by him; he took responsibility for this family, ensured that Margaret was given special rations of tea and sugar, and provided financial support for her widowed mother. He referred to Margaret's brother as his brother-in-law. In 1828 Simpson took Margaret with him on a trip to New Caledonia, and wrote to his friend that she had "been a great consolation to him."

It must have come as a shock to her when Simpson returned from a furlough in England in 1830 with a British bride, his 18-year-old cousin Frances. This repudiation of a country wife in favour of a European woman, by a man as highly placed in the fur trade as George Simpson, marked a profound shift in the mores of fur trade society—and a general decline in the status of First Nations women.

Simpson packed Margaret off to Red River with an allowance of £30. She was essentially forced to marry a servant of the Hudson's Bay Company, Amable Hogue, to rid Simpson of responsibility for

Fort Edmonton. There she met and married Sam Livingston, a gold prospector and trader, in 1865.

The couple set up housekeeping in a shanty at the fort, where the first three of their 14 children were born. Livingston was often away prospecting for gold, hunting buffalo, and trading, leaving Jane to manage the home and family on her own. In 1872 the family moved south to the Bow River. With the disappearance of the buffalo, they settled on land near present-day Calgary and, for the first time, Jane lived in a house with more than one room.

As Calgary grew and more white settlers came, she and her children began to experience discrimination. Once, when she needed medicine in Calgary for a sick child, Jane rubbed flour on her face to pass as white. At that time, all Métis and natives needed a special pass to be inside the city limits.

The Livingstons set up a model farm to demonstrate the suitability of the land for grain as well as cattle raising. Their extended family was large and when Rocky Mountain House National Historic Park was opened in 1979, more than 300 members of the Howse and Livingston families were invited.[HS-1987]

MARIE-ANNE LAGIMODIÈRE

Marie-Anne Lagimodière is perhaps best known as the grandmother of Louis Riel. But she had a more active role in history as the first European woman to accompany a group of coureurs de bois from Quebec to what would become Manitoba, and the first to settle permanently in the west.

Marie-Anne Gaboury was born in 1780 in Masquinonge, Quebec. After her father's death in 1792, she kept house for the parish priest until her marriage in 1806. Jean-Baptiste Lagimodière was a fur trader, a coureur de bois, just returned from four years in the west and restless to depart again. Despite his desperate attempts to dissuade her, Marie-Anne took her place on the floor of the great canoe, surrounded by freight and 10 paddlers, and bid farewell to the home and family she would never see again.

Pioneer women found their hands full. Babies sapped them of their strength and a growing brood always added to their responsibilities as more and more of the ranch business was left to them as their husbands tried new adventures.—Deanna Pederson, Fort Calgary Quarterly, 1980

top left: Indian women on a Vancouver wharf, 1901

below: Jane Howse Livingston

her. She spent the rest of her life there in increasing poverty. Simpson neglected the children he had with Taylor and eventually cut them out of his will.

While Simpson and his colleagues must bear responsibility for their treatment of the country wives, the European women who replaced them also contributed to the stratification of fur trade society, by zealously guarding what they were led to believe was their intrinsically superior status, driving the wedge between First Nations and European women. [HS-1996]

JANE HOWSE LIVINGSTON

Joseph Howse, Jane Howse's grandfather, retired to England in 1815, leaving behind his Cree Indian wife, Mary, and their young son, Henry. Howse had worked for the Hudson's Bay Company as an explorer and fur trader, setting up the first post west of the Rocky Mountains. Mary and her son returned to the Red River Settlement, [now] Manitoba, where Henry Howse married Janet Spence. Jane Howse was born in 1848.

Every year during the buffalo hunts the women followed the men. By the age of 15, Jane Howse could drive an ox-drawn Red River cart, cut up buffalo carcasses, dry the meat over open fires, make pemmican, and sew hides. When Jane was 16, her family moved to Fort Victoria on the North Saskatchewan River near

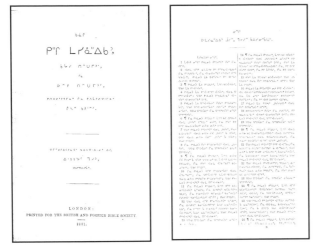

above: Title page and first page of Genesis from first bible printed in Cree

....our grandmothers/ beasts of burden in the fur trade/ skinning, scrapping, pounding, packing/ left behind for "British Standards of Womanhood,"/ left for white melting-skinned women./ not bits-of-brown women/ left here in this wilderness, this colony./ —Marilyn Dumont, 1993

The party arrived at a Métis encampment on the Pembina River in the fall. There Marie-Anne gave birth to a daughter. In the spring, the family left for Fort Edmonton. A boy was born en route in present-day Saskatchewan, and another girl in Alberta. Travelling by canoe and on horseback, pregnant and caring for small children, Marie-Anne experienced to the full all the hardships which befell pioneer women.

The Selkirk settlers were unprepared for the harsh conditions and climate. The presence of Jean-Baptiste and Marie-Anne may account for their survival during the first two winters. The Northwest Company men thought the colony a plot by the Hudson's Bay Company to ruin them. Rivalry between the two groups flared into violence in June 1816. With the help of a Saulteaux chief who greatly respected Jean-Baptiste, Marie-Anne escaped and took refuge with the Indians. But Jean-Baptiste, having delivered an appeal for assistance to Lord Selkirk, was captured and imprisoned in Fort William until the fort was retaken in August.

He was rewarded for his services with a large tract of choice land near present-day Winnipeg. There they built a house and more children were born, including Julie, the mother of Louis Riel. Marie-Anne lived 20 years after the death of Jean-Baptiste in 1855. She witnessed the arrival of the first steamboats, the transfer of Rupert's Land to Canada, and the Métis revolt under the grandson who would become father of the new province of Manitoba. Surrounded by her many children, grandchildren, and great-grandchildren, she died peacefully at 95, ending a lifetime of unfailing courage in the face of constant hardship and frequent danger. [HS-1987]

SOPHIA THOMAS MASON

Sophia Mason was the daughter of a servant of the Hudson's Bay Company and a Cree woman. She received a good education at the Red River Academy and was offered a position as a teacher, but instead she chose to marry William Mason, a young Methodist missionary. They were posted to the Rossville Mission, on Little Playgreen Lake, Manitoba, to work with James Evans, the inventor of syllabic writing for the Cree language. Evans began translating the Bible into Cree, but ill health forced him to retire, leaving the project under the direction of William Mason. Much of the translation was done by a group at the mission, but final editing and polishing seems to have been Sophia's work. She saw the first edition through the press in London. During three years spent in London, Sophia worked on the Bible through her ninth pregnancy and recurring pulmonary problems. She gave birth, saw the completion of the Bible, and died, worn out at the age of 39. [HS-1988]

The last major conflict between Canadians was in 1885 in the North-West, which saw eastern Canadians travelling west on the new railway, believing they were to defend the rights of the Canadian government, to fight against westerners, who believed they were defending their land. The village of Batoche and its residents, in what is now Saskatchewan, were central to that struggle.

CHRISTINE DUMAS PILON

Christine Dumas and her husband Barthélémi Pilon arrived at the Métis settlement of Batoche from the Red River in the spring of 1882. They had recently married in the cathedral in St Boniface (Manitoba). Her widowed mother, Henriette Landry (1822-1909), accompanied her. Many of her brothers and sisters had preceded them to the new "homeland." The young couple settled near their family and began building a comfortable home on their river lot on the South

by the advancing government troops. After the debacle on May 12, during which the Métis defenders were overrun by government troops, she was forced to flee into the woods (Minatinas Hill area) with her young "bibi" (Louis, 18 months old). She was with Mme Riel, who had been coughing blood for three days, and her two children. After days of hiding in the bush, they walked the 18 miles back to Batoche....There they found a stray calf, which they butchered and ate. "Riel returned three times to say adieu to his family before he gave himself up. It was so sad."

Christine and Barthélémi had lost everything. "Il [ne] nous restait que le courage de Canadien et de Métis pour vivre." But they persisted. A new home was built, crops were sown, and a second homestead was acquired. Christine and her "cher mari" celebrated their golden wedding anniversary in 1932. Independent to the end, she died in a little house next door to her daughter Adélaide at the age of 92. [HS-1987]

left: Christine Dumas Pilon, member of the Métis Nation and survivor of the Battle of Batoche, seated, with her two daughters: Adélaide (Mme Ranger) and Octavie (Mme Lepine), ca 1918

Saskatchewan River. Barthélémi pursued mixed farming, and supplemented the family income with freighting and carpentry work. There were many hardships, but Christine was resourceful and was often asked to write personal and business letters for relatives and neighbours.

During the "Guerre nationale" at Batoche in 1885 (referred to as the Northwest Rebellion in Euro-Canadian literature), she defended the actions of Métis leader Louis Riel (a distant cousin on the Landry side). "Ce n'est pas Louis Riel mais le gouvernement lâche qui est venu en guerre chez les pauvres gens," she said, in a poignant account of her trials.

Christine and most of the women and children had sought refuge in dugouts and tents down by the village flat during the heat of battle. Her husband was fighting in the trenches: their new home was burned

Why did you become a Doctor? —We couldn't send 100 miles to Battleford every time we needed one. What did you do when there were murders, suicides, accidents, epidemics...? —What had to be done, of course.

In that brief exchange Dr Elizabeth Scott Matheson exemplifies the pragmatism and resolve of pioneer women. From the medicine women of our Native foremothers, to the contemporary "Dr Mom" television ads for cough syrup, women have been seen as responsible for the care of the sick and infirm, from birth to death. When we forget our history, we forget that the image of the male doctor attended by the female nurse is a development of the last century. Women as central to the healing arts, and the main support of one another in childbirth, is a much longer tradition. That tradition reasserted itself in the pioneer era, especially in western Canada, was submerged again by increasing professionalism and urbanization, and is now being reasserted once more.

Women today who are fighting for the right to the supportive care of a midwife during childbirth are not starting a new struggle but resuming one that their great-grandmothers lost.
—Joanna Dean, 1977

ELIZABETH SCOTT MATHESON

Elizabeth Scott was born in 1866, near Campbellford, Upper Canada. She taught school for some time in Manitoba and attended the Women's Medical College at Kingston in 1887. In 1891 she married John Matheson. The next year they travelled together to the Indian reserve at Onion Lake, Saskatchewan, where Matheson had been appointed missionary for the Anglican Church.

The Mathesons ran the only school in the area, and began boarding children in their own home so they too could attend. By 1895 a doctor was needed in the growing settlement. Elizabeth, with the support of her husband, decided to enroll in her second year at the Manitoba Medical College. Now the mother of two, she gave birth to her third child during that school year. Later, she enrolled in the Medical College for Women in Ontario, and sat her second- and third-year exams in one year, graduating in 1898.

Elizabeth returned to Onion Lake to practise medicine—serving the community and the children in the mission school, as well as mothering nine children of her own. In 1901, as a result of her exceptional work during the smallpox epidemic at Onion Lake, she was appointed Government Doctor for the Indian people.

Elizabeth had been an equal partner with her husband and, when he died in 1916, she continued with the administration of the business, as well as taking over his post as principal of the school. She continued to serve as doctor at Onion Lake until 1918, when she became Assistant Medical Inspector of the Winnipeg Public Schools, a job from which she retired in 1941 at the age of 75. [HS-1975]

MARY AMIRAULT

Born in Bresaylor, NWT, in 1888, Mary Amirault spent the greater part of her life in the historic Fort Pitt district of Saskatchewan, where her work as midwife won her the lasting respect and love of the community. Mary learned the skills of midwifery from her Métis mother

(who had at one time worked with Elizabeth Scott Matheson). From her, Mary also gained a extensive knowledge of medicines and general nursing, which she put to good use during the 1914-18 flu epidemic.

Typically, Mary would drop whatever she was doing when her services were needed, generally travelling by horseback, often many miles from her home. During her career as midwife, which ended in 1941 when a hospital was established nearby, she never lost a baby. It's estimated that she delivered approximately 130 babies.

Her unbounded generosity was well known. She would go where she was needed, often at great inconvenience to herself, particularly when her children were young. She never expected remuneration, instead she would often share her food with those in need. Mary would also look after old people who were no longer able to look after themselves. As there was no undertaker, she also prepared the dead for burial.

Mary was married to a farmer and rancher, and did all the work of pioneer women on homesteads and more—haying, stooking, hunting, trapping, chopping wood, rounding up cattle, plucking chickens, as well as the more traditional chores of cooking, mending, and darning.

Cheerful and physically strong, Mary enjoyed curling and horseback riding (which she did into her 80s), was an excellent ball player, an energetic dancer of the Red River jig, and liked horse racing and sponsored rodeos. She died in 1977. [HS-1979]

above: Elizabeth Scott Matheson, 1887

My "Horse and Buggy Days" were full to overflowing with hardships, thrills, dangers, determination and profit. In looking back, I would not have missed that period for a cool million.—Dr Annie Norman Hennigar, 1925

right: Mary Amirault

This memorable birth experience presumably inspired her decision to become a midwife. She learned her skills by ordering a blue doctor's book from the Eaton's catalogue. "I read that book from end to end. I learned it by heart. At night in my kitchen by candle light." She refused money for her services. "The midwives in those days used to charge. I didn't believe in that. I believed Indians were supposed to help one another." Augusta lost only one patient; the infant of that deceased mother was the first of the many homeless children Augusta raised.

Augusta ended her days in a log cabin with neither running water nor electricity. Her husband had died when she was young and she never remarried, explaining, "Once is enough." She was content living alone, going to church, and sharing her grandmother's stories with her own grandchildren. [HS-1994]

top left: Dr Ella Margaret Strang

I am the rustic type who would rather build a log cabin and carry water from a spring than have Dresden china and broadloom rugs.—Dr Ella Margaret Strang, 1929

MARY AUGUSTA TAPPAGE

Mary Tappage was Shuswap, born in 1888 at Soda Creek, British Columbia. Severed from family and culture at age four, she was taken to a Roman Catholic mission, where she was punished for speaking Shuswap. There she spent nine years, until she returned to live with her grandmother. At 15 she married George Evans. They had four children, two of whom died in infancy. By marrying George, whose mother was Shuswap but whose father was Welsh, Augusta lost her Native status [see p. 67]. Nevertheless, she maintained strong ties to the traditional values of her people. With a belief that Native peoples should always assist one another, Augusta raised numerous children besides her own.

A description of her first child's birth provides insight into the self-sufficient life she led.

"I was out feeding the cattle when I felt my first pain. Well I kept on feeding the cattle, feeding the calves...I was still sick. When that was over I came back to the house. I had to chop my own wood. Well I finally fixed my bed and I was getting ready. I made a big fire and I opened the oven so it would be warm in the house. I kept getting worse and worse. Finally my daughter was born. All alone, I got up and fixed her up...I had to clean myself up....Made some more fire. Well I was there for three days in bed and I got up. Well in the meantime my husband came home. He had been on a spree for three days and came back drunk."

left: Mary Augusta Tappage

I made all our clothes. I sewed them by hand. Dresses were easy, but men's shirts and pants, they were hard! Two women, with a needle and thread, could make a man's shirt in a day.
—Mary Augusta Tappage, 1973

above: Janet Weir

JANET WEIR

Individual proofs of women's work in the West are given at every turn in the great highway. The trail has become a broad and beautiful flower strewn way, and there is no sound heard of the moans which must have been wrung from human, woman hearts in that onward pioneer journey.
—Katherine Simpson Hayes

"Life is for the living" was a favourite expression of Nurse Janet Weir. Indeed, having lost her husband and children to illness and war, she devoted herself to the care and preservation of the health of her community, the Loreburn district of central Saskatchewan.

When she arrived from Winnipeg in 1911, this region, like its counterparts throughout the prairies, had few physicians and even fewer hospitals. Within this context, Nurse Weir provided truly exceptional care. She typifies the many women of this period who were not formally trained, but were nonetheless considered to be "practical nurses." During a confinement or crisis, such as the influenza epidemic of 1918, she would "live in" in order to attend to her patient 24 hours a day, and often assumed the burden of household chores as well. She performed her duties with a customary efficiency epitomized for many by the immaculate, starched white uniform she always wore.

Janet Weir assisted in or presided over the delivery of nearly every child in the area during her career. Although this must have constituted hundreds of births—889 by one account—Nurse Weir kept careful record of all "her babies," faithfully remembering to send each one a birthday card. She continued to serve her community until her death on 7 August 1954, at the age of 85.

That few of her patients can recall details about her personal life is testament to an altruistic nature that never sought accolades or self-promotion. It is also typical of women's history that so little is known about such a significant individual. Loreburn's own "Sunshine Lady" was revered and admired by the numerous generations for whom she was an abiding and benevolent presence. [HS-1994]

As Canada is a young country, although an old land, a large part of our history deals with exploration and development. Ours is a land of wilderness and daring exploits of discovery. Women were bold enough to climb unnamed mountains, journey down uncharted rivers, and set foot in new territory.

Whether it was the lure of the gold rush, new work opportunities in the teaching, clerical, and writing professions offering them independence, or a resurgence of the spirit that had brought immigrant women to this country for centuries and sent Native women travelling along all the trading routes of the continent, Canadian women at the turn of the century were adventurous.

KATHERINE RYAN—"KLONDIKE KATE"

At 24, Katherine Ryan chose adventure over marriage, and left her hometown of Johnsville, New Brunswick, to head west. She was a nurse at a Vancouver hospital when news of Klondike gold finds filtered south in 1898. She went directly to the Hudson's Bay Company, purchased heavy work boots, a mackinaw, and a Winchester rifle, then booked her passage to Alaska.

Ryan was one of the first women to brave the trek to the Yukon gold fields. She earned the respect of fellow travellers, along with the nickname "Klondike Kate." Of this she was proud, though the name caused some consternation later when it was coupled with scandal across North America, thanks to a Dawson City dance hall girl who adopted it, as well as credit for many of Kate's exploits.

Kate eventually settled in Whitehorse, where she helped to build the community. She opened the first restaurant, Kate's Café, in a tent, then in one of the first wooden buildings in the community. She invested

her profits in various claims and took a Free Miner's license to pan for gold.

In 1900 Kate became the first "Woman's Special" attached to the North West Mounted Police, Yukon Department, to serve as matron of the jail whenever a woman was arrested. At six feet tall Kate was an imposing figure, who had little difficulty keeping her prisoners in line. Later, as the only female gold inspector, it was her job to prevent women from smuggling gold out of Canada without paying the royalty.

Kate was a founder of the North Star Athletic Club and a member of the Catholic Women's League, Hospital Committee, and Liberal Association. Her home was headquarters for the Yukon Women's Protective League, whose primary goal was to obtain the vote for the women of the North. During WWI she collected more money for the war effort than any other person in the Yukon. She received a special letter of commendation from the prime minister and was made an honorary life member of the Red Cross.

Kate never married, but became mother to four nephews following the death of her sister-in-law. She spent her last 13 years in Stewart, British Columbia, as active in that community as she had been in Whitehorse.[HS-1994]

NELLIE CASHMAN—
"ANGEL OF THE CASSIAR"

Nellie Cashman embraced danger, adventure, and daring deeds. Born in Ireland in 1845, she spent her adult life on the frontiers of North America, mainly following the latest gold rush, where she invested in mines, ran businesses, and contributed to the community.

Nellie came to Canada in 1874, when gold was discovered in the Cassiar area of British Columbia. Her normal outfit of a mackinaw, men's trousers, and fur hat was practical, if distinctive. She ran a boarding house and prospected for gold, but returned to Victoria for the winter. She soon heard stories of starvation and malnutrition among the miners, so she

above: Catherine Schubert and daughter Rose, who was born en route to the "Cariboo Gold" rush in British Columbia, 1862

"Life amounts to very little in this age if one cannot institute a reform of some worth and we are glad of the opportunity to identify ourselves with the spirit of the times." — Sara Jeanette Duncan, from Brantford, Ontario, in her 1890 account of a round-the-world trip she undertook with fellow journalist, Lili Lewis, entitled *A Social Departure.*

left: Katherine Ryan

I wasn't built for going backwards, when I once step forward I must go ahead.— Katherine Ryan, 1922

organized, stocked and led an expedition into the region. The fresh vegetables she brought saved many from death, and earned the "Angel of the Cassiar" the admiration of miners everywhere.

When she heard of the Klondike strike, Nellie knew she needed to go north:

"I went up in one of the first boats. We went in by way of the Dyea trail. We camped on Lake LaBarge till the ice went out of the Yukon. We built boats and went down the Yukon to Dawson, going through the Whitehorse rapids, the Five Finger rapids, and all the others. Believe me, it's some journey all right...I never want to travel any faster than I did there."

Although she made a lot of money in her various businesses and mining ventures, she gave most away to charity. She also actively collected for charities. A favourite ploy was to find a high-stake poker game; when the pot was high, she would reach into the middle of the table, sweep the money into a bag and say, "Okay boys! This is for the hospital. If you got the money to throw away at poker, you can give it to them hard working Christian women that's takin' care of the sick."

After the Klondike played out, Nellie wandered into Alaska, working her claims until her late 70s. She died in Victoria on 4 January 1925. [HS-1999]

MINA HUBBARD

Mina Hubbard was the first person to explore and map the Naskaupi-George river route through Labrador to Ungava Bay. She became interested in the project in 1903, when her husband, a journalist and adventurer, died in his attempt to complete the trip. Led astray by inaccuracies in government maps of the area, he perished of hunger and cold.

Two years later, Mina hired four men and two canoes, and set out on her own expedition. They left the mouth of the Naskaupi River (near present-day Goose Bay) late in June, and reached their destination, 576 miles west and north, two months later, a few days ahead of schedule.

The journey was dangerous and uncomfortable—the bugs so bad that Mina sometimes masked herself with a waterproof bag—but she didn't mind the physical hardship. Her greatest worry was arriving at Ungava too late to catch the last ship of the season. That would mean wintering somehow in Labrador. Since no one had made the trip before, no one, not even the local Indians, knew for sure how long it would take.

Aside from this anxiety, her biggest problem was with her crew, who were afraid to let her out of their sight. From the beginning she made it clear that she would not take orders as the men expected her to do, and she eventually won freedom of movement too. It was a compromise solution: one of the crew would still accompany her, but he would do so at her command.

Once safely home, Mina recorded her adventures in a book, *A Woman's Way through Unknown Labrador,* which she illustrated with her photographs of the countryside and of the Indians she had met. [HS-1979]

There has always been a West. For the Greeks there was Sicily; Carthage was the western outpost of Tyre...but the West we are entering is the last west....When this is staked out, pioneering shall be no more.— Agnes Deans Cameron, 1909

right: Mina Hubbard

AGNES DEANS CAMERON

Agnes Deans Cameron, born in Victoria, British Columbia, in 1862, was an educator, adventurer, and journalist. She grew up in Victoria and later taught at a number of schools, becoming a principal in 1890, a position she held for 10 years. In 1906, she was elected school trustee for the city, a new and radical departure for a woman at that time.

In 1908, Agnes abandoned her 25-year teaching career and went to Chicago, where she took up newspaper work briefly, and made plans for a six-month, 10,000-mile round trip to the Arctic Ocean. In mid-May 1908, Agnes and her niece Jessie Brown set out from Chicago on their adventure.

They went by train to Winnipeg, the "Buckle of the Wheat Belt," then by Canadian Pacific Railway to Calgary and Edmonton, and by stagecoach to Athabasca Landing; then on June 6 joined the Hudson's Bay Company fur brigade of seven big open scows, or "sturgeon heads," able to carry ten tons each. On these scows, Agnes and her niece journeyed down the Athabasca River and across Lake Athabasca to the Slave River. On July 7, at Fort Smith, they transferred to a steamboat making its maiden voyage and travelled along the Slave to Great Slave Lake, and then down the Mackenzie River to the Arctic Ocean. They returned via the Mackenzie River, Slave Lake, Slave River, Peace River (where Agnes shot a moose), Lesser Slave Lake, and from Edmonton by rail to Winnipeg. Agnes Cameron's book, *The New North,* is an exciting story, vividly describing her experiences, her curiosity, and her patriotic pride.

She spent the following two years in England lecturing and writing about Canada and promoting immigration for the Canadian government. In 1911 she returned to Victoria, continued writing, was active in a number of organizations, and died there in 1912. [HS-1976]

[Agnes was recognized from coast to coast as an inspiring lecturer. In her home province, the [Vancouver] *Province* reported in March 1909 that "Agnes Deans Cameron, the brilliant Canadian lecturer, is still drawing enormous houses where she appears in the United States." A month later she was in Saint John, New Brunswick, where the *Times* reported that "Miss Agnes Deans Cameron not only mentally carried her audience with her on her 10,000-mile journey to the Arctic, but made every native born listener rejoice with her in their Canadian heritage." Eds.]

MIRIAM GREEN ELLIS

Intrigued by the North, Miriam Green Ellis travelled as sole woman passenger down the Mackenzie River to Aklavik in 1922. Instead of staying safely on board, as the men on the boat would have preferred, she annoyed them by acquainting herself with Indian and Inuit people along the way. The result of her audacity was a wealth of information about the northern way of life, and some rare photographic records of the work done by Native women.

She had a firm sense of the personhood of women, and was an outspoken feminist. When men on the Mackenzie trip expressed disgust with women who "aped men's ways" (a dig at her masculine clothing), she wrote: "I told them that for the most part their own estimation of 'men's ways' was quite correct, and no woman with an particle of sense would copy them." Dress was an exception.

After her Mackenzie voyage, "Mary" Ellis freelanced, speaking and writing about a wide variety of subjects. She became especially well known as an expert on agriculture. In 1928 the *Family Herald and Western Star* appointed her western farm editor.

left: Agnes Dean Cameron (right) and niece, Jessie Cameron Brown

right: Miriam Green Ellis

above: Ella Manning

The world takes you at the estimate you put upon yourself, and women have rated themselves too low.
—Nellie McClung, 1915

Stockmen appreciated her unusual ability to photograph prize animals so that their red-ribbon virtues could be clearly seen.

She showed the same sense of adventure building a career for herself in an unusual field for a woman, agricultural reporting. She moved from Toronto to Prince Albert, Saskatchewan, to work as a reporter for the *Prince Albert Post* in 1912, then for the Edmonton *Bulletin* in 1917.

She retired in 1952, but because of her wide range of interests and knowledge of farm matters, she was kept busy as a speaker and freelancer until her death in 1964. [HS-1976]

ELLA MANNING

A telegram which she picked up in April 1938 as she returned home from work dramatically changed the future of a young woman from Nova Scotia. Its message—"If you wish to join me at Cape Dorset this summer for two years I shall be pleased"—was the beginning of a lifelong adventure for Ella. She soon married the sender, Thomas Manning, and almost immediately set out with him to map the hitherto unknown coast of Baffin Island. The two made their way with great difficulty, travelling by dog sled and small boat around the northern coast of Foxe Basin and down the west coast of Hudson Bay to Churchill, where they arrived in February of 1941.

Thomas returned to the Arctic in 1944 to work for the Geodetic Service of Canada. Ella worked with him during two summers. Probably the first white woman to live in the Arctic away from a trading post, Ella became the first female fieldworker for the Geodetic Service. She described her Arctic experiences in two books: *Igloo for the Night* (1943), and *Summer on Hudson Bay* (1946). [HS-1986]

right: Mary Jobe and Bess MacCarthy at Lake O'Hara, Alberta, 1909

HENRIETTA TUZO WILSON

On 21 July 1906, Henrietta Tuzo and her Swiss guide, Christian Kaufmann, stood at the summit of Peak Seven, 3,245 m above Alberta's Moraine Lake. This arduous first ascent marked the greatest achievement of Henrietta's climbing career. Peak Seven was later named Mount Tuzo in her honour.

Henrietta Tuzo was born in Victoria, British Columbia, in 1873, but was brought up and educated in England. She was among the first generation of women to attend university classes, both at Oxford and at University College, London.

In 1898 Henrietta and her mother returned to Canada to visit Henrietta's brother Jack. While there, Henrietta fell in love with the Rocky Mountains. For

several years she regularly returned to climb in and around the Banff area. She was among the earliest serious female climbers.

Henrietta met John A. Wilson in Banff, and married him in England in November 1907. The Wilsons moved to Ottawa, where John became director of air services for the Department of Transport, and Henrietta turned her energies to child rearing and public service. She was for many years president of the Ottawa Council of Women, and via the Council worked with the Consumers' and Household Leagues, precursors of the Consumers Association of Canada. She was involved in the Canadian Council of Child Welfare, and her membership in the Alpine Club of Canada and the National Parks Association reflected her continuing interest in the outdoors. She represented the National Council of Women on the National Fire Prevention Association, and advocated forest fire prevention as well as domestic safety.

Henrietta was president of the National Council of Women from 1926-30, a difficult period for the Council. Like many reformist groups, the Council women had lost much of their pre-war optimism, and the conviction that they could quickly build a better world had faded. Henrietta spent much of her time as president trying to rekindle the old drive and optimism in her followers. In her 1928 president's address she told them, "It isn't lack of time, or lack of money, which handicaps us, it is apathy—throw it off, and in your enthusiasm influence those around you." Her final president's message was a sombre one. She warned, "...while we have the franchise, we have not equality of opportunity with men, and are tending to lose some of our hard-won position." [HS-1992]

MARY SCHAFFER

Mary Schaffer wanted to explore the Canadian Rockies, but in 1904 women weren't being invited to join the expeditions of the adventurous men who were discovering and naming valleys, lakes, and mountains.

Mary and her friend Molly Adams were in Banff that summer, and they saw teams ready their outfits for exploration northwest of Glacier House and Lake Louise, an area made accessible by the newly completed Canadian Pacific Railway line. They watched the men "with hungry eyes as they plunged into distant hills."

By 1906, they were planning their own trip. "We can starve as well as they; the muskeg will be no softer for us than for them; the ground will be no harder to sleep upon; the waters no deeper to swim, nor the bath no colder if we fall in."

With guide Billy Warren (whom Mary later married), they left Banff on 20 June 1907, to explore the headwaters of the Saskatchewan and Athabasca rivers. "Our real object," said Mary, "was to delve into the heart of an untouched land: to tread where no human foot had trod before." They penetrated an area previously unexplored by white people; the following summer they discovered Maligne Lake, in what is now Jasper Park.

Mary's friends back home in Philadelphia were puzzled by Mary's rather strange avocation, and commented that it was "wonderful" she looked so normal. Mary wanted to reply: "Not half so wonderful as that you do not know the joys of moccasins after ordinary shoes, that there is a place where hat-pins are not the mode, and the lingerie waist a dream; that there are vast stretches where the air is so pure, body and soul are purified by it, the sights so restful that the weariest heart finds repose."

After 1911, Mary lectured and wrote about the Canadian Rockies, and is credited with starting the first real flow of eastern tourist traffic to the Canadian mountains. She died in Banff in 1939. [HS-1979]

above: Mary Schaffer

In school [textbooks] women and girls have been shown to be afraid, quiet, and easily given to tears while men and boys have been shown to be brave, strong, and vocal— thus these attitudes became self-fulfilling prophecy.
—About Face, pamphlet of the Ontario Status of Women Council, n.d.

above: Sylvia Stark

right: "Portrait of a Negro Slave, 1786" by Quebec artist François Malepart de Beaucourt

Black women have been part of the history of Canada since the 17th century. They have been pioneers in a double sense, fighting for human rights against the overwhelming prejudice toward people of colour among European settlers, and, like other immigrants, creating communities where there were none. Slavery was abolished in Canada in 1834, and for a time near the mid-19th century, the Underground Railway carried enslaved black Americans to destinations in eastern Canada. However, for black people, and for black women, the struggle began before the establishment of the "railway," and continued after its work ended.

SYLVIA STARK

For Sylvia Stark, Canada promised freedom—freedom from slavery. She was born of slave parents in Clay County, Missouri, in 1839. Her father, after years of effort, managed to purchase his liberty. He tried farming, but the family soon fled after the Ku Klux Klan threatened the life of his neighbour.

After again meeting discrimination in California, they decided to move to British Columbia, attracted by the welcome of Governor James Douglas, who promised Negro immigrants the same rights to land as Whites. With a group of Blacks, Sylvia, by now married, pregnant, and with two small children, journeyed to Vancouver Island. Sylvia's husband Louis built his family a cabin on Saltspring Island, joining the growing Negro population there. Life was not entirely peaceful in the beginning. Indians, who had previously used the island as a summer camp, resented the intrusion of both Whites and Blacks. Their hostilities increased as time went on and the Stark family chose yet another move, to Extension, near Nanaimo, on Vancouver Island.

Tragedy struck with the death of Sylvia's husband, believed to have been murdered. Sylvia, with her oldest son, returned to the original farm on Saltspring Island, where she lived to be 105. Her skills as a midwife and a nurse were in great demand. [HS-1979]

MATTIE MAYES

In 1910 Mattie Mayes homesteaded in the Eldon district of Saskatchewan with her husband Joe Mayes

Joe's death, and continued for many years to serve her community. Her grandson remembers her as a matriarch going off in a stoneboat or buggy, or on horseback, to tend the sick or to deliver babies. Today a fifth generation of Mattie's descendants are growing up in Canada, placing them among the longest-established pioneer families in the West. [HS-1994]

left: Mattie Mayes

NANCY MORTON

Nancy Morton was a Black woman enslaved in Maryland and moved to New Brunswick by her Loyalist master in 1785. In 1807 she brought a writ of *habeus corpus* in a Fredericton court, trying to establish that her slavery was illegal. Although her case failed, she won wide public support. No one in the province publicly spoke in support of slavery after that date.

Until 1834 it was legal to own another human being in Canada, and many individuals were held in slavery in all parts of the country settled by Europeans. The worst abuses of the system were avoided, but only because our climate was unsuitable for a plantation economy. Most slaves were personal and household servants, and the burden of slavery was very hard, especially for the women, who had constantly to fear the breakup of their families and the loss of their children. A diary entry from Prince Edward Island illustrates the situation:

"19th July 1800—I was under necessity of telling my servants Jack and Amelia...that at the end of the year if they behaved themselves well (of which I was to be the judge) and that neither Mrs— or myself wanted them or either of them, I would give them their liberty; that is to say, only for themselves two, not liberty for any children they may now have or hereafter have. But I also told them that if they or either of them misbehaved, they forfeit all expectations thereto. I also told them as long as either of us wanted them they were not to look for or expect their liberty...."[HS-1998]

Women in these times need character beyond everything else; the qualities which will enable them to endure and resist evil; the self-governed, cultivated, active mind, to protect and maintain ourselves.—Anna Jameson

*The pioneer women deserve a monument. They are worthy of the highest tribute we can give them.
—Nellie McClung*

and their 13 children. She had been born a house slave on the Jesse Partridge plantation in Georgia in the US in 1849, and later she and Joe had farmed near Tulsa, Oklahoma. When Oklahoma gained statehood in 1907, the new state legislature began to enact what were known as "Jim Crow" laws, entrenching anti-Black prejudices in state law. Joe, by then a Baptist minister, and Mattie gathered together a party of about 30 people who were willing to try once again for a new life, and moved north to the Saskatchewan country.

They did not receive a warm welcome. According to Murray Mayes, Mattie's grandson, "Some of the settlers didn't want black people and they made it quite clear. Our people almost starved their first winter." But the Mayes and their party persevered. The colony built a sturdy log church, the Shiloh Baptist Church, which still stands next to the Mayes' land.

About two hundred Black people settled in the Eldon district following the Mayes' lead, before racial prejudice in Canada moved the Canadian government to discourage further Black settlement. Mattie became the spiritual leader of the group in the 1930s, after

above: Mrs Brown,
boiling the spuds

The Homesteader was a unique breed of woman—able to withstand physical and emotional hardship, and still find inspiration in her dreams for her future and a vision of her Canada.

LOUISE SMITH CLUBINE

When Louise Smith left her native Toronto in July 1914 for Edson, Alberta, to marry Percy Clubine, she was joining the last great wave of pioneer agricultural settlement in Canada. Percy had taken a homestead near Wembly in 1911; their honeymoon was a two-week trip over the Edson trail to his homestead, 10 miles west of Grande Prairie. She wore out a new pair of walking shoes on the trip. Her observations, recorded in a pocket diary, reflect her spirit, her sense of humour and her curiosity.

below: Peace River
crossing, Alberta,
ca 1910

July 15—Left Edson.
July 17—camped at 7 bridges, put up tent, had supper went fishing. Nothing doing.
July 18—drove 2 miles—got stuck—horse went down—had to use block and tackle...got a cache of oats and drove over very bad road about 6 miles and made camp for dinner. drove 2 miles and lost bed. Perc had to go back for it.
July 19—came to Athabaska River and went over on ferry (35 cts on Sunday)...drove to foot of Fraser

Hill and camped. Started to rain so got tent up first only rained a little but guy ropes got wet and rabbits chewed them up and the tent came down on top of us twice in the night.
July 21—Perc made fire and started out for horses & I had breakfast ready & he wasn't back yet but came soon and said horses have turned back over the trail will have to camp here all morning as he will likely have to go back to 70 mile place [about 5 miles back]. did a little washing in creek & had a sleep.
July 25—Road very bad & walked quite a bit was dumped off the wagon pretty quick once...used block and line twice over very bad holes.
July 27—travelled over very rough roads about 8 or 9 miles & the king pin on the wagon broke about 11. It took all day to fix
August 1—are just ready to leave...will be home tonight. Hurrah!

Louise Clubine was active in her community for a number of years. A history of the Alberta Women's Institutes notes that "Among the splendid pioneer women in the area south of the Peace River was Mrs. P. Clubine of the Wembly district. Her kindliness, her culture, her hospitality were well known throughout that new country where she lived and served her fellows for many years before her untimely death in 1936." [HS-1991]

WAITING FOR THE BOAT

"After we made the portage between Slave Lake and Peace River, we used to have to stop and build a raft of logs to take our goods and horses 300 miles down the Peace River....These rafts would be over one hundred feet long and fifty feet wide. When they had it large enough they would build a corral for the horses at one end of the raft, with a stack of hay for the animals....Next would come the job of loading the foods onto the raft. On one end of the raft would be the year's supply of trading goods, our tent and fireplace, for we cooked, ate, and slept on the raft....When all was loaded they pushed out from shore and we started our 300 mile trip down the mighty Peace to our home."—*Sarah Brock Brick, ca 1896*

Sarah had 14 children, all born at home, attended by "Nurse Weir" [see p. 22]. She also raised three of her grandchildren. In addition to the demands of her large family, Sarah worked in partnership with her husband to build their farm, where they lived for over 50 years. She died in Saskatoon at the age of 97. [HS-1993]

THE RED RIVER CART

Typically associated with the Métis people, the two-wheeled Red River carts were the principal method of overland transportation on the prairies during the last century. Many tons of furs and provisions were carried in the carts, which could be heard long before they could be seen. Each cart, pulled by one horse, could carry the loads of four horses.

It is unclear whether the cart derived from French, French-Canadian, or Scottish tradition. What is clear is that the carts were created exclusively out of materials found in the West. The hubs were made from elm, the rims of the wheels from ash or oak, and the axle from maple. The axles could not be greased, as grease soon mixed with prairie dust and clogged the axle. Nothing was metal; nothing had to be purchased from a trading post.

Carts owned by women traditionally had highly decorated covers. The covers not only protected the cargo, they also provided shade, such as that enjoyed by the unidentified women and children in this photo. [HS-1999]

SARAH DODDS PEARDON

Born in Perth, Ontario, in 1888, Sarah Dodds Peardon moved west with her family to homestead; they eventually settled in Loreburn, Saskatchewan, in 1906. Sarah served as the first teacher in the area, giving classes in her father's house. Married in 1910,

SOD HUT

"As it is now, the pioneer woman, who goes bravely out with her husband to make a home for themselves beyond reach of the neighbours or nurses or doctors actually takes her life in her hands. Many children have been born in far away places where skilled help was impossible to obtain and both mother and child have lived. But again, many a mother and child have died for the lack of proper nursing. The best monument we can build to the pioneer women is to institute a system of rural nursing which will bring help and companionship to these in their hour of need."—*Nellie McClung, 1916*

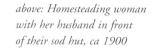

top left: Taking a break from their journey in the lee of a Red River cart, ca 1906

above: Homesteading woman with her husband in front of their sod hut, ca 1900

left: "Kissing bee"— Sarah Dodds Peardon and son, Loreburn, Saskatchewan, ca 1911

WASH DAY

"Washing! What a job that always was. Usually it took me the entire day. In summer I washed outside; in the winter, down in the basement. The boiling, sudsy water had to be carried in pails from the stove to where my tubs were set. More than once I burned myself severely....

"I washed for the hired men as well as for my own family. We were always from eight to fifteen strong, according to the time of year, and since most of the men worked in close contact with the soil, and with animals, there was always an astonishing pile of extremely dirty clothing—mountains of overalls and socks, heavy underwear and flannel shirts, not to speak of voluminous bed linen.

"Drying the clothes was almost as much of a job as washing them, especially in winter. It often took the best part of a week, and for many months during the year, when the weather was cold, the various rooms of our house were made uncomfortable and unpleasant with smelly underwear and clumsy flannel shirts which took not hours but days to air thoroughly."—*Kathleen Strange, from* With the West in Her Eyes, *1937* [HS-1991]

right: Adeline Barberree on a stoneboat pulled by oxen, Beaufield, Saskatchewan, 1909

below: Mrs Joe Mayo, washing clothes on the homestead

The immigrant spirit has been central to Canada's identity in the last century. Like the homesteader heading west, these women were ready and willing to make a home in a new land and to make their new country a better place because of it.

ALICE JOWETT

In 1889, a young widow from Bradford, England, had a vision of life far away from that smoky industrial town. Not content with just dreaming, she and her four children boarded a ship sailing for Canada, via Cape Horn. When she arrived in Vancouver, Alice opened a candy shop on Cordova Street, following the trade she had learned in England. Growing restless in the city and recalling the vision that had sent her to Canada—a place of forests and lakes, where living would be an adventure—she sold her business and moved to Trout Lake in the Interior.

Once there, Alice bought a log hotel, and was so successful that only three years later, in 1900, she was able to build a three-storey hotel which she named "The Windsor." She explained her success: "I had a bartender, billiard room and a very large staff. I laid my tables with linen and the finest silver." Merely running a large hotel in the boom town was not enough for Alice, who decided to file and work mining claims for herself. Although not a geologist, Alice had an uncanny ability to choose sites that would yield gold, silver, and other minerals. Each of her claims rewarded her work with rich returns. With colourful names like "Foggy Day," "Hercules," and "Alice Kootenay," her mines were only slightly less well known than their owner.

An acquaintance told of a trip she made with Alice to one of the claims: "I once walked with her ten miles through the bush to a property. The country was so rough we were not allowed to take horses for fear they would break their legs. That walk nearly killed me, but Alice walked it frequently and always seemed fresh." Alice Jowett worked each claim herself, and, until she was 93, made at least one trip a year to her sites via horseback.

For nearly 55 years Alice ran the hotel at Trout Lake and worked her claims. "Oh, how I loved that country. Loved the trees and the mountains and the lake full of fish at the foot of the hotel." When she was

93 she rode in a plane for the first time in order to see her mines from the air.

In 1953, she admitted to feeling less spry than she once had, and moved to Kelowna, where she died in 1955 at the age of 101. [HS-1982]

MARGARET SCOTT

As a girl in Northumberland, England, Margaret Scott worked outside on the farm with her father, while her older sisters helped their mother inside. In 1910 she immigrated with her family, including her two young children, to homestead near Hanna, Alberta.

One day, while her husband, George, was in town, a prairie fire could be seen racing towards the homestead. Margaret put the three preschool children under a wet blanket in the middle of the plowed garden. She and an older girl fought the fire. They were one of the few families in the district to save their buildings and machinery.

In the years that followed, her husband moved the family several times. In 1923 they were living on a dry farm seven miles from Kamloops. Here Margaret, pregnant with her eighth child, was left to raise her family and to farm alone.

Farm she did, for 34 years, managing so well that she paid off the mortgage on the farm and bought more land in the 1930s.

Margaret was so determined to farm that she would nail an apple box to the tongue of the mower, put the baby in it, and go to the field to hay. At night she would read to her children and knit at the same time. Nothing was wasted. When there was oatmeal porridge left, she added ingredients and made cookies. During those years she worked constantly.

In 1957 she moved to Kamloops, and for the next 20 years kept house for herself and her son. Until less than two months before she died, at the age of 93, she continued to do all her own housework, baking bread and preserving fruit. When she was dying, her major concern was that her daughter preserve the cherries ripening in the backyard. [HS-1980]

above: Margaret Scott

left: Alalia Fancy Stevens, Nova Scotia, early 1900s

You know it's grand, it's beautiful in Canada. I'd do anything I could to help it along.—Alice Jowett, on the occasion of her 101st birthday

above: Moto Suzuki

right: Cleaning salmon, 1975

DOUKHOBOR WOMEN

The famous photo below shows Doukhobor women in southern Saskatchewan hitched to a breaking plow. It was taken in 1902 shortly after the sect arrived in Canada, nearly destitute. Most of the men took temporary jobs to earn a little cash; the remaining men and the women were left to make a start with the stubborn sod. They lacked draught animals, and so the women volunteered.

The Anglo-Saxon community's reaction was unthinking outrage: "But then, what could you expect from those backwards foreigners?" But amongst the Doukhobors, the women's labour was a matter of pride. The land they broke would feed the people; the colony would survive.

The women may also have had another, less matter-of-fact reason for satisfaction. There was an ancient Doukhobor tradition that a settlement could be saved from disease if a guard was plowed around it by 24 girls. Did the Doukhobors have this in mind—that soil broken by women might have special power? [HS-1979]

MOTO SUZUKI

"In the old days there wasn't enough fish for a whole day's work. Whenever the fish came in, they'd let us know by whistle day or night. Sometimes we worked one hour a day, sometimes five hours, sometimes ten hours a day. There was a *mori* house (daycare) where the mothers would take turns looking after the kids when we went to work. I was one of them the year after I arrived.

"When I came (in 1925) I was almost six months pregnant. It was in July, fishing season, so I started work in the cannery almost right away....The fish were cut by machine, Chinese men brought the cans and I packed each can with fish. The work started about June and went to the middle of November. In those days we weren't paid until November....They used books of tickets, each book had 150 tickets. A box contained 24 cans. When you finished one box, they'd punch a ticket. We saved these tickets and in the middle of November we went to the Chinese mess house where they counted the tickets and gave us our money. We used to get $3 for 150 tickets (3,600 cans). In those days, you see, only those who washed the fish were paid by the hour."—*Moto Suzuki, resident of the Japanese-Canadian community of Steveston, British Columbia* [HS-1978]

left: Doukhobor women ploughing

Canada remained a country of pioneers and adventurers throughout the 20th century. Women continued to build lives for themselves and their families on the frontiers—the economic, social and physical frontiers—of our society. In some regions of Canada, the circumstances of subsistence and struggle still persist—as do women. Throughout the country, Canadian women are still pioneering, even as that spirit fades into memory.

ANAHAREO

Anahareo is a seventy-year-old Mohawk who is continuing to lead a vivid and active life. She has been a trapper, prospector, mother, foster parent to beavers, author, artist, and conservationist. Today she continues her crusade to have the cruel leg-hold trap banned.

When Anahareo was 19, she met Archie Belaney, better known as Grey Owl. At first they made their living by trapping, but Anahareo was revolted by this. She took a strong stand and refused to trap. Archie soon followed suit, quit trapping and became a conser-

vationist. At her urging, he began to speak publicly and write books. While he wrote, Anahareo went prospecting. She never did strike it rich, although she did sell some of her claims at a profit.

Their daughter Dawn was born in 1932. Two years later Anahareo began a solo 800-mile prospecting trip from northern Saskatchewan to northern Manitoba, transporting herself and her supplies in a 16-foot canoe. She was gone for more than a year.

After 11 years of marriage, Anahareo and Archie separated. He died two years later, and Anahareo married again in 1939.

She continues her work in Victoria as a conservationist and an ardent spokesperson on behalf of all the animals victimized by the leg-hold trap. "You get involved to stop these atrocities from continuing in our country—or not. But remember this, the animal held fast in the steel jaws of the leg-hold trap has no choice at all. Unless he chews off his foot, he must agonize in thirst, starvation, sometimes gangrene from his injuries, and freezing cold, until death releases him." [HS-1977]

[For the rest of her life, Anahareo continued her conservation and animal rights work and in 1983 received the Order of Canada. She died in 1986. Eds.]

MADELEINE GOULD AND THE YUKON ORDER OF PIONEERS

The Yukon Order of Pioneers is for males only. Madeleine Gould, Dawson resident since 1946, believes women have as legitimate a claim to that title as the men alongside whom they've worked. To prove that, she's had to take her argument to court.

In 1987 Madeleine applied to join the Pioneers, a police force in gold rush days which has over a century become a cultural organization recording Dawson's colourful history—from a male perspective. Her application was rejected.

She complained to the Human Rights Commission, which told the Pioneers to reconsider. The Pioneers' appeal to the Yukon Supreme Court won reversal. An ensuing appeal by the Commission is

It is important for women who are single parents to remember that their children need in them, all the strength and decision-making and planning and independence and competence that they were told girls didn't need and would make them unpopular with boys in the first place.
—Barbara Bloom, 1980

I get annoyed when that phony image of Yukon women is perpetuated. They weren't all dance-hall girls kicking up their skirts in the can-can routine, you know. They were teachers, and store clerks and laundresses, and nurses and typists and hard-working wives and mothers.
—Flo Whyard, author of *Five Pioneer Women*, 1980

As to women's liberation— I am all for it. It is time that women should not be relegated to "chore-boy" in whatever career she may choose.
—Anahareo, 1976

left: Anahareo

above right: Demar Halkett Hastings

What is the importance of rediscovering women's history? The more I thought about it the more I realized how much of the past has to do with the present; to look at one without the other is to miss half the picture.
—K. Linda Kivi, 1992

There are too many history books where, if it wasn't for Queen Elizabeth I and Queen Victoria, you would never realize the human race consist-ed of two genders.
—*Herstory* fan mail, 1993

right: Madeleine Gould

before the Supreme Court of Canada. Madeleine plans to win, her determination buoyed by family support.

Born in St Chrysostome, Quebec, she spent her childhood in Ontario. In 1945 she married Dawson native John Gould, and a year later joined him there. In one of the coldest winters ever, and in a house with neither plumbing nor running water, the 24-year-old bride's mettle was surely tested.

Summers of hauling rocks and scrubbing clothes at the placer mine her husband and his father operat-ed at Hunker Creek proved her commitment as well.

In 1949 the Goulds adopted Jock, and three years later, Susan. Peter was born in 1961. Madeleine raised her three children, later helped with three grandchildren, and operated a tourist campground. She eventually went back to the mine, this time as a cook.

Madeleine divides her time between Dawson and the placer claim high in the Klondike Hills. And she thinks about female pioneers. She's not alone; others are awaiting the court's verdict before they also apply. The one sure thing is: there's no going back. Says Madeleine, "It's going to change human rights. Whether we win or not...it's worthwhile." [HS-1995]

[In 1996 the Supreme Court reached its verdict and, with only two dissensions, denied Madeleine Gould's appeal. Eds.]

DEMAR HALKETT HASTINGS

Demar is a tiny, upright Cree woman, just clearing five feet, with snapping black eyes and thick black hair barely touched with grey. She lives on Besnard Lake in northern Saskatchewan, a few miles north of the narrows where she was born, and has lived a tra-ditional "bush" life nearly all of her seventy years. She fishes and traps small game, gathers berries and other "country" food.

Adaptability is a characteristic of Cree culture. Her life has been one of continuous learning and pride in doing her share.

She tries out additions to the northern culture, such as strains of vegetables adapted to the short growing season, and keeps the northernmost flock of chickens in Saskatchewan. She produces beautiful smoke-tanned garments, starting with the raw hide, and puts up her fish racks every year.

She regrets that much of the native lore is being lost, and as an Elder is always willing to teach. She helped her grandson with his correspondence courses, and her husband with his sensitive role as the only northern member of a public inquiry into a proposal to dam the Churchill River. Her grandson's wife, Betsy, learns bush homemaking as they work together. Ethnobotanists who consult Demar about local plants find they are expected to learn their Cree names as well.

At the narrows, the birch tree that her grandmothers tapped for sap still stands, the first notches now far out of reach. [HS-1989]

ADA MUSKEGO

"I was born and raised from a sacred place. I was born before the white man came, and I saw a lot of nice things. I'm having a lot of worries about my children now. I'm seeing a lot of hardships. I lost many of my grandchildren, but I have many in return. I'm getting paid by God; I have four great-grandchildren. I'm glad of that...I raised many of my grandchildren, and now for the last time, I have a seven-year-old great-granddaughter that I am raising. I talk a lot to my grandchildren, but they don't listen to me, and what will I do now? I am old and I'll never give up my independent life. I still want to encourage my grandchildren. I have a lot to talk about at my age."—*Ada Muskego* [HS-1979]

Instead of complaining of slowness in women's climb into the light, we should each do something to encourage another step. We might start in and with our own lives and those of the women we know best. The personal is (always) political. History and "herstory" begin at home.
—*Herstory,* 2000

far left: Taktu cleans fat from sealskin with an ulu at Cape Dorset, 1960

left: Ada Muskego— 88 years old, Onion Lake, Saskatchewan, 1979

NG the PIONEERS
OF THE
RITORIAL
GROWERS
1905
195
SASKATC
1905

A GREAT RACE OF WOMEN

Once Canada was established as a country, women's work in defining the structure of the nation became political work. Here are the stories of women's increasing demands for formal admission into the governance of their society. This chapter describes important battles in the ongoing struggle, such as the suffrage movement, the Persons Case, Native women's claims for band membership rights, and campaigns for employment and pay equity.

We are so accustomed to the notion that "woman's liberation" is a new concept that we forget our foremothers often exercised considerable political power. Over the centuries women in Canada have continually gained and lost influence in society. Nowhere is this loss more evident than in comparing the lot of the European settlers and immigrants with the power and authority of the First Nations' matriarchies.

Ultimately politics is about citizenship, full membership in the community, and the right to exercise it. Some of the rights we take for granted were hard fought and dearly won. The lesson of the suffrage movement is the lesson of the century—there is no sweeping reform that brings a new world into being; ground is gained case by case, individual by individual.

Formal politics is the most overt way one can seek to affect society. Direct involvement in the political system is crucial to ensure that we build communities in which women's rights and interests are recognized, protected, and respected. Since they won the right to do so, Canadian women have served their country at all levels. In these pages, you will meet women of influence and integrity who understand that women's rights are human rights.

Emily Murphy once said, "I believe that never was a country better adapted to produce a great race of women than this Canada of ours, nor a race of women better adapted to make a great country." We are inclined to agree.

opposite: Violet McNaughton, 1955

right: Mrs. Wolf Child and her daughter, 1906

All real authority rests in the women of the country. The fields and all harvests belong to them. They are the soul of the councils, the arbiters of war and peace, and the guardians of the public fisc.—Father Lafieteau's observations on the five great tribes of the Iroquois

O riginally, Indian nations such as the Huron and the Iroquois were matriarchal: authority, property, and political decision making for the tribe rested with the women. It was only after European settlement that women had to regain the influence they had lost.

IROQUOIS MATRIARCHY

The creation myth of the Huron and Iroquois held that woman was the source of life, and when she died and was buried in the earth "from her body grew the plants that the new earth needed for the people who were to be created."

There is a definite relationship between the position of women in Iroquois society and their image of women as the givers of life. Property and inheritance were passed on through the female line. It was also the responsibility of women to arrange marriages. Women had the power to choose and depose chiefs. However, women did not exercise their power arbitrarily or even individually; Iroquois women acted collectively with their sisters, mothers, and female cousins. [HS-1975]

below: "Iroquois Woman"—aquatint from a drawing by George Heriot, 1807

IROQUOIS WOMAN

"The Iroquois, who, of all the nations of North America, the inhabitants of Mexico excepted, had made the greatest advancement in the social state, assert, that for a series of years they wandered from one situation to another, under the conduct of a female. By her they were led over a great portion of the continent of North America, until they made choice of the tract which they now occupy, whose climate was more temperate, and whose soil was more adapted to the purposes of cultivation than that of any place they had before visited. She there distributed lands among her followers, and thus founded a colony which has ever since retained its station."—*George Heriot,* Travels Through the Canadas....To Which is Subjoined a Comparative View of the Manners and Customs of Several of the Indian Nations of North and South America, 1807 [HS-1992]

NETNOKWA

Around 1745 a girl was born into the Ottawa tribe of the Central Great Lakes region. We know nothing of her early life; she emerges into recorded history in 1790 through the narrative of her adopted son: "Netnokwa, who, notwithstanding her sex, was then regarded as principal chief of the Ottawwaws."

Netnokwa had lost a son and purchased John Tanner, a white captive boy of about 12, to replace him. Tanner remembered, "[Netnokwa's husband] was but of secondary importance in the family, as everything belonged to Net-no-kwa and she had the direction in all affairs of any moment."

The family wintered in the bush, hunting and trapping for food and furs. In the spring they went to

Mackinac to trade. Netnokwa carried a flag in her canoe and when she approached the fort was saluted as a chief. In 1791 Netnokwa decided to lead her extended family and followers west to the Red River area, where her husband's people lived.

The start of this journey was marred by double tragedy: her husband was killed in a drunken scuffle, and Netnokwa's son Ke-wa-tin fell and smashed his knee. As Ke-wa-tin was unable to travel, Netnokwa and her remaining sons stayed with him in the Lake of the Woods region for several months until he died. The family started for Red River the following spring.

Tanner relates that some French traders had borrowed Netnokwa's canoe and refused to give it back:

"...the old woman took it from them without their consent, put it in the water, and put our baggage on board. The Frenchmen dared not make any resistance. I have never met with an Indian, either man or woman, who had so much authority as Net-no-kwa.

She could accomplish whatever she pleased, either with the traders or the Indians; probably in some measure, because she never attempted to do anything which was not right or just." [HS-1999]

POYETTAK, KAKIKAGIU AND AKNALUA

This Inuit family, below, from the Boothia Peninsula was sketched by Captain James Ross in about 1830. Kakikagiu was married to both men and seems to have been the dominant member of the family. Ross relates that Aknalua was her favourite, so it was Poyettak who was sent out to do the hunting for them all. Kakikagiu served as a guide and mediator between the British and her own people and Ross says, "...she was one of the most useful and intelligent in giving us information about the coast, rivers, stations, &c." [HS-1999]

Given the general freedom of tribal life [however low her condition in the eyes of the European settlers], the Indian woman generally had a great deal more independence, security and variety of roles than did her white sister.
—Sherrill Cheda, ca 1975

left: Poyettak, Kakikagiu and Aknalua, sketched by James Ross, ca 1830

Women's progress has not been a steady advance. There have been setbacks along the way, when women have in fact lost rights which would be all but forgotten before they were reclaimed.

THE LARRIÈRE PETITION

right: York Factory, fur-trading post on the shore of Hudson Bay, ca 1840

Quebeckers have often looked back to the pre-Conquest period as the Golden Age, and from the point of view of women at least, this view seems largely justified.
—Caroline Pestieau

below: "Québecoise" by C.W. Jefferys

In the early 20th century Quebec nationalists fought women's suffrage as a threat to their traditional values. However, in 1791 the British government had established the colonies of Upper and Lower Canada, each with a measure of elected government. Voters were defined simply as "persons" who owned a certain amount of property, just "persons," notice, not "male persons." The English-speaking women of Upper Canada apparently knew their place too well to take advantage of the loophole, but their French sisters in Lower Canada, which had a feminist tradition dating back to the 1600s, cast ballots as early as 1809.

For these women, going to the polls must have been an act of courage. Not only were they subject to ridicule, but to legal challenge. In the election of 1827, a number of Quebec City women, including a widow named Mme Larrière, were turned away by the returning officer because of their gender.

Mme Larrière's case was presented to the Legislative Assembly in what may well be Canada's first feminist manifesto. The petitioners pointed to a woman's duties as citizen and taxpayer, and proclaimed her intellectual equality with man. To deny her a say in "the fate of her country, and the security of her common rights" would be "impolitic and tyrannical," they declared.

This was 1828, remember, a generation before the first women's suffrage agitation in Great Britain, and two generations before the movement really got going in Canada.

The Larrière petition (along with challenges to another election because women's votes *had* been counted) was deferred, referred, and forgotten. Women's suffrage was outlawed explicitly by acts

— York Factory —

passed in 1834 and 1849, thereby bringing French Canada into step with the rest of the British Empire.

The right to vote in provincial elections, once lost, was not regained until 1940, and then only after thirty years of persistence and abuse. Perhaps, if Quebeckers had known the true history of women in their province, the struggle would have been shorter and less fierce. [HS-1977]

FEMMES D'AFFAIRES IN NEW FRANCE

Despite the common notion that French Canadian women have always been repressed by church and state and unable to act for themselves, some aspects of French law gave women greater freedom than did English law after the conquest.

The community property and inheritance provisions of the law in New France, essentially "the Custom of Paris," made it possible for enterprising French women to manage property and engage in business. [see p. 6] [HS-1987]

Women who had enjoyed considerable political power in some matriarchal Aboriginal cultures were systematically excluded by the new dominant culture. From the mid-nineteenth century, Native women were subjected to European incursions on their property rights.

CATHERINE BUNCH SONEGO SUTTON

For centuries Canadian Indians suffered oppression at the hands of white colonial settlers. Many strong Native women, women like Catherine Bunch Sonego, struggled against their domination.

Catherine Sonego, born in 1824 on the Credit River in Ontario to Ojibwa parents, was known as Nahneebahqua, "upright woman." Shortly after her birth, her family accepted Christianity and began a Methodist settlement in Port Credit, Ontario. Catherine was very active in the Methodist mission, often taking leadership in the area of education. In the summer of 1846, Catherine and her husband of seven years, William Sutton, temporarily moved to Owen Sound, Ontario, where they settled on about 200 acres of land. After two years in Sault Ste Marie spent as superintendents of a Methodist "Model" farm, and three years improving a mission in Michigan, Catherine and her husband returned to Owen Sound only to find their land had been divided up and was being offered for sale by the government.

The Indian Department refused to recognize the Suttons' claim to their land, and refused Catherine her share of the band's annuities because she had married a white man. Catherine Sutton attempted to buy back her land at a public sale, only to be told that Indians could not purchase their ceded land. Outraged by the Indian Department's discriminatory, unjust behaviour, Catherine Sutton and two Indian men took their concerns directly to the Canadian legislature. They petitioned the elected officials for the title to their land and fair compensation for their loss, but no action was taken.

In 1859, Catherine Sutton took the struggle of her people to England and presented her petition to the Colonial Secretary, to the Duke of Newcastle, and to Queen Victoria. The petition outlined the unjust and dishonest actions of the government of Canada West with respect to land expropriations from Indians and the deprivation of annuity of any Native woman who married a white man. Catherine hoped that her efforts would lead to changes in government legislation which would guarantee land rights and gender equality for Native people. She never could have imagined that her people would still be struggling for such rights 125 years later [see p. 67].

The Suttons were eventually allowed to buy back their land as a result of the intervention of the British government, but nothing was done to recognize other Indians' land claims or to legislate women's equality.

Catherine persisted; in 1861, she called the government's attempt to buy Manitoulin Island "wholesale robbery and treachery." The Island had been promised forever to the Indians in an 1836 treaty. Catherine Sutton continued to be an outspoken critic of government policy regarding Native people's rights until her death in 1865. [HS-1988]

Through our encounters with patriarchal colonial societies we lost a lot of our rights, we lost authority. If women had been part of the treaty-making process, it might have made a big difference.
—Maxine Elliot, 1987

left: Unidentified Métis woman, 1885

The idea of "universal suffrage"—that every adult citizen should have the right to vote—is a relatively recent one. While various groups have historically been excluded, women in particular took up the fight and became the famous "suffragettes." After 24 May 1918, all women who were British, and later Canadian, citizens could vote in federal elections. It wasn't until 1940, when Quebec women finally won "the franchise," that most Canadian women had the right to vote in their own provincial elections. Indian women who were considered "status" and who lived on reserves, however, were not allowed to vote until 1960 (including residents of Yukon, NWT/Nunavit). Here are the dates when provincial suffrage was first won throughout the country.

Manitoba	January 28, 1916
Saskatchewan	March 14, 1916
Alberta	April 19, 1916
British Columbia	April 5, 1917
Ontario	April 12, 1917
Nova Scotia	April 26, 1918
New Brunswick	April 17, 1919
Prince Edward Island	May 3, 1922
Newfoundland	April 13, 1925
Quebec	April 25, 1940

On the Prairies, many women's groups were involved. The Women's Christian Temperance Union, the Saskatchewan Women Grain Growers, and the United Farm Women of Alberta were crucial to the success of the suffrage campaign. Farm women tended to have the support of their men, which may explain why the women in the three Prairie Provinces got the vote before women elsewhere in Canada.

PROVINCIAL EQUAL FRANCHISE LEAGUE

On February 13 1915, fifteen representatives from seven Saskatchewan women's organizations met in Regina to coordinate their fight for suffrage. All were members of one or more groups, notably the Women Grain Growers, local equal franchise leagues, and the Women's Christian Temperance Union, and all felt the time had come for a concerted effort. The women decided to form the Provincial Equal Franchise League of Saskatchewan. They quickly organized a petition, collected signatures in the middle of winter, and on 27 May 1915, sent a delegation to the provincial legislature to lobby for equal franchise. Zoe Haight of Keeler was one of this delegation. From Violet McNaughton, one

right: Canadian Women's Christian Temperance Union Convention, 1946

of the most politically active women in the West, she received useful advice: "I know you will do well. Put it up as a square deal for the asset farm women are. Keep to the justice, do not plead too much."

Premier Scott responded by saying that he was not prepared to introduce franchise legislation in 1915, but hinted that he might reconsider if the women were able to present a petition with even more signatures. The Equal Franchise groups took this as a challenge and set out to collect 10,000 signatures, a huge task in a largely rural province in the days before cars, telephones, and radios. The League members persevered, however, and collected the needed signatures.

On February 14, 1916, women again gathered in Regina, armed with their petition, to lobby for the vote. This time the legislature accepted both the petition and the proposal, and within a few weeks passed the law that enfranchised Saskatchewan women. [HS-1986]

THE CHAMPION

In August 1912 the Political Equality League of Victoria, BC, began publishing *The Champion,* a monthly magazine devoted primarily to the suffragist movement. As the editors noted in their foreword:

"By the exclusion of one-half of humanity from a legitimate share in the counsels of nations there have arisen distorted ideals of human life, and also a double standard (or rather a divided standard) of morality, which, affecting as it does every department of national life, is hindering the highest and fullest development of the race. It is not only the women and children who suffer under the present political system—the result is naturally seen in the lives of men."

The League provided "practical hints" to help "start today an active campaign," including bringing to each monthly meeting "at least one 'anti' or 'wobbler,'" and suggesting supporters "talk to people about suffrage," "read all you can on the suffrage," and "wear the badge always."

right: "Sinking Fast, No Regrets" Grain Growers' Guide, *1916*

Five years later, in 1917, British Columbia women won voting rights. A year later, Mary Ellen Smith became the first woman elected to the province's legislature. [HS-1999]

Women everywhere had to put up with a lot of nonsense from some men and even some women. In 1909, seven prominent Saint John women arrived at the New Brunswick legislature to lobby for the partial suffrage bill under consideration. The lawmakers greeted their arrival with cries of "Help!" "Police!" "Sergeant-at-Arms!" followed by loud clanging of the division bells.

Suffragists had to deal with male politicians who felt that women were not ready for the vote, that women did not want the vote, and so on. Manitoba Premier Roblin's response to a 1914 suffrage delegation is typical of what supporters heard:

"Does the franchise for women make the home better?...My wife is bitterly opposed to woman suffrage. I have respect for my wife; more than that, I love her; I am not ashamed to say so. Will anyone say that she would be better as a wife and mother because she could go and talk on the streets about local or dominion politics? I dis-

above: Inaugural edition, 1912

The real cause of the Woman's Suffrage Movement is that women have come to realize the fundamental truth at the bottom of all progress, that we all have an equal right to live and say how we will live.—Lillian Beynon Thomas

agree. The mother that is worthy of the name and of the good affection of a good man has a hundredfold more influence in molding and shaping public opinion round her dinner table than she would have in the marketplace, hurling her eloquent phrases to the multitude. It is in the home that her influence is exercised and felt."

The women of Manitoba's Political Equality League responded with a brilliant satire—The Women's Parliament.

LAURA McCULLY

THE WOMEN'S PARLIAMENT

On January 27, 1914, a delegation of women petitioned the Manitoba legislature to grant women the right to vote. As expected, Premier Rodmond Roblin refused in a speech filled with chivalrous platitudes.

The next evening the women staged an evening's entertainment at the Walker Theatre, the highlight of which was the Women's Parliament. In this burlesque of the male-dominated parliament, roles of men and women were reversed. Only women sat in the legislature and voted. The idea was not to show parliament as it should be, but to show a parody of what it was.

The climax came when a group of "men" entered asking for the vote. They were met by "Premier" Nellie McClung, who refused the petition with a clever parody of Roblin's speech of the previous day:

"We wish to compliment this delegation on their splendid gentlemanly appearance. If, without exercising the vote, such splendid specimens of manhood can be produced, such a system of affairs should not be interfered with. Any system of civilization that can produce such splendid specimens...is good enough for me, and if it is good enough for me it is good enough for anybody. Another trouble is that if men start to vote they will vote too much. Politics unsettles men, and unsettled men mean unsettled bills—broken furniture, broken vows and divorce."

The play was a roaring success and was presented again in Winnipeg and once in Brandon. The money earned was enough to finance the rest of the suffrage campaign in the province of Manitoba. [HS-1977]

above: Graphic by Cathryn Miller

top right: Laura McCully

"[There is] no particular reason why a woman whose life is spent between child-bearing under adverse circumstances and labour in a sweatshop, should be either too refined or timid to throw stones at windows. Her disabilities over and above men of the same class, are such as would warrant her in trying to improve her position at the cannon's mouth.

"As it is woman remains politically unrepresented. As a result, in the body politic there is a great emphasis on property and corresponding disregard of human life.

"Seeing that men have long had the sole government of affairs and the making of laws, and that they have allowed these to become oppressive to women, so as to force gentle and quiet spirits to revolt, it seems useless to resent the possibility of a woman judge or premier. They may trust her to care for the interests of their sons better than they have done for the daughters of our race."—*from "What Women Want," by Laura McCully,* Maclean's Magazine, *Vol. XXIII, January 1912*

Journalist Laura McCully was an ardent and aggressive advocate of women's rights. At age twenty-two she became the first woman in Canada to hold an open-air meeting in support of the suffrage movement, in Toronto's High Park in August 1908.

She was an accomplished writer; her poems and short stories were published in *Harper's Bazaar,* the New York *Herald,* and other leading newspapers and magazines. Her finest writing appears in a volume of her collected works entitled *Mary Magdalene and Other Poems,* published in 1914. [HS-1977]

Women didn't just want to vote; they wanted their votes to count. They didn't just want to be part of the political process; they wanted to change it.

WOMEN'S FEDERAL PLATFORM

As adopted by the National Council of Women at Saint John, June 1920, for the consideration of Canadian Women.

Basis: Truth, Justice, Righteousness, Loyalty

Political Standards
- Equal moral standards in public and private life
- Abolition of patronage
- Publication of amount subscribed to party funds
- Open nomination of political candidates
- That those who shall hereafter be added to the electorate shall have a speaking knowledge of English or French
- The naturalization of women independently of the nationality of the husband
- The practice of thrift in administration of public and private affairs

Social Standards
- That necessary legislation be enacted to permit of uniform marriage laws
- That there is equality of cause for divorce in all divorce courts—and that there be no financial barrier
- Prohibition of the sale of intoxicants
- Raising the age of consent to eighteen years

Industrial Standards
- Equal pay for work of equal value in quantity and quality [see pp. 62 and 127]
- The basis of employment to be physical and mental fitness without regard to sex
- The principle of co-operation between employer and employed
- The principle of collective bargaining as defined by the Federal Department of Labour [HS-1993]

THE WOMAN QUESTION

"But who shall say, just what woman's sphere is?...Judging by the infinite deal of nonsense uttered on this subject, it would seem that every fledgling in philosophy or religion felt himself fully competent to mark out with entire precision both the general course, and specific actions appropriate to every woman.

"But aside from the fact that hardly any two definitions of woman's sphere fully agree, how impertinent in any *man,* or any *men,* to think of deciding that sphere for her....Very plainly, woman herself alone can tell what her true sphere is. Nor can she *now* tell what it is....Such has been her culture, or rather her want of culture, and her lack of opportunity, and, still more, her lack of stimulus to use her opportunity; such the suppression of her own will and judgment, and her deference to the will and judgment of others, that she herself has no adequate conception of her own powers. Doubtless, a multitude of things which are now popularly reckoned altogether beyond her sphere will hereafter be regarded just as appropriate to her as the care of household, teaching of children, or works of charity.

"[Suffrage] will simply be the opening of another door—the passage into another freedom. It will be a means of education—a stepping stone to a higher level. But to work out her complete womanhood, vastly more is required than the right of suffrage....It is required that her whole nature...should expand and strengthen...into the glad consciousness of acknowledged strength."— *From "The Woman Question," by "M,"* Canadian Monthly and National Review, *May 1879* [HS-1991]

above: Illustration by "Ricardo"

below: "The Door Steadily Opens"—Grain Growers' Guide, *September 21, 1910*

above: Political Equality League presents its petition, 23 December 1915 back: Mrs A. V. Thomas, Mrs F. J. Dickson; front: Dr Mary Crawford, Amelia Burritt

At the end it came without struggle in recognition of women's services during the war. Things often work out that way I find. You struggle and struggle to no direct effect, and suddenly in a lull the whole thing snaps into place.—"A veteran feminist," on the suffrage movement in Nova Scotia. The final bill was recommended for passage, and after a hasty trip through the council, received royal assent on 26 April 1918; no women sat in the galleries that day.

AMELIA BURRITT

"Are not the wives and children equally essential to the growth and prosperity of any country as is the father and the man? Are they deserving of the protection of the law? For these and other like reasons, I willingly spend my latter days in seeking to get what lies at the root of all amendment, the right of women to vote at the polling booths on all occasions, under the same conditions as the men."

With this pledge, Mrs Amelia Burritt set out to help women win the vote, a remarkable commitment for a woman of 93 years.

The granddaughter of a United Empire Loyalist, Amelia was born near Brockville, Ontario, on August 1, 1822. Amelia was certain that "the vote will make [women] healthy, wealthy and wise, better wives, better citizens, and a woman will come to be the glory of the land as she now is of man."

T.C. Norris, Liberal leader of Manitoba, had promised that if women could present signatures amounting to 15 percent of the previous electoral vote, his government, when it came to power, would give them their desired "privilege." The Manitoba Political Equality League was formed in 1912, by prominent Winnipeg women and men, to gather the required number of signatures.

Amelia single-handedly solicited 4,000 of those signatures. Her personal challenge took her to many different people and situations. Daily she walked the streets of Winnipeg and knocked on doors, talking to people about the need for the franchise of women. Of one such visit, she said: "I met a lawyer, who, like a lawyer, said: 'It is all right for the women who live out on the prairie to have the vote, but it is unnecessary for the ladies living in the city.' I replied: 'Please give your reasons for having one law for the city and a different law for the country?' 'So many business men put their property in their wife's name,' he answered. 'Oh,' I said, 'I'm sure that gives you a rich harvest drawing deeds of transfer when they deed it and when they want it back again.' He turned around and said 'Go ahead.' I secured six signatures in as many minutes."

The Political Equality League presented its petition to the government on December 23, 1915. Suffrage for women was passed in Manitoba on January 28, 1916. Along with the right to full political enfranchisement in provincial elections, women gained the right to sit in the provincial legislature. This victory was the direct result of the work of Amelia Burritt and the Political Equality League. [HS-1979]

Women in Canada began to lobby for the vote in the 1800s. However, early suffrage groups in eastern and central Canada were often given names that would not "alarm the men." Newfoundland women had the "Ladies Reading Room and Current Events Club," while women in Toronto founded the "Toronto Women's Literary Club" in 1876.

THE LADIES READING ROOM

After much activity in the 1890s, the suffrage movement in Newfoundland was quiet for a few years, then picked up again. The catalyst for the second wave was a seemingly insignificant event in 1909—a men's club that had allowed women to attend lectures decided to withdraw the invitation. Myra Campbell, one of the banned women, commented:

"Because we had dared to voice our opinion or stand up for Woman Cause, then, if you please, we were debarred for our 'caustic' remarks. At least that's what we are told. We have heard some other flimsy excuses, but we believe the above to be correct....It's just the old prerogative asserting itself which has been in them from [sic] centuries—namely that of the subjugation of woman. Why, that kind of opposition is the very way to make suffragettes."

In December 1909, 10 women gathered at Armine Gosling's home and decided to start "The Ladies Reading Room." It would be a place to listen to lectures, read current literature and meet like-minded women. They rented space on Water Street, stocked it with periodicals and opened daily from 10 until 6. Any woman introduced by a member and willing to pay three dollars a year could join. Within weeks, 125 women had.

The Current Events Club, which met every Saturday, revived the suffrage movement, as Margot Duley notes: "for within its walls, women of influence in St John's were politicized and converted to the cause. [It] functioned virtually as a self-taught liberal arts college in which members gave papers, developed analytical skills, discussed issues, and gained confidence as public speakers."

During WWI, women turned their attention to war work, but by 1920, in spite of fierce opposition from the male establishment and severe depression in Newfoundland, The Ladies Reading Room again became a focal point for the franchise campaign.

Newfoundland women did not get the vote until 1925. It is possible that they might have waited longer had not the Current Events Club helped them to gain the analytical, debating and political skills they needed. [HS-1996]

"19 APRIL 1916"

"The day that woman's suffrage became *un fait accompli* in Alberta, Mrs Jamieson was in Edmonton. When the news came through that the women of the province had been granted the franchise, she rushed to the phone and called up two of her friends, both very prominent women in Canada and tireless workers for suffrage, Judge Emily Murphy and Mrs Nellie McClung...[see pp. 50, 53, and 54] The trio held a caucus and decided that they must celebrate in some way. 'Being women, we couldn't very well express our joy and satisfaction by going out and getting a bottle, so as we walked down Jasper Avenue with our arms interlocked. Mrs Murphy suggested that the most rash thing we could do would be to have our pictures taken.' This picture has become one of Alberta's historical treasures, for it shows three of Canada's outstanding women taken on the most memorable day in the history of Canadian women."—*from "First Woman Magistrate in Canada," by Dorothy Bowman Barker, newspaper and date unknown* [HS-1977]

below: Nellie McClung, Alice Jamieson, and Emily Murphy, 19 April 1916

The battle for suffrage was just the beginning of women's involvement in politics. Since they won the right to do so, Canadian women have served in political office at all levels.

ALICE JAMIESON

right: Alice Jamieson

If women in politics endeavoured to act like themselves rather than in the way they think they should act in order to fit in, then we could conceivably break down the old competitive systems prevalent in politics today.
—Rosemary Brown, 1973

It is not easy to be a feminist. It is even a little frightening, for the understanding of the feminist cause means changes in all domains of life, political and private.
—Margaret Anderson, 1975

I think if women work hard and do not fight amongst themselves, they can accomplish great things. I have great confidence in Canadian women. I know what they can do.
—Florence Bird, 1974

In 1902, Alice Jamieson arrived in Calgary with her husband and four children and soon became active in various women's organizations. In 1914, she was appointed judge of the juvenile court in Calgary and became the first woman judge in the British Empire. She felt this was a giant step toward women's rightful place in public life.

There was opposition and skepticism when her appointment was announced. She later commented: "When I first assumed my duties in the police court, with cold shoulders greeting me on every hand, I said to myself, 'I don't know why I ever came here—I don't have to do this' and then I drew myself up and said, 'Well, I'm here and I'm here to stay.'" Alice Jamieson not only remained on the bench, but she won over her harshest critics with the quality of her decisions.

Alice firmly believed in women's rights. Active in the suffrage movement, she addressed the Alberta legislature, had numerous interviews with politicians, including the Alberta premier, and was one of a group that presented lengthy petitions asking for woman suffrage.

After women had the vote, she actively worked to elect women to the public school board, to the provincial legislature, and to other elected offices. Alice Jamieson retired from the bench in 1932, and died in 1949 at age 89. [HS-1990]

SARAH RAMSLAND

Five dollars to fix a mud hole. That was all the Member for Pelly wanted of Highways Minister Gardiner. He dismissed the request curtly. Out of the question.

"Well," the Member for Pelly said briskly, "I don't know what kind of time you have, Mr Gardiner, but I'm prepared to sit here all day if necessary," and with that she whisked her crocheting from her bag. Besieged, Gardiner gave in, and Sarah Katherine Ramsland, Saskatchewan's first female MLA, got her road work done.

She was elected in 1919 to the seat vacated by the sudden death of her husband during a flu epidemic. With three small children and no money, Mrs Ramsland had to find work. Should she return to Minnesota, where she had taught before moving north in 1907? Should she teach in Canada? Or should she listen to her husband's friends, who kept trying to coax her to stand for election?

A political career had probably never before occurred to her, although she had always shared her husband's interest in public issues. She was a homebody and a contented mother who had never campaigned independently, not even for women's suffrage.

Although the local Liberals backed her unanimously, the party establishment was politely cool. Addressing an election rally on Mrs Ramsland's behalf, the premier outlined the government's accomplish-

ments and intentions—but never once mentioned his candidate by name!

It was a rancorous, brawling campaign. Party loyalties remained intense as the votes were counted, with each side confident of victory, but in the end, Mrs Ramsland won by about 300 votes. She repeated her success in the general election of 1921, but lost to a Progressive four years later. Isolated by her sex, she never displayed the spunk and initiative in the Assembly that she showed on the hustings or behind the scenes. But, hours before the close of her last session, she finally introduced a resolution in her own right, one calling for amendments to the divorce laws so that men and women could apply on the same grounds. [HS-1978]

ROBERTA CATHERINE MacADAMS

Roberta Catherine MacAdams was one of the first two women in the Alberta Legislature. She was elected in 1917 as one of the armed services representatives [see p. 56].

When she enlisted in 1916, she was made a lieu-

tenant and posted to the Ontario Military Hospital in Orpington, Kent, as the dietitian. She was contacted by Beatrice Nasmyth, the only woman agent-general in England, to be a candidate in the upcoming Alberta election, and decided to run. She was the only woman in a field of 21. That year, the Alberta legislature had allotted citizens serving overseas two legislative representatives, both to be elected in the same ballot. Said Nasmyth, Roberta's campaign manager, "I told the Chief [Alberta's premier] if she were returned he would have the finest Member the entire overseas force could offer, and if she lost it would be because our campaign was too honest and unfinanced."

But win she did, 700 votes ahead of her nearest rival. On February 8, 1918, one week after her investiture into parliament, Roberta MacAdams introduced a bill to incorporate the War Veteran's Next-of-Kin Association. This act was the first legislation introduced by a woman in any legislature in the British Commonwealth.

After the war, MacAdams concerned herself with the post-war problems facing returned soldiers, nurses, and their families. In 1919 she worked for the Soldier Settlement Board as a counsellor for war brides going into new homesteads. Roberta retired from parliament in 1921. She involved herself with women's, educational, and social organizations in Calgary until her death in December 1959. [HS-1980]

THE WOMEN'S PARTY

"The Women's Party does not hesitate at handing out advice on any subject in which it is interested," stated the *Grain Growers' Guide* in 1918. It is difficult to find a subject in which the party was not interested, from production in industry to women's rights in India.

In 1918, the year in which the Women's Party was founded in Toronto, many crucial issues faced Canada and the world. World War I was drawing to a painful close, and there was great concern for international security and control. The continuing battle for women's rights and the growing unrest among

left: Sarah Ramsland

below top: Roberta MacAdams campaign poster, 1917

below bottom: Dorise Nielsen campaign pamphlet, 1940

UNITY Means VICTORY

VOTE FOR
MRS. DORISE W. NIELSEN
United Progressive Candidate

right: Agnes Macphail

To have part of life can never be enough, one must have all. That is what I want for women.—Agnes Macphail

Getting into politics is just housekeeping on a national scale.—Louise McKinney

labourers in industry had created an air of tension in the country that few people were willing to disturb.

Not so the Women's Party. Blatant in its condemnation of Germany and disapproval of worker control in industry, the "Programme for the War and After" drawn up by Constance E. Hamilton, Jessie Campbell MacIver, and Sarah A. Ormsby drew wrath from many quarters, most particularly the organized farm women of western Canada. Here the perennial distrust between West and East found voice in lengthy editorials in the publications of that time, heated correspondence between prominent women's organizations, and a general air of scandal that the battered boat of current affairs should be rocked so rudely from its eastern end.

Unhappily, many concerns common to both sides were overlooked in the battle of words across Canada. Prairie women, concerned with the economic realities of agricultural life, were suspicious of what they saw as "mental gymnastics" engaged in by wealthy easterners. Both groups had long since declared their support for such issues as equal pay for equal work, equal marriage laws, and homestead rights for women, but these areas of agreement were often overlooked in the very real disparities then present in Canada. This gulf was exemplified by the comments of Irene Parlby, president of the United Farm Women of Alberta, in 1918: "It would doubtless be well if the women of the whole Dominion could be absolutely united in their work for social betterment, but unity is not possible where difference exists as to fundamentals—sincerity and truth and justice are more important things than unity, and we must first make those secure." [HS-1977]

AGNES MACPHAIL

Agnes Macphail, first woman Member of the Canadian House of Commons, rose from being a country school teacher to a position of leadership in national and international affairs. Born and raised on a farm in Grey County, Ontario, she referred to herself as a "Farmer's Daughter" throughout her career.

During the Ontario provincial campaign of 1919

Agnes was asked to speak in support of the United Farmers of Ontario candidate. She was swept up in the cause, and when offered the nomination by the Progressives in 1921, she took it. Her election in December of that year marked the largest majority recorded to date in that constituency. She was re-elected in 1925, 1926, 1930, and 1935. Her prime interest was the establishment of social justice in the new social order towards which she worked. Cooperation would supplant competition in both business and in politics.

She devoted herself to agricultural problems; to international relations with a view to establishing peace; to greater opportunities for women; and to the reform of the penal system. She was a militant crusader for the removal of the economic causes of wars. In 1929 Ms. Macphail was appointed one of three Canadian delegates to the 10th Assembly of the League of Nations at Geneva. There she sat on the Disarmament Committee, the first woman ever to do so.

International affairs affect women and children enormously and Agnes Macphail felt that women, particularly mothers, should participate in the politics touching their lives:

"Women are born organizers and there is no greater proof of this than the fact that they can keep organizations going that mean nothing....The saddest thing I know, next to the jobless youth, is the woman past 40 whose children have grown self-sufficient and whose husband is off playing golf or otherwise amusing himself. Let such women take off their hats and gloves and scarves and organize for a real purpose." [HS-1975]

WOMEN ARE PERSONS!

This larger-than-life bronze monument was commissioned by the Famous Five Foundation, and created by Barbara Paterson of Edmonton, for Olympic Plaza in Calgary and Parliament Hill in Ottawa.

The Famous Five Foundation educates and inspires fellow Canadians by celebrating women's achievements, commemorating the courage, tenacity, and conviction of the Famous Five, and encouraging women's leadership. [HS-2000]

left: Maquette for a monument in celebration of the Persons Case, the Famous Five, and the achievements of Canadian women

EMILY MURPHY

Emily Murphy was born and educated in Ontario. In 1904 she moved to Winnipeg, where she conducted the literary section of the *Winnipeg Tribune*. Moving to Alberta in 1907, she became very active in civic affairs, especially in the attainment of laws for the betterment of conditions for women and children.

It was her appointment as police magistrate that began the battle she waged for many years in the "Persons Case." Although she spent the better part of her life working for this goal and was recommended for appointment to the Senate, the Canadian government never saw fit to appoint her to the post. She lived to see her obvious claims ignored twice.

Under the pen name "Janey Canuck," she wrote many books and articles mirroring western life. In one of them she said: "Lean on no one. Find your own centre and live in it, surrendering it to no person or thing." [HS-1974]

A tough day in court for Emily Murphy in September 1916 became the foundation for a landmark case which has affected the life of every Canadian woman.

THE FAMOUS FIVE AND THE PERSONS CASE

A few months after the passage of the enfranchisement act in Alberta, Emily Murphy was appointed a police magistrate for the City of Edmonton—the first woman in the British Empire to hold such a post. The very first day she presided over her court, the counsel for a defendant on whom she had imposed a stiff sentence, told "Her Honour" that she was not legally a "person" under British common law and had no right to be holding court anyway. This incident, and Emily's ensuing attempt to gain a Senate appointment, catalyzed a struggle that reached the Supreme Court of Canada, and even the Privy Council in London, England. Learning that any five people could appeal to the Supreme Court of Canada for clarification of the British North America Act, Murphy launched her appeal along with four other campaigners for women's rights: Nellie McClung, Irene Parlby, Louise McKinney, and Henrietta Muir Edwards. Finally, on 18 October 1929, the Privy Council ruled that women were, indeed, persons in the eyes of the law. Following their victory the co-petitioners became known as the Famous Five. [HS-1974, 2000]

right: Judge Emily Murphy conducting juvenile court, 1918

No anthology of *Herstory* would be complete without a tribute to our "matron saint"—Nellie McClung.

NELLIE McCLUNG

Born Nellie Letitia Helen Mooney in 1873 in Grey County, Ontario, she grew up on a homestead near Brandon, Manitoba. Nellie didn't start school until she was 10 years old, but only five years later, she moved to Winnipeg and earned her teaching certificate.

In her first post she boarded with Rev. James and Mrs Annie McClung. Annie was "an ardent champion of women's rights," and Nellie was deeply influenced by this dynamic woman. With Annie's encouragement, Nellie wrote the first of her 16 novels and became one of the most acclaimed writers of her day. She reached a wide audience with her syndicated newspaper column, "Nellie McClung Says."

But she is best remembered as a political activist. Nellie was a fervent Methodist and proponent of the Social Gospel. She fought tirelessly for many of the rights we now take for granted. She was a founding member of the Manitoba Political Equity League, which succeeded in getting women the vote. After moving to Alberta, she joined the Edmonton Equal Franchise League, and in 1921 was elected as a Liberal MLA. In politics she championed old age pensions, mother's allowances, public health nursing, free medical and dental care, birth control, divorce laws and property rights for women. She was one of the Famous Five who battled for women's recognition, achieved in 1929, as "persons" under the law.

Nellie was one of the first female elders of the United Church of Canada, the first female board member of the CBC, and the only woman in the Canadian delegation to the League of Nations in 1938. She was also mother of five children—having married Annie's son Wes in 1896.

On numerous lecture tours throughout Canada, the U.S., and Britain, Nellie used her legendary wit and humour "to drive home at every theatre and community hall her message of justice for women."

She died at her home, "Lantern Lane," in Victoria at age 78. [HS-2000]

Whenever I don't know whether to fight or not—I always fight.—
Emily Murphy, ca 1910

right: Nellie McClung

Women are going to form a chain, a greater sisterhood than the world has ever known!
—Nellie McClung, in the *Countrywoman*

HENRIETTA MUIR EDWARDS

People who stereotype artists as dreamy and impractical would have trouble with Henrietta Muir Edwards. In a day when the vote for women was an almost unheard of idea, she was a leader in the Montreal suffrage movement. Henrietta was instrumental in the formation of a working girls' organization in that city, and used the money she made from sales and exhibitions of her paintings at the Canadian Academy of Arts to further the interests of women in Montreal.

Henrietta knew the need for women to communicate with each other in the struggle for the vote. She did something about it. She and her sister Amélia published one of the early women's papers—*Women's Work in Canada*. Determined that women should know their situation thoroughly, Henrietta published articles on Canadian law pertaining to women, the best

IRENE PARLBY

Eight years before women became "persons" in Canada, Irene Parlby was a cabinet minister in the Alberta government. Her political life began in the community of Alix, where she organized the first women's auxiliary to the United Farmers of Alberta. The UFA approached her to run as a candidate in the 1921 election, and as a constant speaker in favour of women's involvement in the running of the country, she gladly accepted.

The only woman cabinet minister, she became the watchguard over legislation pertaining to women. Since she herself was a farm woman, she was particularly concerned with the lot of rural women in Alberta. She fought vigorously for women's rights to homestead and to share in the ownership of family property [see p. 65]. She introduced legislation to improve the health and welfare of women and children. Irene Parlby was also one of five Alberta women to fight through every court in the land to have women recognized as "persons," having equal rights to fill responsible positions, including that of being named to the Senate.

As both a great politician and suffrage leader, Irene Parlby faithfully carried out her convictions to improve the lives of all Canadian women. [HS-1975]

above left: Henrietta Muir Edwards

All honour to women for what they have done, what they are doing and what they will do.
—Gena Macfarlane, *Winnipeg Free Press,* 1906

known being "The Legal Status of Women in Canada."

In 1902, she moved to Fort Macleod, Alberta. There she became concerned about the welfare of Indians on reserves. She became involved as well in the Alberta fight for social justice for women. As spokesperson for the Alberta Local Council for Women, she went yearly to Edmonton and Ottawa to petition for women's and children's rights. She was generally recognized as one the finest legal minds in the Dominion.

Inevitably, she joined Murphy, McClung, McKinney, and Parlby to fight through the courts for the personhood of women. That battle won with the Privy Council ruling of 1929, she returned to the East and became superintendent of women's suffrage with the YWCA. [HS-1976]

left : Irene Parlby

above:
Louise Crummy McKinney

I believe that women can reach their potential only by planning and working with men to achieve a new balance in the home, in the workplace, in the community, in the world. This new balance can be created through their determination to assume their full rights and responsibilities, not only as women but as human beings.—Grace MacInnis, pioneer CCF-NDPer and the first woman Member of Parliament sent to the House of Commons from British Columbia, 1976

LOUISE CRUMMY McKINNEY

Louise McKinney will perhaps be remembered for her political accomplishments—her election as one of the first two women legislators in the British Empire, and co-petitioner in the 1929 Persons Case—but the basis of her political acts and the prime platforms of her life were her Christian beliefs and her work with the Women's Christian Temperance Union.

Louise was born in Frankville, Ontario, on September 22, 1868. Following her education, she taught school for several years in Ontario and North Dakota. In 1894, she accepted a position as WCTU organizer in North Dakota and, until her death in 1931, she continued to work for this organization with all her dedication. She held many executive positions in the WCTU. In 1898, she was elected the first district president of North Dakota, and when she moved to Claresholm, Northwest Territories, in 1903, she founded its first WCTU local. She was this local's first and until 1931, only president. In 1904, Louise met with other women of Claresholm, Olds, Edmonton, Regina, and Medicine Hat to found the Northwest Territories WCTU. She became the president of this group and continued as Alberta president when Alberta became a province in 1905. She held this position for 22 years and was at the same time vice-president of the Dominion Union. In 1930, she became acting president for the Canadian WCTU, and was host for the 1931 Toronto world convention. At this meeting, she was elected world vice-president.

Louise was also active in her community's church. She supported the Church Union movement of the 1920s, and in 1925 was named commissioner to the First General Council of the United Church of Canada. When the church was formed as Canada's largest Protestant denomination in 1929, she was the only woman to sign the resulting Basis of Union.

In 1917, Louise ran in the provincial election as Claresholm, Alberta's Non-Partisan League candidate. She won, thereby becoming, with Roberta MacAdams [see p. 51], one of the first two women legislators in the British Empire. In her four years of office, she worked to improve the lives of immigrants, to make prohibition more effective, and to bring better legal security to widows and deserted wives. With Henrietta Muir Edwards, she drafted a motion which became the Dower Act, ensuring widows a portion of a deceased husband's property.

Louise Crummy McKinney lived her life with dedication, determination, and sympathy. As Nellie McClung said on her death in 1931: "Mrs McKinney was a great lover of people and because she loved them, she could not look with complacency on any of life's evils." [HS-1981]

Women's traditional involvement in the community and civic politics takes many forms—sometimes they run the city from home, sometimes from the mayor's office.

CHARLOTTE WHITTON

"The nation that fails to enlist the magnificent resources of its women is flying on one wing and bound for a crash landing." Ottawa was spared such a crash landing when Charlotte Whitton took the pilot's seat in 1951. An outspoken proponent of women's rights and equality, she has distinguished herself as both the first woman mayor of a large Canadian city and as a dedicated reformer of the Canadian welfare system.

At Queen's University, where she graduated with a Master's degree in 1918, she had been captain of a hockey team as well as the first woman editor of the student paper. As Director of the Council on Child Welfare, she gained an international reputation for her work in social welfare. She was responsible for totally reorganizing the welfare system, "elevating it from the abyss of casual charity to the broad highway of a profession," according to one government report.

In 1950, after lecturing to a University women's club on the need for more women in politics, she was challenged by the *Ottawa Journal* to run for the

Ottawa Board of Control. Arming a contingency of women supporters with a badge of needle and blue thread, she accepted the challenge and was swept into office with a large majority of votes. When the Mayor of Ottawa died in 1951, Charlotte was unanimously elected mayor by the thirty-one-man council.

During her "reign," council meetings were such hell-raising sessions that the Board of Control became appropriately known as the "Board Out of Control." She did manage, however, to modernize the city's assessment rolls, to get a new city hall, police headquarters, and a cross-city express highway, and to triple the federal government's contribution to the city. [HS-1975]

[Charlotte Whitton died in 1975. Eds.]

FLORENCE McORMOND

Florence Dunlop received her BA from Queen's University in 1907, and taught high school English and history in Ontario before marrying John McOrmond. In 1912 the McOrmonds moved to Sutherland, Saskatchewan (a small CPR town annexed to Saskatoon in 1956), where Florence again taught school. Here she also began her community involvement by organizing the local branch of the Red Cross.

The McOrmonds had three sons and one daughter while Florence continued to be active in community groups. She served on the executives of the local Council of Women in Saskatoon, the Canadian Club, the University Women's Club, the Women's Progressive Conservative Association, and her church's women's group.

In 1936 Mrs McOrmond was elected to the Sutherland town council. In 1937, as the Chairman of the Relief Committee, Florence found that the "head of the family" often spent relief payments on cigarettes and liquor or at the local pool room. She succeeded in having the local pool hall closed and in altering the relief procedure. In 1945 Florence defeated the incumbent to become the first woman to be elected mayor in Saskatchewan—the third in Canada. The press release, carried in newspapers across Canada, praised Florence as the "ideal woman, able to run a home, look after a family, and devote herself at the same time to the exacting business of running a municipality."

While in office Florence McOrmond worked constantly to upgrade the quality of housing, fulfilling her election promise to provide sewer and water connections to at least seventy-five percent of Sutherland homes. She introduced street lights to the town, and petitioned the federal government for fifty wartime houses for her community. Only cities were eligible under the Act; however, Florence travelled to Ottawa and received grants for thirty houses. Mayor McOrmond achieved all this in little more than a year.

Florence McOrmond believed women should be represented at all levels of government, and on councils and permanent government boards. She urged

above: Florence McOrmond

left: Charlotte Whitton, right, with John and Olive Diefenbaker

Whatever women do, they must do twice as well as men to be thought half as good. Luckily it's not difficult.
—Charlotte Whitton

women to discuss politics unashamedly, and to encourage political parties to give them greater recognition. Florence McOrmond celebrated her 100th birthday in 1984; she died in May 1985. [HS-1986]

NANCY HODGES

The goal of women should be to break down, not to build up, the artificial division between women and men in politics. First-class human beings are needed to make our laws and to see that they are carried out, not just women's candidates and men's candidates.
—Florence Bird, 1974

Born in 1888, Nancy Hodges arrived in Canada from Great Britain in 1912. Initially settling in Kamloops, she and her husband operated a newspaper until moving to Victoria in 1916. There she became the women's editor of the *Victoria Times.* Although a respected journalist for over 30 years, with 2,550 columns to her credit, she is most remembered for her distinguished political career.

Nancy Hodges plunged into politics when she was first elected a Liberal MLA in 1941. She served 11 years in that capacity and her outspoken manner and fiery debates in the legislature became legendary.

A strong supporter of women's rights, she often jumped party lines to present a solid front on women's issues. She protested the laying off of single women in favour of WWII veterans, and threatened to campaign for pensions for women at 40 if the practice continued. Inclusion of women in workers' compensation benefits and protection of married women's property rights are among the issues she tackled. She was also president of such groups as the National Federation of Liberal Women of Canada, Victoria's Women's Canadian Club and the Victoria Business and Professional Women's Club. In 1949 she was named speaker of the provincial legislature, becoming the first woman speaker not only in Canada, but in the Commonwealth. She said, "I shan't be able to take part in any of the debates....I'll doubtless find it hard to restrain myself sometimes."

Appointed the first woman senator from her province in 1953, she was quick to share the honour. "I feel that the appointment is a tribute to the women of British Columbia rather than any personal honour to me." After she retired in 1965, she was praised by Premier W.A.C. Bennett. "Mrs. Hodges displayed the

qualities of a brilliant and constructive mind that should rightly earn her the admiration of all the women—and indeed, all the people—of British Columbia." [HS-1996]

CAIRINE MACKAY WILSON

After 10 years of managing three houses and a family of eight, Cairine Wilson was startled by the opinion of her family doctor:

"Never had he seen any person deteriorate mentally as I had he told me; and from an intelligent girl I had become a most uninteresting individual. I have been grateful from that day for his frank words, for it caused me to realize that the work which I had always considered my duty was not sufficient. At once I made a determined effort not to merit such condemnation."

right: Cairine Mackay Wilson

At the age of 36, Cairine plunged into public life. Between 1921 and 1930 she became president of the Eastern Ontario Women's Liberal Association, president of the Women's Canadian Club, a director of the Ottawa Welfare Bureau, a director of the Victorian Order of Nurses, president of the National Federation of Liberal Women for Canada, as well as being active in the YWCA, St John's Ambulance Society, and the Salvation Army. The achievement for which she is best remembered, however, is her 1930 appointment as Canada's first woman senator.

Later critics on both sides of the feminist cause have viewed her background as wife and mother as insufficient preparation for a life in politics, and her appointment as mere tokenism. This is a reduction that disregards an important milestone for all women and negates the accomplishments of a 30-year career in public life. While in the Senate, Cairine championed the cause of refugees and displaced persons, addressed injustices in immigration laws, and was an outspoken crusader against discrimination and prejudice. Notes her biographer, Valerie Knowles, "Senator Wilson not only won respect for herself and a place in Canadian history but by her example, she helped to make a respected place for women in public life in this country. Canadian women...will long remember and pay tribute to her."

Cairine Wilson died on 3 March 1962. [HS-1996]

Throughout the history of Canadian women's political involvement, there have been individuals of great courage and dedication—women who inspire us to act on our beliefs.

THÉRÈSE CASGRAIN

Born in 1896 into one of Montreal's wealthiest families, married to a prosperous lawyer, Thérèse Casgrain could have led a frivolous, easy life. Instead she was at the heart of the battle for women's rights in Quebec, especially the right to vote [see p. 44].

Thérèse Casgrain entered the public sphere during the federal election of 1921, when she conducted a highly successful campaign for her husband, who was incapacitated by illness. In 1928 she became president of the Provincial Franchise Committee (later, the League For Women's Rights)—a position she held for 14 years. In November 1929 she appeared before the Dorion Commission, which had been set up to look into such things as a woman's right to her own earnings and the right to bring law suits without her husband's consent. One of the main obstacles to winning suffrage in Quebec was lack of support from rural French women. She was able to reach many of them through her radio program, "Femina," which was broadcast over French and English networks.

She was also a co-founder in 1921 of the "Comité provincial pour le suffrage féminin," later "La Ligue des droits de la femme." Every year from 1927 to 1939 La Ligue persuaded a member of the provincial legislature

above and below:
Thérèse Casgrain

We are faced with a society that needs to cast off its old concepts of racism, violence, and snobbery. We are too afraid of abandoning old ways of looking at things— when patriotism meant obedience; middle age, wisdom; and woman, submission.
—Thérèse Casgrain, 1972

above: Louise Lucas

*I am convinced that until we
have more women in politics—
openly, flagrantly and
unashamedly committed to the
struggle for the liberation of
woman and determined to
change traditional power
politics to make it more
responsive to the dispossessed of
this earth—we as women are
doomed to many more years of
oppression and exploitation.*
—Rosemary Brown, 1977

to introduce a bill to grant women's suffrage, "an excellent way to obtain publicity to influence public opinion on our behalf." They were finally successful in 1940.

Following the war and the final achievement of the vote, she continued faithfully to press for child protection laws, prison reform, government appointments for women and amendments to the civil code. In 1945 Thérèse used her formidable political, organizational, and social skills to bring about the reversal of a decision to pay family allowances in Quebec to men rather than to women. Other campaigns included fighting for better working conditions and salaries for women teachers and for women's right to sit on school boards and juries.

Her father was a federal Conservative MP, her husband a prominent Liberal. Madame Casgrain ran for parliament as an Independent Liberal, for the CCF and as a peace candidate—always unsuccessfully. She joined the CCF in 1948 and was provincial leader from 1951-1957—the first woman party leader anywhere in Canada. In the 1960's she joined the peace group, Voice of Women, and campaigned around the world against war, getting arrested in Paris for trying to present a petition to a meeting of NATO.

When the NDP succeeded the CCF in 1961, Casgrain continued her active support, holding the position of national vice-chairperson. "I can't imagine a woman who has the best interest of her children at heart not taking an interest in politics," she says.

In 1970 Madame Casgrain was appointed to the Senate, only nine months before her statutory retirement age. She worked tirelessly while she had this chance, including reminding senators that women in Newfoundland and Quebec were not allowed to sit on juries. Throughout her busy life, Thérèse Casgrain took a leadership role, working in co-operation with other women. After her death in 1981, friends created the Fondation Thérèse-F.-Casgrain in memory of her "lifelong commitment to the promotion of human rights and to the defence of the economic, political and social interests of Canadian women." [HS-1974, 2000]

LOUISE LUCAS

Louise Lucas and her husband decided to give up their small wholesale provision business in Chicago and move to the prairies of Saskatchewan, after crooked political bosses in Chicago threatened that they would suffer certain harm if they did not pay them off. Louise thought then that politics was a dirty business and she wanted none of it.

However, ignoring politics was a luxury farmers could not afford in the midst of the Depression. Louise saw families forced to leave their homes, and mortgage companies ruthlessly repossessing everything they owned. She herself became actively involved in politics in order to protect the security of her home and family.

Out of the misery of drought and debt, a coalition of farm and labour groups came together to form the Co-operative Commonwealth Federation—the CCF. Louise, with her bright mind and ability to speak out, and her passion for justice, found herself drawn unwillingly into the "dirty" business of politics. She was much in demand as a speaker for the new party, recording her commitment in such statements as: "I am going on this tour with you and when I collapse you can send me home on a stretcher." Louise Lucas' appeal was to women, challenging them to assume the equality they had been granted in the new political party: "I would be at home with my husband and family on the farm if I thought this job could be done without the help of the women. I am counting on the women to see to it that our movement never becomes just another political party— that they will help keep it a great movement for humanity."

Although she battled for justice, she was without rancour, and always fought to have "the Opposition regarded as human beings with a misguided but honest integrity." Illness interrupted her federal campaign for election to parliament, and she died shortly after dictating her memoirs to a journalist friend. Louise Lucas, the "reluctant debutante" into politics, had become known as "The Mother of the CCF." [HS-1975]

For many years, individual women and women's groups have worked to influence laws affecting them and their children. Since the suffrage battle, women have continued to use the political process to advance their causes.

ELLEN FAIRCLOUGH

When she was sworn in as secretary of state on June 21, 1957, Ellen Fairclough became Canada's first woman cabinet minister in Ottawa. By this time Fairclough had already had a distinguished career and her selection by Prime Minister John Diefenbaker merely confirmed her abilities and talents.

Born in Hamilton, Ontario, in 1905, Ellen Louks had a conventional life in some ways. She married Gordon Fairclough, bore a son, managed a busy household, and became an accomplished musician. Ellen Fairclough, however, proved to have wider interests. She became a chartered accountant, headed an accounting firm in Hamilton, and earned recognition as a tax expert. She was active in the Ontario Young Progressive Conservatives, and served as their provincial vice-president. Active in Hamilton city politics, she sat on city council from 1946 to 1949. Ellen Fairclough was an unsuccessful candidate in the 1949 federal election, but was elected to the House of Commons in a May 15, 1950, by-election. She was subsequently appointed the Tory labour critic, and began to earn a reputation for hard work. In 1953 and again in 1954, Ellen Fairclough introduced a bill in the House advocating equal pay for equal work [see pp. 47, 62, and 127]. When she introduced the 1954 bill she announced it as: "a measure to prevent discrimination against women in respect of their employment by reason of their sex and...to ensure that women will be paid at the same rate as men for similar or comparable work." She went on to point out:

"Since World War I the use of women in industry and commerce, in many instances in so-called men's jobs, has become more and more commonplace. In the factory, in the office, in the school, and in the home women are performing work of a comparable character to that performed by men. As working conditions have improved for all workers, the classifications which were regarded as strictly male have gradually diminished in number."

When the Minister of Labour criticized the bill, Ellen responded: "there is a problem as he admits, and it should be seriously considered and not just brushed

above: Ellen Fairclough with Prime Minister John Diefenbaker

aside lightly with a lot of half-baked excuses about the fact that it should be a matter for collective bargaining; that the time is not ripe." She also urged the government to create a Women's Bureau in the Department of Labour; both ideas were later adopted by the St Laurent government.

Ellen Fairclough was particularly interested in social welfare and labour relations, and was keenly aware of the problems women could face in the workplace of mid-century Canada. It is therefore not surprising that she was the first Member of Parliament to introduce the concept of equal pay for equal work.

Ellen Fairclough served in the Diefenbaker cabinet as secretary of state, minister of Citizenship and Immigration, and postmaster general. She was defeated in the 1963 general election. In 1975 she was named Woman of the Year in Ontario. [HS-1986]

[The title 'The Right Honourable" was bestowed upon Ellen Fairclough in 1992 by Her Majesty Queen Elizabeth II. She was named Companion of the Order of Canada in 1995. Eds.]

EQUAL PAY FOR EQUAL WORK, 1954

On March 2, 1954, Ellen Fairclough, Member of Parliament for Hamilton West, introduced a bill advocating that "women be paid at the same rates as men for similar or comparable work." [see pp. 47 and 127] During that debate, and a second on April 6, both Ellen Fairclough and MP Margaret Aitken spoke eloquently in support of the motion.

Margaret Aitken: Equal pay for equal work is a principle that I believe a young country like Canada should establish forthwith....An artist is judged and paid according to his or her talents. Authors sign the same contract with a publisher irrespective of the author's sex. In fact, such words as "authoress" or "poetess" are obsolete today. In the professions a lawyer or a doctor is worthy of his or her hire. I am proud to say that in my own profession there is no such word as "reporteress" or "editoress."

Yet in one of the most important of all the professions, that of teaching, not only are school boards notably reluctant to recognize this basic principle of equal pay, but so are a good many of the male teachers. One reason for this, and I have heard it many times, is that men teachers do extracurricular duties that women teachers are not called upon to do or are not able to do. If a job calls for the same qualifications, then it seems to me there should be one salary schedule.

...eighty-four out of every hundred gainfully employed women are working because they have to work. While these women may receive one salary for a job, the men receive another salary for the job. And yet the men meet us equally on so many other footings. When it comes to price tags, for instance, there is no discrimination. There is no discrimination when it comes to taxes. When it comes to groceries, fuel, or rent there is no discrimination. Yet we do find insistence upon this discrimination in the matter of payment received for jobs.

Ellen Fairclough: From the standpoint of the women themselves it is a matter of simple justice. It ensures that women workers will receive what they are entitled to receive for the work they do. Those women who are housewives and mothers also have an interest in this type of legislation, because it protects them and their children in that it protects the wages of their husbands. Equal pay affords to men greater wage and job security. It protects them from the exploitation of employers who would hire women for less money or who would replace men workers with women workers at lower prices.

The basic reason for this legislation, Mr. Speaker, is not to protect the woman who is a rare case. It is not to make sure that some individual or group of individuals shall benefit under this legislation. Rather it is simply to protect the great rank and file of women workers, many of whom have no bargaining agents, who have no one to speak for them and...also to abolish the discrimination under which they work at the present time. [HS-1986]

According to the 1981 Census of Canada, full-time women ministers earned $9,249 on the average in 1980, 74% of the average income of $12,555 earned by men of the cloth. Is nothing sacred?
—Herstory, 1986

We were called names, sneered at, scorned... hissed and spit at, but our cause lived to see some of those scorners carry a petition from door to door.
—National Council of Women Yearbook, 1917-18

Canadian women in the 1950s and 1960s had a vision of the Canada they wanted to live in, a vision of a country founded on equality and concerned with human rights, as well as women's rights.

ROYAL COMMISSION ON THE STATUS OF WOMEN IN CANADA

A feminist consciousness was pervading Canada in the 60s; women were making themselves heard on a wide variety of issues crucial to them. In recognition of this new consciousness, and in response to the demands of thousands of women across Canada, the Commission was set up on February 16, 1967.

Their terms of reference were, briefly, as follows:

- to investigate laws and practices concerning the political rights of women,

- to inquire into the present and potential role of women in the Canadian labour force, including the special problems of married women,

- to report on and recommend measures that might be taken by the government to ensure better use of the skills and education of Canadian women.

During 1968-69, the seven Commissioners, led by Florence Bird, travelled throughout Canada and the Territories, receiving hundreds of briefs and presentations from concerned Canadian women. When people couldn't attend the public hearings, phone lines were set up, so that no woman who wished to make herself heard would lack the opportunity.

On September 28, 1970, the Commissioners signed their names to a report that is still being reprinted across Canada, a report that has had considerable impact on Canadian attitudes and laws as they affect women. Few publications of any kind can boast of such a record. In the words of one of its writers: "This report won't be pigeonholed." [HS-1978]

[In 2000, the Ontario Women's Justice Network issued a commentary on follow-up to the recommendations of the Royal Commission by Pamela Cross, "Where Are We After Thirty Years?" Not surprisingly the record is mixed. Some recommendations have been implemented—for example, women can join the RCMP and minimum wages are now the same for both women and men. Other recommendations have been only partially addressed—sports in schools are not equally available to both genders and there are more, but not equal, numbers of women serving on federal boards and commissions. However, some recommendations, such as a national child care program, have been ignored altogether. Eds.]

The harder task... is to make people believe there are causes; it is so much simpler to be content with fussing around over consequences.
—Julia P. Rose, in a WCTU letter to Violet McNaughton, 1939

FLORA MacDONALD

Flora MacDonald's life has been a model for working for a better world through politics. She was a pioneer for women in the House of Commons and has enlarged her constituency to planet size. In 1979-80, the first woman to hold the prestigious portfolio of State for External Affairs, she led the move to admit 100,000 Vietnamese "boat people" to Canada. Since her defeat in 1988, she has been active in over a dozen international organizations promoting world peace and helping those whose lives have been battered by war and poverty.

left: Flora MacDonald

I felt if there were barriers to be broken, I had to be ready to help break them.—The Honourable Flora MacDonald, 1993

right: Flora MacDonald at a Christmas party, 24 Sussex Drive, 1959

She was born in 1926 and attended her first Conservative political meeting at age 11 with her father. After high school she worked as a secretary for over ten years. In 1972, the first woman to graduate from the National Defence College course in Canadian and International Studies, she was elected to represent Kingston and the Islands, a seat she held for 16 years. While an MP she lived and breathed politics. She spent 18-hour days in her Ottawa office, and weekends in her constituency talking and listening to the people she represented. She is one of the best known and most experienced politicians in Canada. Emphatic in her support of "thrift and good sense" in government and her dislike of bureaucracies and red tape, Flora is a firm believer in people and the strength of the community.

Growing up in North Sydney, Nova Scotia, during the Depression, she knew first-hand the plight of the poor and powerless ignored by far-off governments. It is something she has never forgotten and which has influenced all her political actions. Of today's political parties she says: "We have a unique opportunity to deliver politics back to the people, to assure people of their rights, their voice, and their power."

Flora MacDonald did not arrive at her position of national prominence suddenly or by accident. By the time she was elected to the House of Commons in 1972, Flora had participated in nearly forty Tory campaigns in federal and provincial elections. She was executive director of the Progressive Conservative Party for 10 years, from 1957-1966, and a founding member and director of the Committee for an Independent Canada. In 1976, she became the first woman to make a serious bid for the leadership of the Conservative Party.

Compassion and energy are two words that well describe this remarkable woman's career, a career which is her commitment to the people of Canada. "My job is my life," she said while in office, "My constituency is my family." The media made much of her absence from the lists of patronage appointments after 1988. Perhaps too outspoken an advocate for Canadian culture and the world's downtrodden for her

former colleagues, she turned instead to her international constituency, a new career with Vision TV, and travelling the world to turn the eye of media on injustice and suffering. "Every time I come back to Canada from one of my international commitments, I am reminded once again that we are blessed indeed to live here."

She believes globalization and technology will allow the next generation of women to link and work with their sisters. "Now I can be in touch with women all over the world and get to know their problems and their progress....from my point of view. The biggest change for women in the developed world this century is that finally women are accepted and acknowledged as a vital component of the paid labour force. When I began working in the 1940s that wasn't so. There's no turning back now." [HS-1977, 2000]

Property law has long been a concern of women. At one time, a married woman literally owned nothing, not even the clothes on her back—her husband could sell the family home, even if it had been bought with her money, and leave her and her children with nothing.

PROPERTY RIGHTS

Marriage has played a major role in determining the property rights of Canadian women. Unfortunately, that role has often been negative.

In the years just prior to Confederation, the application of English law in British North America ensured that married women could not hold property: "By marriage, the husband and wife are one person in law: that is, the very being or legal existence of the woman is suspended during the marriage." In practical terms, this meant that for a married woman, any action—whether in business or real estate, accepting a donation or inheritance, or giving her children financial aid—was "absolutely null and void, no matter how just, reasonable, or advantageous to her." Her only remaining right was the ability to make a will. In all other aspects, the wife's actions depended upon specific authorization from her husband.

Although between 1875 and 1897 the provinces and territories instituted Married Women's Property acts purportedly to redress this inequity, there was considerable variation between jurisdictions and there remained considerable legalized inequality. For some working women whose property consisted of wages, the husband's consent—or actual separation from the husband—was required before the woman could legally control her own earnings.

In western Canada, disparity between the sexes was demonstrated in the right to acquire property. The *Homestead Regulations* enabled "any male over 18 years of age" to obtain a quarter section of land, but for a woman to enjoy the same right, she had to be "a widow, having minor children dependent upon her." Even her claim to be "sole head of a family"

above: Cap à l'Aigle, Québec

might be reviewed by the federal government before its acceptance.

More recently, property rights—specifically ownership or entitlement—became issues during the dissolution of marriage. Years of joint effort to help establish common assets were considered upon divorce merely the "normal contribution as wife to the matrimonial regime," not a claim to partial ownership of resources. The sentiment voiced by a woman in 1910—that women had no share in anything but the work—might easily have been expressed in the 1970s.

Quebec was the first province to enable both spouses to claim half interest in assets. The other provinces have since followed, and women now realize complete equity in property; today their assets may be vulnerable to alimony claims from former husbands. [HS-2000]

above: Irene Murdoch

How many small farmers could ever eke out a living if their wives did not work? Housewives or farmwives, they are just as surely a part of the labour force as any woman who ever worked for wages.
—Linda Taylor

I am not crazy. I am not scared. Only the ones that have a bad conscience have to be scared. And all the lies will come out.
—Rosa Becker, 1986

PROPERTY LAW

In 1973, Irene Murdoch of Nanton, Alberta, launched a long series of court battles against her estranged husband over her claims to half interest in their ranch. Although Mrs Murdoch had worked as both a housewife and farm labourer on that ranch for twenty-five years, and had often been responsible for its operation, the Supreme Court of Canada ruled that she had made "only a normal contribution as wife to the matrimonial regime." She was awarded only $200 a month separation payment while her husband retained the farm, house, car, and all farm revenue.

Helen Rathwell, of Tompkins, Saskatchewan, was also denied the right to half interest in her husband's farm. Like Irene Murdoch, she had contributed for twenty-four years to both household and farming chores. Mrs Rathwell was granted a divorce and given a maintenance payment of $250 a month. A special 1975 edition of the newsletter, *Network of Saskatchewan Women*, summarized her case:

"Twenty-four years of hard work and literally nothing to show for it but a sizable bill for court costs to fight for one's rights...the facts of the law as they now stand are that no matter how hard a woman has worked to acquire material things for 'us,' she is, in the eyes of the law, only doing her duty, her services are taken for granted."

Even though women like Alberta MLA Irene Parlby [see p. 55] were asking for legislation to institute community of matrimonial property as early as 1925, fifty years later the Murdoch and Rathwell cases clearly represent how the matrimonial law system in Canada often works against women who have contributed to the acquisition and development of family property. Quebec to date has been the only province to respond to Parlby's recommendation. The Quebec government implemented legislation called the "Partnership of Acquests" on July 1, 1970. The legislation recognizes marriage as a partnership of equals and gives both spouses a claim to one-half interest in the other's acquests. [HS-1975]

[Women across Canada now have legal equity in property. Eds.]

ROSA BECKER

Rosa Becker was born in Czechoslovakia on 11 July 1926. While she was still a teenager, she left home for Germany and England, and in 1952, at age twenty-six, emigrated to Canada. Two years later, she met Lothar Pettkus, newly arrived from Germany. He was soon sharing her $12-a-month Montreal apartment and living on what she earned in a lace factory. Pettkus's wages as a garage mechanic were saved in the hope of buying a farm one day. He would brag to his friends that it cost him nothing to live.

In 1961, Pettkus purchased a rundown farm in Franklin-Centre, Quebec. With hundreds of beehive frames they had built during the winter, he and Rosa struggled to establish a beekeeping business. Rosa, slight and frequently ill, shared in the heavy labour, as well as fulfilling the role of wife and homemaker. She adopted Pettkus's name, but when the subject of marriage arose he would reply, "You haven't got the paper but you are my wife—so what more do you want?"

In 1973, in Pettkus's name as before, they bought land in Hawkesbury, Ontario, and built a farmhouse. But life together was becoming increasingly difficult. Pettkus was abusive, occasionally violent, and in 1974, after nearly twenty years, there was a final break between them. Pettkus literally threw $3,000 in ten- and twenty-dollar bills at Rosa, her "share" of their estate, valued at $300,000.

Rosa worked as a babysitter, in a garment factory, and later kept house for a dairy farmer in Franklin-Centre, earning $60 a week. Here she kept her cats, crocheted in her spare time, and made friends. Here, too, she was to claim a historical legal victory over Pettkus, sadly followed by interminable legal wrangling, despair, and tragedy.

The initial ruling gave Rosa $1,500 and forty beehives. However, in 1978, this decision was overturned by Judge Bertha Wilson [see p. 77] on appeal, who awarded her one-half the property and revenue from the business. In 1980, the Supreme Court of Canada upheld this decision. Mr Justice Brian Dickson observed that Pettkus "had the benefit of nineteen

While women in other segments of society continued to make gains, Canada's Aboriginal women were still facing a battle to regain their fundamental rights and identity [see p. 43].

THE INDIAN STATUS BATTLE

For over 100 years after the creation of Canada, the question of who would be entitled to call herself "Indian" was defined by the *Indian Act* of 1876. One of the country's most paternalistic pieces of legislation, it ignored the matrilineal and matrilocal traditions of many First Nations peoples and their right to define their own membership.

left: Alberta church women, 1898

Briefly, if her father was an Indian, and married to her mother, a woman was entitled to be registered as an Indian, regardless of her mother's origins. If she married a non-Indian, she lost her status. But an Indian male who married a non-Indian did not lose his status, and his wife and children gained Indian status.

In 1985, Bill C-31 reversed the *Indian Act,* bringing it into line with the new Canadian Charter of Rights and Freedoms. Native women had lobbied for these changes since Mary Two-Axe Early's first presentation to the Royal Commission on the Status of Women in 1967. [HS-2000]

years of unpaid labour. while Miss Becker had received little or nothing in return."

However, Rosa never saw one cent. As her lawyer, Gerald Langlois, put it: "Pettkus used every legal tree in the forest of the law to evade the award." Six years later, bitter and disheartened, Rosa committed suicide. She left these words, handwritten in German:

"With my death, the law will have to change. And the lawyers too. Don't be sad about my death. It will straighten some things out."

However, new legislation still leaves the rights of common-law spouses in doubt. [HS-1989]

JEANETTE CORBIÈRE-LAVELL

The Department of Indian Affairs and the *Indian Act* state that in order to be registered as an Indian, that person must be "a male person" or "the wife or widow of a person who is entitled to be registered." Consequently, any Indian woman who married a non-Indian man lost her Indian status and all benefits connected with it.

In 1971 Jeanette Corbière-Lavell, president of the Ontario Native Women's Association, tested that

right: Ethel Ewaysecan

Indian Act with respect to marital status. She lost her first battle in the courts, the judge ruling that she was not being discriminated against, since her marriage to a non-Indian had made her the equal of all Canadian women. Later, the Federal Court of Appeals reversed this lower court decision, concluding that the enfranchisement clause of the *Indian Act* was "inoperative and in conflict with the Canadian Bill of Rights."

On August 27, 1973, the Supreme Court of Canada in a 5-4 decision ruled against Ms Corbière-Lavell, demonstrating that the Canadian Bill of Rights does not take precedence over an Act of Parliament simply because that Act is found to be discriminatory on any grounds.

They could take away my number, but in my heart I am an Indian—always have and always will be.
—Evelyn Eaglespeaker Locker, on being reinstated as a status Indian, 1985

Many of the male-dominated Native federations and brotherhoods did not support the movement to change this section of the *Indian Act*. Yet, women such as Jeanette Corbière-Lavell are clear about what they want and are no longer willing to take a back seat. She says: "I believe that a person who has been brought up on a reserve, who speaks an Indian language and considers herself an Indian, is Indian." [HS-1975]

[Jeanette Corbière-Lavell has continued her work with First Nations Women's organizations and with such groups as the Nishnawbe Institute and has served on the Commission of the Native Justice System. She received an education degree from the University of Ontario and became a school principal. Eds.]

INDIAN WOMEN REGAIN STATUS

As long as women are not recognized as the equals of men, humanity as a whole is diminished
—N. Slushbovets, 1974

The *Indian Act* of 1876, in the British legal tradition of defining women as chattels of their fathers or husbands, stipulated that Native women who married non-Natives lost their Indian status and band membership forever. Their children, likewise, were non-status. No such legislation applied to men, although until the 1960s, Indian men as well as women had to give up their status if they wanted to vote or legally buy liquor.

On International Women's Day in March 1984, then-Minister of Indian Affairs John Munro announced legislation that would enable Indian

women to regain their status. The bill was finally passed under David Crombie and received royal assent June 28, 1985, just in time to comply with the new Charter of Rights and Freedoms. Some 16,000 women and 50,000 children were affected, as well as 8,000 Indians who had lost their status for reasons other than marriage.

The new legislation left it up to the home bands to decide whether those reinstated could also become band members again, with the right to live on the reserve, attend band schools, and receive other benefits. It was received differently in different parts of the country. In Quebec, the Caughnawaga Reserve across the river from Montreal jumped the gun on the legislation and was reinstating members while the new minister was still mulling over the legislation. There, Mary Two-Axe Early was the first woman in Canada to be reinstated, at the age of 73. She had fought for the legislation for 20 years.

It is not surprising that the Caughnawaga Reserve acted first. Before the Europeans came, Iroquois descent was traced through the mother's line, and women held the fishing rights, elected and deposed the elders of the governing council, and owned the home to which a man and wife moved after marriage. Divorce took place when a woman tossed her husband's possessions out the door.

On the other hand, the Alberta Council of Treaty Women tried to get a Supreme Court injunction against the bill, and oil-rich southern Alberta bands were not welcoming applications for reinstatement to band privileges. However, farther west, the BC Indians, also with a strong matriarchal tradition, were welcoming women back. Some predict it will be another decade before the full impact of the legislation is felt. [HS-1987]

ROSEMARY BROWN

On August 30, 1972, Rosemary Brown was elected to the British Columbia Legislature—becoming the first Black woman in Canada ever to win a seat in a Legislative Assembly. When a member of the opposition referred to the day the NDP won the election as a black day for BC, Rosemary Brown replied: "As a person who believes that black is beautiful, I'd like to endorse that statement. August 30, 1972, was one of the blackest and most beautiful days for the people of BC."

Political activity has always been part of Rosemary's life; as a child she remembers her grandmother fighting for women's rights. Since then her talents have led her into many fields—social worker, television panelist, ombudswoman for the BC Council on the Status of Women. "No one has a map to guide one's progress through life with certainty," but Rosemary Brown believes "we can shape our des-

tiny by seizing upon...some of the magical or serendipitous circumstances that present themselves to us....Take charge of your life."

Her advice comes of experience. Born in Jamaica in 1930, Rosemary was raised in a family of such capable women that she was "both excited and terrified by my female elders....they seemed overpowering, independent, self-assured and strong." They, in turn, believed in Rosemary's ability, "encouraged and hounded me, and hound me even now."

Arriving in Canada to study at McGill University, however, Rosemary quickly encountered Canadian racism: "polite, denied and accepted." She initially felt her family "should have either protected me or prepared me better for this degradation," until she realized they had: she had not been raised as part of a minority, but had come to Canada "an adult with a formed sense of myself. By then it was too late to imprint on me the term 'inferior.'" In her 1989 autobiography, *Being Brown: A Very Public Life*,

To be black and female in a society which is both racist and sexist is to be in the unique position of having nowhere to go but up.
—Carroll Allen,
from "Black and Female,"
Homemaker's Magazine,
May 1975

...obstacles are put in our path to block us but they don't have to...in fact we can use them as hurdles to achieve even greater things than we thought ourselves capable of.
—Rosemary Brown, 1989

left: Rosemary Brown

above: 52% Solution:
Women for Equality,
Justice, and Peace.

But she wants young women to know she has had fears of inadequacy: "I was constantly running into the mythical Rosemary Brown...and invariably she was taller, smarter, sexier and more powerful than I was." Like all of us, Rosemary has seen her share of tears and depression, problems with kids and family...and failure. But she never gave up. She knew she would have to fight for women and Blacks to play a meaningful part in Canada.

It is a fight she hopes others will take up: "The belief in the equality of women and our right to be treated with dignity and respect is growing and is spreading. Dare to dream the impossible." [HS-1975, 2000] [Rosemary Brown died in April 2003. Eds.]

THE 52% SOLUTION

The 52% Solution: Women for Equality, Justice, and Peace, is a Newfoundland feminist group formed in 1986 which is having a hard look at the opportunities for women in the political party system. They're not very happy with what they see. Women make up 52% of the population, but they're not present when the "rules of the game" are made. They are underrepresented in provincial, territorial, and national legislatures from one end of the country to the other.

she recounts that her "frustration and rage" stemmed from the fact that "my upbringing had not taught me to deal with powerlessness."

Marriage kept Rosemary in Canada and we have all been richer for it. She served for 14 years in the British Columbia legislature. In 1975 she became the first woman to seek the leadership of a national party, coming in second to the New Democratic Party's Ed Broadbent. Since her retirement from provincial politics she has served as executive director of MATCH International and as head of Ontario's Human Rights Commission. As a feminist she wants to see a change not only in laws governing women but in the attitudes of society in general. She believes that the system of "might is right" must be challenged.

The 52% Solution organized a six-day bus tour across Newfoundland in August 1987, to find out whether women outside St John's were interested in getting organized on the issue. They chose to travel in a bright yellow school bus, symbolic of the learning experience they were embarked on and decorated with the green and purple first used by the suffragists. Their takeoff was delayed while they located a woman driver. They weren't going to make the trip with a male driver, not after advocating that women take on non-traditional jobs. The Corner Brook Status of Women Council members greeted them with an old tune and new words that are now famous on the island: "We are 52 per cent/Of the population/If we ever get our way/We'll have a better nation," to the tune of "I'se the B'y." [HS-1989]

With the advance of European culture in Canada came the loss of status for women. Aboriginal women in Canada were often respected and influential leaders—a stature that both they and their white sisters would have to struggle many generations to regain [see p. 40]. Here we see Native women once again successfully leading various levels of government: provincial, national, and international.

NELLIE COURNOYEA

"They used to call us the schemers. We were always scheming, always fighting—for native rights, northern rights, women's rights. Nellie always listens to people, then she goes out and helps them," remembers Agnes Semmier of Nellie Cournoyea and their founding of COPE—Committee for Original People's Entitlement. Cournoyea's proven ability to effect change for northerners was recognized when the Northwest Territories Legislative Assembly elected her government leader, the first woman ever to hold that position, and the first Aboriginal woman in Canada to lead a provincial or territorial government.

The erosion of the traditional lifestyle in the North has created the myriad problems inherent in any transition, but Cournoyea is adamant that solutions will come from northerners, not outsiders. "Our people now are dying mentally because there isn't equality. We are willing to make changes, to adapt two different ways of life together to make a very good one, solving the problems...and making decisions by ourselves. Paternalism has been a failure."

Born in Aklavik in 1940 to an Inuvialuit woman and a Norwegian trapper, Cournoyea received her early education through correspondence courses.

A single parent, Cournoyea waited until her children were older before taking on commitments which included travel. She believes family responsibilities enable women to view larger political issues realistically in terms of their impact on individuals and the family.

Once an announcer and station manager for CBC, Cournoyea was first managing director of the Inuvialuit Development Corporation. She has been a director of several corporations, including the Inuvialuit Petroleum Corporation, and has been MLA for Nunakput since 1979. In addition to her responsibilities as government leader, Cournoyea is minister of Energy, Mines and Petroleum Resources; Women's Directorate, and the NWT Power Corporation.

Practical, tough, and known for her directness, Cournoyea says she does not consider herself out of the ordinary. "If you get to know a whole lot of women from around here, we're pretty much all the same." [HS-1994]

[One of the original negotiators and signatories of the final 1984 land claim agreement, Nellie Cournoyea was elected Chair and CEO of the Inuvialuit Regional Corporation in 1996, with responsibility for administering the land and compensation received. She has won numerous awards, including a National Aboriginal Achievement Award and an honorary degree from the University of Toronto. Eds.]

The harder I fought, the better I liked it.
—Laura Sabia

left: Nellie Cournoyea

above: Mary Simon

MARY SIMON

Since August 1986, the spokesperson for the world's 115,000 Inuit has been a Canadian Inuk, Mary Simon, of Kuujjuaq in northern Quebec. Elected president of the Inuit Circumpolar Conference (ICC), she promised to take the Inuit desire to protect traditional ways to the world stage. A lobbying target is the European Parliament, whose ban on importation of North American seal pelts destroyed the Newfoundland fur industry, and caused great privation and dislocation in many Greenlandic and Canadian Inuit settlements. "Arctic Policy Principles," a document prepared by Ms Simon, will guide ICC directions. She has served with half a dozen Inuit organizations, including Inuit Tapirisat of Canada, and was president of Makivik Corporation, which invests money from the James Bay land claims settlement.

She was born in Kangirsualujuak (George River), near Ungava Bay, in 1947, raised on the land, and spoke only Inuktitut until she went to school. Her mother is Inuk; her father is a white outfitter who spoke several Inuktitut dialects. Her grandmother, Jeannie, was a great influence. Ms Simon remembers her as a determined woman with a strong will. Simon, jokingly referred to as the "Iron Lady" by her co-workers, inherited that spirit.

Much of her adult life has been spent outside the Arctic, perfecting her English and her political and administrative skills. Simon credits her husband's understanding and support for making it possible for her to serve her people.

Ms Simon believes that it is important now for the ICC to have a Canadian leader. It will enhance the visibility of Canadian Inuit when land claims negotiations, the division of the Northwest Territories, and northern development are raising important issues.

"People have often accused me of being a workaholic," she said, when elected. "It might be true, but I enjoy it. This is what I want to do. There is a lot of work to be done." [HS-1988]

[Mary Simon served as president of the Inuit Circumpolar Conference until 1992. In 1994, she became the first Inuk to hold an ambassadorial position as Canada's first ambassador for Circumpolar Affairs. She has been appointed to the Order of Canada, the National Order of Quebec, and the Gold Order of Greenland. In addition to honorary degrees, and the chancellorship of Trent University, in 1996, Mary Simon received the National Aboriginal Achievement Award for her work on behalf of the Inuit of Greenland, Alaska, Russia, and Canada. Eds.]

ETHEL BLONDIN-ANDREW

Ethel Blondin-Andrew is not a stereotypical Canadian politician. The first Native woman to sit in the House of Commons, the Liberal Member of Parliament represents 35,000 constituents in the Western Arctic; she provides a strong voice for northerners and Aboriginals.

Born in Fort Norman, Northwest Territories, Blondin-Andrew speaks Dene-Slavey as her first language. Her ties to the land and to her people have shaped her political views. Her commitment to the preservation and enhancement of the northern way of life is evident in the issues she takes on in Ottawa.

right: Ethel Blondin-Andrew

In November 1989 she presented Bill C-269, an act to establish an Aboriginal languages foundation to accommodate Canada's 53 Aboriginal languages. Blondin-Andrew has opposed the annihilation of the bison in Wood Buffalo National Park, and the construction of pulp mills along the Peace and Athabasca rivers.

Blondin-Andrew has long been a star to her constituents, but in the summer of 1990, she gained national prominence during the Meech Lake countdown. She was a member of the Charest committee which proposed that the First Nations be explicitly recognized in the constitution. "When you look into the constitution, you should be able to see yourself, but...when northerners and Aboriginals look into this mirror of the constitution they don't see themselves reflected."

When the first ministers reached an agreement without incorporating this proposal, Blondin-Andrew was unrelenting in her criticism. "The Aboriginal peoples have been left out, we were depending on you," she told Premier Gary Filmon of Manitoba, in front of national news cameras.

Blondin-Andrew recognizes that her style of politics is not typical. "I was trying to be...your really professional politician who has a firm resolve and doesn't express emotion," she says. "But then I decided, forget it, this is me and this is how I feel and Canada should be able to deal with that."

This attitude has not held her back. She was a prominent member of the Liberal opposition as Aboriginal Affairs critic, and she co-chaired the 1990 Liberal leadership convention.

Blondin-Andrew says her three children are her inspiration. She exemplifies Aboriginal leadership to other young people as well. Students of the 1990 graduating class of Arctic College describe her as "a hero and a role model." [HS-1992]

[Ethel Blondin-Andrew was re-elected Member of Parliament for the Western Arctic in 1993, 1997, and 2000, and has held the portfolios of Secretary of State for Training and Youth, and Secretary of State (Children and Youth). Eds.]

Constitutional issues go to the very heart of Canada's political system. Women have yet to be fully represented in these debates. Fortunately, Aboriginal women have made their voices heard—of only three women to sit at the constitutional table, all were Aboriginal.

ROSEMARIE KUPTANA

The 1990s marked an historic change in the relationship of Canada to its Aboriginal peoples. Rosemarie Kuptana was a catalyst for that change, earning rights for Aboriginals unprecedented in Canada's history. As president of the Inuit Tapirisat of Canada (ITC)—the national voice of Canadian Inuit—Kuptana successfully lobbied for equal participation of Aboriginal leaders

We must look at the world and the future from a distinctly Inuit perspective. Such values as respect for humanity and the environment are too important to keep to ourselves.—Rosemarie Kuptana, 1992

left: Rosemarie Kuptana

The struggle for equality for Native women is continuing today. Native women are emerging in search of the equality once enjoyed by women within Indian society. Traditional Native societies are examples of democracies in which all people were accorded equal rights.
—Verna Kirkness, 1987

at the Constitutional negotiations in 1992—the first time Aboriginal leaders were awarded that status. Kuptana and two other Aboriginals were the only women involved directly in the constitutional negotiations. Kuptana's tenacious advocacy helped establish recognition of the inherent right of Aboriginal peoples to self-government.

Internationally Kuptana has served as Canadian vice-president of the Inuit Circumpolar Conference and co-chair of the International Arctic Council.

Aboriginal peoples were historically self-governing, and Kuptana sees the new recognition of that fact as a means by which the Inuit can "regain control of their lives," enacting legislation to better reflect Inuit culture and re-establishing Inuit language into educational curricula.

Kuptana has been a strong advocate of both human rights and the advancement of Inuit language and culture throughout her career. As president of the Inuit Broadcasting Corporation from 1983 to 1988, she helped create Television Northern Canada, the first all-northern satellite distribution network. She was instrumental in launching Inuktitut educational programming, effectively developing a communications system for the North which reflected Inuit society. At the request of Pauktuutit, the national Inuit Women's Association, Kuptana also began research into child sexual abuse in Inuit communities. Although she found the work "alarming and disturbing," it resulted in a book, *No More Secrets*, published in both Inuktitut and English in 1991.

Kuptana was elected president of the ITC in 1991 for a three-year term. During her tenure, ITC has increased research into environmental issues and human rights, assisted in the settlement of land claims, and developed educational programs.

Kuptana has received the Order of Canada, the Governor General's Confederation Medal, a National Aboriginal Achievement Award, and in 1992 was named Northerner of the Year. [HS-1995]

[Rosemarie Kuptana was president of the ITC until June 1995. From 1995-96 she was also president of the Inuit Circumpolar Conference (ICC), continu-

right: Delia Opekokew

ing the Canadian leadership role begun by Mary Simon. Since then, she has served on the National Round Table on the Environment and the Economy on Climate Change issues and has been a member of the board of the International Institute for Sustainable Development. Eds.]

DELIA OPEKOKEW

Few have achieved as much in political defeat as did Delia Opekokew in the summer of 1994. Opekokew, a lawyer, was the first woman to run for the leadership of the Assembly of First Nations (AFN). She dropped out of the race after losing the first ballot but felt she had nonetheless achieved her goals in running. Simply by her presence, she introduced the possibility of a female national chief, an idea which will likely take a few more elections to be realized. And in so doing, she encouraged other women to get involved in Aboriginal

politics. As well, she sent a message to the current leadership, fewer than a third of which is female. "I told them to keep in mind that...most of the people who are getting highly educated are females and you are going to have to include females, and I may have paved the way for someone."

Opekokew currently lives in Toronto, but she was born and raised on the Canoe Lake Cree Reserve in Saskatchewan and began her political career as a member of the executive of the Federation of Saskatchewan Indian Nations before attending law school.

She graduated from Osgoode Hall in 1977 and shortly thereafter became the first Aboriginal woman to be called to the bar in both Saskatchewan and Ontario. She now runs her own law firm in Toronto, with a client base that spans Alberta, Saskatchewan, and the Maritimes. Much of her legal work has been on behalf of Aboriginal people, individuals and organizations, including land claims. In 1992 she sat as a commissioner, the choice of the local tribal council, on the LaChance Inquiry, which investigated the shooting of Cree trapper Leo LaChance by a self-proclaimed white supremacist [in Prince Albert, Saskatchewan].

Throughout the AFN campaign, Opekokew made clear her support for self-government and put forward her ideas about how it might best be achieved. She expressed the view that the AFN should focus on the needs of individual Indian First Nations rather than on negotiations with non-Aboriginal politicians in Ottawa, believing people cannot become involved in nation-building until they have the resources to meet everyday needs such as housing, employment, and health services: "People have to be strong and healthy before they can exercise self-government fully." [HS-1996]

[Delia Opekokew has continued to represent various First Nations; she has served as general counsel to the Federation of Saskatchewan Indian Nations. She was part of the Royal Commission on Aboriginal Peoples in 1996, and in 2000 was appointed chief federal negotiator to negotiate with the South Slave Métis Tribal Council. Eds.]

The fact has been grasped that human beings can modify their own destiny... this is a tremendous change, and it has an accumulating momentum.—Elizabeth Pauline MacCallum, ca 1954

left: Elizabeth Pauline MacCallum

As women have risen in political prominence, they have heeded the call to the world stage.

ELIZABETH PAULINE MacCALLUM

A lifelong interest in political thought led eventually to a career with External Affairs for Elizabeth Pauline MacCallum, and her appointment to Beirut in 1954 as Canada's first woman chargé d'affaires.

Born in Murash, Turkey, in 1895, to Congregationalist missionaries, Elizabeth MacCallum entered Queen's University, Kingston, in 1913. Poverty interrupted her undergraduate work twice; both times, MacCallum earned enough to continue her education by teaching school in Alberta.

Although MacCallum enrolled in a PHD program at Columbia University in New York, interruptions to her education continued. First came the job of assistant secretary of the Social Service Council of Canada; then a request from the Foreign Policy Association to join their research department for Near Eastern affairs. During her tenure with the Association, MacCallum wrote extensively on the Middle East, including a standard university text, *The Nationalist Crusade in Syria.*

After six years, "feeling as if she were just sliding along the surface of life, as if the substance of her experience was being snatched from her," as one biographer described it, MacCallum bought land near Uxbridge, Ontario. There she remained for the next four years, producing almost all her food from her own garden, and writing during the winter.

Called back by the World Peace Foundation prior to Italy's invasion of Ethopia, MacCallum went to work for the League of Nations, then joined External Affairs in 1942. Called "the government's sole expert on the Middle East" from 1942 to 1947, she also served at the San Francisco Conference which drew up the United Nations Charter, at three subsequent UN General Assemblies, and at the World Health Assembly in 1951. After serving briefly in the Athens embassy during the temporary absence of the ambassador, in 1954 she became the first Canadian woman to carry a lettre de chancellerie, opening the Canadian legation in Beirut. Her posting to Lebanon lasted until her retirement in 1956.

After retiring, MacCallum worked for four years in Istanbul and Ankara, studying Turkish literature and volunteering with village development projects.

MacCallum was given an honorary Doctor of Laws by Queen's University in 1952 and in 1967 was inducted into the Order of Canada. She died in Ottawa in 1985. [HS-1993]

LOUISE FRÉCHETTE

Her appointment as Canada's ambassador to the United Nations marked the first time a woman was given that post, making her Canada's "highest-placed female ambassador," but it was only one of many

right: Louise Fréchette

similar milestones in the distinguished career of Louise Fréchette.

A career diplomat, Fréchette has served Canada in a variety of foreign posts, as well as holding several positions in Ottawa. She has been deputy director of both European Affairs and Trade Policy, and director of Canada's relations with European Summit countries. In 1985 she was named Canada's ambassador to Argentina and given concurrent accreditation to both Uruguay and Paraguay. Upon her return to Canada in 1988, Fréchette was named assistant deputy minister for Latin America and the Caribbean. In that capacity she directed a review of Canada's relations with Latin America, a process which eventually led to Canada joining the Organization of American States. She was then appointed assistant deputy minister for Economic Policy and Trade Competitiveness, with additional responsibility in preparing for Canada's participation in the 1991 London Economic Summit.

Fréchette cites adaptability as one of her main

rights of women. Judicial bodies now recognize that women do not receive equal treatment in the courts and are beginning to take steps to change the system. There have been great gains, including winning the fight to have gender equality entrenched in the Canadian Charter of Rights and Freedoms.

left: Madame Justice Bertha Wilson

MADAME JUSTICE BERTHA WILSON

Women's groups and the Canadian Bar Association were thrilled when Bertha Wilson was appointed to the Supreme Court of Canada on 4 March 1982—the first woman to hold such a position in Canada.

Madame Justice Wilson was born in Kirkcaldy, Scotland, on 18 September 1923. She earned her MA at the University of Aberdeen and emigrated to Canada in 1949 with her husband, John, who became a Presbyterian minister in the Ottawa Valley. Six years later the Wilsons moved to Halifax, where Bertha studied law at Dalhousie University. She joined the Toronto law firm of Osler, Hoskin, and Harcourt, eventually becoming a senior partner and research director in the firm.

In 1975 Wilson was the first woman to be named to the Ontario Appeal Court. Here she gained a reputation as "a liberal judge and a legal innovator." In one case she judged in favour of an East Indian woman seeking the right to sue an Ontario community college for damages in a clear-cut case of job discrimination. In another case she ruled for a girl who had been barred from an all-boys softball team. Both judgments were overturned, out-voted by her two male colleagues. As the first woman appointed to the Supreme Court, Bertha Wilson carried with her the weight of high expectations on the part of many women within and outside the legal community. She fulfilled those expectations admirably, both during her tenure on the Court and through her work in retirement.

On the Court, she consistently rendered decisions which earned her a reputation as an independent judge with a strong social sense [see p. 66]. However, her defining moment as a supporter of gender equity came

strengths. She has been described as "a real behind-the-scenes operator who can get things done in negotiations." Her position in one of Canada's most prestigious diplomatic postings is all the more notable, given that only 15 of Canada's 106 heads of missions are women. Upon her assignment to the UN, colleagues simply remarked, "Of course. She's perfect." [HS-1995]

[On 2 March 1998, Louise Fréchette was appointed first deputy secretary-general of the United Nations, established as part of the reform of the United Nations. Eds.]

Justice is part of the political system, and many women have also carved out significant niches in the legal world. After fighting for admission to law schools and the bar [see p. 140], in the first decades of this century women were appointed to juvenile or women's courts in various parts of Canada [see pp. 50 and 53]. Women are now lawyers, deans of law schools, and judges [see p. 124]. They have formed organizations to intervene in law cases that affect the

when she spoke publicly about gender bias in the Canadian justice system. "I think that a distinctly male perspective is clearly discernible and has resulted in legal principles that are not fundamentally sound and should be revisited as and when the opportunity presents itself."

Following her retirement in 1991, her strong sense of social duty led her to become chair of the Canadian Bar Association Task Force on Gender Equity. The final report of this broadly mandated study of women's participation in the legal profession created an uproar because of its blunt assessment of gender and cultural bias. Bertha refused to accept the criticism that the task force was too radical. "The assumption out there is that male is neutral. We challenge that. Yes, our perspective is female....The big point is a white perspective is not neutral, a male perspective is not neutral, a heterosexual perspective is not neutral."

Growing up in Scotland, Bertha was convinced of the power of education to transform the lives of the poor. This conviction found expression in her interest in human rights while on the Court and her advocacy for the rights of women and of Canada's Aboriginal peoples. She served as a member of the Royal Commission on Aboriginal Peoples, which released a far-reaching report on alleviating the social and economic problems of Canada's Natives. Following her retirement, she also became a board member of the Westminster Institute for Ethics and Human Values, and a scholar-in-residence at the Faculty of Law, University of Ottawa. [HS-1986, 2000]

MADAME JUSTICE LOUISE ARBOUR

"I would be stunned if she is not the first woman chief justice of Canada." When Louise Arbour's former colleague at York University's Osgoode Hall Law School made that prediction, in April 1996, Arbour's report on the 1994 events at the Kingston Prison for Women had just been released, and she was already preparing herself for her next appointment, as chief prosecutor for the United Nations war crimes tribunal in The Hague.

Her investigation of the controversial strip search

Electoral politics touches our lives in a sufficient number of profound ways that no matter what the cost, it cries out for the presence and involvement of women.
—Rosemary Brown, 1989

right: Madame Justice Louise Arbour

and lengthy segregation of eight women prisoners at Kingston was "an enormous wake-up call for the correctional service," according to Kim Pate of the Elizabeth Fry Society. The report upheld Arbour's reputation for "efficiency, pragmatism and candour," and its general acceptance was evidence of her stature in the legal community [see p. 122].

Born in 1947 in Montreal, Louise was called to the Quebec bar in 1971, and to the Ontario bar in 1977. She taught for 10 years at Osgoode Hall, until 1987, when she was appointed to the Ontario Supreme Court. Three years later she was elevated to the court of appeal. At Osgoode, where she spent her summers offering lectures to help judges understand the demands of the Charter of Rights and Freedoms, she was considered a gifted lecturer with a humanitarian view of the law.

Arbour does not regard war crimes prosecution as an academic exercise. The urgency to have the crimes exposed drives her work with the tribunal: "The pile of indictments just kept growing and growing, with no action....I thought this was too passive." In 1997 her office began to issue sealed indictments, to avoid warn-

ing war criminals. "The proliferation of internal armed conflicts emerging from ethnic and regional intolerance and from competition for scarce and unevenly accessible resources will tax the world's capacity for conflict resolution for years to come. I view international criminal law as the weapon of choice in the arsenal of peace." [HS-1999]

[Louise Arbour was appointed to the Supreme Court of Canada on 15 September 1999; on 17 January 2000, Beverley McLachlin became the first woman chief justice in Canada. Since 1999, Arbour has received awards from numerous groups, including Columbia University Law School, the Pennsylvania Law Foundation, the Association of Progressive Muslims of Ontario, Jewish Women International of Canada, the Province of Quebec, and McGill University. Eds.]

WOMEN IN POLITICS

"I was a curiosity, a freak." Agnes Macphail [see p. 52] may well have felt uncomfortable after her 1921 election made her the first—and for many years only—female Member of Parliament. However vital their work behind the scenes has been, few women have succeeded in federal public office: between 1921 and 1993, women won only 2.4% of the total available seats in Parliament. Nearly 80 years after Macphail's victory, does Parliament remain, in the words of former NDP leader Audrey McLaughlin, "an old fashioned men's club"?

Rosemary Brown [see p. 69] recalled that "all the washrooms in the [legislature] meant for the use of elected members had been built with urinals in them." Less amusing was the comment she received from a male delegate who would not support her bid for federal leadership of her party "because he did not believe that a woman should hold a more important job than her husband."

Ellen Fairclough [see p. 61] remembered being asked to leave a cabinet discussion of a capital case involving rape. "I thought, 'Well, the boys want to use language which they don't wish to use in front of me....' They weren't big enough to look at it in an objective fashion."

To say another MP is "scarcely entitled to be a gentleman" has been considered "unparliamentary" since 1876; calling a woman MP a "slut" or a "fishwife" is apparently acceptable. Audrey McLaughlin, former leader of the federal New Democrats, noted this discrepancy and also recalled the press furor when two women cabinet ministers wore the same outfit. The papers could as easily have run the headline: "Two Hundred and Fifty Male MPs Appear in Commons Wearing Same Dark Blue Suit." As columnist Lysiane Gagnon pointed out, a male politician is not "expected to represent all men or be an advocate for any segment of the male population; nor is he expected to embody maleness. Just like every other male politician, he is judged as an individual."

Kim Campbell, Canada's first woman prime minister, noted, "the biggest challenge for women MPs was to bring the reality of women's lives into policy-making....There is nothing subversive about the idea that women's different realities are just as worthy of consideration as those of men."

Regardless of any partisan political considerations, those women who have tried to effect change on behalf of both men and women through public policy deserve our respect and thanks. [HS-2000]

left: The Right Honourable Kim Campbell, Canada's first woman prime minister, June-November 1993, on the hustings.

Every individual is equal before and under the law and has the right to the equal protection and equal benefit of the law without discrimination and, in particular, without discrimination based on race, national or ethnic origin, colour, religion, sex, age or mental or physical disability.
— Canadian Charter of Rights and Freedoms, Section 15, entrenched April 1985

CHAPTER 3

MY SISTER'S KEEPER

W omen have sought to change society both through the formal channels of politics and as independent crusaders. As women were pushing for legal reforms and access to political power, they were also working on local and national reforms to improve the lives of ordinary citizens. Women working as solitary reformers formed groups and organizations to tackle issues such as medical services, food inspection, reproductive rights, violence against women, protection of children, and advocacy for the poor.

In 1974, when the first *Herstory* calendar appeared, birth control information had been legally available in Canada for only five years. The struggle to control their own fertility was only part of the role women played, and continue to play, in the well-being of their communities. The roots of Canada's medicare system can be seen in the determination of isolated rural women exchanging health information over their kitchen tables.

Women's issues are human issues—bearing and caring for children, making a living, fighting for legal status, protecting themselves and their families against violence, working for peace in the world. In this chapter you will learn about both the issues and the women behind the action. Here we feature stories of women who, while not necessarily renowned, were crucial to the success, even survival, of their own communities, as well as women who started at home, but whose energy and commitment took them to a larger stage.

Sadly, many of the issues that women have struggled with over the years have not been resolved. Violence against women is a problem that does not go away, in spite of increasing attention paid it in recent years. But the success stories are equally powerful. Long before they were able to vote or hold political office, women organized to pursue their social goals. Canadian women have recognized the strength and solidarity to be found in co-operation—they have always joined together for friendship, sisterhood and moral support.

opposite: Women in front of the YWCA boarding house, Toronto, ca 1913

*H*erstory is rich with tales of selfless, visionary, and dedicated women—and Canada is richer for them.

MARY TELFORD SHEFFIELD

In the early 1880s Mary Sheffield was a member of the Metropolitan Methodist Church in Toronto, inspired, like many others, by the social gospel vision of the "New Jerusalem," and its hope of creating a better community for all. Born in Quebec of Irish immigrant parents, she had trained as a teacher before her marriage, and had come to Toronto as a young widow. Concerned with the needs of immigrant children, in 1886 she began a Sunday school in the new Orange Hall on Jarvis Street. Her first group, four little boys, had to be persuaded to leave their tobacco "quids" in their pockets before the lesson could begin. Her Sunday school expanded to include recreation nights and gymnasium classes for boys.

right: Mary Telford Sheffield

Working with street children, she became aware that "each evening there would pour into the basement [of a local rooming house]...scores of men seeking a night's lodging." Their accommodation consisted of tiers of 18-inch-wide shelves, without bedding. In 1892 she established the Adelaide Street Mission to offer shelter as well. In 1894 a donation from the Massey family in memory of their son, a former volunteer at the Mission, enabled Mary to purchase and refurbish a warehouse at Queen and Jarvis, the Mission's first permanent home. It was renamed the Fred Victor Mission, and through many changes has continued to this day.

Mary directed the Mission until 1896, when it was considered inappropriate for a woman to fill a salaried position in the now well-established organization. She continued her work under a new, male, director. Women were the founders, but men were the principal beneficiaries, both as clients and as wage earners.

Such missions were central in the vision of building an equitable community at the turn of the century, and most were begun by women. Sarah Libby Carson developed settlement houses across Canada for the Presbyterian Church. All People's Mission of Winnipeg was started, not by J.S. Woodsworth, its best-known director, but by Dolly McGuire of McDougall Methodist Church. Bissell Centre in Edmonton was started by Reta Edmonds and Jessie Munroe. [HS-1994]

THE DAUGHTERS OF ISRAEL

Although they were still unenfranchised and could have no formal participation in public life, many Canadian women at the turn of the century felt responsibility to their communities, and formed clubs and societies to work on improving social and economic conditions. In 1899 a group of Jewish women in Saint John formed the Daughters of Israel. Like many other middle-class Canadian women in this period, the Daughters were expanding their concerns for their own families into the larger community.

The Daughters of Israel was both a cultural and a charitable organization. The women collected the money to construct a *Mikvah*, a ritual bath which provided a religious focus for the Jewish community. Their main concern was to offer material support to less fortunate members of their community. The ladies were careful of the sensibilities of the people they aided; their bylaws stressed that such aid must not be mentioned outside the society, and even in the minute books, recipients are identified only by their initials.

Their resources were limited, so they soon restricted themselves to assisting destitute women and children. Their minutes reveal a fascinating diversity of cases. In February 1906, the ladies took up the case of the "Gs," a young couple with a small baby. They helped "Mr. G" to find work, and when it was discovered that his salary was inadequate, the Daughters continued to support the family. However, by the summer of 1907 "Mrs. G" was seriously ill, and the ladies provided the fee for an ambulance to transport her to the Home for Incurables. Three days later, "Mrs. G" died; the Daughters paid for her shroud and funeral expenses in a final gesture to the diminished and destitute little family. [HS-1991]

LUTIE DesBRISAY

Lucretia DesBrisay had neither humble beginnings nor a humble end. The daughter of a wealthy Prince Edward Island judge, she denounced her family and her inheritance at 16 years of age to devote herself, body and soul, to the Salvation Army. The Salvation Army was the first Canadian organization to accord women equal opportunity. Starting as a captain in charge of small bands of volunteers, Lutie preached, sang, prayed, and worked to eradicate vice and poverty throughout the maritime provinces. In time she became the Army's first woman colonel.

Defying scorn, ridicule, and often arrest, Lutie courageously and defiantly led her troops into the most unlikely places. In Amherst, Nova Scotia, she ignored a law which effectively prevented the gather-

ing of a Salvation Army street meeting, and succeeded in winning enough popular support to have the law repealed. When she was promoted to the rank of district officer, she ordered her workers to hold meetings in the saloons—a very bold and unprecedented step, and one which persuaded at least one hotelkeeper to close his saloon to become an Army supporter.

In the course of her career Lutie DesBrisay organized Salvation Army missionary work in Bermuda, trained women cadets, and supervised the Army's women's social work program. She used this latter post to organize and modernize the Grace Hospitals in St. John's, Halifax, Montreal, Ottawa, London, and Windsor. Twice, when she first took over the post and again four months before her retirement, she commanded the social work program for the whole of Canada.

Following her "retirement," Colonel DesBrisay continued to work ceaselessly at the work in which she believed, travelling throughout Canada and speaking wherever she was invited. She died in 1948, in her hometown of Charlottetown. [HS-1980]

left: Lutie DesBrisay

Volunteers care, and because they care, they are determined to shape the world in which they are living. They are willing to lend a helping hand to their neighbours when there is need; and in taking action, they encourage others to join forces for change.
—Sharon Capeling-Alakija, 1998

above: Agnes Maule Machar

Is it not then a cruel delusion, to foster in girls the idea that in marriage lies a woman's only prosperous and happy career, failing which, life must be blank and objectless? And why, seeing that a single life must inevitably be the lot of so many, should she not be encouraged to possess herself of some means of achieving an honourable independence?
—Agnes M. Machar, 1875

right: Matilda Ridout Edgar

AGNES MAULE MACHAR

Agnes Machar—social gospeller, Canadian nationalist, writer—spent her ninety years tirelessly supporting the causes she believed in. A devout Christian and social activist, Agnes believed that Christian love was best expressed in working to better the lot of one's fellows. As a member of the National Council of Women she campaigned for better hours and working conditions for women and children. Agnes also advocated higher education, and believed in a sound training in household economics for the future wives and mothers of Canada.

In addition to her activities with the Council, Agnes supported her causes in her writing. Her articles advocating social justice and a return of true Christian charity appeared in most of the important Canadian journals of the time. Many of these articles, written under her favourite pseudonym of "Fidelis," advocated fairly radical positions for their day. In 1891 Fidelis wrote, "One thing, however, in which all true friends of the working classes will agree is in the approval of the principle of co-operation and organization among workmen as absolutely necessary to protect their rights in these days of combines of capital."

Agnes also wrote novels and stories for both children and adults. Most of these were strongly didactic, a quality which appealed to the tastes of the late nineteenth century. The best known of her novels is *Roland Graeme: Knight*. This is the story of a young man who loses his Christian faith and finds it again in supporting poor factory workers in their struggles against their cruel and miserly employer.

Agnes was also a Canadian nationalist and a firm believer in the British empire. A true Victorian optimist, she continued to advocate the virtues and benefits of the empire for all its citizens. After the First World War, people no longer believed in simple answers to the world's problems; Agnes's social gospel and her imperialism went out of fashion. By the time she died, in 1927, she was regarded as a quaint relic of a bygone era. Despite the former popularity of much of her work, Agnes Machar was quickly forgotten, both as a writer and as an advocate of social justice. [HS-1989]

MATILDA RIDOUT EDGAR, LADY EDGAR

Matilda Ridout was born in 1844 to a prominent Toronto family. She married James Edgar when she was 21 and spent the next several decades raising their nine children.

Later in her life Matilda took an interest in Canadian history. Her first book, *Ten Years of Upper Canada in Peace and War, 1805-1815,* based on Ridout family letters and documents, was published in 1890. The book was praised by reviewers for providing valuable contemporary views on the War of 1812. Matilda also published a biography of Sir Isaac Brock as part of the *Makers of Canada* series.

Matilda entered public life through her husband's involvement in politics. After James became Speaker of the House of Commons in 1896, Matilda was asked to lend her patronage to a number of charitable organizations. In a biographical note about his mother, Pelham Edgar characterized her as shy, but noted that she contributed her executive abilities to considerable public service. She was associated with the Infants' Home in Toronto, the Imperial Order of the Daughters of the Empire, and the Women's Art Association of Canada. [see p. 216]

After James' death she involved herself more actively in women's issues. Matilda advocated women's

rights to higher education, to suffrage, to adequate income, and to control of their own property, even after marriage. She worked for her causes through the National Council of Women of Canada and was elected its president in 1906 and 1909. [HS-1996]

MARY ANN SHADD CARY

Mary Ann Shadd was born 9 October, 1823, in Wilmington, Delaware. When she was ten her parents took her to Pennsylvania to be educated, since Delaware, as a slave state, offered no such facilities. There, when in her late teens, she opened a school for black children.

She was one of many American blacks who turned to Canada following the passage of the Fugitive Slave Bill which, under its loose provisions, allowed blacks to be "claimed," and so reduced to a state of bondage without redress.

Little is known of her work with the Anti-Slavery Society, which she founded in Toronto in 1851. However, we do know that her prime mission was to encourage independence among refugees, and to "inculcate a healthy anti-slavery sentiment in a country which, though under British rule, is particularly

exposed, by intercommunication, to pro-slavery, religious and secular influence."

Toward this end she edited several publications: *Notes of Canada,* which was circulated widely in the U.S., and the *Provincial Freeman,* a weekly Toronto newspaper. In 1858 the *Freeman* fell victim to the Depression and went under. To carry her message she crossed the frontier and, often with risk to her personal safety, delivered lectures throughout the U.S. As a witty and sharp-tongued speaker, she capably countered most of her opposition.

Following her marriage to Thomas F. Cary in 1856, she resumed her speaking tours, this time in support of the John Brown Movement. On December 27, 1861, at a mass meeting at Chatham, Ontario, she was named and denounced for "begging" on behalf of a mission school.

She went periodically to the U.S. to work, returning to Canada in 1866 to receive her naturalization papers as a British subject. The following year she left for Washington to study law at the newly opened Howard University. [HS-1975]

left: Mary Ann Shadd Cary

Inasmuch as we as human beings need to understand ourselves by placing ourselves in time, to tie ourselves to those who came before us, it is only right that women— and men too—know as much as possible about the lives of their female ancestors.
—Veronica Strong-Boag and Anita-Clair Fellman, 1991

below: Margret Benedictsson and family

MARGRET BENEDICTSSON

When Manitoba became the first province to extend the vote to women, in 1916, credit could rightly be given to the Manitoba Women's Christian Temperance Union (WCTU), active in promoting suffrage for over two decades. Of equal value, however, was the work of the province's Icelandic immigrant women, whose suffrage groups not only paralleled the work of the WCTU, but predated all other women's equality groups in western Canada. One of the leading figures within the Icelandic community's suffrage movement was Margret Benedictsson [see p. 44].

Born in Iceland in 1866, Margret emigrated in 1887 and soon after settled in Manitoba. Of necessity Margret was independent: by age 13 she had had to take care of herself, and put herself through grade school, Bathgate College, and business school. She had a strong sense of social justice. Reading of any oppression, partic-

If you don't stop advocating woman suffrage in your paper you can cancel my subscription. My wife gets the Guide *and reads your articles to me at the supper table and it makes things very unpleasant in my house.*
—Letter to the editor of *The Grain Growers' Guide,* 1913

ularly of "unhappily married women, and unfortunate girls" made her "sorrowful and angered," and "kindled an unquenchable desire to break all chains."

In 1892 Margret married Sigfus Benedictsson, and together they began publishing a magazine, *Freyja* (woman). "The Aims of *Freyja,*" noted in the first editorial, were to be independent, outspoken about human or moral issues, and to support any initiatives leading to the betterment of social conditions.

Freyja's "first and foremost concern," though, was "matters pertaining to the progress and rights of women....Our motto: Humanity and equality. Discuss the subject, but not the person." Canada's first suffrage magazine, it grew to a 40-page monthly publication, reaching over 500 homes in Canada and the United States. Margret wrote most of the articles.

In 1910 Sigfus refused Margret access to the printing press and *Freyja* ceased publication. In a letter written 35 years later, Sigfus took credit for *Freyja*. Margret's name was never mentioned. An article written only four years after Manitoba women received the vote stated that "very little knowledge is available regarding the work done by the Icelandic suffragists." However, it is fitting that when the bill to enfranchise women was given third reading on 27 January 1916, it was moved by Acting Premier T.H. Johnson—son of an Icelandic suffrage pioneer. [HS-1996] [Margret died in 1956. Eds.]

JOSÉPHINE DANDURAND

Journalist and social activist Joséphine Dandurand was the first Canadian woman to be made an officer of the Académie française. She began her literary career in her teens, writing articles for French Canadian journals, including *L'Opinion publique, Le Canada artistique,* and *La Patrie,* among others. In 1890, in her early twenties, Joséphine published a book of short stories, *Contes de Noël,* which were praised for their graceful ease, fine detail, and delicate charm.

In 1892, she founded *Le Coin du feu,* a paper for women in Canada, covering current events, literary critiques, book reviews, and studies of personalities, many

Le féminisme ne doit donc pas être représenté comme une révolution qui boulverse, mais comme une évolution naturelle dans l'ordre providentiel des événements.
—Joséphine Dandurand, 1901

right: Joséphine Dandurand

of which she wrote. "Françoise," a frequent contributor, said this magazine started "in the hope of inspiring young French Canadian women with dignity, self-respect and a taste for intellectual culture." Although it was popular for the four years of its existence, her other interests forced Joséphine to give up the magazine, as it was a virtually one-woman enterprise.

Like many women of her class and time, Joséphine Dandurand was a maternal feminist, believing woman's primary role was nurturing; participation in wider spheres was merely an extension of this maternal role. Typical of Québecoises of her period, Mme Dandurand was a Roman Catholic who kept her vision of women's place within bounds acceptable to her church. The causes she championed were essential to her day and were important precursors of later reforms. She fought for

improved salaries for women teachers, for schools of home economics, and for higher education for women.

Mme Dandurand worked for the National Council of Women in Canada, the Women's Historical Society, and the Victorian Order of Nurses. She also founded a society to distribute literature to the poor and working classes in rural Quebec. She was a founding member of the women's section of the Société St-Jean-Baptiste, an attempt at a feminist organization within the conservative orthodoxy. [HS-1988]

MARIE LACOSTE GÉRIN-LAJOIE

Marie Lacoste was born into a prominent Quebec family. She inherited both her mother's energy and

her organizational abilities, and her barrister father's interest in the law. She spent long hours studying in her father's legal library and continued her studies after her marriage to Henri Gérin-Lajoie, another barrister.

In 1900, Marie joined the Montreal Local Council of Women, which had been founded in 1893. However, the council's nonsectarian stand and predominantly English-speaking membership made it seem a Protestant, anglophone organization. Seeing a need for an organization to unite Roman Catholic, francophone women, Marie and Caroline Béique formed the Fédération nationale Saint-Jean-Baptiste in 1907.

Marie believed that many of women's problems could be relieved by changes in the laws. She wrote on the ways in which Quebec's civil code disadvantaged women, and under her leadership, the Fédération worked to alleviate these disabilities. At the time, Quebec law made a married woman totally subservient to her husband. At marriage a woman gave up all her legal rights; she could not make contracts of any sort, buy or sell her own property, and had no right even to her own wages. The Roman Catholic clergy and most male Quebeckers saw this legal incapacity of women as the necessary foundation of family life and society and were bitterly opposed to any form of feminism, seeing women's emancipation as a force for the destruction of the family and of French-Catholic civilization.

Much of Marie's time and effort as president of the Fédération was spent in working for the reform of these laws. However, both the movement for suffrage, and the efforts for other legal rights were very slow to bear fruit in Quebec. It was only toward the very end of Marie's life that Quebec women won the right to vote in provincial elections.

Marie's charitable and social work was more successful than her efforts for legal reforms. The Fédération worked to provide pure milk and to assist mothers during and after childbirth. They were also concerned with temperance and with ending the "white slave trade." [HS-1989]

The privileges and advantages of civil life which adults, without distinction of sex, enjoy, are forbidden to the married woman. Her personality is blotted out and extinguished, and is absorbed by that of her husband to such an extent that...every act is absolutely null and void, no matter how just, reasonable, or advantageous to her.
—Marie Gérin-Lajoie, 1900

La femme est faite pour aimer des personnes...non pour avoir des idées sur elles.—Un collaborateur féminin de l'Action nationale, 1965

left: Marie Lacoste Gérin-Lajoie

The greatest reform that women had to enact was to reform the thinking of the day.

above: "Le Travail,"
L'Opinion Publique,
Montreal, 2 Nov 1871

I say that Holy Scriptures, theology, ancient philosophy, Christian philosophy, history, anatomy, physiology, political economy, and feminine psychology, all seem to indicate that the place of woman in this world is not amid the strife of the political arena, but in her home.
—Henri Bourassa, 1918

"THE PROPER SPHERE AND INFLUENCE OF WOMEN..."

"There are 'ologies' of which no woman if she is to move in her sphere as she ought to, can afford to remain ignorant. There is the sublime science of washology and its sister bakeology. There is darnology and scrubology. There is mendology, and cookology...the more skillfully its principles are applied its professors acquire the greater popularity and are regarded with a proportionate degree of interest and complacency. Now, all this knowledge must be embraced in any system of female education that pretends to prepare women for the duties of life."—*Reverend Robert Sedgwick, in a lecture delivered before the Young Men's Christian Association, Halifax, Nova Scotia, 1856* [HS-1987]

LE FÉMINISME FRANÇAIS

In 1902 Charles Turgeon travelled to Quebec from France. On the occasion of his 50th birthday, and wishing to renew family ties between the Old and the New World Turgeons, he made a gift of his recent book to Laval University. That book, *Le Féminisme français,* included the following view of marriage:

"Our Civil law in this case is in agreement with theology. It stipulates: "the husband must protect his wife, and the wife should obey her husband." It is a short formula but one that is precise and fair, where you find a summary of the matrimonial charter. Substitute for this mode of Christian marriage the egalitarian role and you have the beginning of a war of secession. If the free-thinker's dream comes true, marriage will become the rapprochement, or rather the conflict of two equal forces, with more rigid pride on the woman's part and less condescending affection on the part of man. And when these two forces, brought together by a temporary attachment, come into conflict that no superior authority can resolve, it will end in divorce since neither spouse will want to surrender. Poor spouses, poor children, poor family."

A few years later, in 1907, Monsignor Paul Bruchesi spoke before the First Congress of the National Federation of St-Jean-Baptiste Societies in Montreal. He echoed Turgeon in his insistence on the dangers inherent in feminism:

"I know that feminism is popular today. When we think of the pretentions shown in some circles to the principles it proclaims, to the reforms it advocates, we have indeed good reason to condemn it, and, for my part, I do not want to see it among us. Our mothers and sisters have so far appeared to us with a halo of kindness, a quiet zeal and a grace which makes us admire as well as love them. We do not want this halo to disappear....The true value of women has nothing to do with this pretentious feminism, egalitarian and selfish. Since the word feminism is now part of our vocabulary I accept it, but I see it with a Christian meaning and I want to define it this way: the zeal of woman for all the noble causes in the area Providence assigned to her." [HS-1985]

THE LIBERATION OF WOMEN

"There is one direction in which women are gradually becoming emancipated which can only lead to good. I mean the direction of actual bodily freedom in the matter of dress and activity. Women's progress in this direction is surprisingly small as yet, but it is encouraging. That women should so passionately demand freedom of action in the world, and at the same time cling so decidedly to the fetters of conventional dress, which render freedom impossible, is one of those instances of unreason which leave the masculine mind in hopeless amazement. There are women who would welcome martyrdom for what they believe to be the cause of personal freedom, who would not accept the freedom of their own natural bodies as a gift."—Bliss Carman, ca 1910

EVERYBODY'S DOING IT

RIDE A RED BIRD
BRANTFORD

Massey   Cleveland   Perfect   Columbia
or other C.C.M. Bicycles

YOU, too, will be more than pleased with the pleasure to be had, the time and energy to be saved, and the glowing health to be gained from riding a first class bicycle.

They look well and run smoothly, not only when new, but for many years.

Ask your local agent for complete illustrated catalogue

Canada Cycle & Motor Co., Limited

Montreal   Toronto   WESTON   Winnipeg   Vancouver

ANNA LEONOWENS

The spunky governess for the court of Siam was also an important figure in Canada's women's movement. Born Anna Harriette Crawford in Wales in 1834, she became a world traveller, author, and political activist. Her husband's early death in Singapore in 1858 left Anna penniless. To support herself and her two children, she worked as the Siamese court governess for seven years, until her physical collapse necessitated her return to England. She immigrated to America in 1867 for health reasons, where she published *The English Governess at the Siamese Court* (1870) and *The Romance of the Harem* (1872), and then followed her daughter to Canada in 1876.

Residing in Halifax from 1876 to 1897, Anna Leonowens established reading and literary discussion clubs for women. She organized a group to establish an art school to commemorate Queen Victoria's Golden Jubilee, creating an Art Loan Exhibition through which she rented international art works from her own and friends' collections for short periods of time, to raise funds for the project. When the Victoria School of Art and Design, now known as the Nova Scotia College of Art and Design, opened in September 1887, Anna served on the first board.

She was active in suffrage work, and in 1894 was invited by Lady Aberdeen to help establish a Halifax Local Council of Women. Anna spoke at the meeting, describing the organization of the first women's council in India 2000 years before, and outlining eloquently the ways in which women could help each other and their children. Anna was elected the Council's first recording secretary. She used her position on the local council and in the National Council of Women to continue to advocate women's suffrage, saying that "while women are refused the franchise they should refuse to pay taxes."

When Anna's daughter Avis died in 1901, Anna moved to Montreal to take over the raising of her grandchildren. She continued to be an inspiring force until ill health and blindness forced her into a more retiring life. She was 75 years old when she gave her

above: Anna Leonowens

The era of sanity in women's costume seems to have dawned. The ideal of womanhood, man's inferior and toy to be indulged and enslaved, is passed, let us hope forever, and with it must gradually pass the standard of women's accustomed dress, devised to emphasize and enforce women's restricted sphere.—Bliss Carman, ca 1910

One bicyclist wearing an advanced costume does more towards furthering dress reform than a score of theorists, writers and lecturers.—The Globe, Toronto, 1895

left: from the National Council of Women Yearbook, 1915-1916

above: Sarah, Charlotte and Elizabeth (Peardon) Holman

Unforgettable is the time when Mrs. Parker began to teach women to read, in a place where there is now a fine college for women. Men sneered and asked, "Are you going to teach our cows to read also?"
—Sarah Holman, 1950

right: Ishbel Maria Marjoribanks Gordon

last lecture on Sanskrit at McGill University. Anna Leonowens died in 1915 and was buried in Mount Royal Cemetery in Montreal. [HS-1980]

[Anna Leonowen's life in Siam was fictionalized in Margaret Landon's 1943 novel, *Anna and the King of Siam,* which later became part of popular culture through the stage musical and film, *The King and I.* Eds.]

THE HOLMAN SISTERS

These three women in late middle age face the camera as resolutely as they faced life. Their shared characteristics of determination and independence, as well as their unwavering faith, set them all on paths decidedly different from most of their contemporaries.

All were born and raised in Prince Edward Island. Elizabeth, after only six years of marriage, was left widowed with three young children to support. She did so by farming on her own for 14 years. In 1903, deciding that her then 17-year-old son should homestead, she packed up the family and headed to Saskatchewan—where they prospered.

Her sisters were also making major life changes. Charlotte had sailed for India in 1900, as a Methodist missionary; in 1906 she convinced Sarah to join her.

In Agra, they quickly decided the greatest need was with the "outcasts," then largely ignored even by other missionaries. As Sarah later recounted:

"The District Superintendent, Dr. Clancy, seeing the pitiful group of undernourished children that I had gathered together said to me, 'Do you think you will get a school out of that?' I replied, 'Yes, I do.'...Dr. and Mrs. Clancy leaned back in their chairs and roared with laughter, 'Miss Holman, when you get a school out of that we will all take our hats off to you.' I answered, 'You will take off your hats then, for I have been appointed to a school and I WILL have a school!'"

She and Charlotte established the Holman Institute, "The first and only school built especially for the depressed classes." In addition to basic education, the school taught technical skills; fed and clothed its

students; provided the community with medical assistance and improvements such as paved roads.

A fourth sister, Louise Fiske, had been left a wealthy widow and was able to give the Institute financial assistance. Childless, Louise opened her home to students attending universities in Boston—and paid their tuition. [HS-1999]

ISHBEL MARIA MARJORIBANKS GORDON, LADY ABERDEEN

Lady Aberdeen believed that wealth and privilege carried an obligation of service. Throughout her life, this remarkable organizer founded and supported associations devoted to social, religious, and political progress. It was Canada's good fortune that Lady Aberdeen spent time in this country and, characteristically, involved herself in the organizing of three associations.

In 1891 Lord and Lady Aberdeen made their first visit, a holiday tour of Canada on the CPR. They were appalled by the bleakness of life and the lack of cultural

and all of Lady Aberdeen's tact and influence to overcome this opposition, but overcome it was, and on 18 May 1898, the Victorian Order of Nurses was established by Royal Charter. [HS-1985]

VON ON THE TRAIL OF 1898

In 1898, shortly after the formation of the Victorian Order of Nurses for Canada (VON), a detachment of four nurses was sent to the Klondike, where the gold rush was underway. Advance publicity suggested that the nurses were "fully aware of the hardships which they will have to face, but count the opportunity thus given to them of succouring suffering humanity under very adverse circumstances a joy, an honour."

The nurses were highly motivated and challenged by the undertaking. Georgia Powell's efforts to write the slogan "Victory or Death" on guideposts into the region "as encouragement to those who came after," demonstrated her zeal. During their travels and upon their arrival in the Dawson district, the nurses provided invaluable medical services. They were quickly affiliated with hospitals in the area where conditions were "degrading enough to make one doubt the blessedness of drudgery," but where their presence was warmly welcomed. This initial expedition introduced the newly established VON into northern Canada and, with accompanying newspaper publicity, helped to strengthen support for the public health nurses. [HS-1988]

left: Four VON nurses sent to the Yukon in 1898, with the journalist who accompanied them

below: The Victorian Order of Nurses first focused on delivering nursing service to districts without access to medical facilities, and on establishing hospitals in isolated areas. The medical conference shown below on the running board of the Model T Ford took place in the Burnaby District of British Columbia sometime in the early 1920s.

opportunities available to prairie settlers. On their return to Winnipeg, Lady Aberdeen proposed an association to send magazines and newspapers to western settlers. A group of Winnipeg women accepted the challenge and founded the "Lady Aberdeen Association for Distribution of Literature to Settlers in the West." With Lady Aberdeen's continuing support, the association flourished. Branches sprang up in other Canadian cities and in Britain. Parcels were shipped free of charge from Britain, and the Canadian Post Office permitted the Aberdeen Association's parcels to be mailed at reduced rates.

When Lord Aberdeen was appointed Governor General in 1893, he and his wife returned to Canada. One of Lady Aberdeen's first activities was to attend a meeting of the World Council of Women in the United States. She was elected president, and, on her return to Canada, was asked to help organize a National Council here. She agreed, in October 1893 chairing the organizational meeting of the National Council of Women (NCW) of Canada. She was elected its first president and remained an interested and supportive "Advisory President" for the rest of her life.

Lady Aberdeen's other great contribution to Canadian life is the Victorian Order of Nurses. In 1896 the Halifax branch of the NCW proposed an organization of district nurses similar to that in Britain. Lady Aberdeen became president of a board to establish the order as a permanent memorial to Queen Victoria's Diamond Jubilee. Many people, especially within the medical profession, were adamantly opposed to the scheme. It took two years of hard work

above: Adelaide Hoodless

It has been said that women are too busy to record their history. Yet admittedly, we are good at preserving—jellies, jams, condiments, relishes, pickles—endurables made from perishable things. It is time that we as women took this approach to recording our own lives, our own stories.
—Carmelita McGrath, 1987

Although nursing, nutrition, and general health and safety were mostly managed within the home by women, opportunities for them to be educated in these responsibilities were severely limited. At the beginning of the 20th century, every mother faced the grim fact that one in 10 children died in the first years of life. The groundwork for the national system of medicare developed in the 1960s in Canada was laid by women's groups working tirelessly to improve health care in their communities.

ADELAIDE HOODLESS

Adelaide Hunter Hoodless believed devoutly that mothers are nation builders. That explains why she devoted twenty years of her life to providing education for homemakers. It does not account for the passion which drove her, quite literally, to work herself to death in service of the cause.

In 1889, the youngest of her four children, a baby of eighteen months, died of tuberculosis because she unwittingly fed him contaminated milk. Lacking a practical scientific education, she hadn't known the risk. If women were responsible for the well-being and strength of mankind, as she believed, it was clearly urgent that they be trained for their work.

Mrs. Hoodless reasoned that since boys and girls were destined to assume different roles as adults, they should not as children receive the same education. In addition to their academic subjects, girls should study scientific nutrition, sanitation, and housekeeping skills. The school board in Hamilton, where she lived, called the idea a "fool fad"; the Ontario minister of education thought it "utterly impractical." But Mrs. Hoodless persevered; she taught classes, wrote textbooks, gave speeches, and made allies until the impractical fad was part of the curriculum in Ontario schools and teacher colleges. She died on a lecture platform in 1910, while raising money for a home economics building at the University of Toronto.

One of her most lasting accomplishments was the founding of the world's first Women's Institute. She was incensed that the Ontario government taught farm men how to breed and raise livestock, without giving a thought to farm women and the breeding and care of human beings. In 1897, she shared this indignation with a hall full of women at Stoney Creek, who immediately organized to study and improve domestic architecture, sanitation, economics, nutrition, and child care. From Ontario the idea of farm women banding together for self-education and community service spread throughout Canada and to Great Britain.

Adelaide Hoodless had no interest in changing the nature of women's work. What she did demand was that both men and women replace cheap platitudes about the importance of motherhood with genuine support and respect for the profession of homemaking. [HS-1977]

SASKATCHEWAN WOMEN'S INSTITUTES

The Saskatchewan Women's Institutes (until 1971 the Homemakers' Clubs), the largest rural women's organization in Saskatchewan, was established at a time when the rate of rural immigration to the prairies was at its peak. In January of 1911 forty-two women from rural communities and clubs met with the University of Saskatchewan extension department to organize the Association of Homemakers' Clubs of Saskatchewan. In 1913 the University hired a Director of Women's Work to organize and supervise the growing network of Saskatchewan Homemakers' Clubs. This woman was Abigail DeLury, a graduate of Macdonald College, who had left her native Ontario to teach Home Economics in Moose Jaw in 1910.

The clubs' work encompassed "all that was for the social and educational welfare of the community." From 1913 to 1930 Abigail coordinated Homemakers' activities. She helped clubs to establish libraries in their districts, organized provincial lecture tours to give rural and city women access to continuing education, and planned and ran the annual Homemakers' Convention and the women's sections of Farm and

Home Week at the University. DeLury and her colleagues were convinced that education was the single most important factor in personal and community development: the short courses and lectures she organized on health care, gardening, food preservation, citizenship, and international affairs were focal points of each convention.

When DeLury retired in 1930 there were 240 Homemakers' Clubs with a total of 5,800 members in the province. The small quiet woman was admired by all she worked with, and was missed when she retired to her hometown of Manilla, Ontario. She died there in June of 1957.

Today's Institutes lobby for rural transition houses for battered wives, and concern themselves with numerous issues, including matrimonial property legislation, the economics of the family farm, pensions for women, pornography, seat belts in school buses, farm safety, and the environment. Times change, but the Institute's aims remain the same: "the promotion of the interests of the home and community." [HS-1986]

HELEN MACMURCHY

A pioneer in recognizing the association between medicine and social work, Dr Helen Macmurchy spoke out against the inadequate housing and slum conditions many of her patients lived in, and argued for medical supervision of schools, stating bluntly that trying to educate children was useless if those children were underfed. Hired by the Ontario provincial government as inspector of hospitals, charities, and prisons, Macmurchy authored one of the first reports on the problem of maternal mortality. When the federal department of health was established in 1919, Macmurchy was appointed head of the Child Welfare division. [HS-1994]

above: Helen Macmurchy

Now, that is our part of the work, the part of the organized women, including the Homemakers, to educate public opinion....—Violet McNaughton, 1916

left: Board of directors, Federated Women's Institutes of Canada, 1921

Women's concern with the health of their community influenced many of the protections and provisions we now take for granted in our daily lives. But there was a time when we were not so well looked after. We owe a great deal to the tireless women who concerned themselves with our welfare and for whom no task was too great or too small.

JEAN McDONALD

Jean McDonald, a working-class heroine, was born in Ireland and raised in Scotland. Before immigrating to Canada in 1907, she aspired to own a dairy farm and to win awards for milk and cheese production. She became instead a boarding-house keeper, police matron, and champion of Calgary's needy.

Jean moved to Calgary in 1910 to support herself and her two children while her husband homesteaded at Munson, Alberta. She worked cleaning houses until she earned enough to buy beds and dishes, then opened a boarding house. Her home became a refuge for the destitute and unfortunate, as she was always willing to share what she had. Jean fought injustice wherever she saw it, writing letters to newspapers and politicians until she got what she wanted. Her reputation for persistence and fearlessness won her many battles. When the Canadian government brought over factory-district girls from Britain to work as low-paid domestics in the 1930s, Jean succeeded in helping them return home. When, as a police matron, she met a woman who had been sentenced to an insane asylum for murdering her cruel husband, Jean had the woman's case reviewed, allowing her to be sent home to her native England. This staunch and steadfast support for neglected causes earned Jean the respect of many, including Prime Minister R.B. Bennett and Calgary mayor Don MacKay.

Jean McDonald touched many, many people. During the Spanish influenza epidemic of 1917-19, she opened her home to the Red Cross to shelter the sick, and served as a practical nurse herself. When the Indian peoples approached her for help, she added their cause to her list. She aided chiropractors to obtain licences to practise, and worked to increase pensions for the elderly.

She did much of her campaigning in the company of other women. In the early 1900s she helped organize the Next-of-Kin Association to agitate for higher allowances for soldiers' wives, formed the Women's Labour League to prod the government into raising pensions, and worked in the local Council of Women and the Victoria Park Community Association to better the lives of Calgary's poor children. She continued her work with the Red Cross and, in her later years, helped form the National Social Security Association to assist the elderly. [HS-1980]

right: The face of poverty. This woman was photographed selling pencils on the streets of Toronto, 18 August 1918. Since that time the old age pension has been introduced, and women's access to higher education, job training, employment, and pay equity has steadily increased. But elderly women are still the poorest of the poor in Canada.

I believed there was no class distinction in Canada, but here it was in full...the exploitation I had left, as I thought, in Britain was right here, with all the traits of snobbishness.
—Jean McDonald

ANNIE GALE

Limp carrots and mouldy cabbage prompted Annie Gale's entry into civic politics. She arrived in Calgary from England in March 1912 with her husband and two sons, and for the next 13 years worked to improve the living conditions for Calgary's citizens. She felt the city should do more than collect taxes; it should also improve society.

In a 1919 memoir, Annie recalled, "I was then [1912] a very conservative woman...but the wrong conditions prevailing here forced me to take note." Those conditions included high land and house prices, and, in spite of the farmland which surrounded the city, expensive produce that "would only be fed to the cows in the Old Country." Annie decided to make changes. Joining like-minded women, she worked to establish a municipal market, and was a leading member of the Vacant Lots Club, which campaigned for unused land to be set aside for community garden plots.

In 1916 she founded the Women Rate Payers Association. More overtly political than many other women's groups of the period, it lobbied for progressive reforms, including municipally funded hospitals, upgraded playgrounds, and improved public transport. In 1917 Annie ran for city office with the support of the *Calgary Eye Opener*: "This lady has all the mental and businesslike qualities requisite for a seat on Calgary's council board." Annie won, thus becoming the first woman to win a city council seat in Canada. In office, she continued to work for the rights of citizens. She advocated that Calgary buy a coal mine as a public utility, and called for equal pay for women in the civic workplace. She served as acting mayor on a number of occasions.

In 1919 she recalled her initial determination to make Calgary a better place to live: "The fighting spirit...engendered by these conditions remains with me to this day, and gives the courage to dare to oppose a full Council of men when the occasion arises." [HS-1996]

above: Annie Gale

THE CONSUMERS' LEAGUE OF EDMONTON

Typically, women are responsible for growing, gathering, or buying food for their families. Although surrounded by farmland, women in turn-of-the-century Edmonton found it difficult, if not impossible, to buy local produce. The Consumers' League of Edmonton, founded in May 1914, saw education of both consumer and producer as their mandate.

The League's first campaign focused on food availability, price, and quality. The League wrote to farmers within a 30-km radius of Edmonton, inviting them to grow fruits and vegetables for a local market. The League also lobbied city council for a central location. The women were successful and so was the farmers' market.

Like women's groups across the country, the League was concerned with the quality of food. They lobbied for laws to regulate the production and sale of bread, and to establish higher standards for milk and abattoirs.

To educate consumers, they advertised in local papers, encouraging Edmonton housewives to know exactly what they required and to realize it was their duty to insist on getting what they paid for.

The consumer movement, now firmly established in Canada, owes its existence to groups of women like these in Edmonton who were pioneers of consumer activism. [HS-1996]

When I come to the closing years of my life I want to feel that I have helped to establish a nation, the standard of which will go down through the ages as equalling or surpassing the traditions of older countries. This is work for women and I am sorry to say that there is much need.
—Annie Gale, 1919

left: Cherry pickers enjoy "tame fruit," Niagara Peninsula, ca 1920

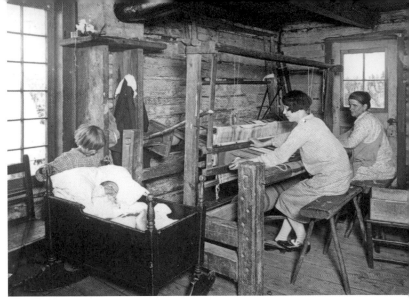

right: Weaving at a loom, Cap à L'Aigle, Québec

The theory that a woman should appeal to a man through her basest qualities— her vanity, her weakness, for which a more honest word is incompetence; her mental dependence which is either ignorance or stupidity, revolts me!—Francis Beynon, Grain Growers' Guide, 1913

below: l to r, Violet McNaughton, Zoe Haight, and Erma Stocking

W omen who advocated for the rights of their gender were truly "a voice crying in the wilderness." Unlike other social reformers, their work promised the betterment of many at the cost of privilege for some. For this reason, their vision of a new world was threatening and they often incurred the derision of some men—and even of some women

WOMEN DON'T WANT TO BE SUPPORTED, THANK YOU

Francis Beynon was one of the most articulate of the early women's-rights advocates. As women's editor of the *Grain Growers' Guide,* she was in a position to influence many people, and her editorials are as valid today as they were in the second decade of the 20th century.

"All my life I have been a woman's woman. I do not hold with [the woman from] Wolf Willow and a great many other women that the Lord made the world for men and then made women to help the men. I believe that the world was made for men and women and they in turn were made to help each other.

"It is all very well for someone like 'Another Mere Man' to sit back smugly and say that there are very few men who will try to beat their wives out of a fair share of the property—'unless there is a good reason....' But that is just the point. The man is allowed to decide what constitutes a good reason....

"Again 'Another Mere Man' shows that he has failed utterly to get our point of view when he says that husbands are compelled by law to support their wives and what more do we want. The attitude of mind expressed in that sentence is one of the things that is driving women to the point of utter exasperation today. He can't see that the progressive, independent woman doesn't want anyone to support her—that all the woman who isn't either mentally or physically lazy wants is a chance to support herself.

"What is still more trying is that he and many thousands of people like him cannot see that you women in the country who work early and late are supporting yourselves right now often without wages, except your board and clothes.

"I consider it downright impertinence for a man on a farm to talk about supporting his wife. When she cooks his meals and sews and mends for him and his children from dawn until dark what is she doing if she is not supporting herself?

"In most country homes the wife not only keeps herself but often contributes the family groceries the year round through raising fowl and making butter. And then her husband talks in a lordly way about supporting her—if he is of the same mind as 'Another Mere Man.'

"Fortunately, there are thousands of four-square men in this country who value their wives and their work at their real worth and who are glad to have them as partners and comrades in the highest sense of the word. We must not forget this fact when our blood boils up at the attitude of the unfair ones." [HS-1982]

VIOLET JACKSON McNAUGHTON

Violet McNaughton was not only key organizer of the farm women's movement, she was also an essential player in a number of progressive causes during the first half of the 1900s. Violet arrived in Saskatchewan in 1909 joining her father and brother on their home-stead; within a few months she married neighbour John McNaughton. Her experiences were similar to other rural women's and informed her activism: she lived in a sod hut on the prairie, slept in a room which served also as a granary, and hauled drinking water 3 km. She also listened to women's stories.

A lengthy hospital stay in 1911 focused her attention on the lack of medical care, especially for women and children; it also left her unable to have children, and she "came to see that her childlessness [gave] her the freedom to dedicate herself to helping create a better life for all children." Although she saw herself as the "small but mighty champion" of farm women and their families, she knew there was strength in numbers. She joined with other Saskatchewan farm women to form the "The Women Grain Growers Association." This politically active, co-operative group campaigned for suffrage, and lobbied to improve rural life, especially for "medical care within the reach of all."

Violet was directly active in provincial and national farm women's organizations between 1913 and 1925. She developed and nurtured groups of women who worked to improve the lives of rural and farm women. Irene Parlby [see p. 55] wrote to her in 1916: "You don't know what an encouragement your letters are to me, as I feel such a hopeless greenhorn at this work; I am filled with interest in it, and enthusiasm but find it so difficult to know how to set about things..."

In 1925 Violet became women's editor of the *Western Producer* and made her pages into a forum for rural women; two recurring topics were medicare and the importance of agriculture in the Canadian economy. She was one of the original signatories establishing the Progressive Party in Saskatchewan, a Canadian delegate to the Congress held in Prague by the Women's International League for Peace and Freedom, and was called to Ottawa during the Great War to act in an advisory capacity with respect to the conservation of Canada's natural resources.

As western vice-president of the Canadian Council of Immigration of Women and Children, she worked to establish women's hostels throughout the Dominion. About the same time, she assisted with the organization of farm women in Alberta, Manitoba, and Ontario, and in 1918, became the first president of the Women's Section of the Canadian Council of Agriculture. In 1934 Violet was honoured by King George V for her services for the welfare of rural women with the conferral of an Order of the British Empire. Violet McNaughton helped shape rural Canada and women's role in it. [HS-1974, 2000]

Resolved that every husband at marriage must sign a contract agreeing to place at least one-third of his income at the disposal of his wife to spend as she may see fit.—Resolution, Public Speaking Class, 1922

MARRIAGE 1927

In 1927, syndicated columnist Inez Haynes Irwin discussed "the marriage problem," describing the changes she would like to see in "this matter of Marriage." Her levelheaded observations are in part reality today, but the ideal Irwin envisioned 55 years ago is still to come:

left: Society of Independent Spinsters, University of Alberta, 1908

right: Adelaide Willson Plumptre

I conclude, then, that all the talk about "woman's sphere," as though it were something as accurately definable as a circle, or a triangle, is equally irrelevant and impertinent.
—"M," 1879

Quand toutes les femmes se rendent compte que...la plupart des femmes mettent leurs énergies au service des entreprises des hommes [et] que ces énergies créatrices pourraient servir à elles— et que ce serait mille fois plus intéressant—alors on a franchi le mur.
—Pol Pelletier, 1981

"It will not be the poet's or the lover's dream of happiness, on the other hand, it will not be a bug bear."

"In a hundred years, perhaps, we shall have learned better than to expect an eternal ecstasy from marriage. At that future time also we shall have learned to make both marriage and divorce as easy as possible. To marry you will only have to go with your partner in the matrimonial scheme to the local city hall and register your intention of becoming married. To divorce you will only go to the same place and register your intention of becoming divorced. The expense, in time and money, and in the case of divorce, the scandal, will be reduced to a minimum....

"In a hundred years from now, social progress will have automatically removed certain inevitable bunkers in the matrimonial game. There are many of these bunkers: money—particularly money...children—for children sometimes push their parents apart instead of holding them together; the position of women in the matrimonial partnership, incredibly inconsistent and degrading; the high pressure economic burdens laid upon the husband—a burden so heavy that often it drains from him all capacity for happiness, curtails his very life....

"Take the question of money. A hundred years from now it will be established by law exactly what proportion of his salary the wife, as his partner in the matrimonial undertaking, may demand of her husband. A hundred years from now, it will be established by law exactly what pension the mother—as the partner in population production with the state—may demand of the state for each child she bears. Many quarrels that now come up between husband and wife in regard to money, will, in these conditions, no longer appear.

"Take the question of children. A hundred years from now a closer and more scientific adjustment of our life along community lines will remove from women much of the care of the household and particularly of the children. The system will give her more leisure for study, the arts, sports of all kinds, entertainment—whatever her body or brain desires. Above all, it will free her for a career." [HS-1982]

ADELAIDE WILLSON PLUMPTRE

"One of Canada's most outstanding women," read *The Globe and Mail* obituary in September 1948. The woman was Adelaide Plumptre, sportswoman, educator, tireless organizer, and committee worker. Born in England in 1874, Adelaide won three scholarships to study at Oxford. Although she passed with honours, in 1900 Oxford still did not grant degrees to women. Adelaide was also an outstanding athlete, winning "blues" in field hockey and tennis. At Oxford, she met and married the Rev. Henry Plumptre, the only man she knew who beat her at tennis.

In 1901 the Plumptres came to Canada to teach at colleges in Toronto. Later, they moved to Montreal, and Adelaide retired to have children and take up volunteer work for the YWCA, the Red Cross, the Girl Guides, and the National Council of Women.

During World War I Adelaide was secretary of the Canadian Red Cross and the only woman to serve on the Canada Registration Board. After the war, Adelaide served on the Toronto school board, becoming the first woman chair. She was elected to city council in 1936 and was the first woman to chair the city's health board, parks committee and housing commission.

Between the wars, Adelaide worked for the League of Nations. She was one of two women to report to the General Assembly. As an officer of the Canadian League of Nations Society, she travelled the country, lecturing in support of the League.

In the Second World War, Adelaide founded and directed the Red Cross Transport Service, which served as a model for the Canadian Women's Army Corps. She also directed the Canadian Red Cross Prisoner of War Bureau, helping Canadian servicemen and their families. For her war work she was made a Commander of the British Empire.

All her life Adelaide used her formidable organizational skills to work on health care and poverty. Both in public office and in charitable organizations, she addressed such issues as housing for the poor, maternal and child care, and public health. [HS-1991]

SAVELLA STECHISHIN

"She promoted the idea that a woman should be a person on her own—free—not just an object in a house." That is Savella Stechishin talking about Ukrainian novelist Olha Kobylanska, but she might just as well be referring to herself.

Ten-year-old Savella and her family emigrated

from eastern Ukraine to a Saskatchewan farm in 1913. At first, life was a hard struggle not only against pioneer conditions, but against the snobbish dominant society which felt that "if you weren't Anglo-Saxon, you just weren't that good." The Ukrainian community was presented with an ultimatum: either adopt British values or accept second-class status. Like many of her people, Savella would not accept those terms. She was "burning to get an education, to be a good Canadian," but without rejecting her own culture.

These ambitions took her to the Mohyla Institute in Saskatoon where she attended public school by day and studied Ukrainian civilization by night. In 1921, when still a student, she married the principal of the Institute, and eventually became dean of women. To share her sense of commitment and self-worth with other young women in residence there, she helped organize the Olha Kobylanska Women's Association, a study group dedicated to self-education and feminism.

Through newspaper reports, the idea spread across the prairies, so that in 1926 a national Ukrainian Women's Association was formed with Mrs. Stechishin as "women's editor" and as national president for nine years. The association, still deeply interested in preserving Ukrainian language and culture, is now associated with the Ukrainian Orthodox Church.

Mrs. Stechishin looks back with satisfaction on the way Ukrainian-Canadians have taken a prideful place in our society without giving up their heritage. "It is a great and marvellous thing," she says, "and the women have helped." [HS-1977]

[Savella received the Taras Shevchenko Medal in 1975, the Order of Canada in 1989, and the Saskatchewan Order of Merit in 1998. She died in April 2002. Eds.]

MARY ANNA "BAY" WIGLEY

"Bay" Wigley arrived in Victoria, British Columbia, at the turn of the 20th century, at the age of 18. After a not particularly happy childhood, she was strongly committed to following her instincts. One of her first decisions was to take a business course and seek

above: Mary Anna "Bay" Wigley

Until women are free, the freedom of all humanity is insecure.
—Charter of Rights for Canadian Women, 1950

left: Savella Stechishin

In writing women's history, there is the tendency to reach far afield for our heroines.... In doing so, we often pass right by those very special women who will never make it into the history books...those strong and beautiful females from whom so many of us gather our strength and courage—our mothers.
—Jessie Collins, 1978

employment—then largely a man's prerogative. As accountant in a prestigious Victoria firm she earned a place in the business community.

She was best known, however, for her social welfare activity. Bay devoted much of her life to others. Whatever the project, she worked long and hard, and was always one of the first volunteers in time of need. She worked particularly to improve life for women and to help them find "their rightful place in a man's world." The issues she took up were varied and often considered unsuitable for women's attention.

In 1921, she and friends started the Kumtuks Club. Its name, meaning "to know and understand," symbolized its founders' intent "to educate members...so that, as intelligent women with the vote, we might know how to properly play our part in the life of Canada—and...also play it." Bay continuously held office or committee positions in this group, which became Victoria's Business and Professional Women's Club.

Another venture, born of the Depression, was the Women's Workroom, with Bay as president. In this ancestor of Goodwill Enterprises, women able to sew, knit, or alter clothing worked to support their families.

In 1936, in her mid-50s, she suffered a stroke and died after a month in hospital. Representatives of almost every social agency and service group attended her funeral. From all sides came praise for Bay as both a private and a public person—for her strong convictions, her sincerity and generosity, her kindness, her ability to inspire others, her organizing skills. She was well-known, widely loved and sincerely grieved. As one contemporary noted at the time of her death, "Quietly and without publicity, Miss Wigley went about doing good....She will be sadly missed." [HS-1991]

There is not very much difference between the murderer and the one who stands by and sees those die whom he could save. The infant mortality rate must be reduced.—Dr Helen Macmurchy, 1911

right: Women's Labour League preparing bundles for Nova Scotia coal miners, ca 1925

"Everyone is guilty of an indictable offence and liable to two years' imprisonment who knowingly...offers to sell, advertises, publishes an advertisement of or has for sale and disposal any medicine, drug or article intended or represented as a means of preventing conception or causing abortion." This 1892 law was on the books in Canada until 1969. Even discussing birth control was illegal. Canadian women who wanted to control fertility were in a desperate state of ignorance.

BIRTH CONTROL

In 1934, a Dartmouth, Nova Scotia, mother of two wrote to Marie Stopes, British birth control pioneer: "I am writing to you as a very ignorant married woman to find out if I too may share your secret...I am taking a great liberty I know, but when one worries so from month to month to find a way out would be wonderful."

Even though it was illegal to even own such material, much less distribute it, in one ingenious scheme, Violet McNaughton [see p. 96] had a friend in England send a new booklet on birth control to her a few pages at a time, as if they were letters. This information was passed along at various women's gatherings, including sewing circles.

Books like *What a Young Wife Ought to Know* (1908) advised twin beds, prolonged breast feeding, and restriction of intercourse to the "safe period," which was mistakenly calculated to fall at mid-month.

Not only were any mechanical contraceptives associated in peoples' minds with a libertine lifestyle and even prostitution, but because of their illegal status, their prices were prohibitively high, and without regulation, their reliability was variable.

As a recourse women shared homemade recipes often containing such unhelpful ingredients as cocoa butter, boric and tannic acids. Ads in women's magazines for household cleaners and disinfectants intimated they could be used for contraceptive purposes.

It was in this atmosphere that Dr Elizabeth Bagshaw established her clinic. [HS-2000]

ELIZABETH BAGSHAW

Dr Elizabeth Bagshaw was the founder of Canada's first birth control clinic. For her trouble, she could have gone to jail. Dissemination of information about birth control and the dispensing of birth control devices were illegal in Canada until 1969. Women's organizations, and women individually, had been asking the government for years for a change in the law, but had got nowhere.

Dr Bagshaw, a practical and hard-headed woman physician, practising in Hamilton, Ontario, didn't wait around for government approval. In 1930, efficiently and without fanfare, she set up a birth control clinic because "both children and mothers were suffering." It provided information and dispensed birth control devices.

It is a sham to pretend that women have equality in our society when control of their own bodies in reproduction is denied. —Dr Henry Morgentaler

Women, who have always been on the front lines of developments in reproductive technologies, will have to be particularly vigilant as the struggle to gain control of our bodies enters new arenas.— Herstory 2000

left: Dr Elizabeth Bagshaw

above: Dorothea Palmer

Implicit within the most fundamental values of our society are the assumptions that women must function within the family, and for the sake of the family, and the fear that society will be in jeopardy if they do not.
—Barbara Roberts, 1979

right: Nurses and babes, Grace Hospital, 1914

"The Depression came on and we had a lot of poor people. There was no welfare and no unemployment payments, and these people were just about half-starved because there was no work....They couldn't afford to have children if they couldn't afford to eat. So the families came to the clinic and we gave them information."

The clinic operated underground for 35 years and Dr Bagshaw was its medical director for much of that time. It is now supported by government grants. How did she get away with it? By "keeping my mouth shut," says Dr Bagshaw. "We didn't advertise...we told our patients to send anybody else they thought would like to come."

Dr Bagshaw also broke with tradition when she, a single woman, adopted a son at a time when such a thing was almost unheard of. She didn't go to Children's Aid because, says Dr Bagshaw, she knew she would have been refused, and instead handled the whole thing herself through a lawyer.

She retired from her medical practice in 1976 at the age of 95. Her philosophy of life was a simple one: "The important thing is to be happy and not to worry." [HS-1979]

[Elizabeth Bagshaw received many honours, including the Persons Award in 1979; a guest lectureship was established in her name by the Hamilton Academy of Medicine in 1981. She died in 1982, age 100. Eds.]

DOROTHEA PALMER

"A woman should be master of her own body," the young woman blazed at the policemen who were interrogating her. "She should be the one to say if she wants to become a mother."

It was not the 1970s; the questioning had nothing to do with abortion. It was 1936, and Dorothea Palmer was being quizzed about alleged infringements of the law which made the advertisement and sale of contraceptives illegal in Canada.

Ms Palmer was a trained social worker who in 1936 was active in the Parents' Information Bureau (PIB) of Kitchener, Ontario, a privately financed agency which supplied contraceptives to poor women at cost. Ms Palmer's job was to visit homes in Eastview,

Ontario, where one-quarter of the 4,000 people were on welfare.

She canvassed door-to-door, talking to mothers, asking about their families, showing them several kinds of contraceptives, and explaining how to use them. Those women who wanted more information were invited to apply to the PIB. In 1936, the bureau employed fifty women, many of them nurses, to do this work in other communities.

Ms Palmer was singled out for prosecution. On paper, her crime was peddling contraceptives. In the courtroom, it became obvious her real offence was bringing birth control information to Roman Catholics. The population of Eastview was Irish and French Canadian; Dorothea Palmer was an English-speaking Protestant. The Crown argued that for her to lure Roman Catholics into the sin of using contraceptives without warning them about the Church's stand was not in the public good.

"The public good" was the key to the trial. The law provided that no crime was committed by those acting in the public interest, but it did not explain what that meant.

The trial dragged on through six months. Dozens of witnesses were called and vitriolic reportage filled the newspapers. Finally, in March 1937, Dorothea Palmer was acquitted. The right of all Canadian women, rich or poor, to accessible birth control had been acknowledged by the courts, if not by society at large. [HS-1976]

WELL BABY CLINICS

The health of mothers and their babies has long been an interest of Canadian women's groups. Women in the late 1800s called for legal reform allowing women more control of their children as well as laws that would protect women and children. Later, they asked for mother's allowances. In the early years of the 20th century, prairie women lobbied for rural nurses and hospitals.

One outcome of this agitation was the "well baby clinic." These clinics were places where women could receive prenatal care, bring their babies for checkups, and take classes on raising children. Initially, these clinics were dependent upon already established women's groups, such as local chapters of the Red Cross, the Women's Institute [see p. 92] or church women's organizations. Later, departments of health became involved. [HS-1993]

left: Mary Panagoosho Cousins, of Pond Inlet, Baffin Island, with child—advocate for the family, her people, and her community for many years.

below: Mother and child at Edmonton clinic, 1928

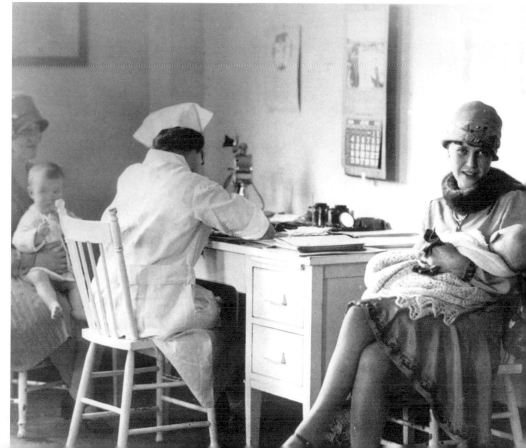

right: Winnifred Stewart

Even when the major battles had been won, such as suffrage and the Persons Case, women in Canada continued to fight for causes that inspired them, provoked them or were simply near to their hearts.

DEPRESSION ERA ACTIVISTS

There is a common misconception that after Canadian women won the vote, the activism of the suffragists dissipated and women went quietly back to their homes, until the renewal of the women's liberation movement in the 1960s. But feminist historians find that women participated in all the great political upheavals of this century. Like most women throughout history, these activists have been belittled or ignored by many male historians.

During the 1930s thousands of unemployed men drifted to Vancouver. Governments' inability and apparent unwillingness to provide decent work or adequate relief drove the unemployed to radical political action. Leftist women organized the "Mothers' Council" to support the unemployed men, but also to take action independently.

The Mothers' Council organized tag days and demonstrations in support of the relief camp workers' strike in 1935. On Mother's Day 1935, the women sponsored a mass rally in Stanley Park. In 1938, the Mothers' Council organized food deliveries which enabled the occupation of the Vancouver Post Office to continue until the men were evicted with tear gas and clubs.

The women also lobbied city council and the provincial government, made speeches at rallies, and led marches in defiance of the police. Inspired partly by their maternal feelings, but also by their sense of the injustice, and belief that everyone had a right to "work and wages," the women of the thirties came out of their homes and took political action. [HS-1993]

WINNIFRED STEWART

Winnifred Stewart refused to accept her doctor's diagnosis that her Down Syndrome baby was beyond help. A nurse, she set to work reading everything available on retardation—not much in 1934—and began to train her son herself. By the age of nineteen, he could shop and travel around the city on his own, participate in sports, was literate, understood basic finances, and had an average vocabulary. At forty-one, he can run

below: Mothers' Council demonstration, Vancouver, 1935

any electrical tool and is proficient in thirty-five crafts. A miracle? No: very hard work, an innovative mind, courage, and a determination never to admit anything is impossible.

Ms Stewart's discoveries about teaching the developmentally delayed would have stopped with her son, had it not been for a chance remark in February 1953 by the administrator of the Physically Handicapped Association. Ms Stewart was in the room when parents of a mentally handicapped child came to him for help and he told them nothing could be done. Snapping bolt upright in her chair, she told him what could be done. He challenged her to pass on her knowledge to others.

Within a week she had formed the Organization for Rehabilitation of Retarded Children. A public meeting a month later resulted in the formation of a school run by ten volunteers. In 1954 Ms Stewart visited the Alberta legislature and was successful in persuading its members to pass legislation to support the mentally retarded, the first such legislation in Canada.

Due to her tenacity and hard work, the Winnifred Stewart School has grown and its program has been copied from Yellowknife to Moscow. In recognition of her service to thousands of forgotten children and their families, Ms Stewart received Edmonton's Citizen of the Year award and the Medal of Service of the Order of Canada. [HS-1976]

[In 1979 Ms Stewart established Cerwood Industries, a vocational training sheltered workshop for the mentally handicapped. With the trend towards integration, the Winnifred Stewart School became the Winnifred Stewart Adult Education Program. On January 13, 1990, the Edmonton Association for the Mentally Handicapped officially changed its name to the Winnifred Stewart Association for the Mentally Handicapped. Eds.]

No matter how busy they may be with their families and homes, women are part of the larger community. They owe it to themselves to develop their abilities and work for a better, peaceful world.—Helena Gutteridge, 1957

CARRIE BEST

"The problems resulting from racial inequality and its limitations have weighed heavily upon me from my earliest recollections....I can say with all seriousness, without regret, and sometimes with prideful humility, that—by the Grace of God and Slavery I am what I am." When Carrie Best wrote these words in 1977, she could look back upon a lifetime of responsible activism aimed at finding solutions to the prejudices she so accurately identified.

Born and educated in New Glasgow, Nova Scotia, Carrie was known as "the woman who swallowed a dictionary." She used her words to help the voiceless: the poor, the underprivileged, and minorities. Always a firm believer in the power of reason and the written word, by 1945 Carrie had begun publishing a broadsheet specifically as a voice for the black community. *The Clarion* eventually grew into a newspaper with national readership; its aim was to help foster interracial understanding and tolerance.

Although *The Clarion* ceased publication in 1956, Carrie continued public service with a radio program, *The Quiet Corner,* carried by four stations in the Maritimes for 12 years. Anger caused her return to print journalism in 1968, when she was informed that a local school principal had refused a scholarship for

One learns as the years bring wisdom that while we cannot ignore our emotions, our intellect will keep them in check, for once the mind is trained, it can evaluate and select its own values.—Carrie Best, 1977

left: Carrie Best

right: Laure Gaudreault

We will emerge from our struggle weakened if we remain turned in upon ourselves with no other horizons but those we have always known and if, led by false teachers, we remain attached to the old traditions alone.—Thérèse Casgrain, in *A Woman in a Man's World,* 1972

Native students, because, in his opinion, "there was not one Indian student who deserved it." The editor of the *Pictou Advocate* gave her a column.

That single column stretched into several years of investigative journalism. She didn't escape envy and criticism, but neither did she back down in the face of adversity. Particularly difficult were the years she spent advising landowners in areas she realized were slated for development.

As a child, Carrie had been advised by her mother: "Society has said you were an inferior being...because you are black. Remember you are a person, separate and apart from all other persons on earth. The path to your destiny is hidden. You alone must discover it. Take the first right turn and go straight ahead."

To her credit, and to the benefit of many, Carrie took her mother's advice. [HS-1995]

[Carrie Best died in 2001. Eds.]

MARY HELEN FROST MOONEN

"It is the women who have often instigated the reforms in this country—in their quiet ways encouraging their husbands. Now we have a generation of women who are prepared to be more vocal, likely because their mothers gave them more confidence in their own abilities...encouraged them to continue their education." So says Mary Helen Frost Moonen, who developed a local Millet, Alberta, Red Cross swim program when a young nephew drowned. She campaigned to upgrade highways, organized 4-H clubs, the Millet Historical Society—to gather and publish a two-volume local history—and the Millet Museum, and remained active in all of them into her 80s. She was active as well in the Friends of the Devonian Garden, the Alberta Lily Association, the Wetaskiwin Horticulture Society, and the Canadian Cancer Society. She also began attending the spring session for seniors at the University of Alberta in Edmonton, picking up other seniors on the way, of course. In 1986 the Wetaskiwin Agricultural Society named her its Citizen of the Year. [HS-1991]

above: Mary Helen Frost Moonen

Women have always been teachers—of themselves and those around them. Teaching was one of the first careers open to women, and almost from the beginning, women educators have sought reform, both within their profession and, by virtue of their dedication to it, through their impact on their students.

LAURE GAUDREAULT

In 1935 the minimum annual wage for women teaching in Quebec's rural schools was set at $300. This was not overly generous for a time when the average Canadian renter paid $366 a year for shelter. But for the seven to eight thousand women who had been making less than $300—many as little as half that amount—it was an unparalleled improvement.

Country school boards, who had to foot the wage bill, were less enthusiastic; they hired women precisely because they would work for so little. When the boards refused to comply with the law, the government took prompt action. It dropped the minimum wage to $250 a year.

Amongst those affected was forty-six-year old Laure Gaudreault of La Malbaie, a small resort town northeast of Quebec City. When only sixteen, she'd taken charge of a class of forty-eight teenagers at several grade levels. Though well qualified, she earned just $125 a year. It was a typical case of poverty and overwork with predictable results—her health broke, and she had to seek other employment.

Mlle Gaudreault took up journalism, and even after her return to teaching in 1931, continued to work as a part-time columnist. When the salary question came up in 1936, she used her access to the press and her public presence to promote the idea of a province-wide trade union for rural women teachers. As a result, the Fédération catholique des institutrices rurales (FCIR) was formed in 1937, with Mlle Gaudreault as president and only paid organizer.

Together, the women fought for six years to secure their $300 minimum wage and to win a small increase to their "insulting and insufficient" pensions. Denied the right to strike, they nonetheless took collective action in 1944 and again in 1954 by refusing to sign contracts until officials acceded to their demands. Inspired by the women's solidarity, other Quebec teachers organized after the pattern of the FCIR. As for Mlle Gaudreault, guiding spirit behind many of these developments, she played a leading role in the teachers' union movement until her retirement at the age of seventy-nine. She died in 1975. [HS-1977]

FEDERATION OF WOMEN TEACHERS' ASSOCIATIONS OF ONTARIO (FWTAO)

"One free moment while wandering along a corridor my curiosity led me to pause at the door of a room filled to overflowing with women. I stepped in and stood along one wall beside several others who had apparently been unable to find seats. So I accidentally attended the organizational meeting of the FWTAO. The woman I stood beside, very attractive in a blue gown and large black hat, introduced herself as Helen Arbuthnot. She kept up a running commentary re proceedings. Miss Johnson of London was in the chair. Miss Adkins of St. Thomas was secretary. I was duly impressed. It seemed just unthinkable that a group of so many women should expect or allow the men to act and plan for them in all professional matters. I was interested in men at the time but still I found some of the comments witty and enlightening."—Edna Clader

At its 3 April, 1918 founding, the FWTAO became the first provincial association of teachers. It is still the only such women teachers' union in the world. The first meeting, described by Edna Clader, who served as president in 1939-40, was a carefully planned event that took place despite outright opposition. Dedicated to the principle of "Equal Pay for Equal Work" and to advancing the interests of female professionals, the women who organized that first meeting would be astounded to see what came of it. The FWTAO is now the largest teachers' group in Ontario, representing over 42,000 public elementary school teachers. [HS-1995]

It is not only prudence which is a virtue; strength is one too.
—Laure Gaudreault, 1967

Did you ever hear of any article in the commercial world having its quality improved and its price remain the same? There is only one product... which I know...is treated in this way, that is, the product of women's brains and women's hands.
—Evelyn Johnson, first president of FWTAO, 1919

left: FWTAO, first board of directors, 1947

Canada's immigration policy has changed over the years, largely due to the political tastes of the day [see p. 135]. Through to the latter 1900s it was standard practice to admit women as adjunct "family," rather than in their own right. There are a number of implications of this policy uniquely affecting immigrant women. They may not have the same access to training and language courses as men, both because of government policy and, sometimes, because of immigrant community pressure. Also, there has been little incentive for governments to offer services in language of origin, which tends to isolate some women. The emphasis on immigrants with money also excludes women, as few have the necessary investment. Reforming and improving the experience of new Canadians has been of particular concern to women.

NANCY POCOCK

At seventy-eight years of age "Mama Nancy" Pocock is relentless in her devotion to refugees. She was first nicknamed "Mama" by those who sought her assistance. Her compassion encompasses all who approach her. "I get calls all the time," she says. "The Salvadorans call me. The Guatemalans call me. Someone told me they even heard my name in Nicaragua." Her work has no boundaries. She offers whatever assistance is necessary. Even her basement serves as a clothing depot. She helps refugees across the American border, then arranges for the hearings needed to grant them landed immigrant status. Once they become landed immigrants she helps them obtain work permits, jobs, English lessons, and lodging. Many young men ask her to help them bring their endangered families to Canada.

Her one-on-one work with refugees began in the 1960s with her late husband Jack Pocock. Their first project was support for the draft dodgers and deserters of the Vietnam war. Young Americans and Vietnamese were welcome to stay in their home over a number of years. Since then countless refugees have found temporary lodging in the Pocock home. "I have this big house and I didn't see why I shouldn't share it." She receives no federal or provincial money; funding comes from the Canadian Friends' Service Committee and private donations.

Nancy is a devoted peace activist. For over 20 years she has been involved with the Canadian Peace Research Institute and the Canadian Campaign for Nuclear Disarmament. She is one of the founding members of the Voice of Women, the Grindstone Island Peace Project, and Project Ploughshares. She serves as moderator for the Commission on World Concerns of the Canadian Council of Churches and is an active member of the Quaker Committee for Refugees.

In 1978 Vietnam gave her a medal for friendship; in 1987 an American group, the Giraffe Project, gave

left: Founded in 1984, Immigrant Women of Saskatchewan
helps meet the special needs of new Canadians

her the Giraffe award for community activism. In 1987 she was the second woman to receive the Lester Pearson Peace Prize medal since it was established in 1979. [HS-1991]

[Nancy died in 1999. Eds.]

VOICES OF CHINESE CANADIAN WOMEN

Records of Chinese Canadian history are limited at best, and what little information there is concentrates on men. In an effort to document women's experience, the Chinese Canadian National Council has conducted an oral history project. Information gathered in over 300 hours of taped interviews will be published as *Jin Guo: Voices of Chinese Canadian Women*.

The project interviewed Chinese women who came to Canada before immigration laws relaxed in the 1960s, women of Chinese descent who have immigrated since 1968, and Canadian-born Chinese women.

"There are stories of the pain of name-calling and doors slammed in the face, of isolation in a strange society that speaks a strange language. Of the struggle to be both Canadian and Chinese, or to be at once mother, wife, and worker, and stories of the joy of parenting or achieving career goals, of working in the Chinese and local community to save Chinatown, build a feminist artist collective, or help senior citizens."—May Yee, 1987

"We had a restaurant and we worked....All we knew was to work. I remember when we were going to high school, I used to work every day until 2 o'clock, sometimes 3 o'clock in the morning, then go to bed—then you get up at 8 o'clock to go to school. And during summer holidays, we worked 14 hours a day....7 days a week."—Mrs L., born in Windsor, Ontario, 1919

"We could never go in our friends' houses. We always called from outside the window—because we were Chinese people. You knew you were Chinese, you knew you were different—nobody had to tell you. So you would sort of try to behave all the time."—Mrs W., born in Hamilton, Ontario, 1919

above: Mrs Hoy Kam Gee and Mrs Jou Lee, 1959

Because of the head tax on Chinese immigrants, and the Canadian government's preference for male immigrants:

"If a woman came, she'd have to disguise herself as a man. She braided her hair [like the men] and wore the black cap Chinese men wore then. They didn't check—you just pay the head tax and you can come. I have a Chinese friend who said that she gave birth at home. She said that all the time that she was here, she had not seen a single person. She was confined because the husband didn't allow her to go out—and she didn't want to either, since she didn't know the language."—Kim, married to a Chinese Canadian man who returned to China in search of a Chinese wife; she immigrated to Canada in 1957. [HS-1989]

In the Canadian context, Chinese women have historically been ignored and forgotten, or at best lost amidst copious academic notes which may grant them vague reference as a prominent someone's wife or mother....It is sad to think that generations of Chinese Canadians have and are continuing to grow up without realizing just how deep their roots are.—Dora Nipp, 1987

right: Leone Pippard

One of Canada's greatest legacies is its natural heritage. Women have played a role in the conservation and environmental movements from the earliest days.

LEONE PIPPARD

Her 1973 introduction to the beluga irrevocably changed Leone Pippard's life. Doing a freelance photo story on the small white whales of the St Lawrence River, she and a friend discovered little was known about these mammals. Captivated, the two women spent months and much of their own money studying the animals. They soon saw that this unique subpolar population was in trouble. Fewer than 500 remained of former thousands. Many were diseased and deformed—victims of pollution and habitat loss.

In 1978 the two released their study. Their lobbying achieved legal protection for the beluga in 1979, and in 1983 the federal government formally declared the whales endangered. A whale autopsy program began in the same year. Never missing a chance to increase public awareness, Leone successfully campaigned for marine traffic regulations and, for 15 years, the marine park and sanctuary now at the mouth of the Saguenay River.

Barely in her forties, "Our Lady of the White Whales," earned the respect of the scientific community. Though she lacks a science background, and was, as a woman, considered out of place on the river by locals, her landmark study is considered the most important work ever done on belugas in the wild.

Building on her conclusions, others have continued studying the beluga's decline. Governments' river cleanup plans have been sparked by Leone's tenacity and ingenuity. Any recovery plan for the beluga will owe much to her. So will the humans who depend on the St Lawrence. Leone was honoured by *Ms.* magazine in 1987 as a "woman of the year." In 1988 she was invited to address an international forum on the beluga. She heads Canadian Ecology Advocates, the environmental group she founded for "ordinary people" to foster responsible attitudes toward the environment. [HS-1992]

[Leone received the Canadian Environmental Achievement Award, Lifetime Achievement, Certificate of Honour, in 1992. She has formed her own consultancy, Leone Pippard and Associates which links planning for sustainable development with effective citizen engagement. Eds.]

Given the range of causes that women embrace and the importance of this work in the community at large, sometimes what they really need, is simply "a room of one's own." Over the past few years, many Canadian women and their organizations have created their own centres in cities across the country. Such centres serve a vital need for women across Canada, and encourage further advancement for women in educational, social, and economic fields of activity.

THE VANCOUVER WOMEN'S BUILDING

"The many women's public welfare organizations of Vancouver require a community home for the unification of their common purpose, a central building from which their social service undertakings may radiate as the spokes from a hub of a wheel. Such a building

---

We can make it right if we want to.
—Leone Pippard, 1990

It has seemed extremely important that children should discover what an interesting world we are living in—interesting in ways that have nothing to do with money or artificial stimulation.
—Mabel Frances Whittemore, ca 1930, mentor to hundreds of southern Ontario's budding naturalists (including Robert Bateman) for whom Canada's premier nature magazine, *Nature Canada,* was established as a memorial.

would prove a fountain head of inspiration, with groups of intelligent women bringing in fresh ideas, collecting and exchanging information as to more effective means of carrying out plans for educational, patriotic, philanthropic, social and domestic legislation."

The ideals that motivated the foundation of the Vancouver Women's Building were first expressed in 1911. On April 12 of that year, the Vancouver Women's Building, Ltd., was incorporated.

Spearheaded by delegates from 12 women's associations in the city, the organization bought a house at 752 Thurlow Street, and opened its doors to serve the needs of Vancouver women. In addition to providing office space and meeting rooms for women's groups, an early project was a free daycare centre for working mothers.

By the end of 1913, 21 women's groups with over 5,000 members were shareholders in the corporation, and many other women's organizations used the building for meetings, offices, and special events. During the first decade of operation, it was apparent that the original frame house was not big enough to serve the needs of the community or the corporation, and the board launched an appeal to raise the monies for an addition.

By 1924, there were over 350 women's organizations in Vancouver. As noted by the corporation, these were not social clubs, but rather were devoted to "philanthropic, religious, educational, and literary purposes, and to social reform."

The fund drive was successful, and on 30 September 1926, the expanded building was opened. The 80 women's groups and 500 individuals who held shares in 1926 were proud of their building, and they had every right to be. For the next 14 years, until the Second World War and changing social conditions forced the building to close, the organization served as a focal point for Vancouver women.

The building served as a training ground for several generations of women leaders. Already by 1924 they were able to claim: "Its roster shows that almost any Vancouver woman who has led public affairs since 1911 at some time or other served an apprenticeship there." [HS-1981]

In 1978, *Herstory* wrote: "Women today are awakening to the subtle sexist oppression in western Judaeo-Christian religions...they are awakening from their passive acceptance of sexist doctrine, and are demanding change." As we look forward into a new millennium, how far have women come on that spiritual journey? Handmaidens no longer, they are assuming positions of influence in many denominations. While many women continue to fight for justice and a place within their faith communities, others seek spiritual homes less in need of reform.

MARY JO LEDDY

Mary Jo Leddy, Roman Catholic nun, journalist, editor, peace activist and teacher, is an articulate spokeswoman for the women's movement, particularly within the church. Her parents' war experiences and her studies have encouraged her to focus most of her energies on the peace movement. Her campaigns for social

...woman is coming into her own. The time has arrived when her intelligence and humanity are needed to help man solve problems of world peace, happiness and prosperity.
—"An Investment in Civic Welfare," Vancouver Women's Building, 1924

My hope is that the women's movement in the church will remain precisely that...for a long time—rather than something which becomes too quickly institutionalized or co-opted. Movements... do transform institutions.
—Mary Jo Leddy, 1988

left: Mary Jo Leddy

reform demonstrate the enormous contribution of church women and draw attention to the restrictions they face in the church.

Sister Mary Jo was born in Toronto in 1946. She has won numerous scholarships and journalistic awards, including the Canadian University Presidents' Award as an Outstanding Young Woman in 1978. She also appeared as a commentator during CBC Television's coverage of the 1984 and 1987 papal visits to Canada.

In 1975-76 she was preaching at the Newman Centre in Toronto as part of a pastoral team. When the Vatican passed a document forbidding the ordination of women, the local archbishop interpreted this as an edict against women preaching. Recalling her PHD studies on the Holocaust, she was not surprised by these restrictions, representing "another example of the inclination to power and domination which have always been prevalent in the church."

At that time Leddy was involved with a small group planning to start *Catholic New Times,* an alternative, independent national Roman Catholic newspaper. Assuming editorial duties, she discovered a new audience, which suggested to her that "women who are working for change in the church, are too often trapped into thinking that the only forums open to them are those which are delineated by the official church. It may be that the most effective forums are those which women help to open up, to create, for themselves and for others."

Leddy has participated in many peace campaigns, including the Christian Initiative for Peace's vigil outside Litton Industries in Toronto, peace pilgrimages to the Honduran-Nicaraguan border and to the Soviet Union, and a fact-finding tour in southern Lebanon. In spite of weaknesses in the church institution, Leddy believes it offers the most hope for peaceful social reform. [HS-1989]

[Dr Leddy has been director of the Romero House Community for Refugees, and adjunct professor at Regis College, University of Toronto. She has authored several books and received the Canadian Council of Christians and Jews Human Relations Award in 1987 and the Order of Canada in 1996. Eds.]

...the kingdom of God worked like the yeast Christ mentioned [Luke 13:20-21] and centuries later, some Christians understood. They worked to abolish slavery and to improve the legal and social status of women and of children.
—Kathie Storrie, 1978

right: Kathie Storrie

KATHIE STORRIE

Kathie Storrie is a Christian feminist with an uncanny combination of toughness and compassion. Within an hour she can discuss why Apostle Paul should be called the patron of the women's movement, and why feminism seems to turn on the issue of child care. "Until you get a situation where men take the role of caring for children as absolutely part of their responsibility, you will not get equal opportunity for women. The institutional church is not at all according to God's will. It's become hierarchical, oppressive; the Submission of Women movement is a total abomination."

When asked why she remains a Christian, she responds: "A few years ago, I went through a spiritual crisis. I thought either God is a God of justice as well as a God of love, or God doesn't exist at all and Christianity is a total sham. I was prepared to give up my Christian faith, but not the sense of justice I knew had to be there."

Her sense of justice was born in the Brazilian cof-

NORMA BAUMEL JOSEPH

left: Norma Baumel Joseph

Norma Baumel Joseph is a Jew, teacher, student, mother, wife, activist, writer, and spiritual leader. One of the things she is most proud of is something she has been working on for over fifteen years. "I have worked long and hard to improve women's situation in many areas but especially in divorce. This is a major accomplishment but I still have a long agenda." Norma is referring to Bill C-61, which amended divorce legislation in Canada to protect Jewish women. Previously it was possible for men to refuse their wives a religious divorce, which made it difficult for them to remarry in spite of having had a civil divorce.

Norma was one of 10 subjects in the film *Half the Kingdom*. She also served as consultant on this brilliant film about women, religion and feminism.

The first group of women to pray at the Western Wall in Jerusalem with a Torah and prayer shawls did so in December 1988. Norma was among them. She is one of six North American women who are party to a lawsuit in Israel's Supreme Court trying to gain the right for women to pray in this way.

As a feminist scholar and Orthodox Jew, Norma looks critically at traditional Judaism. For her, the Talmud reflects the possibility of change from within, without discarding the deep roots of Judaism. She is working for change from inside by rediscovering rituals and stories about women that are long forgotten; through study and interpretation, she knows she will uncover the freedom for women that is there.

"Mostly I love teaching," she says, "especially teaching women. There is so much on our agenda, we have so much to do—but first we must learn, reflect, and study. And then we must share, empower, and act." [HS-1992]

[After a 10-year court battle and violent attacks on the group by ultra-Orthodox worshippers, Israel's High Court of Justice ruled in May 2000 that the "Women of the Wall" have the right to pray at the Western Wall. It is expected that this ruling will be challenged and that the women will have to abide by certain restrictions so as not to offend fellow worshippers. Eds.]

fee farms where her parents were missionaries. Other experiences strengthened that initial experience, including medical social work and sociology degrees in both England and Canada. Kathie now teaches at the University of Saskatchewan, where her Sociology of Sex-Roles class is a powerful and persuasive note for change in societal values; she also counsels students, combining Christianity, feminism, compassion, and her sense of justice.

"We must never underestimate the huge power of the forces ranged against us. We must continue to do the rather dull kinds of things like researching the law, collecting statistics, on top of all the other things we're trying to do, in what we laughingly call our spare time." Kathie's steady, persistent, careful work, whether compiling statistics on battered wives, or planning one of the many speeches she gives each year, is evident. She is an articulate spokeswoman for the Saskatchewan Action Committee on the Status of Women, and for Canadian Women and Religion, which she helped organize.

In spite of her compassion and serenity, the sense of anger remains. "I began to find this Submission of Women literature and I remember throwing one book clear across the room. I was enraged. I was so angry when I began to realize more and more the injustices of the world. I was just as angry on behalf of men, that men should be taught to be such oppressors." [HS-1981]

[Kathie Storrie has retired from university teaching but continues her community involvement. Eds.]

I love being a Jew. I want the community to survive. I want the tradition of Judaism to continue into the future. I want to have a part in that future and I won't be silent.
—Norma Baumel Joseph, 1989

I feel stronger as a human being, proud that I am a woman and proud that there are women who do indeed dedicate their lives to causes and to improving themselves as human beings.—Herstory *fan mail, 1977*

YVONNE PETERS

"I'm...finding that we're having to go through the whole consciousness-raising process....We're still very much in that stage. A lot of disabled people simply believe, are conditioned to believe I suppose, that they're second-class citizens. They wouldn't say that, but the things that they are willing to accept and put up with indicate that they're still willing to allow that second-class citizen treatment."

So says Yvonne Peters, one of the driving forces behind the battle for equal rights for the physically disabled. Her direct involvement began in January 1978 when she took the chair of a committee work-

right: Yvonne Peters

ing to amend Saskatchewan's human rights legislation to include the physically disabled. This change was accomplished by August 1979, following the group's dynamic use of their political force via the media and public lobbying.

Yvonne is convinced of the necessity of lobbying for legislative change. "Educational programs are necessary but they've been around for ages and they haven't made any real significant changes....Until we make it morally wrong for people to discriminate—and that's what laws do—I don't think that we're really going to change things. And so that's a crucial area for us to continue working in—to change legislation."

In 1979 Yvonne was elected provincial president of the Voice of the Handicapped, Saskatchewan's disabled persons' lobbying group. She is also a Saskatchewan delegate to the national group, the Coalition of Provincial Organizations for the Handicapped, and was involved in the campaign to amend the Canadian Human Rights Act to include the physically disabled.

At 18 months of age Yvonne was diagnosed with infantile glaucoma, a disease which resulted in her total blindness by the age of five. The eldest of five children and naturally endowed with stubbornness, she has been independent and determined not to be stereotyped because of her disability, since childhood. Throughout her young adulthood, she used political routes to prevent personal discrimination and to get into the courses of study that she wanted. When she began looking for jobs and realized the extent of discrimination, as well as the legal vulnerability of the handicapped, she decided to become more politically active.

Yvonne is active in both women's and disabled persons' liberation movements, and is interested in the parallel developments in the two. She hopes to see more people who are experiencing minority group problems become elected political representatives in the near future. [HS-1981]

[In 1993 disability became a prohibited ground of discrimination. In 1998 the Act was further amended

left: Shirley Turcotte

since she can remember she endured sexual abuse by her father, who also made her sister pregnant and frequently beat her mother and two brothers. Today Shirley leads a busy, normal life in Vancouver, far from the scene of her childhood horrors, which took place in a remote country home outside Winnipeg. For the last several years she has been helping other survivors of sexual abuse put their shattered lives back together again.

In an act of rare courage, Shirley went public with her story in a powerful National Film Board documentary *To A Safer Place*. Her story of rehabilitation is an inspiration and an unusually intimate view of the human spirit challenging the most painful odds. In the late 1970s she had written a manuscript describing her childhood experiences as a victim of sexual abuse. This script brought her into contact with the National Film Board's Studio D and led to the award-winning film, in which Shirley is both subject and expert, as well as collaborating director [scc p. 238].

Shirley is one of the founding members and executive director of Support, Education and Prevention of Sexual Abuse (SEPSA), an organization formed in 1984. A pioneer activist in this field, Turcotte leads support groups for survivors, and lectures and facilitates workshops on many aspects of child sexual abuse and the healing process. Her work with SEPSA also includes a community outreach program to rural communities in BC and the west.

From 1980-88, Shirley worked for BC Telephones as business engineering support supervisor. She is an expert in telecommunications technology, a field in which there are still few women. Shirley is married and has a son.

Today, as well as working with SEPSA, Shirley is on the advisory board of Kids Help Line which, if established, will be a 24-hour telephone line for troubled and abused kids and teens in Canada. [HS-1990]

[Shirley was successful in launching the Kids Help Phone Line. Every day it is used by over 3000 children across Canada. The number is 1-800-668-6868. Eds.]

If we do not challenge the concept that might is right, then there is no point to this struggle after all.—Rosemary Brown

The average woman is apt to regard national and international affairs as something apart from her own family and life. The tendency has been to accept privileges and not to accept responsibilities. —Hon Cairine Wilson, 1944

to require employers to accommodate the special needs of disabled people. Yvonne was executive director and litigation director of the Canadian Disability Rights Council from 1989 to 1993. She practises as an equity rights lawyer in Winnipeg. Eds.]

SHIRLEY TURCOTTE

Shirley Turcotte was born in 1952 in St Boniface, Manitoba. Her adult life has been a difficult process of coming to terms with living as a survivor of incest.

As a child, Shirley lived a nightmare. Almost

Long before the phrase "global village" came into vogue, reforming women have recognized that concern for the well-being of their community has broad implications.

Health has always been of fundamental concern to women. While basic issues remain the same, threats such as AIDS and breast cancer have recently come into public consciousness.

PEGGY MASON

In the words of her son, Peggy Mason "goes to New York to get rid of guns." She has been Canada's ambassador for disarmament since 1989. Her job has a triple mandate. She represents Canada at the arms control negotiating table internationally. She participates in the nuclear non-proliferation talks in Geneva, and on the First Committee and Disarmament Commission at the United Nations General Assembly in New York.

She is based in Ottawa and charged with consulting with concerned Canadians across the country about arms control and disarmament. Born in Nova Scotia and educated in Ottawa, Peggy practised law for three years before becoming legal advisor and policy analyst for the Canadian Advisory Council on the Status of Women in 1980. She was policy advisor for two Conservative critics before becoming arms control policy advisor to the Minister of External Affairs in 1984.

Peggy knows from polls that Canadian women are concerned with peace and security issues, but does not believe being a woman affects how she does her job. She does believe that "fairly representing the gender of over half of the world's population is absolutely essential." As yet, however, Peggy is one of only a handful of women in the disarmament diplomatic community.

Peggy spends two-thirds of her time travelling. She feels fortunate to be able to do this interesting, challenging, valuable job and also have a family. It is hard on all of them; her son was five when she began. It helps that she has a supportive husband and that she negotiated weekends at home as part of her job. She firmly believes that "if women are going to do these things, the system must be adjusted." [HS-1992]

[Peggy was ambassador for disarmament until 1994. She now chairs a United Nations group on small arms. Eds.]

WINNIPEG WOMEN'S HEALTH CLINIC

"Try and get rid of us now. We're practically establishment," commented Jennifer Cooper, executive director of the Winnipeg Women's Health Clinic, on their move into their third location since their first offices opened in 1980.

The first clinic occupied a modest 750 square feet and employed two people, with a few friendly doctors on call for referral. They now occupy 5,500 square feet in downtown Winnipeg and employ over twenty people, including four part-time doctors, a dietitian, two health educators, reception and medical assistants, a co-ordinator of volunteers, and a specialist in weight preoccupation. There are forty to fifty volunteers, and the clinic is now conducting training programs on self-help groups and public speaking on women's health issues. And all—patients, volunteers, and staff—are women.

Fifteen years ago, today's clinic was not even a dream. The first steps were taken by women in Winnipeg exchanging health information over their kitchen tables. Some felt that the informal exchange on available services and doctors needed more structure. Women were looking for information on birth planning, fertility problems, and how to cope with unplanned pregnancies, but the counselling and information services did not seem to be available.

In 1977 Pregnancy Information Services was incorporated and the training program was formalized. The tiny service was overwhelmed with the response, and in 1980, they launched a fundraising drive to provide capital for expansion. "It has always been a collective vision," Cooper says, and women in Winnipeg rallied to the cause, raising nearly $27,000 in grassroots donations, to transform Pregnancy Information Services into the Women's Health Clinic. In 1983 they were able to obtain funding from the Manitoba gov-

above: Peggy Mason

...instead of arguing with the grownups, who think nuclear weapons are necessary, I devote my time to the children, showing them that the world can be a beautiful and peaceful place.
—Kinuko Laskey, Hiroshima survivor and disarmament advocate, 1986

ernment; by 1988 the annual budget was $500,000.

They have maintained their information-rich, self-help approach to health services. Women have confidence in the clinic, Cooper feels, because it is run by women, for women. [HS-1989]

[The Winnipeg Women's Health Clinic continues to prosper, as their website claims, as: "a feminist, community-based health centre offering a range of services to women from teens to elders." Eds.]

THE LIFE QUILT FOR BREAST CANCER

Each year nearly 18,000 Canadian women learn they have breast cancer; another 5,000 die of it. "The Life Quilt for Breast Cancer" is a metaphor for their struggle—from health to disease to rebirth. Its first section, "Cut in Prime," portrays destruction of the mature forest—diagnosis and disease—through clear cutting. "Call to Rebirth," the second, depicts the destroyed forest now covered by fireweed and other colonizing plants—life continuing in different form. "Green Canopy" shows the new forest—regrowth, integration and healing.

The three central panels were painted by Gay Mitchell, Vancouver-area artist and friend of Judy Reimer, founder of the Life Quilt for Breast Cancer project. Each panel is bordered by 136 small squares created by people across Canada, expressing their thoughts and experiences with breast cancer. As the quilts tour the country, those who add their own stitches come to know the community formed by working together, sharing time and stories, and the warmth and comfort these quilts symbolize. [HS-1999]

[Judy Reimer died in October 2002. Eds.]

FLORA MIKE

Growing up on the Beardy's Okemasis Reserve near Duck Lake, Saskatchewan, Flora Mike never dreamed she would become an AIDS activist. Born in 1926, she lived simply, working on her parents' farm: "It was a happy life. We didn't ask for more than we had."

Married in 1943, she continued to live on the reserve. Over the years she had 12 children. In June 1990, her seventh child, Bobby, called from British Columbia to tell his family he was HIV-positive. Flora was devastated. "I was really hurting inside." When Bobby developed AIDS just a few months later, Flora and two of her daughters flew to British Columbia to bring him home.

Soon after Bobby's return, he and Flora began travelling across Saskatchewan and Canada. They spent 1991 on the road, telling their story to Aboriginal audiences. Flora told her story in the hope that other mothers would accept and support a child with AIDS. "As a mother, I couldn't abandon him. A mother's love is stronger than anything else."

She also felt it was critical to warn Aboriginal people about AIDS. She knew they had little knowledge of the disease. "I didn't know about it myself," she says, until it touched her family.

After Bobby died in 1992, she continued the AIDS prevention work. She takes strength from knowing she is helping change lives. A year after speaking in a Saskatoon centre for street kids, she received a letter telling her one of the girls in the audience had turned her life around, quitting alcohol and drugs.

"I tell young people not to abuse their bodies with alcohol and drugs. And to mothers, I tell them to keep providing love, support, and care for their children." [HS-1999]

above: One section of the Life Quilt for Breast Cancer

The fact that one person can make a difference...is vitally important to me.
—Johanne Morel, 1991

below: Flora Mike

In 1978 *Herstory* wrote: "...marital assaults are not confined to lower class couples: wife-beating crosses all socio-economic lines." Domestic violence was typically seen as a private matter. British law held that a man could beat his wife as long as he used a stick no thicker than his thumb—the so-called "rule of thumb." This was in practice in the 19th century, a time when many British men came to Canada and when our laws and legal custom were established. While some activists spoke out about violence against women in the home or in the community, society as a whole continued to downplay it.

also made us aware that women who are Aboriginal, of colour, mentally or physically disabled, lesbian, or older are at greater risk. At the same time, we are learning the power of healing and forgiveness. In order to heal from violence, we need to learn to forgive.

Recognition of the problem has not always meant increased funding or support. Shelters are forced to turn away women and children. Programs for men who are survivors of child sexual abuse or who are trying to learn nonviolent behaviour are few and far between. We may have made progress since 1974, but we still have a long way to go. [HS-2000]

VIOLENCE AGAINST WOMEN

below: December 6 Women's Grove Memorial on the grounds of the Manitoba Legislature

The Canadian public lost its innocence when a gunman, blaming women for his disappointments, killed 14 young women studying engineering at Montreal's École Polytechnique. After this tragedy, those in power finally admitted there was a problem. The federal government appointed a panel to investigate; its report, released in 1993, legitimized what many had been saying—most women have experienced some form of violence in their lives. The report also expanded the public understanding of violence: all violence is about power over others. Violence is not just physical, but mental, emotional, spiritual, and sexual. The panel

IN MEMORIAM: MONTREAL, 6 DECEMBER 1989

"The events in Montreal certainly and surely upset all of us deeply. They trouble me because any of these young women could have been one of my students, could have been someone I encouraged by saying: 'Look, you can do it. It's a tough turf all right, but there are others. Nothing will change if we aren't there.'

"But these fourteen women are not there anymore....Many say that what happened to them was an act of a madman...that had nothing to with anything except the state of [his] mind....Yes, it was act of a madman, but...how people get mad, how that escalation from prejudice to hate to violence occurs, what and who is hated, how it is expressed, is not unrelated to the world around us.

"When a madman uses easily available weapons and easily available prejudices, it is not totally his problem that will go away when he goes away. At another time, it could have been Jews who were lined up, it could have been black people, but in Montreal they were women, and they were women in an engineering faculty. Killed by somebody who wanted to be an engineer.

"...we remember the fourteen students in Montreal. But we also remember that they were abandoned.... [he]...went into a classroom in which there were men and women. He asked them to separate into two groups and when this didn't happen, he fired a

left: Heidi Rathjen

Science and Engineering, University of Toronto, at the 17 January 1990 memorial service for Geneviève Bergeron, Hélène Colgan, Nathalie Croteau, Barbara Daigneault, Anne-Marie Edward, Maud Haviernick, Barbara Marie Kleuznick, Maryse Leclair, Maryse Legainière, Anne-Marie Lemay, Sonia Pelletier, Michele Richard, Anne St Arneault, and Annette Turcotte. [HS-1992]

HEIDI RATHJEN

Heidi Rathjen was on her way to a career in engineering when the murder of 14 women at L'École Polytechnique transformed her from engineer to activist. On 6 December 1989, when a man with a gun shot her classmates, Rathjen was fortunate not to be in the line of fire. It took some time for her to realize the impact of the tragedy, she says, because it was "too impossible."

The event prompted her to lead a student petition for a ban on assault weapons, a step which she felt was a concrete measure that could help prevent further tragedies. She continued to work on the gun control issue and eventually left an engineering job at Bell Canada to co-found the Coalition for Gun Control with Toronto business professor Wendy Cukier.

Rathjen never went back to engineering. After spending six years with the Gun Control Coalition, which was successful in obtaining stricter federal gun control legislation, she went on to become campaign director with the Quebec Coalition for Tobacco Control.

Working for gun control was challenging and draining, but Rathjen never wanted to quit: "there was never any question of giving up because it was too hard." Although opponents tried to paint Rathjen and Cukier as hysterical man-haters, the two won over the Canadian public and experts with their cool-headed approach.

With the tobacco control coalition, she concedes she is in for a much longer fight because of the size and power of the tobacco industry. But, again, there is no talk of giving up: "It's an issue I feel strongly about that is consistent with my values." She thinks stricter control of tobacco is crucial in discouraging young people from smoking: "public education only goes so far."

The time has come for us to change the question: Am I my brother's keeper?" to a firm commitment: "I am my sister's keeper." —Jean McIllwrick, 1972

Somehow we're always having to make these choices of how to separate what is strictly the Peace movement and what is the Women's movement, what is the Ecology movement and what is the Human Rights movement. I think these movements are alive and effective because more and more of us see these things as interrelated.—Muriel Duckworth, 1987

shot at the ceiling. Then the men left and fourteen women were killed. It is not as much a question of how he got in as a question of how he got out....

"...what does it take to make solidarity real? Is one shot to the ceiling or its verbal equivalent enough to abandon the victims?...Is a joke enough to condone harassment?

"Many...called [it] a 'senseless killing.' Are there killings that are not senseless?...Are there people who can be abandoned?

"...I would urge you...to reflect on what it means that someone is your sister, that someone is a member of that human family. That doesn't mean you have to like them or love them, but it does mean that you and we have to respect their presence as *the right to be there on their own terms,* not by gracious permission of the dominant culture, not only as they keep their mouths shut and go through the prescribed hoops, but, because we are members of one family, by their inalienable right to be and to fulfill their potential."—*abridged text of the address by Ursula Franklin, professor emeritus, Faculty of Applied*

Born in 1966 in Point Claire, Quebec, Rathjen grew up speaking German, French, and English. A natural organizer, she gravitated toward a career that would put her love of math and science to practical use. Although she traded engineering for activism, she is proud to be an engineer and says she has used many of those skills while organizing and lobbying for tougher gun and tobacco control. [HS-1999]

INTERVAL HOUSES

Women and children have traditionally been dependent upon men in our society. Society at large only reluctantly assumes responsibility for those women who, for whatever reason, find themselves outside that relationship, with children to support and nowhere to turn. Until recently, the usual response of social service departments was to house a woman with children in hotels and motels; at best, temporary accommodation particularly unsuited to a family in crisis. Those who did put effort into finding suitable accommodation often found themselves thwarted by landlords who were suspicious and exploitive of single-parent families.

Women themselves have organized to meet this need, to provide resources for women and children in trouble. Dozens of shelters, commonly known as Interval Houses, have sprung up across Canada in the last ten years. Here, women and children can find support and protection for an interim period of time, until the crisis period is over, or until a new life can be made. Relieved of the responsibility of child care for a few hours, and surrounded by the support and company of other women in similar situations, a woman can look for housing, apply for jobs or further training, or simply have the chance to talk over the painful events that have brought her to the Interval House.

A new awareness is growing concerning the inequalities that troubled families face in our country. It is to be hoped that the "stigma" historically attached to those who leave destructive, unhealthy marriage is lessening, to be replaced by developing preventive services. In the meantime, Interval Houses across Canada stand ready to meet the needs of these women. [HS-1979]

above: Illustration by Candace Savage

The more of us there are demanding zero tolerance towards violence, the safer we will all be.
—Tamara's House, 1998

right: Veronica Strong-Boag

Women engaged in research, writing and educating are also reformers. They seek to broaden our understanding—and our minds.

VERONICA STRONG-BOAG

Historian Veronica Strong-Boag considers herself to be one of the "very lucky people" who always knew what she wanted to be, "at least from the time I was six years old." Family influence helped make her an historian; the women's movement of the late 1960s had made her a feminist by the time she took her BA in history at the University of Toronto in 1970. "It was not an intellectual but a political discovery," she recalls.

Intellectual discovery quickly followed. Working on an MA at Carleton University in Ottawa, she wrote a major paper introducing a reissue of Nellie McClung's bestseller, *In Times Like These* (1915) [see p. 54]. Back at Toronto for a PHD, she studied a formative women's organization, the National Council of Women of Canada. [see pp. 84, 86, 89, and 90]

However, history is a notoriously conservative discipline, and Dr Strong-Boag found that many historians rejected her strong feminist orientation. So it was with a sense of homecoming that, after teaching at Trent and Concordia universities, she took up a joint appointment in women's studies and history in 1980 at Simon Fraser University (SFU) in Vancouver.

The Women's Studies Program at SFU is community-oriented and broadly based academically. Not coincidentally, it is also very independent. A Secretary of State grant of $500,000 endowed a chair of women's studies, one of five in Canada. Joy Leach, fund raiser and feminist, was challenged to match the grant: Mary Twigg White and Elizabeth Russ donated $400,000 in memory of their mother, Ruth Wynn Woodward, and over $100,000 in small donations came from the community. "The money has allowed us to do things we couldn't otherwise do, without being cramped by cranky or conservative colleagues and administrations," Strong-Boag observes.

In 1988 her book *The New Day Recalled: Lives of Girls and Women in English Canada 1919-1939* won the Sir John A. Macdonald Prize for the best book in Canadian history. An earlier title, *Rethinking Canada: The Promise of Women's History* (1986), reflects the work and the challenge that Strong-Boag and her colleagues have undertaken. [HS-1992]

[Veronica Strong-Boag is now professor of education studies at the University of British Columbia. She has written and edited numerous books and articles since 1992. Eds.]

JANE JACOBS

For Jane Jacobs, writing is a way of thinking. But, says Jane, "it is not ideas alone that can stop injustice, oppression and idiocies like urban renewal or slum clearance. It is people who have to do that." Jane is not only an outstanding thinker and author, she is also activist and leader. Her research tools are "the eye and heart" and her arena, the world. "I live in Toronto, I also live in the universe. And I am at home in both of them."

Through her books, this woman of strong ideas has changed the way we think about our world. Through personal example, she has more than once galvanized community involvement in city planning, and has been largely responsible for resuscitating the concept of the mixed-use, close-knit neighbourhood.

Born Jane Butzner, in 1916 in Scranton, Pennsylvania, she worked as a writer, eventually ending up in New York, where she married Robert Jacobs in 1944. Love for her Greenwich Village neighbourhood motivated a first book: *The Death and Life of Great American Cities*, in which she criticized the planning that destroys community and creates sterile public housing. It is considered one of the most influential books in the history of city planning.

In 1968, with two sons near draft age, and a daughter, the family moved to Toronto. Jane soon discovered that her new neighbourhood was to disappear under a proposed Spadina Expressway. Believing ordinary people can move mountains, she rallied her community to "Stop Spadina." From this successful campaign came the public participation that is now standard in urban planning.

Jane never completed a formal education and has no professional training in fields where she has unquestioned stature: architecture, city planning, economics, and moral philosophy. She has nonetheless produced a series of books that constitute one of the 20th century's most significant bodies of thought. One, *Systems of Survival*, on reading lists in graduate business schools around the world, has been compared to Plato's *Republic*.

Jane has been honoured for lifetime achievement by the Toronto Arts Awards and is a Member of the Order of Canada. In 1997 in Toronto, a month-long celebration of her ideas culminated in the "Jane Jacobs: Ideas that Matter" Conference. [HS-2000]

left: Jane Jacobs

In the past few years it has become apparent that this tradition of phasing out older women has been exploded, along with a good deal of female mythology related to limitations and helplessness. Menopause is no longer a terminal; the train doesn't even slow down there anymore.
—June Callwood, 1975

No one waves a wand and solves all the world's problems. That's an illusion...don't worry about the big abstract problems that no one, not even government can solve. Deal with problems close to home.—Jane Jacobs, 1997

BLACK WOMEN'S MARCH

"I remember when I used to work part-time in hospitals and I'm coming home at midnight. Always when the subway opens and the subway cars open black women coming in. Similarly we're here going to work at 6:00 in the morning. 5:30 in the morning black women getting out of the subway. Always and you look and these are all the women. And you look and you say God these are our mothers and grandmothers. What the hell are they doing. Like when the whole world, the perfect white world in this country is asleep black women are working."—*Linda Carty, 1991* (below, second from right)

"Here I am I'm a black feminist, I'm a black woman and I've made a conscious political decision to fight against these certain things that are impacting on my life and other black women's lives. Be it racism, sexism, homophobia, elitism....You're taking on this certain kind of identification and you're also saying I'm fighting for these things because I want these things to change and that's a very powerful thing to do." —*Dionne Falconer, 1991* (below, far right) [HS-1994]

below: Toronto Black Women's Collective

Women's relationship with the law is sometimes a matter of politics, sometimes an issue of access, and unfortunately, always an area for reform.

ELIZABETH FRY SOCIETY

The Elizabeth Fry Society was founded in Vancouver in 1939. The name honours Quaker Elizabeth Fry, who assisted women in conflict with the law in 19th century Britain. Today there are 19 societies across Canada that offer a broad range of community and prison programs.

One of the newer societies is the Elizabeth Fry Society of Saskatchewan, founded in 1981 in Saskatoon. Its programs provide services for women in conflict with law in the community, in the criminal justice system, and in the correctional system. As the society believes that female criminality is a status-of-women issue, it also actively lobbies for social change.

A typical woman offender in Saskatchewan is unemployed (90%), has been a victim of sexual abuse (55%), has at least one dependent child (59%), is under thirty (75%), is of Native ancestry (85%), is addicted to alcohol or drugs (79%), has grade nine or less education (72%). Her crime is usually shoplifting, cheque fraud, or a violation of drug and liquor regulations (75%). In a typical scenario, a women is caught shoplifting; finds herself facing charges, but, because of the minor nature of the crime, does not qualify for legal aid; is fined; fails to pay the fine; and ends up in Pine Grove Correctional Centre in Prince Albert. Nearly half (45%) of the woman in Pine Grove (the only prison for women in Saskatchewan) have been jailed for non-payment of fines. Many are not aware of the legal implications of failing to pay a fine, and could not have found the money in any case.

Elizabeth Fry Societies are affiliated across Canada in the Canadian Association of Elizabeth Fry Societies. More job training and affirmative action programs are needed, because when the woman offender is incarcerated, her children are sentenced as well. The Societies believe that fair treatment of women and the prevention of crime occurs when effective and humane solutions come from within the community. [HS-1991]

[While some 10 years later the precise statistics may differ slightly, in the main they are still relevant. Most women prisoners are still "low risk—high need," and the issues they face in and after prison are still the business of the Elizabeth Fry Society, which has grown to 24 chapters across Canada. In 2002, Saskatchewan has three institutions for women offenders, depending on the level and severity of their sentences: Okimaw Ohci Healing Lodge (for Aboriginal women), Pine Grove Correctional Centre, and the Saskatchewan Penitentiary. Eds.]

JOAN LAVALLEE

Born in 1937, of Cree and Saulteaux parents, Joan Lavallee has been part of the revival of Native traditions following the removal of the controversial pass system that confined Indians to reserves, and the closing of the residential schools.

"Grandmothers and grandfathers...wouldn't teach you anything. They were afraid of the reprimand that you might get....You weren't allowed to do anything in a Native ceremony."

At Lebret residential school, Joan encountered harsh discipline, a ban on Native languages, and labelling:

"'Pagans' I guess was the famous word at that time. I didn't think my grandmother and my grandfather were that way at all. So I ended up being a very mixed-up person. I would cringe inside when somebody asked me, 'What are you?'...you denied your heritage or your culture. It took a lot of listening and saying, hey, I'm a good woman, I'm a strong woman, and I'm proud to be an Indian woman."

She was only 43 when she was chosen as an honoured leader to carry her first pipe, a woman's pipe. She was reluctant, but she was reassured: "The grandmothers and grandfathers have chosen you to be the keeper of that pipe."

At first her "biggest fear" was that she would have to give up material things. "Now it really doesn't matter...[when] I was willing to give up anything to walk

above: Joan Lavallee

...that's one of the biggest responsibilities of women, to look after mother earth... If you hear somebody praying...and they say "all my relations" they mean everything—the trees and the grass and the insects that are crawling on the ground, the big animals as well as insects, the big trees and the little trees.
—Joan Lavallee, 1993

left: Women's jail, 1895

this road...all the problem was gone. Everything has come that I need."

Her first use of the pipe outside her home was in the mid-1980s, at Pine Grove Correctional Facility, in Prince Albert, Saskatchewan. The women there are still her "extended family," and part of the pipe when she travels. She travels a great deal now, as an Elder, and as a member of the planning committee for the Healing Lodge which she had moved the Task Force on Federally Sentenced Women to recommend in 1990.

Joan is now a two-pipe holder; the second is for men and women. "I've had a chance to smoke it with my sons. It just really amazes me, at times, the wonderful things I've had happen to me." [HS-1995]

[The Okimaw Ohci Healing Lodge opened in August 1995 near Maple Creek, Saskatchewan, on undisturbed sacred Neekaneet land. The Lodge was established as part of the closure of the notorious Prison for Women in Kingston. See p. 78. Eds.]

MARY ELLEN TURPEL-LAFOND

Mary Ellen Turpel-Lafond's Cree and Scottish heritages were evident when she was sworn in as Saskatchewan's first Aboriginal provincial court judge. The ceremony took place at Wanuskewin Heritage Park near Saskatoon, an ancient meeting place for Native peoples. She wore traditional judicial robes, carried an eagle feather and bathed herself in sweetgrass smoke before the ceremony.

Judge Turpel-Lafond is a member of the Muskeg Lake Cree Nation. She decided at age 13 to study law to find out "how and why the justice system had treated Native people so badly," and has earned degrees from Osgoode Hall, Cambridge, and Harvard. She was chief legal advisor to the Assembly of First Nations for the Charlottetown Accord, and counsel to the Federation of Saskatchewan Indian Nations on the protection of treaty rights.

Mary Ellen has always been involved in the Native women's movement in Canada as an organizer nationally, provincially, and locally. She advocates a strong role for First Nations women in rebuilding their communities and families. She is the proud mother to her young family.

Since her appointment, Judge Turpel-Lafond has been working to bring Aboriginal and non-Aboriginal people together within the justice system. She organized a tour of Wanuskewin for all Saskatchewan judges, as well as the first meeting in provincial history between them and Native Elders. She promises to bring both her heritages to bear in her court work:

"One of the important lessons of my childhood and professional life is that real justice is about healing. The criminal justice process...requires...a holistic healing approach rather than...retribution. My appointment is an affirmation of the perspective that justice is about hope and healing. It must make people broader and more completely realized as members of a community, with a sense of their duty to the community and themselves to reach their potential and not to impair others in the same pursuit." [HS-2000]

Women in conflict with the law are one of the most powerless groups in our society. It is therefore important that all women become familiar with the special problems faced by them.—Saskatoon Association of Women and the Law, 1989

right: Mary Ellen Turpel-Lafond

"I venture to say," wrote Francis Marion Beynon in 1912, "that if men had women's work to do there would have been machinery invented to do nine-tenths of it ages ago."

HOUSEWORK

In 1911 Cora Hind spoke to the founding meeting of Saskatchewan's Homemaker's Clubs, and urged women there to take advantage of labour-saving devices. She argued that men used the latest equipment they could afford, and asked why women shouldn't do the same; the work was equally important and difficult.

The work women do in the home has been a subject of discussion for at least 100 years. "Houseworkers, as unpaid and often unnoticed people in our labour force, have to make do with moral approval." Most families could not afford to pay a "housewife" wage. A study on housework in Nova Scotia concluded that it was worth at least $8.5 billion a year. Until unpaid work in the home is valued for the real and necessary contributions it makes to our society, women will continue to push for recognition of its vital role. [HS-2000]

PAY FOR HOUSEWIVES

1911: "[The housewife] is producing articles of commerce, food, clothing, comfort, service, all coming quite within the scope of economic production. As a buyer for her family and administrator of the family funds, she is performing services as distinctly related to the production of wealth as any similar work done by men in business houses....The burden of her task may be greater in the home than if she worked for wages, and her contribution to wealth is worth money, but because the home is a 'sanctified spot' the wife's labour is not recognized on principle.

"The question demanding investigation is not 'Are wives supported by their husbands?' but 'How far are husbands—men in general—supported by their wives?'"—*Women's editor,* Grain Growers' Guide

1926: "If women *valued themselves,* they would value their own labor for what it was worth, and they would organize to demand a fair price for it."—*J. and V. McNaughton*

1934: "At a recent meeting I heard the economic charter of the CCF discussed. When criticism was invited I pointed out a serious omission in the lists of groups of workers to be paid by the state in the new social order: viz, housewives! This caused some good humoured laughter! The speaker rather put his foot in it by saying that he wanted criticism of fundamentals—not details! Imagine: the question of the economic value of housewives being regarded as a detail...by one who is out to found a new social order of economic security and equality for all the workers!"—*Annie L. Hollis*

top left: Mrs Patten of Midnapore listening to the radio in 1922 while doing the laundry. She was listening to one of the first radio broadcasts in the Calgary area.

My wife will smile when she sees this Bissell Carpet Sweeper.— Eaton's Fall and Winter Catalogue 1893-94

left: Major household appliances from the Saskatchewan Grain Growers' Association's second annual catalogue, 1916

above: Carol Lees

1972: "Of course, paying wives might be hard on the economy, but what good is an economy that is based on an [exploited]...labor force, which is what we have now? It's the same thing as saying that slavery in the South made it possible for the U.S. to have a good economy. It might be a good argument from an economic point of view but it isn't humane."—*Lorenne Smith* [HS-1977]

CAROL LEES

One Saskatoon woman's refusal to falsify her census form may mean that our society will finally value unwaged work.

In 1991, Carol Lees refused to fill out her census form; the Canadian government threatened to send her to jail. While she does not object to the census, Carol was incensed by the question: "When did this person last work, even for a few days, (not including volunteer work, house work, maintenance or repairs for his/her own home)?" As a full-time home manager, Carol knew she worked at least 50 hours a week, yet was required to say she did not work. Also in 1991, Carol prepared an invoice for the prime minister,

reflecting wages for three years of 50-hour weeks. Her $95,843.76 bill was a conservative estimate of the hidden cost of her work, as it did not include overtime or account for additional costs for more than one child.

Born in British Columbia, Carol held several jobs before she married and had children. Since 1977 she has been a full-time home manager, except for a brief time in 1989. She enjoys her work, which she likens to running a small business, but does not enjoy the isolation and the sense of "not working" that go with it. Looking for resources and finding few, Carol started a support group for home managers. The first meeting attracted 35 to 40 women and men; Career Home Managers was born. The group grew and divided into two sections, those who wanted a support group and those who wanted to do advocacy work. The second group organized Canada's first conference on costs and benefits of home management.

In March 1991 Carol wrote to the minister of health and welfare: "Since I have worked full-time within the home for the past 13 years raising three children I take exception to the fact that my labour is not defined as productive." Canada's answer—a threat of jail. After a year, the government dropped the

right: Home economics students in Miss Roberta Gee's class, Junior/Senior High School, Prince George, BC, October 1950

charges; it even organized a conference on unpaid work, though Carol was discouraged from attending. It also prepared test questions about unwaged work for the next census. Unpaid housework and family care were counted for the first time in the 1996 Canadian Census. Carol continues to challenge how our society devalues unpaid work and the policy decisions that flow from that devaluation. [HS-1995]

[Carol now lives in British Columbia and continues her community activism. Eds.]

WAGE EQUITY

"The small wages of the fathers force the young girls out to work early, and the starvation wages of the girls keep them in quest for better pay; while they are seeking improvement of their condition, they are dragged into the net of the white slaver."

This female strike leader defending Montreal women garment workers' agitation for a fair wage in 1910, expressed a common view: women workers were essentially domestic beings—fair wages were necessary only to ward off moral corruption. Radicals like Harriet Hamond Bullock and Mary Oddell of the Montreal Women's Suffrage Society argued, "since they have been driven from home into the stores and factories, they should be on equal footing with men." But most people still assumed that women were not supporting the family but were supported by it and should therefore be paid less than men. Even the groundbreaking Minimum Wage Board, created in British Columbia in 1918 to provide guidelines for living wages for women, failed to demand subsistence wages, according to a bitter report in the union press: "The Minimum Wage Board have thus made it a legislative enactment of British Columbia that parents, as well as their daughters, must contribute to the profits of the boss by helping to support their girls working for a wage not 'adequate to supply the necessary cost of living,'"

It seems that little has changed. In 1953 and 1954, Ellen Fairclough unsuccessfully introduced a bill in the House of Commons advocating equal pay for equal work [see p. 61]. Dorothy Inglis reported that "In Newfoundland, women were not covered by minimum wage legislation until 1955, and even then they were...paid less—fifty cents for men, thirty-five cents for women."

Twenty years later, wage discrimination based on sex was finally outlawed by the Canadian Human Rights Act, but towards the end of the 1990s Statistics Canada reported that the median income for Canadian women was only 60% of men's. Even the government of Canada was resisting full compliance. In 1998, 14 years after the Public Service Alliance of Canada's complaint that employees in predominantly female occupations in government service were paid less than those in male occupations, the government requested a judicial review and announced the possibility of changes to the Act's pay equity provisions.

Dare we hope that changes to the law will improve and not dilute it? [HS-2000]

Do you laugh when you read or are asked: "What will women do with their time when labour saving appliances have secured them so much leisure?" Do you laugh? I hope you do, for I laugh, and I like company.—The Western Producer, 5 February 1931

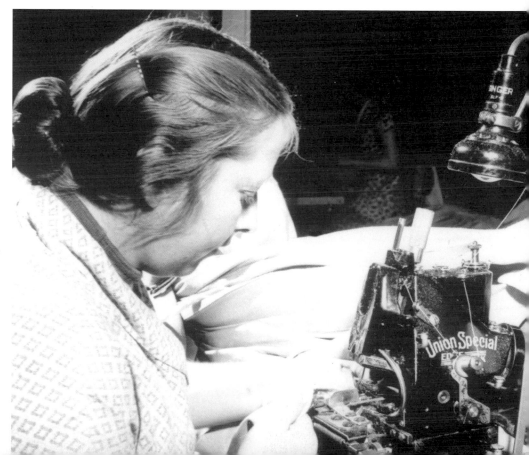

below: Erna Seeghal sewing hems on blue jeans, Winnipeg, Manitoba, ca 1955

CHAPTER 4

THE DOOR STEADILY OPENS

Although the perception is that women have only recently entered the work force, the evidence is that women's work has always been an essential part of the economy, both within the home and in the paid labour force. However, women have often had to fight for access to professions through systemic barriers and obstacles of prejudice.

From the beginning, Canadian women have sought entry into various fields of work and sought recognition, and compensation, for their labours. They have cleaned fish in canneries, built boats, made munitions; they have been civil servants, farmers, stenographers, doctors, lawyers, and Indian chiefs. Women have flooded into the new occupations becoming available to them. They have fought for pay equity, and are still fighting for it. Women are addressing the fact that even in professions where they are predominant, such as education, they are crowded into the lower ranks, and their average earnings remain, shamefully, at just over two-thirds those of Canadian men. Slowly, the realization is dawning that women's full and equal participation in all fields of endeavour is urgently needed.

This chapter celebrates the stories of women who broke down barriers to entering the public sphere. In these pages you will learn about specific obstacles to women train-ing for particular professions and undertaking pursuits for the first time. You will also discover periods when women were "drafted" for public service from which they were previously, and then subsequently, excluded. The Second World War, in particular, provided opportunity for women's forays into a wide range of new experiences, and at the same time ensured that this new independence would only be temporary.

This is yet another example of the ebb and flow of women's history: doors open and close and, eventually, open again. In its 1979 profile of Mary Lucas, the first woman ordained as an Anglican minister in Canada, *Herstory* asked, "could there be any career more difficult for a woman to enter than one dominated by males for nearly 2,000 years?" Here you will meet women in education, law, medicine, religion, science, and business who got their foot in the door, and then pried it off its hinges.

opposite: Mount Allison University graduates, 1875

above: Elsie Hall, first woman law graduate at the University of Saskatchewan, 1920

Ladies having regularly matriculated and completed the course of study prescribed by this board shall be entitled to receive degrees in the arts and faculties upon the same terms and conditions as are now or may hereafter be imposed upon male students of the college.
—Minutes of the College Board and Senate, Mount Allison University, 1872

right: Mary Electa Adams

For more than 100 years, Canadian women have been fighting for equal access to education. *Herstory* has recorded a few of the "firsts" in that struggle. Although we know the names of these pioneers, many others, whose names have been forgotten, persisted in obscurity and isolation. To them, modern women owe their opportunities to study and work where they please.

Once they won the chance to receive an education, women still had many difficulties to overcome. Some were discouraged by their families, others made to feel like outcasts, even by their own sex. They took strength from within themselves and from other women striving to learn.

The lone woman in the photo at the opening of this chapter is Grace Annie Lockhart, first woman in the British Empire to receive a bachelor's degree from a recognized university. Since the founding of the Ladies' Academy at Mount Allison, in 1854, women students had followed a program which emphasized high intellectual standards. Women were admitted to regular classes in 1862, and in 1872 were given the right to take degrees at the college. [HS-1994]

MARY ELECTA ADAMS

Mary Electa Adams was a pioneer of women's higher education in Canada. She directed women's academies for fifty years, always insisting that her students were intellectually equal to male students and that they could meet the same academic standards.

In 1854 Mary became "Lady Preceptress" of the new female academy at Mount Allison. During her three years at Mount Allison, Mary established high academic standards for the women. In an editorial in the college's newspaper, Mary wrote that their education tended to produce "that impatience of thought, that tendency to the desultory and the superficial, which are proverbial failings of young Ladies." Mary's students pursued as rigorous a course of studies as their male counterparts. She continued, "The ornamental branches, without being depreciated or displaced, will always be pursued in subserviency to the solid studies."

Mary's father died in 1856 and she returned to Upper Canada to help look after her mother. However, the intellectual tone she set at Mount Allison was maintained and helped influence the decision, in 1872, to allow women to enrol in degree programs.

In 1861 Mary became the first principal of another women's college. Again she established high academic standards for the Wesleyan Female College in Hamilton. Mary served as principal until 1868, when her mother's death gave her and her sister Augusta the freedom to travel to Italy.

Returning to Canada in 1872, the Adams sisters established their own school in Cobourg. Brookhurst Academy was near Victoria College, and one of Mary's ambitions was to have her students take degrees at the college. There was considerable co-operation between the two, and Brookhurst students attended classes at Victoria, but Mary and Augusta were forced to close the school before any of the women were actually admitted for a degree. However, the historian of

Victoria College credits Mary's efforts as the first step in women's admission to Ontario universities.

Mary spent the next 12 years as principal of yet another ladies' college. In 1892, at the age of 69, she retired from teaching and moved to Alberta, where she and Augusta helped one of their nephews establish a cattle ranch. [HS-1993]

MARTHA HAMM LEWIS

In 1849 Martha Lewis, the 18-year-old daughter of a New Brunswick widow, made the revolutionary decision to attend the Teachers' Training School in Saint John. She herself had been educated by private tutors and in a boarding school. According to family legend, she had tutored some of the young men from the Training School and realized that she would make just as good a teacher as they.

She applied repeatedly for admission to the Training School, established and run by Edmund Duval. He repeatedly refused to allow it, on the grounds of custom and expediency. No doubt he, and almost everyone else, expected the matter to end there. He was not taking into account Martha's determination.

She wrote to the lieutenant governor of the province, who decided that she could not be excluded. The council ordered that she be admitted to the Training School, but Martha was warned that the council could not "be held responsible for any adverse consequences of her decision."

Undeterred by these veiled forebodings, Martha enrolled. Duval, who obviously had fears of his own, set down very harsh regulations, which Martha alone had to follow. She was to enter the lecture room 10 minutes before the male students and leave five minutes before the end of class. She was to curtsy to the teacher and sit alone at the back of the class, wearing a black veil at all times. She was forbidden to stay in the school after classes and was never to speak to her fellow students.

Martha endured these rules for the whole of the

year-long course. In 1850 she graduated successfully and was licensed to teach at the nearby village of Upham. In 1853 she moved to a school in Saint John. In 1856 she married Alexander Peters and retired from teaching to raise a family.

Though she taught for only a few years, Martha's strength of will opened the doors of training schools to other women. Only three years after Martha's admission, Duval's school had changed. By 1853 over 50% of the students were female, and within a decade there were women on the teaching staff.

Martha lived on in Saint John until her death in 1892. We hear no more of her as a crusader for women's rights, but at least one of her daughters, Mabel Peters, became a suffragist. No doubt Martha felt well content to be responsible for the effects of her youthful decision. [HS-1995]

above: Nisbet School, 1908

Without aggression, without any noisy obtrusiveness, a few Canadian women by deep thought, by clear vision, or by honest service have prepared the way for those who will follow, and have proved the right of all to work as they are able.
—National Council of Women, 1900

above: Miss Georgina McGill taught 14 students in this sodded frame schoolhouse in Saskatchewan, 1909

Woman stands today the confessed peer of her stronger brothers in all that pertains to intellectual endowment, her brilliant record in the Colleges having banished the last shadow of doubt upon that point.
—Principal B.F. Austin, 1889

right: Mary Matilda Winslow McAlpine

RULES FOR A FEMALE SCHOOL TEACHER—1915

You will not marry during the term of your contract.

You must be home between the hours of 8:00 p.m. and 6:00 a.m. unless attending a school function.

You are not to keep company with men.

You may not loiter downtown in any of the ice cream stores.

You may not travel beyond the city limits unless you have the permission of the chairman of the school board.

You may not ride in any carriage or automobile with any man unless he is your father or brother.

You may not smoke cigarettes, cigars or a pipe or chew tobacco or take snuff.

You may not dress in bright colours.

You may not under any circumstances dye your hair.

You must wear at least two petticoats.

Your dress must not be any shorter than two inches above the ankle.

To keep the classroom neat and clean you must: sweep the floor at least once a day; scrub the floor at least once a week with hot, soapy water; clean the blackboards at least once a day; start the fire at 7:00 a.m. so the room will be warm at 8:00 a.m. [HS-1994]

MARY MATILDA WINSLOW McALPINE

Tilly Winslow was the first Black woman to attend the University of New Brunswick. She graduated in 1905 with a Bachelor of Arts degree and a prize for excellence in classics. Unable to find work in Canada, although her family had lived here for over 100 years, she moved to the United States. She was for a time dean of the education department at Central College in Alabama and later moved to Springfield, Massachusetts. [HS-1997]

Though women were always responsible for the care of family and community, the right to qualify as licensed physicians was long in coming. The women who broke barriers in choosing a career in medicine showed tremendous courage. It is impossible to appreciate fully how difficult it was to obtain the freedom of choice we now take for granted, and how much we owe these trailblazers.

EMILY HOWARD STOWE

Emily Howard Stowe was born in Norwich, Ontario, on May 1, 1831, one of six daughters of Quaker parents. They considered education as important for girls as for boys, so she was taught at home by her mother. In 1853 she received her teacher's certificate and secured a position at Brantford Central School, which she held until her marriage to John Stowe in 1856. When he became ill with tuberculosis, she applied to the University of Toronto for admission to their Medical College. She was refused because of her sex, the president telling her that "the doors of the University are not open to women and I trust they never will be." Emily is said to have replied, "Then I will make it the business of my life to see that they will be opened, that women may have the same opportunities as men."

She then enrolled in the New York Medical College for Women, leaving her three children in her sister's care. In 1868 she graduated and moved her family to Toronto to become Canada's first female practising physician. Because there was great prejudice against women doctors, she did not receive her formal licence until July 1880.

In addition to her medical practice, she lectured in and around Toronto on women's rights. In 1877 Dr Stowe attended a meeting in Cleveland of the American Society for the Advancement of Women, which inspired her to form, on November 3, 1877, the Toronto Women's Literary Club, later to become the Toronto Women's Suffrage Club [see p. 48]. She was an officer in this organization, as well as president of the Dominion Women's Enfranchisement League—a post she retained until her death. [HS-1974]

QUAKER WOMEN

Quaker women have known they were first-rate citizens since 1802, when the first Canadian Preparatory Meeting of the Society of Friends began. From that beginning, women had the right to travel and minister for their faith, and their counsel was respected on a level with that of men.

In 1842, girls in the Society of Friends attended co-educational Pickering College, which had both a principal and a lady principal. By 1917, however, the surrounding culture had influenced Quaker decision makers to favour male students in the face of scanty financial resources.

The society's stress on careful, inclusive decision making has ensured that all voices are heard. The process has preserved freedom and strength for Quaker women. A peculiar Canadian flavour to that freedom had already developed when Elizabeth Comstock, an American visiting Canada in 1854, observed, "Women here seem to be treated with much greater respect than in England."

Women Friends were leaders in the struggle for Canadian women's suffrage and equal rights, for they

above: Quaker women

These days demand women
not too young in thought
And not too old.
Women with a sense of
youthful power;
Who love life as pioneers,
whose hands
Know much of homely
tasks made beautiful
Whose minds run not
in fleeting fads, but
Draw upon eternities.
—When Women Work Together

left: Emily Howard Stowe

above: Augusta Stowe-Gullen

It is not always pleasant to be a pioneer. No one knows, or can know, the furnace we are passing through these days at college. We suffer torment, we shrink inwardly, we are hurt cruelly.
—Elizabeth Smith-Shortt

right: Elizabeth Smith-Shortt

wished all women to share the equality with men which they enjoyed as their Quaker birthright. Emily Stowe had her Quaker tradition to sustain her in her long fight for recognition as the first Canadian female doctor, and in her organization of the Dominion Women's Enfranchisement League in the 1890s.

Today, Quaker women are still independent souls, strong women and gentle Friends. At the 1975 Canadian yearly meeting, women Friends celebrated their womanhood in a warm and welcoming support group, a Quaker invention of several years' standing. The women expressed their concern that men Friends recognize the pain they cause women by their many careless acts and words, a concern which Quaker men responded to with heightened awareness.

In other areas, the heritage of social concern and integrity is evident in the many women Friends who are leaders and spokespersons, not only in the Society, but throughout the Canadian community. [HS-1977]

AUGUSTA STOWE-GULLEN

Augusta Stowe-Gullen, only daughter of Emily Howard Stowe, entered the Toronto School of Medicine in 1879, and became (in 1883) the first woman to graduate in medicine from a Canadian university. When the first Women's Medical College was formed in that year, she was appointed Demonstrator of Anatomy and later, Professor of Pediatrics, which post she held until the College amalgamated with the University of Toronto in 1906. In 1882 she was elected to the Toronto School

Board, and in 1896 she and her mother participated in a mock parliament called the Ontario Legislature of Women, which was organized by the Women's Christian Temperance Union. She followed in her mother's footsteps, avidly supporting woman's suffrage. Upon Dr Stowe's death in 1903, Augusta became president of the Toronto Women's Enfranchisement Association. She was appointed to the senate of the University of Toronto and was vice-president of the National Council of Women, remaining chairperson of its citizenship committee throughout her life. [HS-1974]

ELIZABETH SMITH-SHORTT

The organizer of Canada's first women's medical course was a woman of intelligence, wit, ambition, and great energy. When Queen's University opened its doors to

women, Elizabeth Smith-Shortt decided to forfeit early graduation from an American institution in order to take her training in Canada. She advertised in the Toronto newspapers for other women wanting to study medicine and arranged with Queen's a summer medical course for herself and the respondents.

Upon successful completion of their first year, the five women fought to gain admittance into the regular medical programme. They succeeded in October 1881. This was not to be their last fight. In their third year of study, Elizabeth and her classmates found themselves the centre of Canada's first student revolt. Their male classmates demanded the women's expulsion, claiming falsely to the press that certain "sensitive subjects" were not taught in sufficient detail with the women present. The men threatened to quit en masse if their demands were not met. The university compromised by establishing separate classes for the women and agreeing to accept no more female students. In this battle, the citizens of Kingston supported the women, who had proved themselves devoted and able students.

After their graduation in 1884, these five women founded the Women's College in Kingston, again enabling women to study in Canada. Elizabeth established a medical practice in Hamilton, and later returned to teach in the medical college she had helped institute.

Following the birth of her three children, Elizabeth left the active medical practice she had fought so hard to attain, devoting herself to community, suffrage, and welfare work. She maintained an involvement in medicine through writing. "Often in the early part of the night, I lay awake and planned a paper. Then, when everyone was asleep, I got up and wrote it."

The list of Elizabeth's community projects is very long, including agitation on health issues such as tuberculosis prevention, milk pasteurization, and treatment of venereal diseases. She also led the campaign to establish mothers' allowances for needy widows.

Dr Elizabeth Smith-Shortt died in 1949, just before her 90th birthday. [HS-1980]

Since the beginning of European conquest, France and later England devised immigration policies to further their interests in North America. The "filles du roi," dowered by the King, were intended to marry as soon as they arrived and to bear children to populate New France. Britain too wanted to establish communities and claim the riches of the new world.

In the 19th century, women were encouraged to immigrate if they were the "right sort." Just what that meant depended on the politics of the time: middle-class women of British stock to marry the hordes of single men in the west; sturdy peasant women from central Europe who, with their families, would work the land in exchange for little but clothes and food; and there was always room for working-class servants (who should be properly grateful). Women were wanted, but they were not wanted to be too independent [see p. 108]. Fortunately, they were anyway, and eventually claimed some of the riches of this new world for themselves.

What men had done for themselves in agricultural pursuits on the prairie, women could also do for themselves. Woman can earn for herself independence and, in time, wealth.
—Georgina Binnie-Clark, 1914

The Land Commissioner of the Canadian Pacific Railway Company again reminds us that the great want of the Northwest is more women...a few thousand loyal and sensible women would probably do more to make that country than any other influence that could be brought to bear on it just now.
—Daily Nor'wester, Winnipeg, 1896

left: This girl represented Canada at the Exeter, England, Carnival in 1907. She took first prize.

HOMESTEADS FOR WOMEN

Honest working girls are in great demand, not only as help, but the country being overrun with bachelors no one can hope to keep a girl more than a few months, and in many cases, but a few weeks, when she is married and away.
—Mrs Sutherland, 1886

"Why hasn't a Canadian woman a birthright in her country?" That question was posed by Isabelle B. Graham in the columns of the *Grain Growers' Guide* for November 1909. Why, asked Mrs Graham, was a Canadian woman not entitled to take up a free homestead on the same basis as a Canadian man? According to the Dominion Lands Act of 1870 (and all subsequent revisions): "A homestead entry for one quarter section, containing 160 acres, more or less, can be obtained by any male over 18 years of age on payment of a fee of $10. A woman who is a widow, having minor children dependent upon her, is entitled to a homestead entry."

This provision, which excluded all single and married women, was bitterly resented by many western women who believed they were as capable of proving up their quarter sections as their menfolk. The cause was taken up by "Lilian Laurie" (in private life, Lilian Beynon Thomas) in her column in the *Manitoba Free Press.* "LL" also printed letters on the topic from her readers. One woman, who signed herself "Magna," reported that she had obtained a homestead and worked it herself, and could recommend farming as an excellent way for a woman to make her own home and living. "Magna" pointed out that women homesteaders, even if they did not fulfill all their duties, would still do more for the country than the speculators who were taking up land and holding it to sell at inflated prices.

Some letters in the *Free Press* reflected less enlightened views. One writer thought if women wanted to homestead, they should marry (male) homesteaders. This was the view taken by a succession of ministers charged with administering the Act. Many women pointed out that the Dominion Government used the free land provision as a lure to attract male settlers from other countries. As one woman rather bitterly put it, women were to have no share in anything but the work.

Despite the agitation in 1909 and 1910, the Dominion Lands Act was never revised to allow women homestead rights. In 1930, when the Prairie Provinces took over administration of their own Crown lands, Manitoba and Saskatchewan abolished the right of free homestead. Only Alberta had enough unclaimed land to allow homesteading to continue, and here the right was made available to all persons (a term which by this date was acknowledged to include women) [see p. 53]. [HS-1988]

A CARGO OF HOME-LOVING GIRLS

When Canada gained control of the prairies, it wanted to prevent a U.S. land grab similar to that which lost it the Oregon Territory. This meant creating transportation links and a government, and populating the area with settlers who owed allegiance to Britain. As the rails pushed west, the Canadian and British governments, and the Canadian Pacific Railway (CPR) actively encouraged settlement.

right: Canada's Call to Women.
This poster is representative of those used to convince British women to emigrate to western Canada between 1885 and 1930.

WHITE STAR LINE

CANADA'S CALL TO WOMEN.

SERCOMBE & HAYES, 9, South Street, DORCHESTER

By 1885 it was apparent that this policy was only partially successful. Men came, but communities did not develop as anticipated. The government concluded this was due to the lack of women. The Winnipeg *Daily Nor'wester* of 1896 commented, "The bachelor farmer is...the greatest drawback to the prairie country. His house is unkept and his life unsweetened by human companionship save that of his own sex." At the same time, there was an "over-supply of women" in the British Isles.

Britain had too many women; western Canada desperately needed them. Thus, the government and the CPR began a propaganda campaign mainly directed at British women, encouraging them to emigrate to western Canada in order to "civilize" it. In 1889 the Manitoba government declared: "Of all classes, those for whom there is the greatest demand are women. The demand for women is practically unlimited."

To this end, the CPR published a number of leaflets describing the lives of individual women in various parts of the West. Almost without exception, these were rosy accounts, though women admitted to cold winters. The railway also encouraged British writers to come and to report back to British women.

One such writer was Jesse Saxby, who was convinced of the superiority of the British race *and* of its moral duty to colonize North America. She wrote enthusiastically of women's opportunities in western Canada, as domestic help, working women, or wives:

"I believe the old country would confer no greater boon upon this fine young nation than by sending it thousands of our girls to soften and sweeten life in the Wild West. The want of feminine influence tends to make men...restless, dissatisfied, reckless, and godless." A Canadian gentleman of influence said "Better even than money...should be a cargo of home-loving girls."

Women did come west. Many were teachers, nurses, or domestic servants, and many, did, in fact marry and help build "British" communities in the West. Others remained single by choice. Many had more satisfying lives than they would have had in Britain. Like all women, of whatever origin, they helped shape what is now western Canada. [HS-1996]

above: *Immigrants for domestic service, 1911*

Today and yesterday, and probably tomorrow, women have the responsibility for domestic work, whether they earn a living by it, or have it as an unpaid addition to gainful employment. Employment as a domestic is still an avenue for women seeking admission to Canada as landed immigrants, as it was at the turn of the century.

DOMESTIC SERVICE

Domestic service in the 1880s in Canada was a major source of employment for working-class women. Servants often worked sixteen to eighteen hours a day for either low wages or simply room and board. At this time, there was no legal minimum wage or regulations covering the hours of work.

Domestic service freed middle- and upper-class women from household tasks and allowed them to become involved in social and recreational activities, charitable organizations, and higher education. The power that employers had over their servants can be illustrated by the case of Ellen Porter, a young girl who had been brought to Canada in 1891 at the age of fifteen for domestic service, and who told of working for two years without receiving any wages.

Legal recourse for servants was out of the question—even if they had been able to afford the legal fees, the laws were often more favourable to the employer than to the employee. As late as 1920 it was still possible for a servant in Ontario, Manitoba, or British Columbia to be commited in service under one master for as long as nine years.

As industrialization increased, more and more women began to leave domestic service to work in factories. The loneliness, lack of freedom, and constant supervision, as well as long hours and poor wages paid for domestic service, were all factors that influenced women to seek alternative employment in the public workforce whenever possible. [HS-1975]

ELLA SYKES

In 1911, Ella Sykes decided to investigate, first-hand, the "openings there might be in the Dominion for educated women." This well-travelled, highly educated British woman went to Canada and attempted to support herself as a domestic servant. *A Home Help in Canada,* Ella's narrative of those six months, is an interesting commentary not only on British attitudes toward their empire, but also on Canadian attitudes toward the British.

Sykes is highly sympathetic to the Canadian viewpoint. "I was an incompetent amateur trained to do nothing properly that the country wanted." She stated that if she had to earn her living she would immigrate to Canada. Nonetheless, she cautioned, "...it is

well for a woman to know, in Canadian parlance, 'what she will be up against' if she crosses the Atlantic. Much of the literature treating life in the Dominion [is] so roseate-hued that the fact that WORK, and usually very *hard* work, is the order of the day there is sometimes ignored. The girl who is a failure in Great Britain will most certainly not be a success in the Dominion."

She was highly impressed with the progress of settling western Canada. "I felt the splendid vitality of it all, and rejoiced to think that my own race was still at its work of empire building." Ella worked in five situations in several parts of the West, and from each she drew conclusions about the life and opportunities for women in the area. She felt the prairies were extremely hard on women, as they were often confined to their small shacks and became virtual slaves to the homestead. Chicken farming, on the other hand, was a good occupation for a woman who had a small amount of money, since the work was well within the physical abilities of women, and the eggs and chickens were needed in all parts of the West.

An early example of investigative reporting, *A Home Help in Canada* was a realistic assessment of women's work in western Canada. Ella Sykes was frank about the problems and the drawbacks of life in the Dominion, but felt that if a woman was willing to work hard, there was little she could not do. [HS-1985]

When the doors of opportunity opened, women flooded in. Despite their successes in many fields of endeavour, women were believed generally unable to meet demanding physical standards or the performance levels of men already in place.

These barriers of prejudice still persist. They range from personal choice for marriage and family often still believed incompatible with a demanding career, to inadequate career counselling and poor teaching in the schools, to resistance from the professionals themselves.

WORKING TOGETHER, PLAYING TOGETHER

After the turn of the century, white-collar work of all kinds became open to women. From being virtually confined to domestic work, in their own or someone else's home, women began to find places in the "public" workforce. Social attitudes changed more slowly than economic opportunities, however, and until after the Second World War large-scale employers of women were expected to, and did, act *in loco parentis* to their female employees, providing housing and a supervised social life for them. The new occupation of telephone operator came into being just as the trend from home to office was beginning, and was almost at once overwhelmingly a woman's job. BCTel was particularly active in providing the infrastructure for a "home away from home" for its women employees, who had access to many sports, social, and cultural activities through the company. [HS-1993]

TELEPHONE OPERATORS

Since 1888, when women replaced men at the switchboard, the Bell Telephone Company has been a major employer of women. "Boys" were at first employed, as "running a switchboard required a brilliant technical mind." The feisty nature of their male workers, however, soon attracted the Bell to women. "Girls are usually more alert than boys and always more patient. Women are more sensitive, more amenable to discipline, far gentler and more forbearing than men." Thus, women were hired for their submissiveness and willingness to handle impolite customers.

The telephone company expected its "girls" to be models of purity and decorum. Applicants needed three character references, including one from their clergyman. Once hired, operators needed to maintain their moral perfection—they could be fired for such indiscretions as dancing the tango at a staff party. Physical strength was also required, to bear the six-and-one-half pound headset on their shoulders.

Many heroines emerge from the history of telephone operators. In national and regional disasters, such as the Regina tornado and the Halifax explosion, operators continued to work through danger and discomfort. Local emergencies often underlined the courage and resourcefulness of "Central." In 1928, for example, Dorothy Smith of Ferintosh, Alberta, won a hundred-dollar reward for calling all the farmers on appropriate roads and coordinating a posse that trapped bank robbers before they could escape.

Operators went on strike against Bell Telephones of Ontario in 1907. The issues were hours and wages, as Bell was increasing shifts from five to eight hours daily with only a slight increase in wages. A Royal Commission was appointed to study the problem while the women returned to work. The women who had joined the International Electric Workers Union during the strike were required to resign from the union on threat of firing. Thus, by the time the Royal Commission report was released, half of the striking women had been replaced. The report charged Bell with causing their employees bad "nerves" with line overload-

left: A swimming group at a British Columbia Telephone Company chief operators' picnic, Vancouver, ca 1915

What is more important, the happiness and health of your children or a house that is spotless? ...Don't try to do it all. —Irene Grant, 1991, who became the first woman in Winnipeg's school division to teach legally after marriage. She used her success to lobby for others, as well as for equity in pay and retirement age.

above: Turn-of-the-century telephone operators in British Columbia

Every moment in our lives is a fresh beginning. Whatever it is we are fighting for, now is the time to see about getting it. —Nellie McClung

But having once taken their place in the industrial, commercial, and professional life of this country [women] were loath to relinquish that place, and indeed industry, commerce and the professions were loath to see them go.—Ellen Fairclough, 1954

right: Clara Brett Martin

ing, flashing lights, and breakneck work pace. In particular, the report cited medical evidence showing that former employees had nervous breakdowns and raised nervous children. Wages and unionization were ignored. The report, in fashion typical of the time, focused on women as mothers rather than as serious workers.

The Canadian telephone system continues to be a major employer of women, and although equipment and conditions have been improved since early days, the job of a telephone operator is still one of the lowest paid and lowest status jobs in the company. [HS-1980]

CLARA BRETT MARTIN

"Clara Brett Martin single-handedly opened and made respectable the profession of law for women in Canada and the British Empire."

That may be overstating the case a little: if Clara Martin had really managed to make law "respectable" for women, she would have had an easier and a happier life. But it is true that she was the first woman lawyer anywhere in the British Empire, and that she fought her battles alone.

In 1891, when she first applied for admission to Osgoode Hall, Clara was only 17, though she already held an honours degree in mathematics. Her qualifications were impeccable—except for her sex. The authorities kept her waiting for a year, and then turned her down, arguing that women were not legally "per-

sons" and thus were not eligible for the privilege of studying law [see p. 53].

As a result of the ensuing controversy, an act was passed in 1892 which permitted Ontario law schools to accept female students. But would they? Not voluntarily. After another rejection, this time on the grounds that it was "inexpedient" to admit women, Clara went straight to the top—the Attorney-General of Ontario. With his help, she finally won the right to begin her studies.

However, the legal profession had not given in. When Clara graduated in 1896, she was at first refused accreditation as a barrister. Only after another fight was she finally admitted to the Bar.

The years that followed were weary ones for her. Other women were disappointingly slow to take advantage of the opening she had created for them. Male lawyers were often cold and unkind; her assignments were largely routine. In her determination to prove herself at least as strong and competent as her colleagues, she ruined her health with work, and in 1923 she died, only 49.

Since 1941, when Quebec modernized its regulations, all ten provinces have permitted women to practise law. Clara Brett Martin would be glad to know that and gratified, perhaps, by the knowledge that without her, it would have taken even longer. [HS-1979]

KIT COLEMAN

major international exhibitions, Queen Victoria's Diamond Jubilee, a number of sensational trials—and the Spanish-American War. They were well repaid for their departure from convention: Kit was a bold, resourceful journalist who brought in more than her share of scoops.

In 1911, she quit the *Mail and Empire* after being its major selling point for 20 years. The editors wanted her to write a front page column in addition to her regular page, but refused to raise her $35 a week salary. Undismayed, Kit wrote a column, the first to be syndicated in Canada, and sold it to dozens of papers across the country.

By the time of her death in 1915, Kit was recognized as "a pioneer in journalism" who had improved the scope and status of women in the profession. In 1934 the Canadian Women's Press Club, of which she was the first president, established a scholarship in her honour. [HS-1976]

left: Kit Coleman

The low economic standing of women is not on a pin-money or waiting-for-marriage or no-dependent basis. It is founded on custom, prejudice, the women's timidity, and lack of confidence, their poor bargaining ability... their habit of not valuing their work.—Helen Gregory MacGill, speaking at a minimum wage conference in BC, 1918

EDITH BERKELEY

The first woman war correspondent did not come by the job easily. She had to win the approval of her paper, the Toronto *Mail and Empire;* then she had to convert the American secretary of war, who frankly laughed at the idea; and finally, she had to badger the authorities to let her on a boat to the battlefield after her colleagues were on their way.

"I'm going through," she vowed to her readers, "and not all the old generals in the old army are going to stop me. I beat them in Washington and I'll beat them here."

She did. The year was 1898; the battleground, the Spanish-American War in Cuba. The reporter's name was Kathleen Blake Watkins (later Coleman), better known as "Kit of the *Mail.*" Every week for nine years, she had written an entire eight-column page of comment, book reviews, poetry, character sketches, sports, and advice to the lovelorn. "Woman's Kingdom" as the page was known, was so popular that the *Mail's* editors occasionally freed her from food and fashion to cover

At age 14 Edith travelled unaccompanied from Tasmania to England via Cape Horn. She had already journeyed from South Africa to England, to India, and to Tasmania. With a scholarship to the University of London, she completed a pre-medical course, and chose to work in pure science—chemistry and zoology. In 1898 she met Cyril Berkeley, whom she married in 1902. They returned to India, where Edith helped in Cyril's research. She bore a daughter, Alfreda, who was left with Edith's mother in England [see p. 183]. India's climate proved too much for Edith, and the couple moved to British Columbia, where Cyril began farming in the Okanagan. Realizing that their interests still lay in scientific research, both joined the staff of the fledgling University of British Columbia, and later, the Pacific Biological Station at Nanaimo. Edith began work on polychaetes (marine worms), which established her as a world authority.

Edith worked as a volunteer from 1919 to 1963. Her work at the Station brought considerable prestige to the institution, though she was never officially on staff.

below: Edith Berkeley

right: Carrie Derick

The first women working in the natural sciences in Canada did not fear to enter a man's world....Although they were few in number... they opened the door for other women to follow.
—Lorraine C. Smith, 1976

Volunteerism has declined with modern lifestyles. In Edith's day, however, female volunteers had advantages over paid scientists. Volunteers could do fieldwork, whereas government and academe did not hire women. Married volunteers were not expected to give up their work; paid scientists were. Academic institutions enforced nepotism rules, and the scientist-wife was often a "footnote" in a two-person single career—the husband's.

Volunteers worked more or less as they wished. Edith did fieldwork and in 1923 began publishing. In 1930, Cyril, also a volunteer, gave up his research to help her. Edith published a dozen papers under her own name; together the Berkeleys produced 34 papers between 1932 and 1964. Many organisms have been named for them.

Edith loved her garden, and spent much time among her flowers. She suffered a great deal when Alfreda died in 1951, but lost neither spirit nor direction, continuing research until her death at age 88. [HS-1988]

I believe that even a doubtful privilege in the hand is better than a rankling feeling of injustice in the heart.
—Nellie McClung, 1916

CARRIE DERICK

In the early 1900s, when the professor of botany at McGill University became sick, his assistant of nine years took over all his duties. After his death a year later, it seemed natural that the assistant should succeed him, except that she was a woman. And so a man was awarded the professorship, and the assistant, Carrie Matilda Derick, got a grand new title to glorify her unchanged status.

That was in 1904. Eight years later she finally became professor of comparative morphology and genetics at McGill, the first woman promoted to a full professorship by a Canadian university.

According to a 1915 interview with one of her close friends, Carrie Derick worked for everything she got, "and never a woman harder. It is conceded that she is clever, but...where others might arrive at conclusions by intuition, Carrie had to plod for them...[where] others forgot what they learned, she remembered. For years she never took a holiday,

[Women must] accept responsibility for themselves as human beings. This means no longer deferring to bullies no matter if it is in the form of injustice encapsulated in the law or injustice encapsulated in the living-room conversation.
—Mary Van Stolk

spending her summers at a science school."

This is not to imply that she was a dull drudge. In fact she was a brilliant student, an inspiring teacher, and an adventuresome scientist. For her, botany spanned everything from plant folklore to heredity. Her course on evolution laid the foundation for the study of genetics at McGill.

Nor was she an ivory tower academic. Through the local and national Councils of Women, she advocated greater participation by women in national affairs, the opening of agriculture to women and the recognition of domestic service as a profession [see p. 126.]

The first woman appointed to the Protestant Committee of the Council of Education for Quebec, she concentrated on the training of retarded children. In 1913, she became president of the Montreal Suffrage Association, and after it disbanded in 1919 in favour of bilingual organizations, she remained active in suffrage campaigns through her membership in the

returned to the Philadelphia hospital, and completed training with a female doctor there.

When she returned to Toronto, no hospital would give operating privileges to a woman. Her first operation took place in the patient's kitchen, where, attended by other female doctors, she removed an ovarian tumour.

"There were more women in medicine, and more women specializing in various fields. We felt the need of a hospital of our own in which to do our work." Dr Smillie joined with other female doctors to open the first Women's College Hospital in a small rented house in 1911. They met with financial difficulties in the early days. "I remember once when we women doctors sat at a meeting of farmers' wives, collecting vegetables with which to feed our patients." In 1935 the Women's College Hospital opened on its present site on Grenville Street.

Dr Smillie served as chief of gynaecology for many years and continued to be active in surgery until retiring in 1948. "I worked as hard as I could go."

Jennie had set aside marriage for her busy career. When she retired at age 70, she married Alex Robertson, a man she had met while teaching, and who had "seen her off to medical school with tears in his eyes." He died after 10 happy years of marriage.

Dr Smillie Robertson died in 1981 at the age of 103. [HS-1987]

left: Jennie Smillie Robertson

I first met the man I was to marry many years earlier, in 1898, while I was teaching. At that time I was planning for medicine, not marriage, and didn't think I could have both.—Jennie Smillie Robertson, 1978

below: Women's College Hospital, 1915

National Council of Women. For many years, she was in great demand as a speaker on botany, feminism, and social reform.

Carrie Derick died in 1941 at the age of seventy-nine. [HS-1976]

JENNIE SMILLIE ROBERTSON

In 1883, at age five, Jennie Smillie asked her mother if women could be doctors: "She told me they could and from then on I knew that is what I would do." Jennie first became a teacher. She saved enough from her $300 a year salary to enrol in the Women's Medical College of Toronto in 1903.

Jennie graduated in 1909, and interned in Philadelphia before returning to Toronto to set up practice. She tried to train in surgery, but no Toronto surgeon would take on a woman. Undaunted, she

top right: Ethel Mary Cartwright

ALICE WILSON

Alice Wilson started work for the Geological Survey of Canada as a clerk in 1909, determined to become a geologist. But it took her 36 long, struggling years to be recognized as such.

She had to fight for herself. In the field, people remember, she was always first: the first to spot a wild flower, a high flying bird, the gathering storm, always the first over a farmer's fence. Of course she was first; she had to be. She must show them that being a woman made no difference to being a good geologist, even if, when she got home, she couldn't eat for exhaustion.

If you can't beat them, join them and work to improve them from within.—Ethel Mary Cartwright, ca 1920

She started doing fieldwork in 1913, but the Survey, wanting to keep her in her "place," wouldn't give her a car; "when they were being issued to all the men, they gave her a bicycle." Undaunted she bought her own car, strapped the bicycle to the side, and "drove off down the Ottawa valley."

After asking for educational leave from the Survey for ten years without success, she was finally given permission to compete for a fellowship. She won, and at the age of 45, went to Chicago to work for her doctorate, which she received in 1929. The Survey, however,

did not see fit to make her a full geologist until one year before she retired in 1946.

She continued working, however, until her death at the age of 83. In 1947 she published a book on geology for young people, *The Earth Beneath Our Feet.* And in 1948 she became a sessional lecturer at Carleton College, where she enjoyed teaching and was well-loved. [HS-1974]

ETHEL MARY CARTWRIGHT

That McGill University's Board of Governors should have agreed to create a Department of Physical Education in 1919 was largely due to the considerable accomplishments of Ethel Mary Cartwright. Hired as Physical Director by McGill's Royal Victoria College in 1906, Cartwright had established both intramural and intercollegiate athletic competitions and had made physical education a requirement for undergraduate women at the college. More importantly, Cartwright had worked

right: Alice Wilson

to shift the emphasis in physical education away from the military-based Strathcona Trust plan, toward recognition of the need for physical education specialists trained through universities and normal schools. Based in a small women's college, Cartwright initiated an undergraduate physical education program that even the authorities recognized as setting a standard it would take the men some years to attain. Nevertheless, Cartwright was overlooked when McGill chose a director for its new Department of Physical Education: instead the job went to a man who had been associated with the McGill physical education program for only one year. Cartwright was excluded from any policy-making position.

Born in England in 1880, Cartwright had emigrated to Canada in 1904 and taught at the Halifax Ladies' College prior to joining McGill's Royal Victoria College. Cartwright remained at McGill until 1927, when she and a friend retired to a small farm.

The president of the University of Saskatchewan had taken note of her abilities, however, and persuaded Cartwright to accept a position as assistant professor. Although her arrival in 1929 coincided with the depression and difficult years financially for the university, by 1933 Cartwright had succeeded in establishing a School of Physical Education. Under her influence, women students formed an autonomous women's athletic directorate at the university, and she continued her fight to employ women coaches and officials for women's sports.

At her retirement in 1943 she was awarded the rank of Professor Emeritus. She died at her home in Quebec in 1955. [HS-1994]

It must be realized that [women] are not seeking escape from marriage and the home as much as searching [for] satisfying use for the talents and training they possess, escaping the sense of waste and frustration and futility that so breed unhappiness where there is idleness and underuse of endowment and skills.—Charlotte Whitton, 1946

left: Black women graduates

From her first arrival in Nova Scotia, the Black woman has been immersed in a struggle for survival. She has had to battle slavery, servitude, sexual and racial discrimination, and ridicule. Her tenacious spirit has been her strongest and most constant ally; she is surviving with a strong dignity and an admirable lack of self-pity and bitterness. She is surviving, but not without struggle.
—Sylvia Hamilton, 1982

right: Grace Hutchison (l) and Nellie Carson (r) standing next to a Gypsy Moth DH6O that belonged to the Saskatoon Aero Club. Hutchison set a world altitude record over Saskatoon in 1935.

The freedom of flight has always been a compelling image. It resonates deeply with women who long to follow their dreams, and see where their spirit will lead.

WINGS FOR THE LADIES

Eileen Vollick of Hamilton, was the first woman in Canada to secure a Dominion Government pilot's licence. Eileen S. Magill of Winnipeg, was the second. Gertrude De La Vergne of Calgary, was the third Canadian woman pilot.

Helen Harrison was the first licensed woman flying instructor in Canada. She flew in Canada, South Africa, Australia, and England and insisted "that a woman instructor should not be considered a novelty, that a capable woman should make just as good an instructor as a man."

Violet Milstead was the only woman in the world to instruct at a school for bush pilots (in the 1940s). Besides having taught over 100 men, she has flown more than 50 types of aircraft. When she appeared for her flying test at the age of 18, she had only 9 hours dual instruction behind her. Since then she has piled up an impressive number of hours in the air, much of it during the two years she spent with the Air Transport Auxiliary in England.

The Flying Seven was organized in Vancouver in 1937, by a group of women pilots who felt the need of an organization to encourage women interested in flying, and to facilitate communication between women pilots. Rollie Moore, president, has given aerobatics displays in Canada and has won several awards for flying. [HS-1974]

[After the war the Flying Seven disbanded. However, six years later, the Ninety-Nines, an organization for women pilots founded by Amelia Earhart, established a branch in Canada. Today there are nine chapters. As the Flying Seven noted in their heyday: "Aviation is one field in which women have entered on the ground floor and we intend to rise with it." In 1995 Violet Milstead was inducted into the Bush Pilots Hall of Fame. Eds.]

below: Eileen Vollick (left, Eileen S. Magill (centre), and Gertrude De La Vergne (right)

ADA MACKENZIE

The winner of more golf titles than any other woman of her day, Ada Mackenzie dominated the Canadian golf scene for more than half a century. Her career started in the 1920s, when private golf clubs weren't anxious to give women much time on the courses. Frustrated with the starting times she was assigned and with the strictures on women, she decided to build the first women's golf club in the world. In six weeks she raised over $30,000 to buy land near Thornhill, Ontario, on which the Ladies' Golf Club of Toronto was built in 1924. She managed the club for five years after its completion; it remains the only golf club in the world built and owned by women.

Ada's recipe for championship golf was to start young and keep at it; Ada started at the age of ten. At school she distinguished herself in cricket, basketball, tennis, hockey, and figure skating, but golf was always her first love: "I used to stay so long after practice they made a special rule that students had to clear out by 5 p.m." At thirteen she played and won her first golf match; at nineteen she took the Canadian Ladies' Open.

In more than fifty years of tournament play, Ada won the Canadian Open five times, the Closed five times, the Ontario title nine times, the provincial Seniors twice, and the Toronto and District Championship on ten occasions. She was runner-up in ten national Opens and three Closed.

When she became frustrated with the inappropriate woman's golf costume of her day, Ada opened a ladies' sportswear shop in Toronto which she managed for twenty-eight years.

In 1929 she became the first Canadian to play in the British Ladies' Open when she played on the Scottish National Team. She was named Canada's outstanding female athlete in 1933 after winning every major golf championship in the country. When the Canadian Golf Hall of Fame was established in 1970, she was one of the first two women included. The second was Marlene Stewart Streit, the only other Canadian woman to match Ada's record. [HS-1975]

[The Ladies' Golf Club of Toronto is still the only golf club in North America reserved for women. Eds.]

left: Plane and lady aviator, August 1929

Among women who do participate in sports it is the female professional who is most discriminated against, just as the prospects of the female as breadwinner are most frustrating in other areas of paid work.
—Abigail Hoffman

PHYLLIS MUNDAY

Long before mountain climbing became an accepted pastime for women, Phyllis Munday, née James, would ride the Vancouver streetcar and ferry to the bottom of Grouse Mountain, hide her skirt under a log, and scramble up one of the routes in her bloomers. Today in her 80s, she maintains an active interest in the western Canadian mountains and in nature.

Phyllis Beatrice James was born of English parents on September 24, probably in 1898, in Ceylon, where her father managed first Lipton's, then Ridgeway's Tea. Upon arriving in Canada, the family settled in the Vancouver area, and Phyllis was soon exploring the nearby mountains. In 1909, she was the first girl in Vancouver to join the Girl Guides, and she has spent her lifetime actively supporting the organization. She set up a Girl Guide camp at Lake O'Hara in the Rocky Mountains in 1926, and met young girls from across

Take the woman whose usual occupation is a sedentary one...put her on a train and send her to the mountains. The imperfect glances of this peak and that gorge are small foretastes of what she is going to enjoy, for no one knows the mountains who sees them only from the car window.—Mary E. Crawford, turn-of-the century mountain climber

There is no salvation for women but in ourselves; in self-knowledge, self-reliance, self-respect, and in mutual help and pity.
—Anna Jameson, 1838

the country at the small train station. For many of the Guides, it was their first experience of seeing Canada.

In 1920, demanding more challenge in her climbs, she joined the British Columbia Mountaineering Club (BCMC). In the same year, she married Don Munday, whom she had met while working in the military annex of the New Westminster Hospital. For the next thirty years, until he died in 1950, Phyllis and Don were a unique climbing team.

In 1924, Phyllis became the first woman to climb Mount Robson, the highest peak in the Canadian Rockies. Conrad Kain, famous for his guiding abilities in the early days of mountaineering, led her and Don up to the summit. For Phyllis, it was a "most wonderful experience." Phyllis and Don spent much of their time at their cabin on Grouse Mountain with their daughter Edith, who was born in 1921. At least twice, Phyllis came to the aid of an injured climber. Once, she carried a teenage girl down the mountain on her back. Another time, she looked after a young man for several weeks in her cabin after he received head injuries due to a fall. For this, she was awarded the Bronze Cross for Valour from the Guides.

For eleven years, beginning in 1925, Phyllis and Don explored the northern reaches of the coastal mountains. In 1925, they spied the highest peak in the Coast Mountains, and although they never reached the top, they mapped out the surrounding region, noting plants, animal life, and geographical formations. In 1927, a neighbouring mountain received the name Mount Munday.

Phyllis has contributed much time and effort to the Alpine Club of Canada (ACC), the BCMC, and the Girl Guides. She has received the Silver Rope Badge from the ACC, and in 1971, was elected Honorary President. In 1967, she became the first woman to be an Honorary Member of the American Alpine Club, and that same year was awarded the Centennial Medal. The St John Ambulance Association appointed her Dame of Grace of the Order of St John. Her greatest recognition came in 1973, when she was awarded the Order of Canada. [HS-1985]

[Phyllis Munday died in 1990. Eds.]

MONA AND AGNES HARRAGIN

"I've never been afraid of anything. I don't know why, but it's true. Guiding turned out to be a lot of trouble and hard work. But for me, it was worth it. Just to know I could do the job."

Mona Harragin and her sister Agnes were the first women trail guides in Canada's national parks. From 1928 to 1930 they worked out of Jasper, wrangling, packing, and guiding "dudes" on trail rides, some of which took them into the mountains for weeks at a time.

right: Mona Harragin, one of the first women to guide in a national park in Canada, loading up for the trail, ca 1929

Born in 1904 and 1906, they were raised on a small farm near Salmon Arm, British Columbia, and grew up loving the outdoors and working with animals. Agnes, the younger sister, was especially fond of horses; a friend suggested she might enjoy guiding. However, every outfitter she wrote to at Jasper and Banff turned her down. They didn't hire women guides.

Fred Brewster, at Jasper, offered the women jobs as camp cooks. They took the chance to get a foot in the door, and spent the 1927 season at Medicine Lake on the Maligne Lake trail. They taught themselves wrangling, getting up at three a.m. to round up the horses, bring them in, saddle and doctor them. The guides happily slept in and let them practise.

The following season Brewster offered them any camp they would like, but the sisters replied they wanted guiding or nothing. They would have compromised, but Brewster agreed to let them guide on the circle trip from Jasper to Maligne Lake. Later they learned that Mrs. Brewster insisted they be given a chance, saying she would far rather make the trip with "one of her own kind."

They confronted the park authorities, got their badges, and met their first big test the day they started work. The male wranglers and packers who were to assist them to get their 35-horse string ready for the trail didn't show up, protesting the hiring of female guides. The women did their own wrangling and packing, standing on stumps and boxes to heave the loads up.

Although Mona and Agnes were popular with the dudes, the Depression was affecting business and they were replaced in the 1930 season by a man. Brewster offered them desk jobs, with the chance to take day trips out from Jasper. Preferring the "real thing," they went to work for another outfitter. In 1930, Mona married Charlie Matheson, a park warden who later became an outfitter, and Agnes married Mark Truxler, who joined the park service after working with local ranchers and outfitters. The sisters retired from guiding, but stayed in the area and used their trail skills working with their husbands. [HS-1988]

That women have faced opposition in their desire to be fully active participants in their religious faith—to follow their own path in praise and worship rather than to be merely led—is perhaps one of the most poignant struggles of women's emancipation.

LYDIA GRUCHY

Lydia Gruchy's decision to enter the ministry was a characteristic reaction of strength to pain. During the First World War her brother, ready for ordination, was killed. Lydia converted her grief into a determination to dedicate her life to the ministry.

Her graduation started a thirteen-year controversy in the church over the propriety of ordaining women. While the battle raged around her, Lydia began her ministry as a lay preacher among new Canadians in the Kamsack area of Saskatchewan, where her ability as a linguist was much needed.

I did my coming-out sermon. I told them about my orientation, how I felt like I was being treated like a weed in a rose garden.... I knew I was not a weed, and I wasn't sure that they were all roses.—Sally Boyle, United Church Minister, 1989

Christ was a true democrat. He was a believer in women and never in his life did he discriminate against them. Nellie McClung, 1916

Women are held back by various social and economic considerations from doing what they might do and becoming what they might become. —Margaret Gould, 1936

left: Lydia Gruchy

Some day, all women may say of their church that it will "welcome all of me, my spirit, my intellect, my whole being; not just my body and the fruits of my labour."
—*Herstory 1975*

But I believe that a competent performance by a woman in any field reflects favourably on other women who are seeking recognition. If I can do a good job of it, then it will be easier for the next woman who comes along the path.
—*Flo Whyard, 1980*

As long as women were at the stage of demanding equality on paper, the process, however slow, was relatively easy. But now that women have been legally recognized as, and publicly affirmed to be, equal citizens, words are no longer enough.
—*Ginette Busque, 1986*

right: Drawing by Sylvia Regnier

Lydia first requested ordination in 1926, then repeated the request every two years until 1936, meanwhile proving by the work she was doing that she was clearly competent for ordination. She took over pastoral charges which ordained men shunned because of the work involved. She often started the furnace in churches whose walls breathed cold from a week of prairie winter. She never gave in to blasting prairie heat, bone-shaking roads, or blizzards.

Colleagues and members of her congregations continued to request her ordination. Finally the lethargy of the male-dominated United Church was broken. Even though, as Nellie McClung put it, some church dignitaries seemed to have made up their minds "that nobody wants the ordination of women anyway," many presbyteries supported her ordination, and the policy of the United Church was changed to allow it.

Lydia Gruchy was ordained in 1936. From 1938 to 1943 she served in Toronto as executive secretary on the Committee on Deaconess Order and Women Workers, and for a year during that time was acting principal of the United Church Training School.

In 1953, she became the first Canadian woman to receive the honorary degree of doctor of divinity. It was well-earned recognition for a life of physically hard work and emotional and spiritual strength. [HS-1976]

MARY LUCAS

Could there be any career more difficult for a woman to enter than one dominated by males for nearly 2,000 years? In 1976, after many years of opposition and struggle, the Canadian House of Anglican Bishops gave individual bishops the power to admit qualified women to the priesthood. Although a few more countries are moving in this direction, Canada was second only to Hong Kong to officially recognize women in this field. Even in Canada where it is now officially recognized, opponents of the change are still bitter.

One must then admire a pioneer in this field: Mary Lucas, a Christian feminist, who has persisted in the face of opposition and was ordained November 30,

1976, in the Niagara, Ontario, diocese.

Mary's interest in the church began when she was about ten years old, and along with her decision to know more about God and to study religion, came a growing awareness of a commitment to God. She knew that women weren't priests, but she felt strongly that she had a vocation and there was nowhere else for her to go. Before Mary became an ordained deacon in 1975 she obtained a master of divinity degree, *cum laude,* from Harvard Divinity School. She also had two years of experience teaching in a mission school in Japan. As a deacon she was assigned a part-time hospital chaplaincy in St Catharines. Added to this was a part-time position as curate at Grace Church, St Catharines. Mary admits that she never assumes now that "anyone...will approve of her." She adds, "Nobody wants to be different. It means being very lonely and isolated."

Women seeking a vocation as priests have known isolation, uncertainty, anger, and, many times, disappointment. Mary's success is certainly encouragement for us all. [HS-1979]

[Since her ordination to the priesthood in 1976, the Reverend Mary Lucas has been involved in parish ministry both in Canada and the United States. She has also engaged in community action work with a variety of social justice organizations. Currently, she resides in Ontario. Eds.]

The employment demands of the war industry in the twentieth century forced a change in the role of women in Canadian life.

WOMEN IN THE WAR INDUSTRY

To attract them into the workforce during the two world wars women were offered higher salaries, government-sponsored daycare, specialized training, and more challenging employment. Women went to work in such industries as aircraft manufacturing and munitions, obtaining positions as welders, boilermakers, mechanics, technicians, chemists, radio physicists, production experts, and job supervisors. Much to the surprise of the Canadian employer, women proved to have very definite advantages over male workers: better eyesight, dexterity, and speed; they were more careful and alert; and they had lower accident rates.

Throughout Canada, working women were celebrated as "the Heroines of Canada." Women, it was said, were having the time of their lives with their newly acquired status. They had gained economic independence, more personal freedom, and a greater sense of their own worth as Canadians. With the end of the war, the return of the soldiers, and the threat of the mass unemployment of men, the Canadian woman was

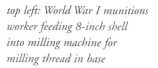
top left: World War I munitions worker feeding 8-inch shell into milling machine for milling thread in base

abruptly removed from her wartime position.

Through various forms of media propaganda, she was urged to return home to help create the "baby boom." Discrimination against women in hiring and firing practices helped to eliminate those women from industry who hadn't been swayed by the media. Along with the closure of government sponsored daycare, it became almost impossible for women to continue the careers they had pursued during the war. [HS-1974]

"They are killing us off as fast as they are killing the men in the trenches," declared the spokeswoman of a deputation of women munitions workers who came into the Star *office yesterday morning. "We are working six days a week from seven till seven and on Sundays from seven till four, and now they want us to work fourteen hours a day."—Toronto Daily Star, 27 July 1917*

bottom left: Women's lunch room, British Munitions Supply Co., Verdun, Quebec, 1916-18

above: WWI munitions factory

MUNITIONS FACTORY, WWII

"Women between the ages of 18 and 35 and in good health are wanted to work in eastern war plants. 'Keep 'em firing' is the motto used. The kind of girl we want is the girl with a good head on her shoulders. We take girls absolutely unskilled in war industries and train them right at the plant. A Saskatchewan girl—whether she's a farmer's daughter, domestic servant, waitress, clerk, stenographer, college graduate or debutante—if she is willing to learn—has the qualities of a good war worker. Wages are 35¢ an hour for a 48 hour week. Time and a half for all overtime. At the end of 4 to 6 weeks, the rate of pay will be increased according to the individual's ability."—The Leader-Post, *Regina, December 5, 1942* [HS-1985]

right: Women shop stewards in Burrard Dry Docks canteen, North Vancouver, 1942

DEPARTMENT OF LABOUR—WWII

The Second World War offered many Canadian women their first opportunity to enter the labour force, and to work in occupations formerly reserved exclusively for men. For the most part, management viewed these new workers with ambivalence, and government policy-makers reinforced this attitude.

"The average woman would rather stay on a familiar job with fellow workers, a foreman and routine she is used to than be promoted, if promotion means changing to a new environment. A man is eager for any change that means getting ahead.

"Women take brusque criticism much worse than men. Reproofs must be sugared up: 'You certainly do a wonderful day's work when you are here, Jane—now why can't you manage to get here oftener?'

"Competition, with prizes, stimulates men and often lifts a whole department's output. It's just bad medicine for women. They become tense, get too excited—and those who fall behind become so discouraged that they stop trying altogether and so do worse than before the contest.

"The too pretty girl is a nuisance. If she does outstandingly well and the foreman promotes her, the other women interpret his motives cattily. If she is reprimanded, she is likely to take it as a personal affront.

"Rough kidding in the bluff, hearty manner that goes

CANADIAN WOMEN'S ARMY CORPS, 1941-46

In summer 1941 Canada was one of the last countries in the British Empire to sanction female enlistment in its military forces. Female enlistment was a more palatable solution to the "manpower" shortage than was conscription this early in the war. But Canadian women determined to aid the war effort had been pressing government for some time. They were quick to volunteer. Throughout World War II over 45,000 women volunteered, 22,000 in the Canadian Women's Army Corps (CWAC).

Many ex-servicewomen cite patriotism as their primary reason for enlisting, but there were other motivations. Some women were bored with their jobs and looking for a change. Some wanted adventure, as one female enlistee recalls:

"You enrolled for adventure. At seventeen, who had much experience? I lied about my age and told them my birth certificate was lost. That was in '42 when we'd already been hearing war songs for three years. I was working in Montreal and every day I had to pass a recruiting office. Take part in the war? Be a patriot? Replace a man? Perhaps, but for me it was really more for the fun of it and to see new places."

After six weeks of basic training the women took up a variety of trades. Initially most were related to domestic or clerical work, but by the end of the war

above: From the National Council of Women Yearbook, *1917-1918*

top left : Three factory women

over big with men won't do at all with women. They want the courtly touch.

"Women are more willing than men to admit mistakes and to ask advice. But they will do badly on a job in which they have to make decisions. There should never be two ways to do an operation which a woman worker performs. It takes her too long to make up her mind which course to follow.

"Of practical importance are various odds and ends: women do not work well with tools that require rotary motion, such as screw drivers. Keep them off high platform jobs; their sense of balance is poor. They are faster and better than men on light rhythmical jobs.

"Investigation of man-girl trouble among employees showed the woman the aggressor, or initiator, three times out of four."—Excerpt from "A Fair Day's Output from a Fair Day's Work," Department of Labour manual, n.d. [HS-1985]

left: CWAC Recruiting poster: Canada Calls her Womanhood for Service Anywhere in the Canadian Women's Army Corps. *A candidate for enlistment...must be minimum height five feet; weight not less than 105 pounds, no dependents; must have Grade VIII, must be between the ages of 18 and 45 and be a British Subject.—Advertisement in the* Edmonton Journal, *13 February 1943*

top right: CWAC service-woman, WWII

What my mother has given me is the desire to find my own path, a path that takes the long way, threading through wild land and between the lives of people, avoiding the highway.
—Beverley A. Brenna, 1989

Canada's war effort, rather than any consideration of women's right to work, determined the recruitment of women into the labour force.—Ruth Pierson, 1977

To my parents, who never once said, "Please don't go to sea."—dedication to *Deep Sea Sparks: A Canadian Girl in the Norwegian Merchant Navy,* by Olive J. Carroll, 1993

right: Olive J. Carroll

over 50 trades were open to women to release men for combat duty.

In addition to the anticipated hardships of hard work, lack of privacy, highly regimented lives, boredom, and physical danger, enlisted women faced considerable public disapproval. They were seen by some as "camp followers."

One former CWAC member speculates: "I just wonder, if you could turn the clock back, with so many more women being educated today, what it would be like. I think it would be much different—an entirely different ball game—because men dominated the whole thing then."

By the end of the war, however, senior army officials declared that "women in the service had put men 'on their toes,'" and that they had "been of great service to [their] country and an honour to [their] sex." Colonel C.P. Stacey called the formation of the CWAC one of the most successful military innovations of World War II. Most CWAC members returned to civilian life with increased self-confidence and heightened ambitions. [HS-1994]

OLIVE J. CARROLL

"Good God, no!" Even during WWII, when women were routinely undertaking many occupations previously considered the sole preserve of men, the reaction of one Canadian official to women serving at sea was unmistakable: "We have enough trouble on ships now without having women on board!" In spite of that opposition, at least 17 Canadian women served both during and after the war as wireless operators (or "Sparks")—all on foreign vessels. That we know their stories at all is due in large measure to the research of one of them, Olive J. Carroll.

Ten Canadian women served as ship's Sparks during the war. Olive worked in Intelligence, using her wireless training as an interceptor operator—but she and six other women eagerly accepted appointments on board vessels after the war. The Norwegian Merchant Navy had no reservations about hiring women; in their telegram confirming a position for Olive, they had only one request: the names of any other available operators.

A ship's Sparks was the essential communications link with the outside world. As sole Sparks aboard, Olive was on call whenever the ship was at sea. In addition to her wireless duties, Olive was also purser and secretary, and after an accident at sea, she served as nurse as well.

"Equality was one of the pluses of life at sea"; the Norwegian crews she sailed with considered her "just one of the officers." Sailing also offered Olive the chance to see the world. She witnessed a magnificent, albeit staged, welcome for Eva Peron; walked into a Communist revolution in Chile; and was one of the few people in the immediate post-war years to see countries behind the Iron Curtain.

The Canadian women who sailed on foreign vessels more than proved their competence. One captain Olive sailed under remarked that she was the best radio operator he had worked with in his 41-year career.

Four years without a holiday, and the poor diet aboard ship—particularly the lack of fresh fruits and vegetables—finally took their toll, and Olive signed off on her doctor's recommendation. She left the service, "grateful to the Norwegians" for the opportunity: "I wouldn't have missed the experience for anything." [HS-1996]

above: WWII Poster

top left: Kathleen Jeffs— Member of the Order of the British Empire for her distinguished service as a wing officer in the RCAF

left: Warrior's Day Parade at the Canadian National Exhibition in Toronto, 1920. The women were from Earlscourt, an area in Toronto near present-day Dufferin and St Clair. They were representing their dead soldier-sons in the parade commemorating the end of WWI.

above: Mary Doyle

*right: Toronto Transit Conductor
"Doris and I went to the TTC
in September 1942....I was so
withdrawn before I went to work.
After I got that job I was just a
babbling brook. It gave me all
the confidence in the world....I was
able to cope with everything."
—Anonymous, n.d.*

The civil service was another employment opportunity opening up to women, but not without limitations.

MARY DOYLE

In 1914 Mary Doyle was president of the Women's Branch of the Civil Service Association of Ottawa. She had worked in the civil service since 1892—all but six months of those twenty-two years as a permanent clerk in the office of the Minister of Marine and Fisheries.

Throughout this period Mary remained single, at times supporting a sister and her widowed mother in a house she owned in Ottawa. In other years she boarded with friends or strangers. Whether or not Mary considered marrying is unknown. Female civil servants were bound by custom (although not by law) to resign once married, and perhaps the threat of losing her job kept Mary single.

By 1907, Mary was one of nine women who had achieved the second class clerk's level—the highest level to which women were then appointed. A total of 241 other permanent female employees remained in positions below her. Mary earned $1,300 that year, the second highest salary paid to a woman.

Mary Doyle is one of the hundreds of women who worked in monotonous clerks' jobs for very little money in the early years of the civil service in Canada. Contrary to the popular view at the turn of the century, she eventually made a career out of it—a notable achievement given the attitudes and constraints of the time. She was atypical, however. Many women could not move beyond temporary status, and of those who did, only a few attained Mary's level of pay and responsibility. [HS-1986]

THE "PROBLEM" WITH WOMEN IN THE CIVIL SERVICE

In 1907 the federal government appointed a three-man royal commission to investigate the efficiency of the civil service. Several deputy ministers and senior officials—all male of course—were called to testify. Most commented on female employment as the "problem" at the root of many different concerns. The following are excerpts from the Commissioners' questions, and the testimony given in answer.

Q: *All over the service there are exceptional women, but as a body do you think women will be able to take the higher positions?*

A: I am not prepared to say offhand that they are not. My own view—it may be a prejudice— would be rather to have the superior positions filled by men.

Q: *It is not prejudice, it is the result of observation?*

A: It is the result, very largely, I think, of the experience that the superior positions have hitherto been filled by men and not by women .—*Frank Pedley, Deputy Superintendent of Indian Affairs.*

Q: *What is your opinion generally as to the desirability of employing women?*

A: For certain branches of our work they are good up to a limited point.—*R.N. Coulter, Deputy Postmaster General*

Q: *Would you suggest as a matter of fact that there should be a limit of pay for women?*

A: Yes, second class. In the employment of women there is this disadvantage; though they may know as much as the men clerks, you cannot utilize them in the same way. You cannot confide outside business necessitating travelling, and they cannot transact certain business which would be done by a man having their knowledge.—*F.F. Goudreau, Deputy Minister of Marine and Fisheries*

Some of these people [are temporaries who] have been with us for twenty to thirty years, and they are getting exactly the same remuneration as those who came in during the last three or four years.—*T.C. Boville, Deputy Minister of Finance*

My own opinion is that the employment of women in the service has closed the avenues for young men, and that we are not training young men for the higher positions in the service as we should do.—*James McKenna, Assistant Indian Commissioner*

When girls enter first at the age of seventeen or eighteen, or it may be from eighteen to twenty-three or twenty-four, they are inspired with the idea either of getting married or of something happening that they can get out of the service. They do not usually take the same interest in their duties that a man does who feels that it is his life's work and he is going to remain at it.—*W.W. Cory, Deputy Minister of the Interior* [HS-1986]

All too often, women who have fought for access have worked as volunteers or have remained nameless, in the shadows of men whose work has appropriated theirs.

LUISE OETTINGER HERZBERG

In spite of time and place—Germany, in the first part of the century—and pressures to be "feminine" from her well-to-do Jewish family, by the time she was 27, Luise Oettinger had studied engineering and physics. She had also married Gerhard Herzberg, a fellow

From woman's right of self-determination follows also the correlative right to enter any employment or profession for which she has the taste and qualification.
—"M," 1879

left: Luise Oettinger Herzberg

physicist with whom she was collaborating in spectroscopy, as well as conducting the independent research which led to her doctorate.

But it was 1933; the Nazis had been in power since January. Her PHD, granted in August, may have been the last received in Frankfurt by a Jew under that regime. By 1935 she and Gerhard were refugees, accepted into a reluctant Canada due to a colleague at the University of Saskatchewan, John Spinks. Four years later her parents joined them. For the next 20 years, she worked in the shadow of her increasingly famous husband, continuing their collaboration, but often shut out from the technical talk by the prevailing assumption that she "had to prepare tea in the kitchen and was usually expected to talk to the ladies." She was burdened as well by family responsibilities which included catering for a vegetarian husband and caring for a father who expected his daughter's complete attention.

Gerhard Herzberg accepted an appointment at Yerkes Observatory near Chicago after the war, and, although Luise "being a woman and a wife, could not, at that time expect a paid position," she was allowed to work for nothing as a "voluntary research associate." She developed an interest in astronomy, and when Gerhard moved the family to Ottawa to take a post with the National Research Council, she joined the Dominion Observatory, paid first as a "summer assistant," although she was working year-round, but finally, after four years, as a full-time "scientific officer." Recovering from surgery for breast cancer, she moved to the Radio Physics Laboratory at Shirley Bay, Ontario, in 1959, and worked there until her death in 1971, just months before Gerhard won the Nobel prize—"a success which he could not have achieved without her devotion and support," according to their son Paul. She continued to publish and lecture to the end of her life, against all odds making lasting contributions to both spectroscopy and radio physics. [HS-1996]

right: Nellie Greenwood Andrews, first woman in Canada to graduate with a Bachelor of Science degree, from Victoria College, Toronto, 1884

One of the more sobering revelations of historical investigation is that many of the causes remain the same: at one hundred years' distance one can still hear the same pleas for equal access to education, to training and the professions, for daycare, for shared family and household responsibilities.
—Alison Prentice and Susan Mann Trofimenkoff, 1987

I am happy that my daughters (and sons) will be able to take advantage of the increased general respect and sensitivity for what women can offer to society. Our youth are such a rich resource; no barriers should diminish their ability to contribute and fulfill their dreams."
—Connie Eaves, 1998

WOMEN AND THE SCIENCES

In the '50s both "environmental pressures" and personal goals were identified as the major barriers to women's entry into traditionally male fields like engineering and the natural sciences. Inadequate career counselling in the schools, poor teaching, and the attitudes of women themselves, who appeared to prefer the typewriter to the microscope, or who were more interested in getting an "Mrs" than an MSC once they did get to university, were named as barriers. However, the resistance of the professions themselves to the entry of women was not identified as a factor.

Today, many still believe that the recruitment of

women to the sciences has moved slowly because women are more likely to put establishing a family ahead of establishing a career. However, a recent survey shows that 74% of the women responding who had PHDs in sciences, psychology, engineering, or mathematics had worked steadily, usually full-time, since receiving their doctorates. Gaps in their work records were often due to the inability to find work rather than to family commitments.

More women are qualifying: between 1969 and 1984, doctoral degrees in biology awarded to women in Canada rose from 10% to 29%; from 3% to 22% in chemistry and biochemistry; from 0% to 18% in geology; and from 4% to 7% in physics. By the end of the '80s nearly 50% of graduates in the biological sciences were women, even though only 8% of their professors were. The hiring of women faculty members proceeded much more slowly: only 5.3% in mathematics and physical sciences in 1985 were women, up only 0.9% from 1970. Engineering is one of the fields least welcoming of women. By the end of the '80s women were approximately 10% of undergraduates, but only 2% of faculty members. By comparison, close to 45% of medical students were women, as were from 3% to 15% of medical faculty members.

A 1957 survey of women in the "scientific professions" found that "Low salaries, slow promotion and little or no recognition of work done by a woman are mentioned again and again." Even today, a top engineering graduate who is female still has to fight to escape clerical assignments. While more than half (60%) of male engineers between the ages of 25 and 39 have supervisory positions, only 33% of women engineers the same age do. Canada is facing a severe shortage of science professionals in the '90s. Earl Dudgeon, vice-president of engineering for the National Research Council, says, "We can't afford to ignore half the population." [HS-1991]

[In 1999, Statistics Canada noted that only 20% of natural sciences, engineering, and mathematics professionals were women—only a slight improvement from the 1987 figure of 17%. Eds.]

In whatever field they choose, when women "step up to the plate" they do so with pride, determination and, invariably, success.

MARY "BONNIE" BAKER

They hit homers and stole bases wearing rose-coloured skirts. They played up to 140 games per season, seven days a week, with double-headers on Saturday, and earned $75 to $125 weekly. At night they attended charm school. They attracted up to 1,000,000 fans per season. They were women who played for the All-American Girls Professional Baseball League (AAGPBL) between 1942 and 1954.

Fifty-three Canadians played for the league. Former schoolteachers, models, students, and stenographers, they came from every province west of Quebec. And ironically, it was a Canadian, Mary Baker, who epitomized the all-American player.

The media dubbed her "Bonnie" for her bubbly per-

I thought everybody's mom [played baseball]. She taught me how to catch. She also taught me the mental aspect. She taught me you never give up and you always play hard.—Casey Candaele, 1988. Her mother, Helen St Aubin, nicknamed "The Female Ted Williams," played for the Fort Wayne Daisies.

left: Mary "Bonnie" Baker

The union, the women's movement, time and experience have led me to believe that every woman's place is where her interest lies.
—Addie Wyatt, Vice-President, United Food and Commercial Workers

sonality and beauty. She appeared on the cover of *Life* and acted as spokesperson for the league on many occasions. Mary also starred on the field, finishing second in batting in 1946. She was twice an all-star catcher and became the only full-time female manager in 1951.

Chicago Cubs owner P.K. Wrigley started the league in 1942; the war had depleted the ranks of the major leagues and he sought another attraction. His original four teams later expanded to eight. Wrigley and the male board of directors set the rules.

Players were expected to embody "the highest ideals of womanhood" and were required to "dress, act, and carry themselves as befits the feminine sex." In public the dress code was skirts, dresses, and shoulder-length hair. Instructors from the Helena Rubenstein beauty school trained the women in poise, posture, and makeup. Smoking and drinking were forbidden and the players were closely supervised by chaperones in pseudo-military uniforms.

"They expected us to look feminine but play like men," recalls a teammate. In fact, what really kept the fans' attention was the calibre of play. The AAGPBL played hardball, used knock-down pitches, upended shortstops sliding into second, argued with umpires and usually played hurt because of their short skirts and bare legs.

The AAGPBL prospered following the war until the major leagues revived, the novelty wore off, and the women were encouraged to return to family life. Mary Baker returned to Regina and her husband, played champion-level softball throughout Canada and became the first Canadian woman sportscaster in 1964. [HS-1991]

[In 1992, a Hollywood film, *A League of Their Own,* told the story of this first women's baseball league. In 1998, Mary and her AAGPBL colleagues were inducted into the Canadian Baseball Hall of Fame. Eds.]

HENRIETTA GOPLEN

Henrietta was 10 years old when she joined the first speed skating team at the Saskatoon Lions Club in 1942. Before long she became one of Canada's top speed skaters. In 1947 she was second overall in the Canadian championships held in Sudbury, Ontario. She ended her skating career in 1950, when she began her home economics degree at the University of Saskatchewan. In 1955 she made a comeback, and won the senior ladies' provincial title. Her dream was to skate in the Olympics, but women's speed skating events were not held in the Winter Olympic Games until the 1960s. Instead of dwelling on this disappointment, she says, "I would rather work so that the next generation will have opportunities...I'm happy to see someone else go."

Sports are character building...one learns that things don't come without work.
—Henrietta Goplen, 1990

right: Henrietta Goplen

She was the first woman speed skating coach in Canada when she began coaching in 1975. Many of her young skaters have made the national team, including her son Gordon, who skated in the 1988 Winter Olympic Games. She was thrilled to take part in the same Olympics as an official. "As soon as they said the Olympics were going to go to Calgary, I said 'I'll do whatever I can to get there,' and I didn't know at the time that my son was going to compete."

Her appreciation for speed skating is evident in her book *The Saskatoon Lions Speed Skating Club: 45 Years of History.* She writes, "The sight is beautiful to watch, they glide to a certain rhythm with a minimum of movement on shiny long blades, around the large ice surface. Even the smaller ones, with stiff legs and arms precariously swinging, have their own beauty."

Henrietta is an honorary life member of the Saskatoon Lions Speed Skating Club. In 1988 she was inducted into the Saskatoon Sports Hall of Fame, and in 1989 received the Canadian Amateur Speed Skating Association's 3M coaching award for her role in the formation of young athletes. [HS-1991]

[Henrietta retired in 2000 after 60 years of practising and coaching speed skating. She was president of the Canadian Amateur Speed Skating Association from 1994-96, and in 2002 was given the John Hurdis award for volunteering with Skate Canada, one of only five such awards in 112 years. Henrietta considers "it an honour and a privilege" to have coached Catriona LeMay Doan for eight years (1980-88.) See p. 206. Eds.]

ALL-GIRL RODEOS

The western-clad young lady leaning admiringly on a fence post watching her man tame that unbreakable bronco is often Hollywood's view of cowgirls. That is certainly not the view of the members of the Canadian Girls' Rodeo Association. These women are competitors, not spectators.

The CGRA is responsible for 12 All-Girl Rodeos that take place each year in western Canada. All-Girl Rodeos are composed of six major events: barrel racing; team roping; calf roping; goat tying; steer undecorating; and cow riding. The events are reminiscent of the men's events. They have been modified somewhat to compensate for the difference in size and strength between men and women, but that doesn't make them any less exciting or any easier. The cows used in the women's cow riding may be smaller than the bulls in the men's event, but they are no less mean.

Another major difference is the size of the winning purses. A man can be a professional cowboy and make a reasonable living, but a woman as yet cannot. This does not mean they are any less dedicated. These women travel thousands of miles in a season and may attend two or three rodeos in a weekend. They put in endless hours training their horses. They do it for the love of horses, the excitement, and the close comradeship with other competitors. [HS-1982]

WOMEN IN THE ROYAL CANADIAN MOUNTED POLICE (RCMP)

On May 24, 1974, RCMP Commissioner M.J. Nadon announced that women, both married and single, would be accepted into the Force. The decision was the result of a number of pressures: the evolution of women's roles, the Royal Commission on the Status of Women, which caused women to question why they

below: RCMP women

right: Deanna Brasseur

*I didn't begin with
proving anything
to anyone but myself.*
—Deanna Brasseur, 1989

*In the really small
communities they welcome
and respect the police.
In a place like Paulautak
[NWT], you can fly in to
charge somebody, in one
breath you are compelling
them to court for their
wrongdoings, and in the
next breath you are
socializing with the same
individuals, coffeeing
and spreading good will.*
—Corporal Pat Harrish,
first female RCMP corporal
in the NWT, 1992

weren't allowed to join [see p. 63], and the RCMP's need to attract recruits with a university education.

Thirty-two women were chosen from among 292 candidates. Those selected were expected to be "mature and well adjusted," at least five feet four inches tall, "with a proportional weight," and a minimum educational level of grade eleven.

The women were selected from across the nation. There were former teachers, nurses, college students, secretaries, and sales clerks, and women who had been in other areas of police work. News reports of the day noted: "During their six months of training—the same given male recruits—the women showed skill and will in unarmed combat and did better than their male counterparts in criminal psychology, social situation analysis, public relations and criminal investigation."

In March 1975, Troop 17, the first contingent of women Mounties in the 102-year history of the Force, graduated from the RCMP training depot in Regina, Saskatchewan.

The 30 women, aged 19 to 29, were immediately assigned their first postings. [HS-1979]

[1999 marked the 25th anniversary of women in the RCMP. At that time, there were 2,045 female regular members, representing roughly 14% of the total Force. Eleven members of the original Troop 17 were still serving. Eds.]

DEANNA BRASSEUR

In 1972, Deanna Brasseur, a clerk in the Canadian Air Force, wanted a challenge. She applied for officer training and became an air weapons controller. Her work introduced her to the field and the missions, and she often flew "back seat" in the planes.

That experience sparked her interest in flying. She took private flying lessons, but didn't aspire to a military flying career until 1979, when positions of pilots, navigators and flight engineers opened to women on a trial basis. She applied immediately.

Brasseur found that male pilots in their thirties and forties encouraged her. It was the nineteen- and

twenty-year-old men training alongside her who complained that women didn't belong in the air. She completed the program and moved on to train pilots at CFB Moose Jaw. She served on the Charter of Rights and Freedoms task force, which recommended women be allowed to fly jet fighters in battle. That decision came in 1988. In 1989, Deanna and Jane Foster graduated as the first two women fighter pilots. Foster left the program in 1990.

Few people become members of a fighter squadron, but to be a woman member is even more isolating. "It's a scary concept. I don't really have a professional peer group." Still, there is a family feeling as they bond together to get through tough times.

Along the way, media attention has often interfered. "Political pressures, more than anything, initiated the trial programs....At each section of the course, we were isolated, extracted for a press purpose. It caused a rift." The press works against her too. Major Brasseur did not go to the [Persian] Gulf immediately with her squadron in January 1991. The headline "Ready, willing...but unable: Nerve problem grounds our only female jet pilot," seemed to question her ability and confidence. Buried in the article was the real story: operations on nerve endings in her left elbow had grounded her, as they would have grounded a male pilot, with no resulting press. [HS-1993]

[In 1994, Deanna retired from the Canadian Air Force and formed, trained and assumed leadership of the all-woman Canadian Precision Flying Team. In 1998, a tree was planted in her honour in the International Organization of Women Pilots Forest of Friendship, at the birthplace of Amelia Earhart, in Atchison, Kansas. Chosen as one of *Maclean's* magazine's outstanding Canadians in 1999, Deanna received the Order of Canada that year and the Queen's Jubilee Medal in 2002. She has applied to become a member of the reserves, and will be once again in uniform. Eds.]

CHRISTINE BERTRAM SILVERBERG

In October 1995, Christine Silverberg stepped into the top job in the Calgary Police Service, the first woman to be appointed chief of police in a major city in Canada. She has sometimes shaken up the traditionally conservative Alberta community, but has also earned new honours, including the name "Bluebird Lady" from the Piegan Nation, and a Platinum Podium Award from Toastmaster's International for leadership through communication. Murray Billet, a director of Gay and Lesbian Awareness in Alberta, says, "This is a progressive police chief who believes in the citizens of her community. She's saying, 'Don't be afraid to deal with police officers.'"

Her disarming appearance belies her status as a veteran of nearly 30 years of policing, and her determined overcoming of obstacles in a service dominated by men. She waited eight hours for an application form to join the Mississauga, Ontario, police force in 1971. Women were not allowed on uniform patrol, the usual starting point for new recruits. Assigned to the youth bureau instead, Christine became involved in abuse investigations, undercover work, and criminal investigations, and distinguished herself in community services, working her way through the ranks to inspector by the early 1980s.

She also took numerous courses in police operations, management, and administration, completed an MA in criminology at the University of Toronto in 1983, studied executive development at Queens University, and earned her accreditation in public relations.

In 1990 she took a senior position in the Ontario ministry of the Solicitor General, the first woman to do so, then returned to the service as deputy chief of the Hamilton-Wentworth Regional Police.

She has blazed a trail. As she observes, "Today there is no field which should be inaccessible to women. We have proven our competency in numerous areas of policing, from tactical to all kinds of investigations, to canine units to motorcycle units. And we are seeing more women in management positions."

Chief Silverberg is active in community and professional organizations, from the Chamber of Commerce to the National Coordinating Committee on Organized Crime, and the International Association of Chiefs of Police. She and her husband Dr Ben Silverberg, whom she married in 1971, have two children. [HS-2000]

[Christine Silverberg retired from the Calgary Police Service in October 2000, leaving behind her a long list of distinguished contributions to both the Service and her community. Eds.]

Every individual is different and it has nothing to do with gender.—Shirley Robinson, 1997

In order to know where you are, you have to look and see where you came from—and celebrate those successes.—Christine Bertram Silverberg, 1999

left: Christine Bertram Silverberg

above: First-year carpenter apprentice, Antoinette Morteas

I would say that the single largest factor that has given me confidence in my skills as a carpenter, in my right to call myself carpenter and be proud, was working with another woman on our own jobs.
—Kate Braid, 1984

right: Women workers near Baddeck, Nova Scotia, 1914-18

As the nature of work that women do for wages expands, the sense that women have of themselves, as women and as workers, changes as well.

LINDA SKOMOROWSKI

Canada's first woman journeyman plumber and licensed gas fitter grew up in Canora, Saskatchewan, in the 1960s, thinking that she might become a kindergarten teacher. After high school she tried office work, and a year of university, but both bored her and left her feeling that such pursuits led nowhere.

Linda decided to do something different. In fact it was so different for a member of her sex that she made history, but Linda's story is riddled with the humiliations women experience when they enter all-male domains.

"I chose one of the three hardest trades to get into. It's not an easy job. And I had to fight just to begin."

Linda's career began in 1972 with a ten-month pre-apprenticeship plumbing course in Manitoba. To get around a long waiting list for the course at Winnipeg's Red River Community College, she decided to go through Canada Manpower. Manpower threw a major discriminatory obstacle in her way. She was told to get a medical from a doctor who was also a plumber; none of the male applicants for the same course were required to get medicals. Linda took her case to the Human Rights Commission and the medical was waived, but she was still only on the waiting list.

In the meantime Linda was able to enroll immediately in the pre-apprenticeship course at Brandon's Assiniboine Community College. She completed the course and won three awards for excellence, including top marks in plumbing. In May of 1973 Linda began her five-year apprenticeship, and received her journeyman's papers in March of 1979.

"I have to deal with cold weather, lots of mess, mud, and heavy lifting. But I'm proud of my work and I certainly consider myself a lady."

Linda lives in Norquay, Saskatchewan, with her husband Joe and their son Trent. Joe is also a journeyman plumber, and together they run the Joe-Lin Plumbing and Heating business. [HS-1981]

[More than twenty years later, Linda is still in the plumbing and heating business. She and Joe have added premises—the shop in Preeceville is very much "a going concern"—and sold the original Norquay shop. Eds]

KATE BRAID

Kate Braid believes she is living proof that anyone can start without any knowledge of a trade and become proficient in it. When she started on her first construction site, Kate had to wield her sixteen-ounce hammer with two hands. The bubble in the level was a mystery to her, and six-foot ladders simply didn't get moved. For the first two weeks she stumbled home for a nap before rising to eat and then returning to bed. Nonetheless, Kate instantly loved being a labourer.

That was in 1977. Kate has since been a successful carpenter in Vancouver, preferring union work such as building high rises, condominiums, and Rapid Transit stations.

A few years ago, Kate would have stressed the problems of being the only woman, if not first woman, on every job. However, she realized that many of her difficulties were shared by male apprentices. She stopped expecting to be treated badly and developed confidence in her skills. "I have never found the physical demands of the job a problem, though that is always the first question I am asked. You grow stronger, you learn how to handle materials, you ask people to help you, you don't try to prove how strong you are by wrecking your back."

Kate Braid became a certified journeywoman on July 15, 1983. In her words, "That is a date you don't forget!" [HS-1986]

[Kate Braid is now a writer and poet. Her first book of poetry, *Covering Rough Ground*, which is about her 15 years as a carpenter, won the Pat Lowther Prize. She also teaches creative writing at Malaspina University-College in Nanaimo. She does carpentry only for herself. Eds.]

NON-TRADITIONAL WORK AND SELF-IMAGE

Traditionally, women's work experiences have confined them to domestic and public service roles. However, more are entering occupations usually identified only with the male sex, in industries such as logging, mining, and construction. For many women, their new role in the workplace gives them a welcome sense of inner strength.

In her study of women in non-traditional work in British Columbia, Kate Braid says that one of the greatest attractions of such work seems to be its effect on a woman's sense of well-being, both physical and emotional. "In spite of the fact that they are generally assumed incompetent when they begin, these women very often experience strong positive gains in their perception of themselves, in their ability to be assertive, self-confident and competent."

"I got strong," a mine mill operator told Braid. "I felt better working hard. And it was good to feel hungry and tired after work. You don't feel frustrated. I'd rather be tired physically than uptight." A forklift driver commented: "I think my personality has strengthened a little bit because I can shoot off my mouth better. I had never yelled at people before, or had a good argument. When you're sitting in an office you've got to sit still while your boss tells you what to do. You can't talk back or express your feelings or tell him that he's wrong. But at this job you can. You can even make suggestions to your boss. So it changes you."

Braid says that unlike traditional women's jobs, non-traditional ones offer a sense of beginning and end, and a final product. One labourer told Braid: "You wash the floor, tomorrow it's going to be washed again. It never shows—nothing ever shows. At work there's something there, you know? According to my son I built that road over there....It's gratifying."

For one single mother, the job had increased her respect within the family and community. "I was my kid's idol. We went to get him some shoes and he said, 'Get me some workboots just like yours, Mom.'"

The women in non-traditional occupations are on-the-job leaders in the campaign to challenge and eradicate stereotypes. Their performance in the workplace is evidence that women can do work outside the domestic and public service sectors. Further, their newfound confidence, competence, and physical strength exhibit behaviour not usually considered characteristic of the female gender. [HS-1981]

EXCEPTIONAL PURSUITS FOR WOMEN

Women worked in non-traditional occupations even before the turn of the century in Canada. The National Council of Women included a statistical table of "different occupations" in their report compiled for the Paris World's Fair of 1900. Among them were:

	PEI	NS	NB	QUE	ON	MB	NWT	BC
Agents (insurance)			2	1	3			
Livery Stable Keepers		1	1	1				
Photographers			3	6	18	1		
Physicians & Surgeons	1	6	5	17	50	3	2	5
Publishers (Census, 1891)	3			20	3			
Sextons (Census, 1891)	1	5	8	7	18	3		
Theatrical Managers (1891)		1	1	3	1			
Barbers			1	1	7			
Butchers			1		9			1
Coal Merchants	1			1	2	1		
Flour, Grain, Feed Dealers		3			17			
Hardware Dealers		1		3	3			
Tinware & Stove Dealers					2			
Undertakers				3	3			
Watch and Clock Makers					4			
Wines & Liquors Dealers	1	10	1	6				

[HS-1987]

above: Regina Women's Construction Co-op, 2000

Families headed by women aged 15-64 have incomes which average half those of families headed by men. —Statistics Canada, *Women in Canada, 1985*

I don't know what feminine is, but being more confident, more capable, happier as a person, makes me feel strong as a woman.—anonymous carpenter in Kate Braid's *Women in Non-Traditional Occupations in British Columbia, 1979*

THE LONG DISTANCE RACE

What did women do once they had obtained access to new realms of endeavour? They strove for, and achieved, excellence. They excelled not only in the new professions to which they had gained admittance, but also in the traditional domains of women's expertise. This is not a recent development. Women have always achieved great things, and the stories told in *Herstory* show us that there is ultimately no limit to what they can accomplish.

This chapter features women who showed great resourcefulness and determination in taking advantage of, and broadening, the opportunities made available to them by women who had gone before. This is a celebration of diverse achievement covering a wide range of professions and pursuits. You will find here stories of women who made outstanding contributions in their field. The only common theme is women going where they haven't gone before and doing very well once they got there!

The discipline and accomplishment of athletics best typifies the initiative, resolve, and talent of the women in this chapter. An 1899 commentator suggested that "muscular capacity in women is almost evidence of disease." Nearly a century later, Canadian women athletes can still anticipate headlines like the one describing Olympic medalist Silken Laumann as "too pretty to row." But in the interim, Canadian women have more than proven their spirit and abilities. Sharon Wood, the first North American woman to reach the summit of Everest, echoed the experience of many of the women featured here: "I went beyond where I'd gone before, pushed harder, reached deeper than I've ever had to do and I still had something left. It makes you wonder what our limits really are."

opposite: Mary Morris Vaux, 1 July 1900—First ascent over 10,000 feet by a woman in Canada, Mount St Steven, British Columbia

Amid the snippets of "useful and entertaining knowledge" contained in the *Canadian Home, Farm and Business Cyclopedia* are several articles on rearing daughters. For its day, much of this material is remarkably progressive. The articles focus on bringing up not just nice, well-mannered girls, but women who are educated and trained to make their own way in the world. *Herstory* shows us many examples of women who did just that.

CANADIAN HOME, FARM AND BUSINESS CYCLOPEDIA

"If the commercial distress which visited this country between the years of 1873 and 1879 had brought us no other benefit, amidst the vast deal of suffering and ruin which occurred to a people who had been living too fast, it did this immense good: it taught women that they could work and could earn money. It has been no uncommon thing for the wife and the sister to support the family during those dreadful years, now happily past.

"Men are broken and discouraged, when the ordinary business of their lives fails them. They have not the versatility of women, they have not woman's hope. It probably seemed to many a ruined father that there was little hope in the accomplishments of his daughter. She could paint a plaque very prettily, perhaps write tolerable poetry; 'but that would not pay the butcher.' The fact remains that it did pay the butcher. One delicate woman during these dreadful years has supported seven men—seven discouraged, ruined, idle men, and she has done it very well too.... Therefore, we can never say what a woman cannot do."—*from J. S. Brown & Sons of Paris, Ontario,* Canadian Home, Farm and Business Cyclopedia, *1883.* [HS-1990]

HANNAH MAYNARD

Hannah Maynard was not one to sit idly by while her husband was exploring the gold fields of British Columbia during the rush of the 1860s. At home in Ontario, she studied portrait photography. When her husband returned to prepare to move to Victoria, she packed up her camera and equipment, planning to set up a photographic studio out west.

Her advertising said: "Mrs R. Maynard, Photographic Artist and Dealer in all kinds of photographic materials." She soon was so busy "shooting" wealthy miners and naval officers who visited the mining camps, that her husband gave up his shoe store to join her enterprise. In addition to the studio portraits she continued to do, Hannah and her husband travelled by stage coach, sternwheeler and canoe throughout British Columbia, photographing outdoor scenes. Unfortunately, many of Hannah's photographs were attributed to her husband, as people of the day didn't expect a woman to be so skilled.

While Mr Maynard was away exploring, Hannah continued in her craft, making daguerreotypes while raising her family. [HS-1979]

right: Self-portrait by Mattie Gunterman, ca 1900

In 1894 Susie married Petrus Rijnhart, who had served as a missionary with the China Inland Mission. He had been stationed in Lanzhou, the westernmost mission station in China, and had decided that his ambition was to bring the Christian gospel into Tibet, at that time still almost totally unknown to Westerners.

Shortly after their marriage, the Rijnharts embarked for China as independent missionaries, sponsored by a Toronto church. Landing at Shanghai, they spent six months trekking over 3,000 km across China to Lusan, a small town in Qinghai province on the border with Outer Tibet. At Lusan they survived a bloody rebellion. Susie's medical work won them friends, but they were unable to win a single convert.

They later moved to Tankar, a trading town closer to Inner Tibet. Their goal was still to penetrate as far as Lhasa, to "proclaim the gospel" in the capital of the "Sealed Land." In May 1898 the Rijnharts and their baby son set out for Lhasa, accompanied only by three Tibetan guides.

During a nightmarish journey the baby died, the guides deserted, and the party was attacked by robbers. In September Petrus left Susie, with her revolver in hand, while he attempted to cross a river to enlist help from some nomads. She never saw him again. After waiting for three days, Susie made her way back to China alone. She appeared, two months later, at a missionary station in Kangding in Sichuan province.

Susie returned to Canada, where she lectured on her experiences at churches across the country. While in Canada she wrote *With the Tibetans in Tent and Temple*. The book is both an account of the Rijnharts' missionary work and travels and a record of Susie's knowledge of Tibetan culture.

In 1902 Susie returned to Kangding to found the Disciples of Christ Mission to Tibet. While in Kangding, she married James Moyes, another missionary. They worked for several years in China, but Susie's health failed and they returned to Canada in 1907. She died in hospital in Chatham, attended by her sister Jennie. [HS-1996]

left: Self-portrait composite by Hannah Maynard

Feminists are asking for fundamental social and cultural change, and so I believe we must prepare ourselves for the long distance race, not for the sprint.
—Ann Dea, 1976

[Maynard's biographer, Claire Weissmen Wilks, notes that "by the mid-1890s she had moved into an eccentric universe of her own, achieving an aesthetic statement unmatched by photographers until the 1920s." Eds.]

SUSANNA CARSON RIJNHART

Susanna "Susie" Carson was born in Chatham, Ontario, in 1868. She was a member of the second class of the Women's Medical College in Toronto, graduating with an MD in 1888. Her sister Jennie also became a doctor and the two women practised together, first in London, then in Strathroy, Ontario.

For as long as people have been farming, women have been among the farmers. Indeed many Native Canadian women were the primary agriculturists, and it was only with the arrival of Europeans that women farmers were seen as unnatural. When Cindy Murray, sole operator of a Manitoba farm, went to get a bank loan in the 1980s, the bank manager insisted on classifying her occupation as "farmerette." It was not until the 1991 census that Statistics Canada recognized the individual contribution of women to the family farm.

POLLY BARBER SCOVILL

But even in the 19th century there were women of European ancestry who defied convention and oppression to become successful farmers.

"The most prosperous farmer of Sutton" was born in 1803 in Saint-Armand, Lower Canada. By the time she was 17, Polly Barber was teaching younger children and weaving to help support her family. In 1834 the Barber family moved to Sutton, in the Eastern Townships. Here Polly taught school for a weekly salary of $1 plus room and board.

Shortly after moving to Sutton Township, Polly married Stephen Scovill, a farmer with large landholdings. The couple devoted their time and energy to developing their farm. Besides the crops, they had a flock of sheep, from whose wool Polly wove substantial amounts of cloth. In 1846 the Scovill's properties were valued at $1,450.20—then a considerable sum.

Although the Scovills were successful farmers, their personal lives were marked by tragedy. Several of their children died young and in 1847 Stephen died, leaving Polly with three small children and a fourth on the way.

In this crisis and in later years, Polly proved her strength and determination. She increased the farm's

below:"Farmerettes" —Women haying near Souris, Manitoba, 1916

production of crops and livestock and even opened a clothing factory which employed several people. By 1861 her farm was valued at $5,000 and her annual recorded production figures were remarkable: 1,300 lbs of maple sugar, 1,100 lbs of butter, and 60 yards of woollen fabric.

Polly successfully raised four children, making sure that her daughters were educated, then helping them and her son get themselves established. During her lifetime she provided several of her children with land and homes. In her will she left her remaining property to be divided equally among the four children. She also stipulated that her daughters' legacies must never be included in community property agreements.

Toward the end of her life, Polly gave the original farm to her daughter Judith, and retired to live with another daughter and her husband in neighbouring Scottsmore. Polly died in 1898 at the age of 94. [HS-1996]

CORA HIND

Agricultural expert Cora Hind arrived in Winnipeg in 1882 at the age of 21. When the *Winnipeg Free Press* refused to hire her, she learned to type on the first typewriter west of the Great Lakes and worked as a legal stenographer for $6 a week before opening her own public stenography office.

Cora made her first wheat inspection in 1898, became known for her expertise, and in 1901 was at last hired by the *Free Press*. In 1904 a promising wheat crop in western Canada was attacked by black rust. Chicago wheat "experts" were called in and predicted a yield for the season of 35 million bushels. The *Free Press* wanted to challenge this estimate, which it believed was made for speculative purposes, and sent Cora Hind to make an inspection. Her estimate was 55 million bushels, which turned out to be nearly exact.

Her analyses of the size and quality of the wheat crop were so uncannily accurate, they helped determine the prices paid for Canadian wheat every year for

left: Cora Hind

As a group women have been defined and delimited, not so much by a lesser capacity for work or determination or thought, but by patriarchal custom and male authority.
—Veronica Strong-Boag and Anita-Clair Fellman, 1991

a quarter of a century. Those forecasts were not divining, but hard-headed judgments of an agricultural expert with a deep love for, and commitment to, the West.

Cora earned an international reputation, and in her seventies received an honorary degree from the University of Alberta. In her 74th year she was sent by the *Free Press* to look into the agricultural conditions of the world "wherever a study of them would be of interest and advantage to Canada." She visited 72 countries, taking two years for the journey. In addition to her newspaper reports, she wrote a book about her journey and her findings. [HS-1974]

Women have always taken responsibility for the health of those around them. The women featured here have pushed the boundaries of medicine, education, and research. They have risen to the top of their professions, and, in the process, improved health care for all of us.

MAUDE ABBOTT

Dr Maude Abbott was born in a small town in Quebec in 1869, and was raised by her grandparents. She loved the challenge of learning and matriculated brilliantly from high school with a scholarship to McGill University. She was an outstanding Arts graduate, and applied to medical school. McGill would not admit women medical students despite public support and money for such an enterprise. However, Bishop's Medical College offered to take Maude as a student. She graduated with the Chancellor's Prize and Senior Anatomy Prize in 1894, and then went to Europe to study for three more years.

Back in Montreal, Maude set up practice and continued to research and write. She was gaining respect for her work on cirrhosis and heart murmurs, and was invited into the all-male Medico-Chirurgical Society.

In 1898 McGill appointed her assistant curator and then curator of the university's medical museum. Her work and demonstrations were so thorough and popular that they were placed on the curriculum as a compulsory part of the course. Maude continued to research and write. She became internationally famous, particularly for her work on congenital heart diseases.

In 1910, eight years before women medical students were admitted, McGill awarded her an honorary MD CM and appointed her lecturer in pathology. By 1923 Maude was assistant professor of medical research.

Maude died in 1940. She had published 104 medical writings and two books. She was remembered for being the world's greatest authority on congenital heart disease, a giant in her profession, and a pioneer for the acceptance of women into the medical field. [HS-1978]

right: Maude Abbott

ETHEL JOHNS

English by birth, Ethel Johns was a young girl when her family settled on the Wabigoon Reserve in northern Ontario in 1892. Here she acquired a self-reliant nature as well as a sense of humanity which became a trademark throughout her illustrious career.

She graduated from the Winnipeg General Hospital Training School for Nurses in 1902, at a time when classroom teaching existed more in name than in fact. Young students were exploited by the hospitals as a source of cheap labour in exchange for a nursing certificate.

During the years immediately following her graduation, Ethel held a variety of positions. Perhaps the first indication of her future success came with her appointment as staff nurse of the newly created x-ray department at the Winnipeg General Hospital.

It was not long before her literary, oratorical, and organizational skills placed her in the vanguard of her profession. She sought and achieved the formation of an alumnae group at her alma mater. From here she undertook a more politically charged battle when she began to lobby for the registration of nurses. This was attained in Manitoba in 1913.

Determined to elevate her profession to a level more in keeping with the responsibilities inherent in nursing, she began a campaign, following a year at Columbia University, to secure university training for nurses. She became a relentless crusader against a predominantly male medical profession which was bitterly opposed to this objective. Largely through her efforts, the obstacles were overcome with the formation of the Department of Nursing at the University of British Columbia. Miss Johns was appointed director of nursing service and education in the department.

With this achievement behind her, she went on to broaden her nursing experience. She served with the Rockefeller Foundation, both in the U.S. and Europe. In 1929, she worked with the Cornell Medical Association project, and in 1932 was appointed to a committee to examine the grading of nursing schools.

left: Ethel Johns

...we still retain a notion that because women bear and suckle children they must be something more or less than plain ordinary beings.
—Dorise Nielsen, 1944

She returned to Canada to assume the position of editor of the *Canadian Nurse*. She worked tirelessly in this capacity to improve the dissemination of information related to health care. Following her resignation from the journal, she was involved in several projects and published a series of booklets entitled *Just Plain Nursing*. By invitation, she compiled a history of the School of Nursing at Johns Hopkins. She eventually retired to Vancouver and lived there until her death on September 2, 1968, at the age of 89. [HS-1985]

right: Maud Leonora Menten

MAUD LEONORA MENTEN

Maud Menten spent her life doing medical research, primarily at the University of Pittsburgh, from 1918 until she retired at age 71 as head of its pathology department. She was particularly recognized for cancer research and for publications—nearly 100 papers spanning 50 years of brilliant and intense effort.

Born in 1879 in Port Lambton, Ontario, she spent her early years mostly in British Columbia and finished high school in Chilliwack. She travelled alone from this small farming community to university in Toronto.

Maud graduated from the University of Toronto in 1907 as a bachelor of medicine. An outstanding student, she had already published a year earlier. In 1911 she was one of the first Canadian women to receive her medical doctorate.

By 1916, she had a PHD in biochemistry from the University of Chicago, and had co-authored another paper which is still considered fundamental to understanding the behaviour of enzymes. The Michaelis-Menten Equation, developed during research in Berlin with Dr. Leonor Michaelis and published in 1913, embodied a revolutionary biochemical concept which brought its authors immediate and lasting international recognition. Their discovery is considered even more important today than when it was made.

This was only one of many major contributions by Dr. Menten. Whether viewed as a scientific genius, a hard-working and well-trained researcher, or an admired teacher who demanded excellence, Maud Menten has left her mark in biochemistry as have few others.

Nor did her accomplishments stop with medicine. She was a student of languages and astronomy. She played clarinet. She painted. Loving the outdoors, she explored ocean beaches, swam in the Pacific, climbed and camped out in the Rockies. In her zest for life, age and gender presented no barriers.

After retirement she spent two years in research in Vancouver before ill health forced her to stop. She died in 1960 in Ontario; her ashes were interred in Chilliwack.

In 1979, the centennial of her birth, hundreds of scientists from around the world took part in the unveiling of a plaque to her memory at the University of Toronto. [HS-1991]

FRANCES EVELYN WINDSOR

Evelyn spent her life practising medicine, often in unexpected places. During WWI, she successfully applied to serve overseas. Her arrival in London was met with dismay; Canadian officials had assumed Dr. Windsor was *Mr* Windsor and had made no provisions for a "lady doctor." Evelyn was seconded to the British army, which had such provisions, but worked at the Canadian hospital. In June 1917 she married Teddy Leacock, a Calgary suitor who had followed her to London.

Evelyn continued work, but in 1918, she realized that she would either have to take leave or resign—she was pregnant. The military authorities tried to ignore her condition; in her eighth month, she had a mild illness and was immediately granted a discharge. She returned home with her son in 1918.

Back in Calgary, Evelyn resumed her practice and had two more children. By 1927, however, it was apparent that her marriage was over. She found a temporary post at the Blackfoot Reserve in Gleichen, near Calgary, and reassumed her birth name. She remained superintendent of Blackfoot Hospital and resident doctor there for over 20 years.

Evelyn had an advantage over her male colleagues. The Blackfoot women would not go to a male doctor, but they had no hesitation about going to Evelyn, who soon gained their confidence. The infant mortality rate dropped. She encouraged families to visit patients and worked with band council and Elders to improve medical conditions, but at the same time, she respected Blackfoot customs. Because she was paid by the band, not the Department of Indian Affairs, she was able to spend her time working with patients, not government bureaucracy.

When she accepted the job in 1928, it was not a

desirable one, but by the early 1930s, it was. Not only did she have a salary, but food from the band allotment; unlike some physicians in Calgary, she did not worry where her next meal was coming from. Some male doctors in Calgary wanted the suddenly attractive job and tried to get her fired. They failed because the band council was happy with her work and, as a war veteran herself, she could not be ousted by anyone claiming preference as a veteran. Evelyn retired after 20 years' service in Gleichen. [HS-1996]

FRANCES McGILL

Born in Manitoba, Frances McGill received her medical degree at age 37. Like many other women who became doctors during the early years of this century, she taught in order to earn money for medical school. In 1915 she graduated from Manitoba Medical College with the gold medal for the highest average, the Dean's prize for general proficiency, and a prize in surgical history.

Frances interned in Winnipeg, and in 1918 became the provincial bacteriologist for the Saskatchewan Department of Health. A few years later, she became the provincial pathologist. Since the RCMP in Regina had not yet established a forensic laboratory, Frances did their forensic pathology. In an era when women were not considered capable of difficult, tiring work, Frances McGill travelled with RCMP officers to investigate cases even when it involved long and arduous journeys. She travelled by car, train, horseback, and boat. She was not deterred by snow, sleet, or dust storms.

An honorary member of the RCMP, she frequently lectured on forensic medicine at the RCMP College in Regina. Her hard work and dedication, combined with her knowledge and curiosity, gave her a well-deserved reputation for excellence.

After retirement, she consulted and opened a private practice. Shortly after her death in 1959, she was honoured when Lake McGill, north of Lake Athabasca, was named for her. [HS-1987]

I have what I call Franklin's Earthworm Theory of Social Change...[it] does not come like an avalanche down a mountain, but from prepared soil. Many types like myself in the sciences spend our lives earthworming through the hard soil because we cannot accept that things are hopeless.
—Ursula Franklin, 1987

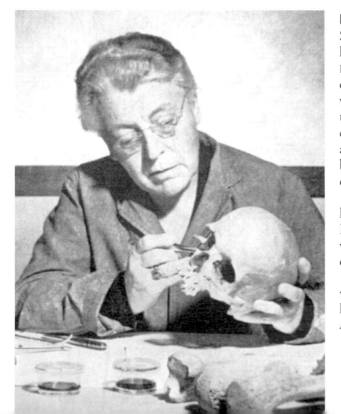

left: Frances McGill

above: Lucille Mulhall, champion woman steer roper of the world

Throughout the 1920s and '30s within Canada, women athletes achieved a status not regained to this day. Women's baseball was a major spectator sport; basketball games were carried live on radio; newspapers hired reporters whose exclusive beat was women's competitive sport.
—Abby Hoffman, 1976

right: The Edmonton Grads, ca 1915

Some of the most outstanding players through the years were Noel McDonald, Etta Don, Gladys Fry, and Margaret MacBurney. These women helped to win over ninety-six per cent of the Grads' games. [HS-1975]

[Basketball's Canadian inventor, Dr James Naismith, said simply, "The Grads have the greatest team that ever stepped out on a basketball floor." The Grads disbanded in 1940, having become household names across Canada, and having amassed one of the best records of any sporting team. None of the Grads was ever paid. Eds.]

FANNY "BOBBIE" ROSENFELD

The story of Fanny "Bobbie" Rosenfeld is one of courage and indomitable spirit. Described as a natural athlete, the talented and versatile Bobbie was named Canadian woman athlete of the first half-century by the press in 1950, and elected to the Canadian Sports Hall of Fame for her achievements in national and international competition.

Born in 1903 in Russia, Bobbie came to Canada with her family as a child. Her athletic prowess manifested itself early, and the young woman became the star of championship basketball, ice hockey, and softball teams in Ontario in the 1920s; she also excelled at golf. In 1924 she won the Toronto grass court tennis championship and a year later astounded spectators at the Ontario Ladies' Track and Field Championship when, as the sole entry of the Patterson's Athletic Club of Toronto, she placed in every event on the pro-

Much has been said to discourage women from competitive sport. Fortunately, many of them didn't listen.

THE EDMONTON GRADS—
BASKETBALL'S REAL "DREAM TEAM"

Basketball was invented by a Canadian in 1891. By 1900 women were playing the game. In 1914, J. Percy Page began coaching a girls' basketball team at McDougall High School in Edmonton, which later became the world famous Edmonton Grads.

Between 1915 and 1940, this team of women students and graduates of McDougall played 522 games in Canada, the United States, and Europe, winning 502 and losing only twenty (two to men's teams).

They won the international Underwood Trophy so consistently, defending it forty-nine times, that in 1940 they were given permanent possession of it. From 1924 to 1936 the team attended four Olympic Games, playing twenty-eight exhibition games and winning them all.

duced a column that was as outspoken, spirited, candid, and humorous as its author. In the 1950s she gave up writing and transferred to the newspaper's promotion department. She retired in 1966 and died three years later, after a valiant struggle against her debilitating disease. [HS-1979]

left: Fanny "Bobbie" Rosenfeld

THE 1928 OLYMPIC RELAY TEAM

In 1928 a contingent of seven women—six of them track and field athletes—were the first women to represent Canada officially at the Olympic summer games. Those Games also marked the first time track and field events were open to women in Olympic competition.

It was a development that did not meet with wide approval. The manager of the Canadian team argued that women were neither strong enough physically nor tough enough emotionally to stand the strain of competition. Nevertheless, with two gold medals, one silver, and one bronze medal to their credit, the 1928 women's track team was more successful than any Canadian women's track team has been since.

According to a 1970 study, eighty-seven percent of Canadian sports stories are about male athletes, "a striking anomaly... since...Canadian women have always done better than men in international sport."
—S. F. Wise and D. Fisher, Canada's Sporting Heroes, 1974

gramme—four firsts and two seconds—in events as diverse as discus, long jump, and hurdles. At the 1928 Olympics in Amsterdam, Bobbie won a silver medal in the 100-metre sprint (with another Canadian entry, Ethel Smith, coming in third) and a gold medal as a member of the women's relay team, which set an Olympic record of 48.4 seconds for the 400-metre relay.

But for Bobbie, tragedy followed triumph. Only one year after her victory in Amsterdam, she was crippled by arthritis. She spent eight months in hospital and more than a year on crutches. Refusing to concede defeat, the young athlete fought her way back to health. Two years later she was again leading her softball league in number of home runs. "What was I supposed to do, become an invalid?" she asked.

Bobbie eventually turned to coaching, then joined the Toronto *Globe and Mail* as a sports columnist in the early 1930s. For the next two decades this "strong-minded, outgoing individual with a broad sense of humour," as she was described by contemporaries, pro-

below: The 1928 Olympic relay team: Florence Bell, Myrtle Cook, Ethel Smith, Fanny Rosenfeld

right: Alexandria High School women's hockey team, ca 1928

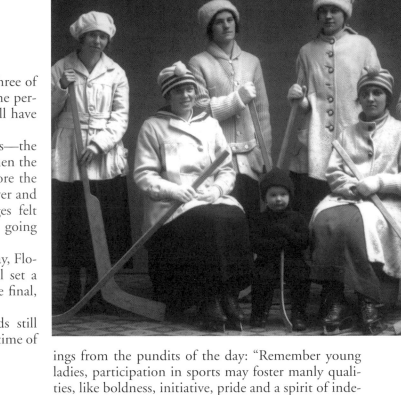

Members of the relay team accounted for three of those four medals. Indeed so outstanding was the performance of the Canadian team that it may well have ensured that women's events were retained.

Prior to the very first event—the 100 metres—the predominately male audience were unsettled when the three Canadian finalists hugged and kissed before the race. Fanny Rosenfeld and Ethel Smith won silver and bronze, in a finish so close that several judges felt Rosenfeld had won, the dispute eventually going before the League of Nations to be settled.

In their primary event, the 4x100 metre relay, Florence Bell was running injured. The team still set a world record in their heat, broke it again in the final, and won the gold. [HS-1999]

[Their world record time of 48.4 seconds still compares favourably with the 2000 gold medal time of 41.59. Eds.]

below: Ethel Catherwood

ETHEL CATHERWOOD

Ethel Catherwood, the first woman Olympic Gold Medal winner in Canada, broke the world record in women's high jump at the Amsterdam Olympics in 1928, by jumping 5 feet 3 inches. Besides being the world champion woman high jumper, she also excelled in baseball, sprinting, basketball, and javelin, in which she held the Canadian record.

The Saskatoon native was named to the Amateur Athletic Union of Canada's new Hall of Fame in 1950 for her outstanding athletic achievements. [HS-1974]

WOMEN "HOCKEYISTS"

While Canadian Manon Rheaume was rightly celebrated on 13 December 1993 as the first woman to play in a regular-season professional hockey game, history seems to have forgotten that Canadian women have, in fact, been playing hockey since before the turn of the century.

These pioneers faced social censure and dire warn-ings from the pundits of the day: "Remember young ladies, participation in sports may foster manly qualities, like boldness, initiative, pride and a spirit of independence." In this environment, it is a wonder that any female athletes of exceptional ability emerged. However, numerous women's clubs thrived. Throughout the 1930s the Preston Rivulettes were the undisputed national champions, compiling an astounding 348-2 win/loss record.

Since that time, women's hockey has achieved an increasing prominence and popularity. The Ontario Women's Hockey Association, established in 1975, is unique in the world and epitomizes the co-operative approach that women have taken to promote their game while emphasizing "fun, friendship and fair play."

The Canadian Women's National Team has repeatedly won the International Ice Hockey Federation's World Championship. The number of Canadian women participating in the sport has increased dramatically and acceptance of women's hockey as a full-medal sport at the 1998 Olympics will likely encourage this trend. [HS-1996]

[Canadians celebrated when their women's hockey team won the Olympic gold medal in Salt Lake City in 2002, no longer "hockeyists" but athletes in their own right. Eds.]

As women become CEOs and entrepreneurs in ever greater numbers, we can be inspired by the stories of those who fought for, and achieved, independence, power, and success.

DOROTHEA MITCHELL

The advertisement read: "Desired, an educated young woman as Companion-help to Superintendent's wife in mining camp, N.W. Ontario. Some office duties." And that was how Dorothea Mitchell, newly arrived in Canada after being raised in England and India, found herself at Silver Mountain mining camp. Dorothea's job as "Companion-help" was short-lived. Silver Mountain mining camp soon shut down, but Dorothea promptly created her own job. She persuaded the CNR to take her on as agent and caretaker of the Silver Mountain railway station, as well as taking on the duties of the local postmistress and storekeeper.

This later position led to Dorothea becoming the "lady lumberjack." Men who ran logging and milling operations in the area often paid for supplies with lumber when they were short of cash, and Dorothea soon found herself finding buyers for her own and other people's wood. She soon established herself as an astute businesswoman. The first time a buyer tried to cheat her on a lumber contract, she travelled to Winnipeg, conducted her own investigation, sued, and won her case.

By 1914, Dorothea Mitchell was running a logging camp of 20-30 men, and had bought her own sawmill. She managed her own business completely, trekked out on snowshoes or skis to inspect her own lots, and often stacked lumber on railway cars herself. Dorothea was also determined to become a woman of property. Undaunted by the current policy of granting land only to men, Dorothea applied for homestead rights north of Port Arthur. Her application was reluctantly accepted by the Crown agent, and she became the first single woman to be granted homestead rights in Ontario.

At age 44, Dorothea went into the real estate-insurance business in Port Arthur, ending twelve years in the Canadian bush. She continued to be very active in local business and community affairs, going in and out of retirement as new projects caught her interest. She died in Victoria, BC, at the age of 94. [HS-1978]

Other days, other ways— and these are other days, when a woman is not regarded as an oddity if she expresses in practical affairs some talent for getting things organized and underway.—Dorothea Mitchell, 1967

IRMA WRIGHT
TORONTO
4 TIMES CANADIAN CHAMPION
WORLD'S AMATEUR
CHAMPION 1928

left: "The Fastest Fingers in the World." Irma Wright was billed by the nation's press as "Canada's top secretary" but she was not content to remain in that role. A forceful woman, she kept her maiden name after marriage when it was unfashionable to do so and encouraged secretaries to seek executive positions.

MARY PICKFORD

Gladys Louise Smith was born in Toronto on 8 April 1892. Better known as Mary Pickford, she became "America's Sweetheart," and the most powerful woman in the fledgling film industry.

Despite the innocence of her silent film persona, she shrewdly managed her career in an era that treated film actors as labourers. Offered five dollars a day for her first job with D.W. Griffith in 1909, Mary demanded ten: "You realize I am a stage actress and an artist." She consistently maintained this unprecedented stance of artistic integrity, accepting work only on her own terms. By 1917 she was commanding an astounding $350,000 per film. At the age of 25 she was writing screenplays, overseeing editing and even producing her own films. Her company, Pickford Corporation, aggressively marketed films in other countries, increasing immeasurably the scope and impact of cinema.

In 1919, with Douglas Fairbanks, Charlie Chaplin, and D.W. Griffith, she formed United Artists. It was her strategy to avoid the stranglehold of an impending monopoly that would undermine actors' efforts to gain artistic control over their productions. Despite her commitment to the integrity of her craft, Mary was always humble about her own talents. Her failure to make the transition from silent films to "talkies" was due less to limited acting ability, than to the practical recognition that her popularity had been based on mastery of the childlike ingenue that was now out of fashion: "I decided...that if I were only to be a semi-precious gem, to be frankly that rather than a paste imitation of something more glittering and gorgeous." She continued producing movies for 15 years.

Mary Pickford was the first and possibly the most powerful female movie mogul ever. She pioneered the first era of Hollywood filmmaking, seized and held power longer than any other woman in movie history. [HS-1996]

I've worked and fought my way through since I was twelve, and I know business.—Mary Pickford

...women belong in the corridors of power. The more women are seen as a legitimate part of the business power structure, the more equal our society will become.
—Heather Reisman, 1985

right: Mary Pickford

called Olive: "a sturdy pioneer nurse with the true missionary spirit. In a little log house, with one end equipped for 2 hospital beds and the other for her own living quarters, this intrepid worker cares for the sick, nurses patients in the district, shows mothers how to care for their children, and brings into her place those which she cannot nurse in their own homes."

Olive's work was typical of that done by nurses in areas with few, or no, doctors [see p. 20]. Not only was their work vital to their communities, it allowed them to use their skills—and satisfy their love of adventure. [HS-1991]

MOLLY LAMB BOBAK

Critics have described her work as "exhilarating, even astonishing," with "an expansive and celebratory spirit," but what surely makes Molly Lamb Bobak's art so accessible is the sincerity she brings to her work, painting "out of sheer joy."

Molly was born in Vancouver in 1920. Her father was an early supporter of the Group of Seven; Molly grew up in a household where artists were frequent visitors and art was regularly discussed. At the Vancouver School of Art, Jack Shadbolt was one of her teachers. He took Molly's art seriously and that proved to be the catalyst for her: "I never looked back after he came....I knew exactly what I wanted to do forever."

top left: Olive Ross

In four years of war, nursing sisters from Canada had earned a high reputation while making their special contribution to the cause of humanity, justice and freedom.—G.W.L. Nicholson, 1975

below: Marching to the train at Victoria, BC, August 1915. Nursing sisters of No. 5 Canadian General Hospital begin the long trek that would take them to Salonika.—G.W.L. Nicholson, *Canada's Nursing Sisters,* 1975

Women served with distinction in the war efforts of the last century, whether on the home front, or on the front lines.

NORTHERN NURSES

Thousands of Canadian nurses served during World War I. After the war, many, including Olive Ross, went west to seek new adventure.

Olive Ross was born in Edmonton in 1881 and trained at Montreal's Royal Victoria Hospital. When World War I broke out, she went overseas as a member of the Ninth Canadian General Hospital Unit.

After the war, Olive, like other veterans, needed adventure. She combined her love of challenge, her faith, and her profession when she accepted the position of nurse and hospital director at the Presbyterian Women's Missionary Society Hospital in Fort McMurray.

In 1930, the Women's Missionary Society, in *Healing the Sick: Our Hospitals and Foreign Work,*

right: Molly Lamb Bobak

*I cannot imagine
a more beautiful life.*
—Molly Lamb Bobak, 1978

*Despite the heavy workload...
I believe that most farm
wives are happy to stay on
their farms. What they find
frustrating is that their
labour is neither recognized
nor adequately rewarded.*
—Norma Taylor, 1976

below: Plucking chickens

In 1942 Molly enlisted in the Canadian Women's Army Corps (CWAC) [see p. 153] and began a journal: "W1 10278: The Personal War Records of Private Lamb M." Observant and humorous, these journals detail the ordinary routine of life in the CWAC. Gradually, Molly's art came to the attention of the Committee for War Records Artists. Her "headline" of 24 May 1945 says it best: "LAMB'S FATE REVEALED! 2/LIEUTENANT REELS IN STREET! TO BE FIRST WOMAN WAR ARTIST! 'THIS,' SAYS OFFICER, 'IS IT.'"

Molly was sent overseas with the other Canadian war artists. She did not see any fighting, but was witness to the aftermath of war: "...grim...everyone was exhausted, frustrated, and poor....There was much black marketing and violence...the Europeans just wanted to pick up what they could of their lives and be left alone."

As Canada's first female war artist, Molly achieved national prominence, although it is fairer to say her own dedication and commitment to her craft brought her recognition. After the war, with a young family, Molly found time to pursue her art when she could: "I think of my kids and the garden and the houses we built by hand. I didn't paint that much....I had great energy, but I had kids and a house and I taught night school...."

Molly takes her subjects from events and objects around her: crowds, wildflowers, interiors. She has become an internationally recognized artist. Shadbolt described Molly's work as capturing "the everyday poetry of life." She states simply, "I want people to share it and it's an absolute delight to me that they do." [HS-1996]

A FARM WOMAN'S WAR

The years of the Second World War were busy ones for farm women. Able-bodied men were scarce—most of them had gone off to war—and women were called upon to take their place. In addition to her regular chores in the home (and the garden, and with the chickens, and all those other duties handled by the farm wife), she now shouldered the work of the hired hand.

A number of women even took on the whole responsibility of the farming operation, and managed handsomely until fathers or husbands or brothers returned from the front line.

"Three years ago today my father died and a year later my brothers left to join the forces. I took over the farm and have carried through the cold winters and hot summers. I specialized in pigs and have sold as many as 100 hogs in six months, which should be some bacon. I have increased the beef cattle to 50 head and started in registered Herefords, besides getting some sheep. Last but not least come the chickens. I raised 200 last year and sold eggs all winter, as well as canning 50 quarts of cockeral [sic] meat for the summer.

"I am a very busy woman, but I love it...mother carries on and does the housework which for a lady of her age is something, but yet, that is her part. We managed to can 65 quarts of vegetables and 100 of fruit.

"As I write this I feel if my Dad could see the old home and the improvements...he would be very proud to think a girl of his could put on overalls and keep the home together until the war was over and the son came back."—*Gertrude Forbes, Two Hills, Alberta, in the* Western Producer, *1943* [HS-1978]

polychaete taxonomy. [see p. 141] Edith's daughter, Alfreda Needler (kneeling) received a doctorate from the University of Toronto in the early 1930s and researched red tide marine organisms until her untimely death in 1951. Fourth generation daughter, Mary Needler Arai (toddler) has ably carried on the tradition of scientific research and teaching and is presently full professor in the Department of Biology, University of Calgary. [HS-1988]

[Mary Needler Arai has now retired from teaching. Eds.]

left: A family of scientists

The beautiful phenomena attending moonrise and moonset and sunrise and sunset, the annual showers of shooting stars, Venus as evening star, the old moon in the new moon's arms—all these and many more were just as enjoyable and just as attainable for me as they would be if a giant telescope were standing at my side.
—Dr Helen Sawyer Hogg, astronomer, The Stars Belong to Everyone: How To Enjoy Astronomy, 1976

ALICE VIBERT DOUGLAS

A distinguished scientist and warmly human person, Dr Allie Vibert Douglas was outstanding both as an astrophysicist and as dean of women at Queen's University. Born in Montreal in 1894, Douglas began her university career as a student at McGill. During the First World War, she worked as a statistician for the British War Office and was made a Member of the Order of the British Empire in recognition of her service.

After the war, she returned to Montreal and completed her BA and MSC at McGill. In the early 1920s she returned to Britain to study at Cambridge under A.S. Eddington, one of the most distinguished astrophysicists of the day. In 1925 she completed her PHD at McGill. She lectured in astrophysics at McGill from 1923 to 1939, when she was appointed dean of women at Queen's. She was also a professor of astronomy at Queen's from 1946 to 1963.

Her research and writing centred around her interest in the spectra of the very hot A and B type stars. She served a term as president of the Royal Astronomical Society of Canada and was a fellow of the Royal Astronomical Society (UK). She was also frequently a Canadian delegate to conferences of the International Astronomical Union.

During the twenty years she held the position of Dean of Women, "Dr D." was known as a good friend and unfailing source of help and understanding for

below: Alice Vibert Douglas

S cience, unfortunately, is still an area where women are a relative rarity. The contributions of these women show what a loss that is.

A FAMILY OF SCIENTISTS
Martha (Treglohan) Dunington (seated in the photo above) married when a career was not believed compatible with a woman's family role. She never actively pursued a science career, but she made certain her daughters had a good education. She encouraged Edith (standing) to study science. Edith Berkeley taught zoology at the University of British Columbia in 1916 and became a world-recognized expert in

right: Elsie Gregory MacGill

As women have become better educated, choice overlaps necessity. Educated women want to work, ideally at a job that corresponds to their intellectual skills.
—Myrna Kostash, 1982

Queen's women. She was influential in persuading Queen's to open medicine and engineering to women students. In recognition of her scholarly work and her work for women, Dr Douglas was the first Canadian president of the International Federation of University Women. She was made a member of the Order of Canada in 1967 and was named one of ten "Women of the Century" by the National Council of Jewish Women.

After her death in August 1988, as a final tribute to a loved and respected colleague, astronomers named one of the recently discovered minor planets "Vibert Douglas." [HS-1990]

MARGARET NEWTON

Cereal grain farmers all over the world owe a large debt to Margaret Newton. One of the first two women in Canada to study agriculture at university, she became interested in cereal grains during her academic career. While an undergraduate at McGill, Margaret discovered the "presence of physiological races in rust." Her discovery was essential in conquering the wheat rust that destroyed over 100 million bushels of wheat in 1916.

She received her PHD in 1922 from the University of Minnesota and by 1924 was the leading Canadian authority on cereal rusts.

In 1925 she was invited by the Minister of Agriculture to head a team at an agriculture research centre in Manitoba. She accepted the appointment and her reputation grew.

She was frequently invited to speak around the world. In 1930 she travelled to Russia to train 50 students in the problems of rust research. She was asked to take charge of their research program, but declined in order to stay in Canada.

Margaret Newton received many honours, including a fellowship in the Royal Society of Canada. She was the first woman to receive the prestigious Favelle Medal of the Royal Society of Canada. [HS-1987]

above: Margaret Newton

ELSIE GREGORY MacGILL

Elizabeth Muriel (Elsie) Gregory MacGill was a pioneer in Canadian aviation. She graduated from the University of Toronto in 1927, the first woman with a BSC in electrical engineering, and in 1929 received a Master's degree in aeronautical engineering at Michigan. In 1929, she also contracted acute infectious myelitis, and was told she would never walk again. Elsie returned to Vancouver, where she worked to regain her health and wrote articles on aviation. Later, Elsie continued graduate work.

In 1934 Elsie became assistant aeronautical engineer at Fairchild, where she worked on the prototype of the first Canadian all-metal airplane. She also became the chief aeronautical engineer at Canada Car and Foundry, heading the project that developed the Maple Leaf Trainer, used extensively by Commonwealth air forces.

Soon, she had a more challenging task. Only weeks after the start of WWII she was assigned the task of building Hurricanes—the aircraft that would be crucial in the Battle of Britain. Within a year she had renovated an old factory, staffed it with 4500 workers and was producing three Hurricanes a day.

Newspaper interviewers in the 1940s seemed amazed at Elsie's feminine appearance and that she enjoyed bridge, knitting, clothes, and parties. She was described as "a pint sized girl in a modish suit, with a mop of curls and a piquant face." A 1941 *New York Herald Tribune* headline proclaimed "No Job for a Woman," reporting her appointment as head of the Hurricane project. Her response was, "I'm an engineer, and I do what all engineers do, that's all."

In 1943 she established a consulting company in Toronto and married Bill Soulsby. In 1946, Elsie became the first woman to serve as a technical advisor to the International Civil Aviation Organization, and in 1947 was appointed chair of the stress analysis committee. Elsie received many honorary degrees and professional awards, was inducted into the Canadian Aviation Hall of Fame, and became an officer of the Order of Canada in 1971.

Elsie's belief in equal opportunity and equal pay was evident throughout her career. A member of the Royal Commission on the Status of Women, she impressed fellow commissioners by her astute analysis and by her strong feminism. She died in 1980. [HS-1989]

ELINOR F. E. BLACK

Elinor Black entered medicine at the University of Manitoba in Winnipeg in 1924, at 19, in spite of opposition from every member of her family except her sister Charlotte. Her brother Donald, also a doctor, told her that women were a nuisance in medical schools.

But she stayed, and established a string of firsts for Canadian women: member of the Royal College of Obstetricians and Gynecologists (1938), and Fellow (1949); head of a major medical department (Obstetrics and Gynecology, University of Manitoba/Winnipeg General Hospital (1951); president of the Society of Obstetricians and Gynecologists of Canada (1961).

Six feet tall, with the erect bearing of an athlete, Elinor could be intimidating, but she was also a woman of passionate friendships, inspired by women like Dr Lillian Cringan-McIntyre and Dr Geraldine Oaldey, who had held regular clinics in the Calgary public schools when Elinor was a pupil there.

Her family moved to Winnipeg when she was twelve. There she joined the Canadian Girls in Training, and later, as an undergraduate, met Gertrude Rutherford, who developed the Student Christian Movement. Her lifelong friendship with Rutherford, who had faith in women as professionals and policymakers, helped counteract the negative attitude of her family to her work.

Elinor entered practice at the beginning of the Depression, in a basement office in Winnipeg, on money borrowed from friends. In later years she was unstintingly generous to students, colleagues and friends. The university took four years to accept her

I speak to over 1,000 school children each year (many in rural settings) and still get gasps of amazement when "Dr Hickson" appears and lo and behold, Dr Hickson is a woman! I hope that in my lifetime "Dr" or "PhD" won't immediately conjure up a male image.
—Catherine J. Hickson, vulcanologist, 1993

I need a car...it's for Dr Black. And tell the driver—Dr Black is a woman.—Elinor Black to dispatcher

left: Elinor F. E. Black

right: Sylvia Fedoruk

resignation, and was obliged to greatly increase the budget of the department to replace her. She had been subsidising a salary of less than $6,000 from her private practice, and had been doing without secretarial or lab assistance.

Her writing in the 1940s often focused on the potential dangers and abuses of the hormone therapies then coming into fashion in gynecological practice. It was not until the 1980s that women's health movements began publicly to raise the same questions. She did not live to see it; she died in 1979. [HS-1995]

SYLVIA FEDORUK

In 1986, medical physicist and champion curler Sylvia Fedoruk became the first woman chancellor of the University of Saskatchewan. Characteristically, she described university administration as a team effort and herself as a new recruit to the team.

There is risk involved in everything we do.
—Sylvia Fedoruk, 1986

Enrolling at the university in 1946, Sylvia graduated with distinction and high honours in physics in 1949. She was awarded the Governor General's Gold Medal for most distinguished graduate, the Spirit of Youth Award for top female graduate, and shared the Copland Prize awarded to the top scholar in the College of Arts and Sciences. Excelling in athletics as well, she played on 12 inter-university championship teams. She has been inducted into the Canadian Curling Hall of Fame, the Saskatchewan Sports Hall of Fame, and the University Wall of Fame.

One can but have one's heart and hands full, and mine are. I have love and work enough to last me the rest of my life.
—Anna Jameson

Upon completing a Master's degree in medical radiation physics in 1951, Sylvia began lecturing at the University and helped develop the first cobalt therapy unit, now used in cancer treatment around the world. It was a team effort again, in 1962, when she helped design and build a super-sensitive scintillation camera to detect cancer cells. In 1965, she became Director of Physics with the Saskatchewan Cancer Foundation, responsible for the Regina and Saskatoon clinics.

Recognized as one of the country's leading medical

physicists, Sylvia served as the first woman on the Atomic Energy Control Board of Canada. She was named YWCA Woman of the Year and received the Saskatchewan Award of Merit. [HS-1988]

[Sylvia Fedoruk served as Lieutenant Governor of Saskatchewan from 1988-1994. She has received many accolades for her outstanding career, including honorary degrees, the Order of Canada, the Saskatchewan Order of Merit. The Sylvia Fedoruk Prize is given annually to the best paper in medical physics by a Canadian, published worldwide. Eds.]

MABEL TIMLIN

"I am satisfied that my life as a whole has been a 'plus' rather than an 'equals' or a 'minus' and that should be enough for anyone."

In 1912, Mabel Timlin began a career as an elementary school teacher. After several years she joined the University of Saskatchewan as secretary to a professor. Later she became a professor herself—in the field of economics. Her book *Keynesian Economics,* published in 1942, gained her an international reputation. In

1959 Mabel Timlin became the first woman elected president of the Canadian Political Science Association.

Regarded as an authority on economic theory, monetary policy and immigration, her retirement did not mark the end of her research and writing career. The Canada Council invited her to accept a special fellowship to conduct research into Canada's immigration policy. [HS-1976]

[Mabel Timlin died in 1976 in Saskatoon, the city where she had worked for so long as a distinguished researcher, scholar, and teacher. Eds.]

Herstory is proud to reclaim the achievements of women whose work behind the scenes was often overshadowed by those they influenced and supported.

DAISY PETERSON SWEENEY

Like many other black women in Montreal in the 1930s, Daisy Peterson Sweeney began her working life as a domestic, taking the only job available to her,

left: Mabel Timlin

for $4.50 a week. Racism was so pervasive that even a job cleaning toilets at the children's hospital was denied to her. She recalled "...they weren't the worst of times, but these were attitudes you had to rise above."

Daisy rose above them. Her parents bought a piano at the beginning of the Depression, realizing that the family would not be able to afford any other entertainment. They taught Daisy to play and she taught her younger siblings. At 19, she was paying more than half her weekly wage for music lessons with well-known pianist, Paul de Marky; at 25, she had earned a diploma from the McGill Conservatory and was teaching full-time.

Although widely regarded as an accomplished musician, Daisy did not seek a career as a public performer, due to her father's constant pressure to excel. Once, just before she was to play a solo, her father repeatedly admonished her not to make any mistakes. "Well, I made a mistake at the beginning, middle, and end. And I always remembered it. And from that time on, if I had to play, I was just a bag of nerves. I never enjoyed playing in public again."

Fortunately for more than one generation of Montreal children, Daisy chose to teach. She is credited with the formative musical training of a number of Montreal's jazz greats, among them Oliver Jones and her own younger brother, Oscar Peterson. "She was the strongest musical influence I had," states Oliver Jones.

Daisy refuses to take credit for her work with such famous musicians. "I hate to say I taught Oliver, because whatever you gave him to do, he came back with it accomplished—he was such a gifted person. It was the same thing with Oscar."

She remembers, rather, a student who had difficulty learning music: "I didn't have a clue how I was going to teach her." By the year-end recital, they were able to play a duet. "That, I think, was my greatest achievement."

In 1987 Daisy Peterson Sweeney's accomplishments were recognized by Laurentian University with the award of an honorary doctorate. [HS-1992]

I have taught simply because I think music plays such an important part in a child's life.
—Daisy Sweeney, 1987

Where both male and female teachers were available—at all levels of study—it was frequently the women who had the highest reputation, judged not only on student achievement, but also on the reports of the individual students.
—Sandra Gwyn

right: Helen Creighton

Traditionally, women's creative output has been considered craft rather than art, and hobby rather than profession. Canadian women, however, have made their mark in cultural industries from the Junos to Juilliard and from Lynn Lake to Las Vegas.

HELEN CREIGHTON

Dr Helen Creighton is internationally known as a collector of folklore, especially folksongs of the Maritimes. Since 1943 she has recorded more than 4,000 folk songs, as well as folk tales, games, dances, instrumental music, and samples of dialect. Four honorary degrees are some measure of the recognition accorded her.

Dr Creighton was born in 1899 in Dartmouth, Nova Scotia. While on a writing assignment in 1928, she asked fishermen in that province if they knew any pirate legends. One old man commented that when he died many of the yarns and songs he sang would die too. She realized that these songs should be written down—they were part of Nova Scotia's history and portrayed the lives, experiences, and thoughts of the people.

Her first tools were pad and pencil; at first it was difficult work to set down the tune. Someone then gave her an antique melodeon, a small organ on which she could pick out the tunes; she toted it around for four years. Helen had no income during this time, but her parents shared her enthusiasm and paid her expenses. By 1931 she had enough songs to make up a fat volume, and the following year *Songs and Ballads of Nova Scotia* was published. The book was not a best seller, but it was highly praised by critics and firmly established Helen Creighton as a folklorist.

After 14 years of effort in this field, Helen was finally financed when she was awarded a scholarship by the Rockefeller Foundation. She was later awarded two more scholarships, and after that, the Library of Congress in the United States subsidized her until she was engaged as a field worker by the National Museum

below: Lily Inglis

of Canada in 1947. During this time she also received Canada Council grants. In 1967 Helen retired from the National Museum in Dartmouth.

She has written numerous books, articles, and stories, has lectured extensively, broadcasted and recorded many songs. Her autobiography was published in 1975. [HS-1976]

[Helen Creighton died in 1989 having received many accolades for her life's work, including six honorary doctorates, appointment as Honorary Life President of the Canadian Authors' Association, and the Order of Canada. In her home province, both a Folklore Society and a Folklore Festival have been named in her honour. Eds.]

LILY INGLIS

As a young girl in Milan, Italy, Lily Inglis developed a strong interest in architecture. During a childhood illness she was confined to her bed, where she spent hours drawing and constructing three-dimensional miniature buildings from paper. She is now a partner in the Kingston, Ontario, firm Inglis and Downey Architects Inc., a Fellow of the Royal Architectural Institute of Canada, and winner of numerous awards for renovating and recycling old buildings praised particularly for their seamless incorporation into their environment.

As a 12-year-old, Lily was sent to a British boarding school. When the Second World War broke out she found herself in Britain, having finished school and wanting to be an architect. Determined to pursue her career, Lily apprenticed with a Cheltenham firm before attending the University of Edinburgh's School of Architecture. In 1953 she married James Inglis, an Edinburgh psychologist, and began a six-year architectural practice in London. At night, she also studied landscape design.

Lily's career took a new direction when the Inglises moved to Kingston in 1959. The large number of stone buildings in the city impressed her and she was inspired to preserve this heritage by incorporating it into functional designs. She chose to work out of her home while caring for two daughters, but found that "as an architect in North America, working out of the house and being a woman meant two strikes against you."

Over the years, Inglis has developed a more aggressive attitude in her professional life. She finds she must re-establish her credibility with each new construction job, especially when the workers don't expect a woman. "They don't take you seriously until the work gets underway and technicalities come up and you can actually solve the problems with them." Her buildings testify to her talent, determination, and sensitivity to architecture's importance to the quality of life. [HS-1988]

[Lily Inglis continues to work as an architect and advocate for the preservation, restoration and re-use of heritage buildings. Eds.]

ELEANOR MILNE

Eleanor Milne, federal government sculptor since 1962, must wait until members of parliament leave for the day before her crew can install the works prepared in the workshop. In her position, Milne is responsible for all new and historic statues and carvings in federal buildings in Canada and abroad.

Eleanor was chosen through a national competition. They sought an artist who "could work with wood, glass, plaster, stone; offer advice on restoration, interior decorating and building materials; research historical themes; and make written and verbal presentations."

She began her studies at the Montreal Museum School of Fine Art. Thinking a painter should know about the human form, she studied anatomy at the McGill School of Medicine. While she was there, renowned brain surgeon Wilder Penfield asked her to sketch his operations and document his research.

Eleanor moved to England, planning to be a wood engraver and book illustrator. Realizing that publishers preferred photographs, she instead studied sculpture

below: Eleanor Milne

right: Mary Scorer

*My parents didn't attend
any of the award ceremonies.
They expected me to do well.
If I came second they asked
why I didn't come first.
If I came first, well then,
I should have anyway.*
—Eleanor Milne, 1989

and stained glass as her "other media." Her graduate studies with Yugoslav sculptor Ivan Mestrovic at Syracuse University determined her focus. As a sculptor she was versatile and prolific, winning rave reviews.

Before her appointment in 1962, Eleanor received commissions for wood engraving, book illustrations, stained glass, oil painting, and watercolours. She won many awards and prizes and participated in exhibitions.

While overseeing construction of the family country house for her father, an accomplished marine engineer, she became comfortable with construction sites and crews. Media reports which focus on her distinction as a female sculptor and ignore the men who work with her on every project have created her only problems with the crew.

Eleanor has designed stained glass windows for the House of Commons, and completed many smaller projects for Parliament Hill and other legislatures in Canada. She has completed designs for sculptures in the Parliament Buildings and is committed to stay on until each one is in place. The citation at her investiture in the Order of Canada in 1989 said her works "have added immeasurably to the beauty of one of Canada's great national treasures." [HS-1991]

[Eleanor Milne was Dominion Sculptor until 1993. She lives and works in Ottawa. Eds.]

MARY SCORER

In 1959, Mary Scorer opened her bookstore on Kennedy Street in Winnipeg. A woman starting a business was unusual then, but Mary Scorer Books proved to be a unique idea whose time had come. Mary eagerly supported and encouraged writers and poets of the prairies, and the shop became a meeting place for book lovers of all kinds: "Writers came to discover other writers; historians spent hours thumbing through journals and books of days gone by. It was a store where the general public, visiting dignitaries—even members of the Royal Family—found a good book to read," recalls her protege John Oleksiuk.

In 1967, Mary established one of the first publish-

below: Jean Sutherland Boggs

ing firms in western Canada, Peguis Publishers, and challenged traditional approaches by promoting local history and Native issues. In 1973, after Peguis was up and running, she sold the bookstore to John. There are now three Mary Scorer bookstores in Winnipeg and one in Saskatoon.

When Mary died at the age of 77, the reading public lost a friend. John remembers her dedication and generosity: "She had a passion for literature and cared deeply about what people read. She worked with librarians, historians, teachers, ministers and students and even gave free advice to those thinking of opening their own bookstores." [HS-1990]

[In 2001 Peguis Publishers was renamed Portage & Main Press "as the Aboriginal connection no longer exists," according to new owner Mary Dixon. The bookstores have closed. Eds]

JEAN SUTHERLAND BOGGS

When Jean Sutherland Boggs headed the National Gallery of Canada from 1966 to 1976, she was the only woman in the world to hold such a position. It is interesting to note that the gallery was founded by a woman—Princess Louise—and that Boggs' appointment was made by yet another woman, Judy LaMarsh, then Secretary of State.

SHEILA FISCHMAN

left: Sheila Fischman

Sheila Fischman has been translating books from French Quebec for 17 years, and loves it. Perhaps the best-known Canadian translator, she may be the only one to make a living from her work. She has translated over 30 titles, including almost all of Roch Carrier's, and has received the Canada Council Translation Prize twice.

Sheila was reading by age four and spent much of her childhood deep in the world of books, more to her liking than helping in the family store in Ontario. After earning degrees in chemistry and anthropology, she married and moved to Quebec's Eastern Townships, where translating seemed the perfect way to improve her French. When a friend suggested a book she might start with, Sheila accepted. The book was *La Guerre, Yes Sir,* by Roch Carrier, then unknown outside Quebec. Sheila's "carrière" was launched.

She often works seven days a week, six hours a day without a break, steeping herself in a text. After hours of polishing, a third or fourth draft may begin to read as if it had been originally written in English. Or, she may spend hours looking for "le mot juste" and wind up going for a walk or heading for the kitchen—"ceiling dusting," she calls it, "anything which helps put off a stubborn passage."

Hers is highly disciplined, solitary work. She tries to be true to the spirit and the original text. She does not tinker with authors' ideas, regardless of her own feelings. Says Sheila, "That's the difference between being a translator who is content to be a translator and one who is a frustrated writer." Canada Council grants pay about ten cents a word, double what they were ten years ago. Sheila doesn't translate for the money, but for a love of books and a sense of place in a bicultural country. For Canada to have a truly national literature, French and English must be mutually accessible. That requires translation. Her satisfaction lies in making Quebec's literature available throughout Canada while staying hidden herself, like a good actor deep in a role. [HS-1988]

[Sheila has translated more than 100 Quebec novels, among them all of Roch Carrier's novels and sto-

Rire. C'est la seule façon de survivre. —Sheila Fischman, 1986

I rate success differently from just making money. I see it as being able to do lots of things that improve the quality of life. —Lily Inglis, 1985

Under Boggs' direction, the National Gallery blossomed. During that time over sixty per cent of all acquisitions were Canadian. She stressed the importance of the relationship between museums and the community: "there should be a strong regional flavour expressed in buildings, staffs, programs and collections," she said. She believes that "meaning rather than beauty, justifies a preoccupation with works of art."

Preparation for her position included studying with Arthur Lismer at the Montreal Museum of Fine Arts, museum training under Paul Sachs at Harvard, thesis study in Europe, and teaching in American colleges and universities. She has an international reputation as an author, art historian, and hard-working administrator. She has written four books, one of which, *The National Gallery of Canada,* has received wide acclaim.

Jean Sutherland Boggs has suggested that "Canada is almost a haven for women in the arts." Certainly the National Gallery was during her tenure, when 44 per cent of the professional staff were women. [HS-1978]

[After leaving the National Gallery, Jean Sutherland Boggs continued her distinguished international career as art historian, curator, and museum director. As CEO of the Canada Museums Construction Corporation, she oversaw the construction of both the new National Gallery building and the Canadian Museum of Civilization. Although there was not another female director of the gallery until the 1987 appointment of Dr Shirley Thomson, women continue to be well represented at the National Gallery as curators, directors, managers and on the Board of Trustees. Eds.]

ries; she has received numerous awards for her work, including, twice, the Governor General's Literary Award for Translation. In 1989 and again in 1990, she received the Félix-Antoine Savard Translation Prize given by Columbia University. She has received honorary degrees from the universities of Ottawa and Waterloo, and, in 2000, was named to the Order of Canada. Eds.]

DIANE THORNTON DUPUY

On the first day at school in Hamilton, Ontario, Diane Thornton was called "a retard" because she was a little different. That insult struck home and she never forgot it. As a small child she developed her already vivid imagination with the help of a puppet theatre. From her mother she learned how to work hard. Perhaps her most important assets were an amazing determination to get her own way, coupled with a boldness that allowed her to accost important people and badger them into doing what she wanted.

right: Diane Thornton Dupuy

In 1974, the 26-year-old Diane decided to create a professional puppet theatre company called the Famous People Players (FPP), whose members were mentally handicapped. She had first to overcome the fears and reluctance of the parents and agencies responsible for these young adults. Next, she had to get the company recognized and supported by the professional entertainment world. Her first and greatest supporter was Liberace, whom she got to a performance by devious means. He was immediately won over, and invited the Famous People Players to work with him in Las Vegas.

From this beginning the company has continued to succeed. It regularly tours the United States and Canada, has been to China and, in 1988, had a show on Broadway. Diane herself has received the Order of Canada and the B'nai B'rith Woman of the Year award. She was the first Canadian to receive the Library of Congress Award and the first winner of the Ernest Manning Award for "developing a unique idea or concept without association with a professional laboratory or research facility."

Diane admits she can be very demanding of the people who work for her. Because she expected the highest professional standards of her players, they achieved them. Because she refused to treat them as less than other people, the Famous People Players is not a sheltered workshop. Because Diane Dupuy demanded of everyone what she expects from herself, they are a professional theatre company. [HS-1994]

[Famous People Players continues to attract celebrity support. Using proceeds from Paul Newman's Newman's Own products, and the contributions of musician Phil Collins, FPP established in Toronto the first dinner theatre in the world for people with special needs. It provides skills training for both new members and those retiring from performance. A second troupe continues to tour worldwide. The company has received an Ontario Lieutenant Governor's Award for the Arts (1995). Diane Dupuy has authored two books: *Dare to Dream* and *Throw Your Heart Over the Fence*. Eds.]

MAUREEN FORRESTER

Maureen Forrester has been triumphantly acclaimed in the United States, throughout Europe, the Scandinavian countries, Russia, and Australia, as well as at home in Canada. Jan Peerce, the American tenor, said of her: "It is a rare pleasure to see and hear such a performer in action. This lady is a great pro, a delightful colleague, and a glorious artist."

Born in 1931, in Montreal, Maureen quit school at thirteen, and worked at a variety of jobs. At one point she was working at a switchboard in the morning, taking vocal lessons in the afternoon, and entertaining in the evening. She sang in the Montreal St. James United Church Choir, and spent two years singing for Les Jeunesses Musicales du Canada, touring and performing on both sides of the continent.

The turning point of her career occurred when she attended a concert given by the Dutch baritone, Bernard Diament, for whom she later auditioned. He took her on as a pupil in 1951, and continued to coach her throughout her career. Her formal Canadian debut was at the Montreal YWCA in 1953. By 1956 she was prepared for her debut at New York City's Town Hall. The reviewers were unanimously enthusiastic. She then set out on a triumphant European tour, singing with the leading orchestras of London, Berlin, Amsterdam, Oslo, and Paris.

She speaks four languages and sings fluently in nine. In addition to giving concerts, singing the lead in operas, and making numerous recordings, she has also taken on pupils herself. Her career has been interrupted only briefly by the birth of her five children. [HS-1975]

[Among the most superb interpreters of Mahler's songs the world has ever known, Maureen is celebrated as "one of Canada's musical ambassadors." She has made more than 130 recordings, received countless awards and honours—among them over 30 honorary doctorates—and a place in the Juno Hall of Fame. She was made a Companion of the Order of Canada in 1987 in recognition of her outstanding contributions to Canadian music. In the 1980s, she chaired the Canada Council and served as chancellor of Sir Wilfrid Laurier University, which has established a music scholarship in her name. In 2000, Maureen received the Ruby Mercer Opera Award. Eds.]

JANINA FIALKOWSKA

Born in Montreal in 1951, Janina began piano lessons with her mother before she was five. At 10 she appeared with the Montreal Symphony, and by 17 she had completed her bachelor of music and master of music degrees at McGill University.

The next year, 1969, she won first prize in the Radio Canada National Talent Festival and moved to Paris to study. In 1970 she entered New York City's Juilliard School of Music. Eventually, convinced she had no future in music, she applied to law school. But first she travelled to Israel to compete one last time in

I can sing the morning I'm giving birth, and even during. It doesn't bother me....It's just the conductors who get nervous.
—Maureen Forrester

left: Janina Fialkowska

the Artur Rubinstein International Piano Master Competition. She placed third, but Rubinstein said about her playing, "For me she was a revelation. I have never heard any pianist play the great Liszt Sonata with the power, the temperament, the understanding, the beauty of tone, and above all, the emotion and the complete technical command she has shown in her performance." She forgot about law.

Rubinstein invited her to New York and asked her to play Bach, Beethoven, Schumann, Chopin, Liszt, Ravel, Debussy, and Prokofiev. Janina played for hours, to the point of physical exhaustion. Rubinstein became her mentor, tutoring her in structure, rhythm, articulation, and projection to the audience. "He took me completely under his wing and launched my career." His manager arranged appearances for her, and her ability soon established her reputation. Following in Rubinstein's footsteps, however, was major pressure for a young pianist and for six months Janina could not perform because of nervous exhaustion.

Rubinstein died in 1982, and Janina has become a prominent pianist, performing to critical acclaim with major orchestras around the world. Of her performances critics say: "There is no grandstanding, only detail and balance," and "...one was almost afraid to breathe for fear of breaking the spell cast by Fialkowska."

She is renowned as a Liszt virtuoso. In 1990 she was invited to perform the world premiere of a newly discovered Liszt concerto with the Chicago Symphony Orchestra. Hers is the thrill of interpreting a musical work for the first time, and having all future performances measured against hers. [HS-1992]

[Janina Fialkowska continues to record and perform and has founded "Piano Six," a group of internationally renowned Canadian pianists committed to bringing affordable recitals of important classical music to Canadian communities where such performances are rare. She tours regularly and is a guest artist with many of the world's best known orchestras. In 1992, Janina was the subject of a television documentary film which received a special jury prize at the San Francisco International Film Festival. Eds.]

right: Lynn Johnston

LYNN JOHNSTON

Most of the 40,000,000 readers of the family comic strip "For Better or For Worse" would be surprised to learn that it originated in the small community of Lynn Lake, Manitoba, more than 800 km north of Winnipeg. Its creator, Lynn Johnston, arrived there in 1978 with her husband Rod; Aaron, a son from her first marriage; and Katie, three months old. Lynn had been employed as a medical artist, sometimes doing freelance work as well, and had already produced three volumes of cartoons. *David, We're Pregnant* sold more than 100,000 copies.

Lynn's work caught the interest of Universal Press Syndicate, which initiated a 20-year contract for a daily cartoon strip. "For Better or For Worse,"

in northern Manitoba, the Johnstons moved to North Bay, Ontario. Though she sometimes worried about so minutely examining family life where traditional roles are magnified by climate and distance from the outside world, Lynn expressed regrets about leaving Lynn Lake. 'The isolation...the variety of friends... and the closeness of the people...provided the perfect environment in which to work and raise children.'

Whatever Lynn's uncertainties, they seem to provoke the "sort of tension that breeds invention," as one commentator noted. "Lynn...is the first syndicated cartoonist to portray the laughter and tears of family life from a woman's perspective. She does it with a sensitive and a knowing élan." [HS-1985]

["For Better or For Worse" now appears in more than 2,000 newspapers worldwide in 22 countries and eight languages, reaching over 220 million readers in print. Lynn has published over 28 books and inspired television specials, videos, and merchandise. She was the first woman, the first Canadian, and the youngest artist ever to win the National Cartoonists Society's prestigious Reuben Award for Outstanding Cartoonist of the Year in 1985, and in 1992, received the Best Syndicated Comic Strip Award from the NCS. In 2001 Lynn was awarded the B'nai Brith Canada, Media Human Rights Special Award for her sensitive portrayal of diversity and human rights in her cartoon strip. Eds.]

left: Marie-Louise Gay

MARIE-LOUISE GAY

In 1985 Marie-Louise Gay, one of Canada's best children's illustrators, won Canada Council illustration awards in both French, for *La Drôle d'école,* and English, for *Lizzy's Lion.*

Her lively, provocative drawings, highlighting her own stories, enchant children on both sides of the Atlantic. *Moonbeam on a Cat's Ear* (Canadian Library Association Prize, 1987) was immediately translated into French *(Voyage au clair de lune)* by its bilingual author. *Rainy Day Magic (Magie d'un jour de pluie)* and *Angel and the Polar Bear* followed. In French or

appeared in 1979, bought even before its debut in 120 newspapers around the world. Lynn works at home, spending each morning sketching with impressive speed. She generally submits several weeks' cartoons at one time.

From the beginning the comic strips have been "an unabashed ripoff" of Lynn's own family life. Almost anything husband or children say or do is likely to turn up in the lives of her cartoon characters, Elly and John, whose domestic life emerges with a tender yet lightly sardonic turn.

In 1984, facing the uncertain economic situation

English, they appeal directly to the "universal language of children."

Marie-Louise had a nomadic childhood and an early education entirely in English. She hesitated between being an actress or teacher. At eighteen she "got the design bug—and was off." She studied graphics, then spent two years at the Montreal Museum of Fine Arts. She freelanced and did a children's book simply because she hadn't done one. "I was just having a good time."

In San Francisco, she realized that by addressing children she could do more than just have a good time. More books followed, along with a return to Montreal. No longer satisfied to work on stories written by others, she began to illustrate her own. The third, written for six-month-old son Gabriel, grew into *La Drôle d'école,* Canada Council prizewinner.

At the Bologna International Children's Book Fair, Marie-Louise revelled in imagery and took to heart a comment on her work—"It's beautiful, but it's not your own life." She started drawing what she saw, felt, knew best. Her little people aren't beautiful, with their big heads and small hands, but to her young readers they are real. Children are captivated by and identify with the fantastic world which emerges from Marie-Louise's pen.

Marie-Louise talks with youngsters and gets ideas from her own sons, Gabriel and Jacob. She likes writing for three- to eight-year-olds who "are open to everything...their imaginations...still fluid."

Gay also teaches illustration, designs puppets, costumes, and sets, and illustrates children's clothes. She nourishes her own spirit through travel, from each place "stealing a little colour and light," but her first love is creating children's books. [HS-1989]

[Still in Montreal, Marie-Louise has now written and illustrated 30 books (published in over a dozen countries), and her drawings have been exhibited in major cities around the world. She has received many honours, including two Canada Council awards, two Governor General's Awards, Mr Christie's Book Award, the Ruth Schwartz Award, and the Elisabeth-Mrazik Cleaver Award. Eds.]

I didn't enter the business world with any kind of notion that I wanted to be one of the establishment boys or I wanted to beat the system. That wasn't ever part of my agenda. I just wanted to find something that satisfied my desire to accomplish things in this world. Really, that's my prime motivator. I just wanted to get things done.
—Ellis Galea Kirkland, award-winning architect and urban planner, 1992

right: Pauline Jewett

"Life is just too short to do things you can't stand." These are the words of Louise Chevalier, the first Canadian woman to train as a test pilot. This is also the spirit of countless Canadian women who have followed their bliss and achieved great things along the way.

PAULINE JEWETT

The 1974 appointment of Dr Pauline Jewett as president of Simon Fraser University makes her the first woman in Canada to head the administration of a large coeducational university.

Born in St Catherines, Ontario, in 1922, Dr Jewett received her BA and MA in politics and economics at Queen's University, completing her PHD in government at Harvard and her post-doctoral work at the London School of Economics. She taught at three universities and held four administrative posts, including Director of Carleton University's Institute of Canadian Studies from 1967-1972.

Her interest in public policy resulted in several publications and an active role in politics, She was a Liberal MP, vice-president of the Liberal party, vice-chair of the Committee for an Independent Canada, and, in 1972, a federal NDP candidate.

In her university role, she envisions the institution as an essential organ for social change—a place for the research necessary to make change possible and for discussion of social policy and the role of government in education. She is working to take the university to the community, to make its resources available to a broader segment of the population. She also advocates the hiring of more Canadians and more women to faculty and senior positions in Canadian universities. [HS-1976]

[Pauline Jewett died in 1992 leaving a legacy as a respected scholar, social reformer and role model to many women. In 1993 Carleton University renamed its Institute of Women's Studies in her honour. Eds.]

ELLEN BRUCE

Old Crow, an isolated Gwich'in community in the northern Yukon, has been Anglican for a century. For more than half those years, Ellen Bruce has served her people. Licensed as a lay reader in the early 1980s, she became a deacon in 1985. In 1986, she received an honorary Doctor of Divinity degree from Edmonton's St Stephen's College. In 1987, Ellen became the first northern Native woman to be ordained in the Anglican Church.

Reverend Doctor Bruce was born in 1911 at Rampart House, a small trading post. Living in a tent, her family moved about following caribou and moose. Religion was vital, particularly for Ellen, whose grandfather had been a lay catechist trained by the first Anglican missionary to the Gwich'in. Ellen's father carried on his work and passed on that knowledge to Ellen.

Her involvement in the organized church began in 1929, when a native minister came to Old Crow and taught in the people's own language. Ellen led the Women's Auxiliary and readied the church for services.

left: Ellen Bruce

Ellen, her husband, and children hunted and trapped in the bush, spending only summers in town, until 1949. Ellen took more responsibility in the church, helping her father and later taking his place, speaking in church, visiting the sick, and conducting services in homes.

Since 1925, 10 white and three Gwich'in ministers have served in Old Crow. Through all the changes, the people have maintained their traditions and Ellen has gradually become spiritual leader. She continues to be a source of strength and stability for a community undergoing rapid social change.

Old Crow's young people describe the encouragement and support "Auntie Ellen" embodies, and their dependence on her. For all her people, she is a model to follow with pride. [HS-1990]

[The Rev. Dr Ellen Bruce was honoured for her lifetime contribution to her community with membership in the Order of Canada in 1991. Eds.]

One of the ladies that I'd written about had passed away and her family requested that a couple of wardens be there in dress uniform because her husband had worked for Parks... We were standing outside when a fairly elderly woman from near the park came up to me and said, "It's good to see one of our own doing this job."
—Cyndi Smith, National Park Warden, founder of Coyote Books and author of *Off the Beaten Track*, a chronicle of women mountaineers, 1991

right: Joan Donaldson

JOAN DONALDSON

Joan Donaldson was the driving force behind the creation of CBC Newsworld. She dreamed of highlighting the regions in Canada, of letting them tell their stories to each other.

Joan began her career as a switchboard operator on an open-line radio show in 1964. "Aggressive and curious," she found that she was passionate about news, especially "passionate to get it right." She moved to the CBC in 1967 as an editor with *National Radio News,* soon becoming Senior Editor of *The World at Six, Sunday Morning Magazine,* and various news specials.

Joan produced the evening news show in Winnipeg, and *Newsmagazine* in Toronto, before spending five years as field producer for CTV's *W5.* Tiring of the "selfless grind of manufacturing television news," she taught broadcast journalism at Ryerson and in the Journalism for Native People program at the University of Western Ontario. Her students work across Canada and around the world.

Donaldson returned to the CBC in 1983, as coordinator of regional programming. "My job took me coast to coast and I was really knocked out by the quality of the programs in the different regions. At the same time, it was very frustrating, because a lot of really good work was being shown once in one location and never seen again."

Donaldson, then 43, was appointed head of CBC Newsworld in 1987, and built the network from scratch. Although born there, she made sure that Toronto played a minor role; most of the major programs were based in other locations. She hired newscasters to satisfy her concern that women and minorities be prominent on the channel.

Colleagues describe her as a "cut-the-crap" journalist who cherished folk art and doted on her cats, a demanding leader who won admiration and friendship among her staff, a workaholic administrator who always found time to offer a friendly ear or counsel former students.

Joan's career ended suddenly in 1990 when she was hit by a cyclist in Montreal. The accident caused a brain injury that brought on a coma. Joan eventually

I think that people have lots of ideas and views to share with each other that have nothing to do with politics, but with the realities of their lives.
—Joan Donaldson, 1988

Women are emerging as the solution people.
—Susan Nelson Pier, 1991

recovered from the coma, but remains severely impaired and unable to resume her career.

The staff of Newsworld carry on without her, working to fulfill her dream. [HS-1993]

[The Joan Donaldson Newsworld Scholarship was established in 1999, to "honour a person who can serve as an icon for the increasing numbers of women reaching positions of power in the media." Eds.]

MAY EBBITT CUTLER

Tundra Books has gained international recognition for the quality of its art and children's books. This reputation can be attributed to its founder, May Ebbitt Cutler.

Outspoken, innovative, and uncompromising, May Cutler stressed the importance of quality of design and production as well as content. The results have been a noticeable improvement in the quality of children's books available in Canada, and an impressive string of awards for Tundra Books.

May founded the press in 1967, having concluded that "people, especially women, don't get anywhere unless they establish their own businesses."

A graduate of McGill University and the Columbia School of Journalism in New York, May first worked as a journalist on a major Montreal newspaper, and then taught English at McGill.

Following marriage and the birth of four sons, she continued to juggle the demands of family and a writing career. One of the first books published under the Tundra imprint was an essay for which she won first prize in the Centennial Commission Literary Competition.

May's passion for excellence has sometimes made her critical of her fellow Canadians, whom she sees as a people generally dedicated to the pursuit of mediocrity. It is not one of her sins. [HS-1978]

[May Ebbitt Cutler ran Tundra books for three decades before selling it to McClelland & Stewart. From 1987 to 1991, she was the first female mayor of Westmount. Her 1997 attempt to stage her own children's musical inspired a campaign for greater support of Canadian content in the performing arts. In her 1998 Hugh MacLennan Lecture, delivered at McGill University and titled "Fear of the Original: A Canadian Phobia," she derides the timidity of Canadian producers and asks: "are we going to grow up, to demand, to dare, to recognize, to nourish and appreciate?" Eds.]

WENDY CLAY

The appointment of Wendy Clay to the post of Surgeon General, the first woman to be so honoured, is only the latest in a series of firsts she has achieved throughout her 29-year career in the Canadian Forces. Since graduating from the University of British Columbia in her home province and completing an internship in Toronto in 1968, she has been unstoppable.

She was posted to Trenton, Ontario where she trained as a flight surgeon—the first woman ever to do so. She then became base surgeon at Canadian Forces Base Moose Jaw, Saskatchewan, where, in 1974, she was the first woman to earn pilot's wings in the Forces. As a specialist in aviation medicine, she felt it was important "to get a better understanding of the stresses [facing] air crews." She flew Tudor jets, the same type of aircraft used by the Snowbird aerobatic team, and still cites her pilot's wings as her proudest accomplishment.

Wendy advanced steadily through the military ranks, becoming lieutenant colonel in 1977, colonel in 1982, brigadier general in 1989, Deputy Surgeon General in 1992, and finally major general and Surgeon General simultaneously in 1994. She is the only woman ever to have reached the rank of major general in the Canadian Forces. She also held a number of important administrative posts throughout this time, among them command surgeon at Air Command Headquarters in Winnipeg and commandant of the National Defence Medical Centre in Ottawa.

Her career has also taken Wendy beyond Canada's borders. She was assigned to a six-month peacekeeping tour in the Middle East.

The role of women in the Canadian military has changed dramatically in the past quarter-century, and Wendy is cited as an exemplar of that change. As her colleague Commodore Michael Shannon, who predicted in 1989 that she would one day be named Surgeon General, has said of her: "She has blazed the trail—a very impressive lady." [HS-1996]

[Major-General Wendy Clay retired from the Canadian Forces in June 1998. Eds.]

above: Wendy Clay

Can we hope that the day is not far off when our achievements will be judged on their own merits, rather than over-praised because we are women?—Mrs Dawson, *Ladies Alpine Club Journal*, 1931

left: May Ebbitt Cutler

right: Denise Verreault

DENISE VERREAULT

A woman is at the helm of Verreault Navigation in Les Méchins, Quebec. Denise Verreault, her sister and mother inherited the family's shipbuilding company when her father died suddenly in 1982.

Denise knew nothing about shipbuilding except what she had learned as a child watching her father repair his fishing boats. Only twenty-four years old, she had completed her BED with the intention of teaching school. "We started by going to the filing cabinet and looking inside." The company's work eventually earned the confidence of initially reluctant clients and it prospered, moving from the repair of small fishing boats to large ships with steel hulls.

La société a beaucoup évolué et elle ne voit pas pourquoi une femme ne réussirait pas aussi bien qu'un homme dans un même domaine. L'évolution de la société fait qu'aujourd'hui autant une femme qu'un homme peut saisir une opportunité qui se présente.
—Denise Verreault, 1989

With about 85 employees, her company is the major employer in the Les Méchins area. While waiting on repairs, ships' crews remain in the area for four or five weeks at a time; local hotels, taverns, and restaurants benefit. Denise feels the economic health of the community is more important than her company's profits: "Je sais très bien que les opportunités d'affaires sont plus nombreuses dans une région comme Montréal ou Québec, mais j'ai la région à coeur. C'est mon coin de pays et je considère que j'ai une mission de développement ici."

Denise instituted a welding course at the local polyvalente to train women for her company. She feels women can work as well as men, using different, sometimes better work skills. This policy was not initially popular with the male staff, but her reassurances and their faith in her leadership soon allayed their fears.

If it is true that satisfying work liberates, then I became a truly liberated woman.
—Thérèse Casgrain, *A Woman in a Man's World*, 1972

Denise firmly believes that the company's success is rooted in the mutual respect between her and her employees. She has absolute confidence in and profound respect for their work: "Nous sommes tous embarqués dans le même bateau. Le balayeur qui voit à ce que les planchers soient propres est aussi important que moi à l'administration." [HS-1991]

[Verreault Navigation has expanded with Denise Verreault still at the helm as president of Groupe Maritime Verrault, Inc., which wholly owns and operates four companies specializing in ship construction, conversion, and repair. In addition, Denise has served on numerous boards and committees including the St Lawrence Seaway Management Corporation, and the minister's advisory council on oceans. She was named Woman of the Year for her business acumen in both 1991 (Montreal) and 1995 (Matane), and Businesswoman of the Year in 1999. Denise was named "chevalier de l'Ordre national de Québec" in 2001. Eds.]

ROBERTA BONDAR

Roberta Lynn Bondar, neurologist, clinical and basic science researcher, and Canadian astronaut, pursues her scientific studies with dedication and enthusiasm. Since her selection as a member of the Canadian astronaut team in 1983, her schedule has become more hectic, but she enjoys the "chance to fulfill my lifelong dream of an adventure in space."

Born on 4 December 1945 in Sault Ste Marie, Ontario, Roberta grew up in a supportive home environment. She credits her parents for giving credibility to her childhood interests, and her sister for providing sustained support. Roberta earned a PHD in neurobiology from the University of Toronto in 1974, and an MD from McMaster University in 1977. In 1981 she was admitted as a fellow of the Royal College of Physicians and Surgeons of Canada. She has won numerous fellowships, scholarships, and awards, including a Career Scientist Award from the Ontario government in 1982. An honorary member of the Girl Guides of Canada, Zonta International, and the Canadian Federation of University Women, Roberta was selected as an Outstanding Young Canadian by the Jaycees of Canada in 1985.

Roberta's participation in the Canadian Astronautic Program includes parachuting, flying, and training at the Johnson Space Centre. She is also a research fellow at two Toronto hospitals, is on leave from McMaster's Faculty of Medicine, spends three days a week on clinical work, and serves on several professional committees.

When speaking about the space program Roberta stresses the peaceful uses of space technology, including its potential "for land resource management and the provision of medical care to remote communities." She also speaks to schoolgirls to encourage them to participate in science programs, recognizing that social factors continue to influence and discourage women's participation in science-related fields. [HS-1989]

[In 1992, Roberta Bondar became the first Canadian woman in space as payload specialist aboard the space shuttle Discovery. She has been made an Officer of the Order of Canada and is the recipient of over 20 honorary degrees. She has returned to her scientific and personal interest in photography, publishing, most notably, *Passionate Vision,* a millennial commemoration of Canada's National Parks. Eds.]

Women are indeed in the long distance race. *Herstory* celebrates with these athletes the triumph of women's victories over tremendous odds and daunting obstacles. Most of all, we cherish their successes.

VICKI KEITH

By the time Vicki Keith retired from marathon swimming in the summer of 1991 at the age of 30, she had set 14 world records, raised more than $800,000 for charity, and achieved the status of a national hero.

Growing up in Kingston, Ontario, Keith was an unlikely athlete: "I had never been good at any sport in my life; I was the last pick for team sports. I had no reason to believe I could do my first swim." But she had the necessary strength of will to attempt the impossible, and she was never one to turn down a dare. In 1985, inspired by the *Guinness Book of World Records* and egged on by friends, she set her first world record with a twelve-mile butterfly swim in Lake Ontario.

Keith followed her first effort with one new challenge after another, notably a double crossing of Lake Ontario in 1987, and a crossing of all of the Great Lakes in the summer of 1988, both firsts in marathon swimming. Subsequently she completed several daunting international swims using the butterfly stroke, including: the English Channel, the Juan de Fuca Strait, and the Catalina Channel.

Keith's secret is the ability to focus on her goals and to maintain her faith in herself. She relished the challenges, "the fight—with yourself, with the elements—making it through adversity." She never underestimated the elements. Prior to the Lake Superior leg of her Great Lakes swim she described herself as "very respectful of the lake," and before salt water swims she made "a pact with her hosts," abstaining from seafood for the preceding six months.

She has persevered against high winds, dangerous currents, jellyfish, sharks, and hallucinations induced by sleep deprivation and hypothermia. Her closest call

I found a long time ago that the best way for me to learn about myself is to measure myself and my limits during all sorts of situations, whether I'm flying, or scuba diving, or backpacking in the Rockies .
—Captain Louise Chevalier, 1978, first Canadian woman (and youngest person ever) to be enrolled at the United States Jet Test Pilot School at Edwards Air Force Base

left: Roberta Bondar

was in the 11°C Juan de Fuca Strait, where she finished her swim in an advanced state of hypothermia. She considers it her toughest swim and the one she is most proud to have achieved.

Keith has developed a lasting association with Variety Village, a Scarborough athletic facility for disabled children to which she donates money. She has worked with disabled children, teaching them to swim, since she was 10 years old. "Water is freedom for them; they can move around for the first time. Pools are essential." [HS-1993]

[One of the greatest female swimmers of our time, Vicki Keith has set 17 world records. She has received numerous honours, including the Order of Canada (1992), has been inducted into the Swim Ontario Hall of Fame (1993), and, on the 10th anniversary of her record-setting swim across all five Great Lakes, the city of Toronto named "the most famous arrival and departure point" for her Lake Ontario swims, Vicki Keith Point. Vicki continues to raise thousands of dollars for young people with special needs. Eds.]

You do not really know who you are until you know what you can fully achieve. That is what makes living worthwhile.
—Sharon Wood, 1986

right: Vicki Keith

SHARON WOOD

On 18 May 1986, Sharon Wood celebrated her twenty-ninth birthday—on the north face of Mt Everest, two days away from being the first North American woman to reach the summit. Only four other women had stood at the top of the world before her. But shyness almost cost her the opportunity. Exhaustion, cold, and thin oxygen had taken their toll on most of the climbing team, as they prepared to make the final assault. Sharon hung back until the group leader urged her to speak up: "For God's sake, don't be so Canadian. If you want it, let's do it!"

Sharon was born in Halifax and raised in Vancouver from age six. She began rock climbing in Jasper at age seventeen. Training the mind as well as the body is important in a field where life-threatening circumstances are commonplace. Climbers also learn from their mistakes. For Sharon, climbing Mt Huascaran, the highest peak in Peru, in the heat of the day, was one of them. The sun had softened the ice and snow, dislodging a rock which broke her shoulder: "I found that as long as I held together mentally, I could do it. I had significant pain and I used the right arm for climbing, but it was the kind of pain I could transcend. It was fascinating for me. I could survive."

It took twelve hours for Sharon and fellow climber Dwayne Congdon to reach the summit of Everest, battling winds of more than 150 kilometres per hour: "We hugged each other....We looked around and then Dwayne gave me heck for holding one of the flags upside down as he took pictures." But the descent nearly ended in tragedy. They became separated when Dwayne ran out of oxygen and had to move more slowly. They rendezvoused at their campsite, suffering from frostbite and hypothermia. There the pack stove exploded, singeing Sharon's face and setting the tent ablaze. They completed the descent the next day: "I feel very privileged to be the first North American woman to get to the top....But it's hard to feel special when I'm around eleven [others]...who worked just as hard to make this a success."

Sharon has other notable achievements. In 1977 she was a member of the first all-woman team to climb Mt Logan, Canada's highest peak. In 1983 she conquered Mt

McKinley, North America's highest, and the following year Mt Makalu in Nepal. She has also scaled Argentina's Mt Aconcagua, highest in the western hemisphere. Sharon, the first winner of the Breakthrough Award for women in Canada, feels that the Himalayas may yet hold some challenges for her: "I went beyond where I'd gone before, pushed harder, reached deeper than I've ever had to do and I still had something left. It makes you wonder what our limits really are." [HS-1989]

[Sharon Wood became the first woman to be certified a Canadian Climbing Guide, and to be admitted to the International Association of Mountain Guides. She received the inaugural Tenzing Norgay Award as "Professional Mountaineer of the Year" from the American Alpine Club and the [New York] Explorers Club, and was also recipient of a Governor General's Award for meritorious service, and an honorary doctor of laws degree from the University of Calgary. She has parlayed over 20 years of climbing experience into a career as a professional motivational speaker. Eds.]

JACQUELINE GAREAU

In 1980, Jacqueline Gareau won the Boston Marathon in 2:34:28. In the 1982 Boston race, where she placed second, her time of 2:29:27 put her on the list of the world's ten fastest female runners and achieved a new Canadian women's record. Her 1983 performance at the World Championship Marathon in Helsinki earned her fifth place in the 42-km race, and fifth place on the world list. In 1984 she won an International Marathon in Los Angeles.

Jacqueline feels she was born to do just what she does. She began to run at the age of 20. In her job as a respiratory technician in Montreal, she saw people whose every breath was a major effort. She sought change in her own life as the importance of good health became more and more apparent to her. "I felt I was suffocating in the city, always surrounded by four walls. Then I realized I was shutting myself in. I began to walk to work, to go bicycling, camping, climbing, skiing, and quietly, I began to run."

She ran quite casually at first, only one or two miles a day, gradually increasing her distance. Those who watched her run were quick to realize that she was special. She thrived on distances which casual joggers couldn't face. Little by little, the idea of running competitively began to grow, and in 1977 she entered her first marathon. Her time was 3 hrs 45 mins.

She never stops wanting "to do better the next time...to be the best in the world." To reach that goal she trains daily; her weekly distance of 160 km and more includes hill training, sprinting, and endurance work. A former coach says that his biggest problem was always stopping her from doing too much: "She'll cycle 60 kilometres, run 40 kilometres, and then swim for a couple of miles."

Three years after her first marathon, she entered the Boston Marathon and became famous both for winning and for having to wait a full week to be declared the real winner, over another runner who appeared in mid-course, crossed the finish line first and claimed the victory. [HS-1985]

[Jacqueline's first place finish marked the last time a

left: Joan Oliver at Needle Peak, Lake Louise, 1936

In life, the great thing is to have challenges, no?
—Jacqueline Gareau, 1980

Canadian has won the prestigious race. More than 20 years after winning the Boston Marathon, Canada's Female Marathoner of the Century, is "semi-retired," but still running. Eds.]

SILKEN LAUMANN

Whenever you are given a gift, whether it be in music, art or sport, it is wonderful if you can experience it to the fullest.... I want to see how fast is fast for me, and discover how good I can get.
—Silken Laumann, 1991

On 16 May 1992, Silken Laumann was at the zenith of her rowing career. As defending world-champion single sculler, the 27-year-old Mississauga, Ontario, native was competing in what should have been a routine pre-Olympic meet in Germany. However, less than three months before the Barcelona games, Canada's uncontested gold-medal hopeful and female athlete of the year was the victim of a freak accident during warm-ups. In a collision with a German pairs team, her boat was destroyed and her right leg injured so extensively that doctors told her she might never row again.

right: Silken Laumann

Such predictions underestimated Laumann's determination and drive. Less than month after her accident and still unable to walk without a cane, she was back in her boat training to compete in the Olympics: "I remember the doctor in Germany telling me I'd have to accept that I wouldn't be coming to Barcelona. They seemed very concerned that I was still keen on rowing, but I just couldn't envision not going."

This kind of tenacity is not exceptional in the life of an athlete who has had to defy convention in a traditionally male sport. Although she was successful enough to train with the men's team, Silken Laumann had to prove to herself that the increased physical demands of the sport did not undermine her femininity: "There is a conflict between having a muscular body and being a woman....On one hand, you want to get strong and be the best but people think that bigger means uglier...now I look at my muscles, and I think it's great. I think it looks good. It's taken me a long time to get that way." Well before she reached Barcelona, Laumann had already battled headlines such as "Too pretty to row," and limited funding in a sport which is not as marketable as the more "feminine" pursuits of gymnastics and figure skating. [HS-1994]

["Canada's Comeback Kid" went on to win a bronze medal at Barcelona and silver at the 1996 Olympics, before retiring from the sport. In 1997, Silken Laumann was the first non-American to receive the Wilma Rudolph Courage Award. She was inducted into Canada's Sports Hall of Fame in 1998. Eds.]

SYLVIE FRÉCHETTE

"You watched me swim, now watch me dance," were the words of Sylvie Fréchette on learning she had been awarded an Olympic gold medal for solo synchronized swimming—14 months after the competition. The events leading to this unusual circumstance are a testament to Fréchette's perseverance and dignity. There was apparently no resentment that "le plus beau jour de ma vie" was so long delayed.

performance of my career," a judge's computer error mistakenly awarded the gold medal to her closest competitor. The erroneous decision was upheld, and Fréchette returned home in the wake of a series of personal tragedies which included the suicide of her fiancé one week before the games: "There have been times this past year when I was afraid to cry because I knew that if I started I might never be able to stop."

Fréchette's refusal, then or since, to criticize or complain has earned her world-wide admiration. The gold medal the Olympic Committee finally awarded her on 6 December 1993, was an overdue accolade for a woman who, in the eyes of the world, had already earned gold for a display of courage and self-control befitting not only a gifted athlete, but a sporting legend. [HS-1995]

[Sylvie Fréchette went on to win silver at the 1996 Olympics in a team event. Since retiring from competition, she has performed with Cirque du Soleil and was inducted into Canada's Sports Hall of Fame in 1999. Eds.]

left: Sylvie Fréchette

My mother always said if you worked hard and were honest in life, good things would happen.
—Sylvie Fréchette, 1993

DENISE MARTIN

Born in Rosemount, Quebec, in 1967, Fréchette discovered synchronized swimming at age seven. Julie Sauvé was her first and only coach, and, under a tutelage which stressed the artistry of the sport, she became known as an innovator who brought emotion to her routines. Winning her first Canadian junior competition at 13, Fréchette began a promising career, but for years was overshadowed by former world and Olympic champion, Carolyn Waldo.

Fréchette stepped out of that shadow with a record-setting performance in Australia, producing seven perfect 10s to win the world championship 18 months prior to the 1992 Barcelona Olympics. It seemed her 18-year climb to the Olympics was nearly over, with sports reporters already declaring that "it looks like a coast to the gold medal." But this was not to be. Despite Fréchette's nearly flawless routine and her confidence that "I knew I had just given the best

On 26 May 1997, Denise Martin became the first Canadian woman to reach the North Pole. "I would have done it if I had been the 100th. I had the time of my life. I loved every minute of it."

Denise has been challenging herself in the outdoors since the age of 17, first through Katimavik, and later, over nearly a decade as an instructor with Outward Bound. She was well-prepared when a group of British women contacted her with their idea of reaching the Pole by relay. Each team was on the Arctic ice for two to three weeks, but Denise and her co-leader, Matty McNair, completed the entire expedition—a total of 81 days. "It's not as flat and boring as people would imagine. The world underfoot was ever changing. The ice was incredible colours. I found it fascinating and beautiful. Life on the ice becomes simple and deeply satisfying and revolves around the three themes of food, shelter and companionship."

above: Denise Martin

It's not just a medal
or how much money you make
that makes you successful.
It's setting goals and taking
care of what's inside of you.
You have to be healthy
in body, mind and spirit.
—Catriona LeMay Doan, 1999

right: Catriona LeMay Doan

CATRIONA LeMAY DOAN

With power, speed, and grace, Catriona LeMay Doan has captured international success in speed skating and the admiration of young women across Canada.

She is happy to be a role model. "I've helped make known that it is okay to be very muscular and strong and yet still be feminine." She feels this view of women is becoming more accepted in all areas. Women are demonstrating that it's possible to be powerful on many levels: in physical pursuits, in their careers, and in their spiritual lives.

She is also an optimist about the future of young female speed skaters. The sport has become better known over the last decades, due to the success of the Canadian team at the 1998 Nagano Winter Olympics. Catriona earned the gold medal in the 500-metres and a bronze in the 1000-metres. She is also world sprint champion, World Cup champion in both the 500- and 1000-metres, and a world record holder. The personal success of Catriona and teammate Susan Auch, and the friendly rivalry that has spurred both of them to outstanding performances have sparked an interest in the sport for many young women.

After the camaraderie of the quest, arriving at the Pole was anti-climactic. "I was actually quite sad to get up there because I just really loved the trip. I don't think I've laughed so much. It was quite something to be involved with such a team and such an idea."

Denise's experience challenges other assumptions about the heroism of daring expeditions: "We don't have any epics to talk about and that's a good thing. It was well done in that we didn't have any problems, really no safety issues at all. Women perhaps do things differently from men, who would probably think more about goals and distances and such. I think we paid more attention to our emotional well-being, and how we could encourage each other. A group of women out on the ice need to be creative about some of the physical problems we encountered. We relied on each other. And we made just as good time as some of the male trips." [HS-1999]

Growing up in Saskatoon, Catriona began speed skating at 10. Although she was already involved in ringette, soccer, and track, speed skating soon captured her devotion. "It is fun, but at the same time it is very graceful and powerful." But she didn't give up her other sports. She competed at the 1993 Canada Summer Games, winning two bronze medals and one silver in track and field.

Catriona lives and trains in Calgary. After competing at the 2002 Olympics, she may pursue coaching or motivational speaking in the hope of continuing to inspire other women. [HS-2000]

[When Catriona won the 500-metre race at the 2002 Olympic Games, she became the first Canadian to successfully defend an Olympic gold medal. She has broken the world record eight times. Catriona ended the season as the world, Olympic, and World Cup 500-metre champion, "a dream season." Eds.]

WOMEN IN SPORT

This photo of Sandra Schmirler's 1998 Olympic gold-medal-winning curling team highlights an unprecedented development for women in sport. The teammates returning home to Regina from Nagano, share the spotlight with their young children, whom they have not seen since leaving for Japan. With their gold medals around their necks, the women are clearly elite competitors. With their children in their laps, they show that women can combine this achievement with their role as mothers. [HS-2000]

[In March 2000 Canadians were saddened by Sandra Schmirler's death from cancer. The not-for-profit Sandra Schmirler Foundation has been set up to help families with children challenged by life-threatening illnesses. Jan, Joan, and Marcia have continued to curl competitively. Eds.]

So many Canadian women have done so much, yet it is only in recent years that their accomplishments have come close to being noted with the same diligence and coverage routinely given male athletes.
—Wendy Long, 1995

My question is not: Who's winning the war between the sexes? But: Who's creating peace between the sexes? And How? How can we enable each other to have fun, develop athletic skill, and enjoy each other's company?
—Mariah Burton Nelson, 1991

left: Canada's Olympic women's curling team, 1998: l to r, Sandra Schmirler, Jan Betker, Joan McCusker and Marcia Gudereit.

CHAPTER 6

VOICES AND VISIONS

All the women in this book have had an impact on Canada's culture. In this final chapter we highlight women's contributions to the arts. Here you will meet writers, artists, performers, musicians, and filmmakers. Their biographies illuminate the ways in which women develop their unique voice, express their imaginative vision, and create new worlds just as their foremothers did before them.

Canadian women diarists and journalists, fiction writers, publishers and poets, painters, sculptors, musicians and actors have been portraying our lives since before Confederation. Working in both official languages and the many other languages Canadians speak, they articulate what it is like to be here, and they show us the meanings that emerge in the lives of Canadian women. Some have been, or are, famous; others have been all but forgotten.

Artistic images have always reflected the world around us, but traditionally women have been only the object of art's gaze. It is heartening, therefore, to see women increasingly on the other side of the lens, the canvas, and the quill, creating their own vision.

Unfortunately, the traditional creative work of women's hands has often been marginalized as "craft." "Women's work" has been considered practical rather than artistic, the product of industry rather than genius. *Herstory* seeks to redress these omissions of the past, bringing to light women of accomplishment who might otherwise be ignored by the exclusionary practices of history.

Throughout this book you have had only glimpses into women's lives. In weathered photographs you have seen their faces and wondered in turn how they saw themselves. You have followed along as women in Canada sustained their families, established communities, fought for reform, won new freedoms, and achieved acclaim. Now you will meet women who reflect on that experience of the world, women who mould and communicate their lives through their art.

With this chapter, we close our story of women in Canada, celebrating the accomplishments and contributions of Canadian women in the hope that they will inspire you to dream of new possibilities.

opposite: l'Orchestre des Ursulines, Quebec City, 1890

Writing has been women's work, and joy, for more than four millennia. *A History of Reading* points out that the first author named was Princess Enheduanna, born about 2300 BC. In the 19th century, most women wrote without much hope of financial reward, as very few authors of either gender made money in Canada's small literary market.

SUSANNA MOODIE

The Strickland family of Suffolk, England, was remarkable for the number of its members who were devoted to writing. Of the eight children, all but one of the six sisters became famous through their books. The household was highly intellectual, Mr. Strickland educating his children personally from his extensive classical library.

Susanna, the youngest of the Strickland sisters, published a volume of verse in 1830. A year later she married John Moodie, and in 1832 they emigrated to Canada with their infant daughter. They were to spend the next six years farming in the backwoods of Upper Canada. Susanna continued to write and documented their experiences:

"We found that manual toil, however distasteful to those unaccustomed to it, was not, after all, such a dreadful hardship; that the wilderness was not without its smile. If we occasionally suffered severe pain, we as often experienced great pleasure, and I have contemplated a well-hoed ridge of potatoes on that bush farm with as much delight as in years long past I had experienced in examining a fine painting in some well-appointed drawing room."

In 1838 Susanna was invited to submit work to the *Literary Garland,* a newly-formed Montreal magazine dedicated to encouraging Canadian literary talent. "I actually shed tears of joy over the first $20 bill I received from Montreal. It was my own; I had earned it with my own hand; and it seemed to my delighted fancy to form the nucleus out of which a future independence for my family might arise."

above: Susanna Moodie

...the letters of great men become great correspondences; the letters of women remain letters, however "charming" and "moving."
—Margaret Anderson, 1972

In 1840 they moved to Belleville, where Susanna became the chief contributor to the Literary Garland. In 1852 she published *Roughing It In the Bush,* which became one of the most widely read books on pioneer life in Canada.

Susanna Moodie raised seven children, wrote eight full-length novels, and published enough verse to fill two or three volumes. [HS-1975]

ROSANNA ELEANORA MULLINS LEPROHON

Rosanna Mullins was born in 1829 in Montreal, and educated at the convent of the Congregation of Notre Dame. She published her first poems in 1846, while still a schoolgirl. Much of her early work was published by the *Literary Garland.* This was an appropriate debut for a writer who was, in her own way, one of Canada's first literary nationalists. Her country's history and the need for understanding and co-operation between the French and English are recurring themes in Mme Leprohon's writing.

In 1851 Rosanna married Dr Jean Lucien Leprohon, a member of a distinguished French-Canadian family. During the almost thirty years of her married life, Rosanna produced 13 children, and a number of romantic tales of love, intrigue, and betrayal. Although sentimental, her novels still retain some of their appeal for the modern reader. In *Antoinette de Mirecourt* for instance, Lucille d'Aulnay, Antoinette's more worldly cousin, remains an amusing and rather charming portrait. It is Mme d'Aulnay's accommodation to the English fact that introduces one of the novel's more serious themes. The English conquerors are here, therefore, says Lucille, one must accept them and get on with one's life. In her resignation to the changed circumstances, Lucille is in marked contrast to Antoinette's father, who swears that he will have nothing to do with the English and threatens to disinherit his daughter if she marries an English officer.

Antoinette de Mirecourt is part of a trilogy of novels set at the time of the English conquest of New France. All three novels, *The Manor House of de*

Villerai, Antoinette de Mirecourt, and *Armand Durand,* were first serialized in English language magazines, then quickly translated into French and published as separate novels. Mme Leprohon retains her place as one of the first Canadian novelists who was successful and popular in both official languages. [HS-1987]

FÉLICITÉ ANGERS / LAURE CONAN

Félicité Angers was born in La Malbaie, Quebec, and spent most of her life there. She was educated by the Ursulines in Quebec City, where the Bible and the writings of the fathers of the church became her favourite reading matter.

At the end of her schooling, she returned to La Malbaie and set up housekeeping with her sister and brother. Her private life was very quiet; she was a good aunt to her numerous nieces and nephews and was known in the neighbourhood mainly for the beauty of her rose garden.

However, this quiet recluse lived a second life as Laure Conan, one of the most popular writers and journalists of her day. Her first published work, the novella *Un amour vrai,* was serialized in *La Revue de Montréal* in 1878. Several years later, in 1881-82, her best known work, *Angéline de Montbrun,* also made its first appearance as a serial.

Angéline was recognized as the first psychological novel written in French Canada. It tells the story of a lovely young girl, adored by her widowed father, and courted by handsome young Maurice Darville. For the first half of the novel, Angéline seems to have everything a young woman could want. Then, her adored father is killed while hunting, and she herself suffers an accident that scars her face. Shattered by her father's death, and sure that Maurice can only pity her now that she is no longer beautiful, Angéline returns to her country house and shuts herself away from the world. The second half of the novel examines Angéline's attempts to come to terms with her grief and loss, and her struggles to achieve peace in the contemplation of her religion.

Many critics have seen the novel as at least partially autobiographical. Did Félicité Angers suffer the loss of her love? Did she too struggle to achieve the consolation of faith? This intensely private woman permitted no one to know. When H.R. Casgrain, one of the most influential writers in Quebec, wrote the preface for *Angéline's* appearance in book form, Félicité was adamant that not the slightest clue should be given about her real identity. Later critics have seen the relationship between Angéline and her father as the central love story of the novel, and have analyzed the oedipal and masochistic aspects of Angéline's character in a way that would have profoundly shocked the author and her contemporaries.

After *Angéline,* Laure Conan turned to journalism, history, and popular piety. She wrote articles for journals as diverse as local parish magazines and *Le Journal de Françoise.* She wrote a number of historical novels, drawing her themes from the early history of French Canada. The most successful of these, *L'Oublié,* told the story of Lambert Closse, Maisonneuve's lieutenant in the founding of Ville-Marie. *L'Oublié* was awarded the Prix Montyon by the Académie française, an unusual honour for a Canadian. [HS-1989]

left: Rosanna Eleanora Mullins Leprohon

Canadians should not be discouraged from trying to form and foster a literature of their own... if Antoinette de Mirecourt *possesses no other merit, it will, at least, be found to have that of being essentially Canadian.*
—Rosanna E.M. Leprohon, 1864

Des femmes commencent à dire et à écrire. Cette écriture, contrairement à la tradition littéraire de ce siècle, sait dire plus facilement les peines d'amour, les chicanes de ménage, les rancunes d'amoureux, les peines d'enfants, et la vie autour de soi.
—Le Collectif Clio, 1982

above: Emma Albani

In the nineteenth century it was even more common than today for Canadian performers to find recognition in England or the United States rather than at home. But there were exceptions.

EMMA ALBANI

Emma Albani was born Marie-Louise Emma Cecile Lajeunesse on September 24, 1847, at Chambly, Quebec. She was taught at home by her parents and appeared as a singer, harpist, and pianist from the age of nine, sometimes composing her own music. From her first public appearance at Mechanics Hall in Montreal in 1854, her audiences were astounded by her unusually fine voice.

In 1866 she moved to Albany, New York, where she accepted the position of soprano soloist and later organist at a Roman Catholic cathedral. By means of concerts and community assistance she raised the money to study in Paris, leaving in 1868. There she studied under Duprez and Benoist, then with Lamperti in Milan.

Her Italian debut was in Messina in 1870; here her stage name was chosen in honour of an old Italian family. She travelled to England in 1872 to make her first oratorio appearance, followed by tours in Paris, St Petersburg, Moscow, Berlin, and New York—16 countries in all—and became the leading oratorio singer in England.

She returned often to make tours of Canada, her last being in 1903. She trained two other Canadian singers of repute: Eva Gauthier and Sarah Fischer. She repeatedly sang for Queen Victoria, and entertained at the coronation of King Edward in 1902.

Emma's last concert was in 1909. She received many honours from royalty and was made Dame Commander of the British Empire in 1925. A few cylindrical recordings of her voice, made in 1904, remain—a testimony to her greatness. [HS-1974]

MAUD ALLAN

Maud Allan was born in Toronto on 27 August 1873. Although she implied otherwise in her autobiography, Maud had a fairly normal working class upbringing. She studied piano at the San Francisco School of Music and received a degree from Cogswell College.

In 1894, Maud went to Berlin to study music, and in 1901 became one of a select group studying with the renowned pianist, Ferruccio Busoni. About this time, Maud decided to switch to dance. She made her public dance debut in 1903 at Vienna's Theatre Hall of the Royal Conservatory of Music. Although not an overnight hit, Maud continued to study and perform.

In 1907, Maud created her most famous dance, *The Vision of Salomé.* The piece, danced to music by Marcel Rémy, became her signature. That same year she danced at Marienbad before Edward, Prince of Wales.

That engagement led to the London stage, and in March 1908, she began a long run at the Palace

right: Maud Allan

In 1918, however, she became entangled in a trial involving Oscar Wilde's *Salomé*. As a result, her reputation was severely damaged. She continued to dance, though without the success of earlier years. She acted in several plays in the 1930s, but retired to California in 1941, where she lived in near poverty until her death in 1956.

Her dance career spanned thirty-three years, and, as one dance historian has noted, at the height of her success, she was certainly as famous as Isadora Duncan. Although not so well-known today as other pioneers, Maud Allan, "The Canadian Dancer," helped to define and expand the world of dance. [HS-1990]

left: Charlotte Nickinson Morrison as "Melanie" in Napoleon's Old Guard, *with her father, Major John Nickinson, ca 1855*

CHARLOTTE NICKINSON MORRISON

Born into the Nickinson theatrical family in 1832, by 1852 she is said to have taken her birthplace, Quebec City, by storm. She was applauded by theatre audiences and critics alike. "The more we see of her," one reporter wrote, "the more cause do we perceive for Quebec's being proud of her daughter." In Toronto, her father leased the Royal Lyceum Theatre, where she was the leading lady. Her repertoire enlarged to include "all the Shakespearean roles, with other characters."

After her marriage to a prominent journalist in 1858, Charlotte retired from the stage for a time, but was back at work by 1864, under contract to J.W. Buckland of Montreal. She went into business for herself after the death of her husband in 1870, managing the recently constructed Grand Opera House in Toronto. One of her achievements was a centennial production of Sheridan's *School for Scandal,* prepared under the patronage of Lord Dufferin, the Governor General at the time.

After regaining her reputation as a "talented and sterling actress," Charlotte returned to charity and church work. She undertook the presidency of the Toronto Relief Society, and was prominent in the newly formed National Council of Women. [HS-1976]

Theatre. Maud was soon the toast of London society. She also published her autobiography, *My Life and Dancing.*

In 1910, Maud, who always billed herself as "The Canadian Dancer," made a triumphal North American dance debut. She toured throughout the world during the next eight years, achieving great popularity in Europe, South Africa, and the Far East, as well as North America. In 1915, she stopped in California long enough to star in a silent movie, *The Rugmaker's Daughter,* in which she performed a small segment of *The Vision of Salomé.*

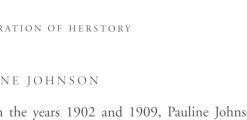

top right: Two women with camera

PAULINE JOHNSON

Between the years 1902 and 1909, Pauline Johnson travelled back and forth across Canada providing entertainment in Canadian towns and cities from High River, Newfoundland, to Pincher Creek, Alberta. She became known as the "Mohawk Princess" and did dramatic presentations of her own plays and poems.

The Corn Husker

Hard by the Indian lodges, where the bush
Breaks in a clearing, through ill fashioned fields,
She comes to labour, when the first still hush
Of autumn follows large and recent yields.

Age in her fingers, hunger in her face,
Her shoulders stooped with weight of work and years,
But rich in tawny colouring of her race,
She comes a-field to strip the purple ears.

And all her thoughts are with the days gone by,
Ere might's injustice banished from their lands
Her people, that today unheeded lie,
Like the dead husks that rustle through her hands.
[HS-1974]

Women's photographs have always been autobiographical: they have always been the ones to maintain a chronicle of their own and their family's lives in the family photo album.
—Isobel Harry and Shirley Puckering, 1973

The new medium of photgraphy provided some women with career opportunities. And others, both professional and amateur, with the means to create records of their own lives.

GERALDINE FITZGIBBON MOODIE

In 1878, while visiting in England, Geraldine Fitzgibbon married her distant cousin, John Moodie, thereby doubling the Moodie connection she already claimed through her well-known maternal grandmother, Susanna [see p. 210].

Two years later, the couple was in southern Manitoba, bent on farming. With the Riel Rebellion of 1885, however, John joined the North-West Mounted Police (NWMP) and after various western postings, the Moodies came to Battleford, Saskatchewan, in 1891. There Geraldine undertook to perfect the craft which was to make her famous—photography. She was operating her own studio by the time John was transferred south in 1896. Undaunted

right: Pauline Johnson

at starting over, she opened a new studio in Maple Creek and, within a year, a second one in Medicine Hat, 100 km to the west.

Drawing subjects from the culture around her, so unlike that of her Ontario birthplace, Geraldine soon became a strong presence in a male-dominated commercial world. She was as well mother to five children, caring for them alone much of the time, as John was often away.

In 1903 Moodie was assigned to set up the first NWMP post in the Hudson Bay region. The next year Geraldine sailed north with him, ready for a new adventure just as she was turning 50. She was about to begin her finest work.

Geraldine found the intricate Inuit costumes of the west coast of Hudson Bay fascinating, particularly the women's beaded and decorated parkas, works of art by any definition. Photo after photo focused on them, most of them portrait-style and done indoors, restrictions due perhaps to her reliance on glass negatives and heavy cameras. They remain some of the most outstanding photographs of Inuit.

left: "Self-portrait by Frances Benjamin Johnston, taken 1896, with three symbols of rebellion: proper Victorian women did not smoke, drink beer or show their petticoats.

It is important for women to look at other women, because the kind of image many male photographers have of women is certainly very different from the way we see ourselves.
—Erica Lennard, 1975

Her work is not only beautiful, but of uncommon historical interest. She was always careful to record the names of her subjects, and today these names are a major key to the past, particularly of women and children, who had almost always remained nameless, or known only by a husband's name, in traditional photography.

Geraldine's death in Alberta in 1945, just days before her 91st birthday, ended, as one biographer noted, "a lifetime of adventure and a career that few other women of her time could even imagine."

A particularly poignant story lay behind Geraldine's portrait of the startlingly beautiful Koo-tucktuck (left). Attuat, an Inuit elder, pronounced her name "Kusiqtut," perhaps a corruption of the Inuktitut word Oqajuittuq—the one who cannot talk—but added, "We knew her as Qanimirat—they sometimes have two or three names." As a deaf mute, what kind of life had she? "She was a very happy person. She could do anything she wanted to do—the only thing she couldn't do was speak. She even used to try to sing." [HS-1996]

There are those who watch it happen, those who make it happen, and those who don't know what's happening. I intend to make it happen.
—Kaaydah Schatten, ca 1991

bottom left: Koo-Tucktuck, photographed by Geraldine Fitzgibbon Moodie, ca 1905

right: Mary Dignam

*In the arts, "feminine" means
small, delicate, intuitive
emotions. "Feminine"
materials are those found in
the home, used by women....
"Feminine" is appropriate for
women, problematic when
applied to men, whereas the
universal, to which we have
been taught all good art
aspires, is generally a form of
the masculine.—Daphne
Read, Rosemary Donegan,
and Liz Martin, 1982*

*I have become convinced
that female brain-power is
probably the greatest unused
resource in this country.
—Gwen Matheson, 1976*

*Quilts are made with more
than the decorative arts in
mind; they express emotion,
beliefs....Every quilter prizes
her quilts, hands them down
to her family, treats them with
a sense of reverence which
indicates the importance of
them to her sense of self.
—Mary Conroy, 1983*

Once, while teaching at the Alberta College of Art, painter Marion Nicoll was asked how she felt being the only woman out of a staff of 165. She replied, "Almost outnumbered."

THE WOMEN'S ART ASSOCIATION OF CANADA

The Women's Art Association (WAA) of Canada was founded in Toronto in 1887 to foster the work of Canadian women in the arts. In 1890, the Association obtained a national charter and began to establish branches across the country. The Association was one of the first affiliates of the National Council of Women and remained an active participant in the Council until the 1970s. At the time of its widest influence, the Association was affiliated with the International Lyceum Clubs and had branches extending from New Brunswick to Alberta.

The WAA interested itself in all branches of the arts: fine, performing, and applied. They established a gallery and held shows and sales of the works of female painters and sculptors, as well as women's work in such media as weaving, lace-making, pottery, and embroidery. The Home Industries Department of the WAA had an early appreciation for many craftswomen, giving them both a source of income and a means of reaching public view. The WAA had an early appreciation for the arts and crafts of Native women, Canadiennes françaises, and immigrant women of various cultures. Through WAA shows and sales, many of these women were encouraged to maintain their own artistic heritages, and other Canadians were introduced to the beauty and value of these traditions.

Emily Carr's first solo show in eastern Canada was held in the WAA's Toronto gallery in 1935 [see p. 218]. Sculptures by Florence Loring and Frances Wyle [see p. 217] appeared frequently in the WAA gallery. Loring served as president of the WAA in the '30s. The WAA also patronized music, dance, and literature, holding concerts and readings and offering scholarships to young performers.

For many years the Women's Art Association of Canada worked hard and successfully, as the *National Council of Women of Canada Yearbook* of 1919 noted: "to create a general interest in art, to encourage art handicrafts and home industries, and to establish art lectures and exhibitions of painting, sculpture and design. In this way it hopes to supply in some measure that great need of the artist: a public able to understand and trained to appreciate the best in art."[HS-1991]

MARY DIGNAM

The following excerpts come from a history of women's art in Canada by painter Mary Ella Dignam (1860-1938), a founder of several women's art programs in Ontario and the driving force behind the Women's Art Association. In 1886, she and twenty other women artists banded together to share studio space and to hold exhibitions. Thanks to Mrs Dignam, this Toronto collective was soon affiliated with a thousand more artists and art lovers in other Canadian cities.

At a time when Canadian society took little interest in art, and less in local artists, these women organized classes, shows, lectures, and sales with the triple objective of public education, co-operation amongst women artists, and support for Canadian craftswomen. Although still in operation, the association was most vigorous before World War I.

"The earliest art work to be recorded in Canada is the pottery made by the Indian women...excellent in form and good in decoration....In weaving and dyeing, in beadwork, and in many other ways the Indian women made a creditable beginning in handicrafts and home industries.

"[The handwork of pioneer women], tidies and tablecovers, rugs and rag carpets not only displayed a desire for comfort...but showed more than anything else the innate love existing in women under all conditions for artistic expression. Many wrought in this homely way, who in other times would have fashioned rare tapestries or intricate embroideries."—*Women of Canada, Their Life and Work", 1900* [HS-1977]

FRANCES LORING AND FLORENCE WYLE

Frances Loring and Florence Wyle met at the Chicago Art Institute in 1908, and spent the next sixty years living and sculpting together. Both sculptors worked in clay, wood, and stone. They arrived in Toronto in 1912 and after 1920, their church-studio became the centre of activity for sculpture and sculptors in Canada.

Frances Loring contributed monumental sculptures to Canada, including the figure of Robert Borden for

Parliament Hill and the Lion for the entrance to the Queen Elizabeth Way in Toronto. Her last piece, *Eskimo Woman and Child,* was done when she was seventy.

One of Florence Wyle's finest pieces is a nude torso, completed in 1930. She created portrait busts of the artists Frederick Varley and A.Y. Jackson, and is known for the many garden pieces of children that she sculpted.

Both women died in 1968, Florence at age eighty-seven and Frances at eighty-one. They lived to see their work exhibited in a joint show at the Pollock Gallery in Toronto—a final tribute to two great artists. [HS-1975]

MARY RITER HAMILTON

Mary Riter Hamilton was born in Ontario in 1873. She painted and drew from childhood, but seemed to be destined for the traditional role of wife and mother. Married at eighteen, she was widowed at twenty-three and decided then to pursue a career as an artist.

Mary took art lessons in Toronto, and in 1896 went to Europe to study in Germany and Paris. She studied under some of the most prominent teachers of the day, who assured her of her talent and encouraged her to exhibit her work. In 1905 and for several years after, she exhibited paintings at the Paris Salon. The Parisian critics and public liked her emotional work and she was able to return to Canada as a European success.

In 1911 she came back to Canada to nurse her mother, who had moved to Winnipeg. While in Canada, Mary arranged for an exhibition of 150 of her paintings, to be shown across the country. These paintings were well received critically, and Mary was hailed as Canada's top woman artist. She travelled across the country herself, painting portraits and landscapes.

The outbreak of World War I made it impossible for her to return to Paris, so she remained in Victoria for the duration of the war. Here she had a studio where she taught and accepted commissions, including portraits of several lieutenant-governors of British Columbia.

After the war, she was commissioned to paint a series of pictures commemorating Canadians' contri-

Listen, female babies are not any less strong or creative or intelligent than men. It's the bloody education that conditions us from first grade to be feminine, soft and unaggressive —knocking us on the head and telling us it's not ladylike to want to be a winner. —Rita Letendre, painter, former member of the Montréal Automatistes, considered "a leading exponent of the abstract colorist movement." Her work has been exhibited around the world and can be found in public and private collections throughout North America.

I've been really envious of men for the uninterrupted periods of time they get. People feel very differently about interrupting a man at his work than about interrupting a woman.—Alice Munro, 1975

left: Frances Loring and Florence Wyle

right: Painting by Mary Wrinch

There are two kinds of art. Man art and woman art. They are two different kinds of people, so their art comes out differently.—Joyce Wieland

I still find...that when people wish to be particularly complimentary, they say that my work looks as though it had been done by a man!
—Patricia Fulford, *Eclectic Eve, 1974*

below: "Market Among the Ruins of Ypres," by Mary Riter Hamilton, 1920

butions. She returned to Europe in 1919 and for three years travelled the battlefields, painting the horrors and devastation that remained after the conflict. It took great courage to travel with the work parties who were still burying bodies and collecting live ammunition from the wasted battlefields. The 350 pictures Mary painted during this time—stark, grim, impressionistic records of death and destruction—are testimony to the profound emotional effect of the scenes she witnessed.

Her war paintings were exhibited in Paris and London to considerable acclaim. The French honoured her with the Palme Académique and made her an officier d'Académie. But Canadians wanted no reminders of the desperate conflict they had put behind them, and Mary's style was out of step with that of the nascent and popular Group of Seven. As a consequence, Mary's paintings were largely ignored in Canada. Although she received offers of purchase from Europe and the United States, she wanted the collection to remain in Canada, and eventually donated them to the National Archives.

She returned to Winnipeg in 1926 and spent the rest of her life there and in Victoria. She died in poverty in 1954, blind and almost forgotten in her own country, despite the fame and honours she had received in Europe. [HS-1989]

MARY WRINCH

Mary Wrinch was born in England in 1877 and came to Canada at the age of seven. As a youngster she developed a great love for the country which she later displayed in her career as a painter.

She began painting Canada's scenic landscapes years before the Group of Seven made Canadian themes popular, yet received little credit for her artistic foresight. Her work was shown with that of Harris, Jackson, MacDonald, and Thomson at the Art Gallery in Toronto in 1926. The Group of Seven and its members are well-known names in the history of Canadian art. Mary Wrinch is not.

Once again, the question is not why are there no great women artists, but rather why is there so little known about great women artists? [HS-1977]

EMILY CARR

The great British Columbia forests and mysterious Indian totems are themes that occur often in the work of Emily Carr. However, Emily Carr's struggle was not merely to skilfully capture these forms on canvas; it was to delve into the very soul, the very essence of these subjects and of herself, and to portray this essence in

her art. Emily Carr was born on December 13, 1871, and grew up in Victoria with four sisters and one brother. For a woman to decide to be a serious artist in "Victorian" Victoria was no easy thing—but then Emily had always described herself "as contrary from the start." Having shown talent for drawing in her youth, she was to study art in San Francisco and later in London and Paris. Always she returned to her beloved Canada and the west coast where she was born.

During the early years of the twentieth century, she received little encouragement or remuneration for her work and took to other endeavours in order to make a living—renting rooms, growing fruit, raising hens and rabbits, breeding dogs, potting, and running a ladies' boarding house. She painted little during this time.

However, in 1927 she was invited to show some of her work in the exhibition "Canadian West Coast Art, Native and Modern," which took place in Ottawa. For the first time her work received nationwide attention. During her trip east she met the Group of Seven. She found their work inspiring, and was much encouraged by the acceptance and praise which she received from these kindred artists.

It was on her return to the West that she began to create her finest works and entered her most prolific period. She journeyed up the Nass and Skeena Rivers, to the Queen Charlotte Islands, and into the deep forests—living and sketching in the places she loved. Though she began to receive steady recognition, money from sales of her paintings did not bring her financial security until she was in her late sixties.

During the late 1930s and early 1940s she suffered a series of heart attacks and strokes. This curtailed her journeys to the forests, but she continued to paint and became more involved in her writing. The next few years brought successes for both her writing and her painting. Her book *Klee Wyck* won the Governor General's Award in 1941, and 57 of 60 paintings were sold at an exhibition in Montreal in 1944. Emily Carr died on March 2, 1945, at the age of 73. [HS-1982] Excerpts from *Hundreds and Thousands: The Journals of Emily Carr:*

"Yesterday I went to town and bought this book to enter scraps in, not a diary of statistics and dates and decency of spelling and happenings but just to jot me down in, unvarnished me, old me at fifty-eight—old, old, old, in most ways and in others just a baby with so much to learn and not much time left here but maybe somewhere else. It seems to me it helps to write things and thoughts down. It makes the unworthy ones look more shamefaced and helps to place the better ones for sure in our minds. It sorts out jumbled up thoughts and helps to clarify them, and I want my thoughts clear and straight for my work."—*Nov. 23, 1930.*

"What's the good of trying to write? It's all the unwordable things one wants to write about, just as it's all the unformable things one wants to paint—essence."—*April 24, 1934.*

"I wonder will death be much lonelier than life. Life's an awfully lonesome affair. You can live close

It is wonderful to feel the grandness of Canada in the raw, not because she is Canada but because she's something sublime that you were born into.
—Emily Carr, *Hundreds and Thousands: The Journals of Emily Carr,* 1966

There lies a country, fresh from the dawn, pulsating with life and colour just awaiting the painter's brush.
—Euphemia McNaught, painter, ca 1927

left: Emily Carr

I had a thought about Cinderella the other day. The real reason that Prince Charming chooses Cinderella over the other two sisters is that she is the only one who can do housework.
—Margaret Atwood, 1975

below: Maud Dowley Lewis, outside her painted house

against other people yet your lives never touch. You come into the world alone and you go out of the world alone yet it seems to me you are more alone while living than ever going and coming."—*July 16, 1933.*

"B-a-a-a, old sheep, bleating for fellows. Don't you know better by now. It must be my fault somewhere, this repelling of mankind and at the same time rebelling at having no one to shake hands with but myself and the right hand weary of shaking the left. Stop this yowl and go to your story and enter the joy of birds. Wake thy old sail up, hoist it up into the skies on lark songs. Fill it with thrush songs and blackbirds, and when the day is petering out wrap the great white owl's silent wings round it and let the nightingale sing it to sleep."—*April 6, 1934.* [HS-1974]

MAUD DOWLEY LEWIS

In adversity and deprivation, Maud Lewis found beauty and joy. Her paintings—bright, unusual, often humorous, glimpses of rural life and nature—reveal a fond nostalgia for the fleeting happinesses of childhood.

Maud was born in South Ohio, Nova Scotia, in 1903—with hands deformed and shoulders hunched; her misshapen chin touched her chest. Often taunted, she quit school after grade 5. With her mother's help she began painting.

When her parents died, her brother claimed the family inheritance and Maud was forced to re-enter the outside world. In 1938 Maud married Everett Lewis, a taciturn fish peddler seeking a housekeeper. His tiny house had no kitchen, no running water, no electricity, and no telephone.

But Maud could paint in it, and paint she did, with whatever brush and paint available—but never on canvas. She covered every flat surface in the little house, including stove, windows, and door, with fanciful butterflies, animals, and flowers. A "paintings for sale" sign by the road lured passersby to look, and purchase. When she was well, and had paints, Maud did two paintings per day, sometimes selling them wet to customers. Her Christmas cards sold well on Everett's routes, bringing in welcome cash—though he is said to have kept the money himself.

Suffering from rheumatoid arthritis, Maud could finally do almost nothing without help. Yet she still sat by the window and painted; her easel a TV tray, her palette sardine tins.

In 1968 Maud broke her hip and never fully recovered. She died on 30 July 1970, having never travelled farther than an hour from her birthplace. She was buried in a child's coffin, her graveside ceremony the "best attended in decades." Everett had "Maud Dowley" engraved on his family's stone; another 26 years would pass before Maud had her own monument.

After long effort to acquire it, the Art Gallery of Nova Scotia is restoring Maud's painted house. In 1997 they mounted a highly successful travelling exhibition of some 200 of her paintings. [HS-1999]

PARASKEVA CLARK

Harold Townsend, artist and long-time friend, describes Paraskeva Clark: "She had a strong rough way of putting things down. Her personality was so fierce, she was so irascible. She wasn't content to make pretty pictures. She aimed for power. At its best, her work is as tough as she is."

Born in St Petersburg, Russia, in 1898, she studied painting in the evenings while working in a shoe factory. In post-revolutionary Russia she was able to study in the "Free Studios." Her first husband died tragically, shortly after their son was born, and she moved to Paris to work as a housekeeper for her in-laws, painting in her spare time. A chance meeting in 1931 led to her marriage to Philip Clark and her move to Canada. Paraskeva and Philip had a son in 1934.

Paraskeva is perhaps best known for her self-portraits. She painted seven, as one reviewer noted, "Not out of vanity, but because it was easier than asking someone else to pose and perhaps because she was trying to understand who the person in the mirror was." She claimed "The face is more complicated than anything else. It's not form only but character." In Canada she had to struggle to get her paintings shown on the walls of conservative Canadian galleries accustomed to the Group of Seven. She was unimpressed. "Landscapes, landscapes. I don't even paint still lifes."

Paraskeva struggled to achieve the political and social awareness for which she had gained a reputation in the 1930s and '40s with paintings like *Petroushka* and *Presents from Madrid*. But she also struggled with societal expectations that she spend her time cooking meals and caring for her family. After her eldest son was diagnosed a schizophrenic in 1943, she painted less and less. She gave up painting altogether at the age of 80 in 1972.

Saddened by the things that cannot be changed, and by those that have changed, Paraskeva Clark wore her long years fiercely. Artist, sometime socialist, sometime feminist, she was her own woman at her own cost. [HS-1991]

[Paraskeva Clark died in 1986. Eds.]

left: Paraskeva Clark

There is just cooking, cooking, cooking. Loblaws, Dominion; Dominion, Loblaws. What's a woman's fate? What has the Lord created us for? Just to produce more men. I can't forgive him for that.
—Paraskeva Clark, 1983

PRUDENCE HEWARD

Born in 1896, Prudence Heward became interested in art at an early age, and studied under William Brymner at the Art Association of Montreal. While there she won scholarships for drawing and for painting. During World War I she and her mother worked for the Red Cross in London while her brothers were stationed overseas. She later returned to Montreal to study under Randolph Hewton, then completed a few months of training at the Academy Colarossi in Paris. In 1929 Prudence won the Willingdon Arts Competition for her painting *Girl on a Hill*.

Though Prudence progressed slowly in her early years of painting, she persisted, and continued to develop her skills and her ideas about art. She was dedicated to art and her artist friends, and in 1933 became one of the founding members of the Canadian Group of Painters, for which she served as vice-president for a time. She spread her enthusiasm for painting to others as well. Her family's summer home near Brockville became the scene of many "painting picnics." Prudence and the neighbouring Eliot family, sometimes joined by other friends, would gather together to sketch and paint the surrounding countryside. Unfortunately, her career was brief and was often interrupted by illness; in 1945 she could no longer continue, because of illness, and two years later she died at the age of 51. [HS-1978]

below: "Girl on a Hill," by Prudence Heward, 1928

W omen have been central to the development and success of the performing arts in Canada.

GWENETH LLOYD AND CELIA FRANCA

These two women, who emigrated to Canada from the Sadler's Wells School of Ballet in London, England, can be credited to a large degree with the success of dance in Canada.

Gweneth Lloyd arrived in Winnipeg, Manitoba, in January 1938 and established an institution which has earned worldwide recognition—the Royal Winnipeg Ballet. Celia Franca came in 1950 and produced in the National Ballet Company a standard of

If members of my sex appear at times to be inadequate, it must be because a wise God created them to match the men.
—Cora Hind, *...And Mighty Women Too,* 1975

When you thought you were training your body, in the end it turns out that you were training your whole self, your whole being, to be a dancer.
—Veronica Tennant, acclaimed dancer with the National Ballet of Canada for 25 years.

right: Celia Franca in Giselle, *1956*

excellence that seemed impossible at the time.

Both women struggled against great odds: they worked with almost no personnel or resources, their dancers had received only haphazard instruction. Celia Franca worked as a file clerk at the Eaton Auditorium, rehearsing her dancers at night. Gweneth Lloyd wrote four ballets a year for the first few seasons, and five in 1942. During the war years her company performed to record audiences, and became the first dance troupe in the British Commonwealth to bear royal designation.

Franca began modestly, then launched her company on a career that can only be described as fantastic— a local tour in the first season, a national one in the second, and international ones in the third and succeeding years, to almost invariable critical and popular acclaim.

In addition to founding and directing the Royal Winnipeg Ballet, Gweneth Lloyd has long been a member of the Royal Academy of Dancing, and principal of the Canadian School of Ballet with branches in Winnipeg, Toronto, and throughout the valley towns of the Okanagan. For twenty years she was head of the ballet division of the Banff School of Fine Arts, during which time it became one of the largest ballet schools in Canada. [HS-1974]

[In 1978 Celia Franca became co-artistic director of the School of Dance in Ottawa, continuing her mentorship of young artists. She became a Companion of the Order of Canada in 1985 and was awarded the Governor General's Performing Arts Award in 1994. Celia has been on the boards of the Canada Council and Canada Dance Festival Society, as well as the board of governors of York University.

Gweneth was made Officer of the Order of Canada in 1977, and received the Dance in Canada Award in 1984, not long before her retirement from the Royal Winnipeg Ballet. In 1991, the Royal Winnipeg Ballet staged a revival of *The Wise Virgins,* one of the most famous of the 35 pieces Gweneth Lloyd produced for her company. She was awarded a Governor General's Performing Arts Award in 1992 and died in 1993. Eds.]

tion is strictly contemporary but she is not an extremist....There have been great executive artists among women but you could count the composers on the fingers of one hand....Here is strong, austere music, characterized by contrapuntal mastery, economy of means, and loftiness of purpose." [HS-1975]

[Violet Archer received numerous awards and honours, including the Order of Canada in 1983. She died in 2000 at the age of 87. During her lifetime she composed more than 290 works, and was a tireless advocate for contemporary music education. Eds.]

left: Violet Archer

If you want to be an artist and you are a woman, you have to be strong in some sort of way—either in your head, or physically or both...and if you're stubborn enough, and you have some talent, you may make it.
—Nancy Hazelgrove, Eclectic Eve, 1974

VIOLET ARCHER

Violet Archer is one of Canada's most prolific composers; a creative pioneer since her work in the 1940s.

She was born Violet Balestreri, of Italian immigrant parents, and subsequently changed her name to the English equivalent—Archer. From early childhood her main interest was music: "I always adored music and I always wanted to study it even before I could hardly talk." Following her graduation from McGill University in 1936, with a Teacher's Licentiate and a BA in music composition, she continued her studies at Yale under a Quebec government scholarship.

She established her reputation in the United States as a professor of composition and judge of state and nationwide composers' contests. Since returning to Canada in 1960, she has served as a professor of theory and composition at the University of Alberta where she heads the Music Department.

Her output has been truly remarkable. The catalogue of her work lists compositions for orchestra, opera, solo and chamber music, and pieces for choir and solo voice. Although her fame rests upon her sophisticated concert works, much of her music is meant to be played not in the concert hall but at home, in class, or in church.

A music critic wrote: "Miss Archer's musical dic-

PORTIA WHITE

She was frequently billed as "The Marian Anderson of Canada," but contralto Portia White was a magnificent singer in her own right.

Born in Truro, Nova Scotia, in 1910, Portia began singing at age six, the youngest member of the choir in the Baptist church where her father was pastor. When she was in her teens, the family moved to Halifax and Portia began singing in the local music festivals. By the time she was 17 she had decided to make music her career.

Financial constraints prevented her from realizing that objective immediately. She began teaching kindergarten in a village near Halifax, and once a week hiked the three miles to the train which took her into the city for voice lessons. In the late 1930s she enrolled in the Halifax Conservatory of Music.

Portia made her debut in Toronto in 1941. Within a few years she had made concert appearances all across Canada. She received international acclaim following a recital in New York, where she was hailed by critics as "one of the finest contralto voices to reach New York since Marian Anderson." In the years that followed, Portia toured extensively in Latin America and was so popular there that on the occasion of her performance in Panama, a medal was struck in her honour.

At the time of her death in 1968, she was teaching music at Branksome Hall, a private girls' school in Toronto. [HS-1978]

above: Portia White

KAREN KAIN

I know what life is all about, the pain and the joy. Through my dedication I hope to bring it to the stage.
—Evelyn Hart, 1982, principal dancer with the Royal Winnipeg Ballet.

The most striking thing about Karen Kain, next to her madonna-like features and exquisitely graceful body, is her single-minded commitment to her art.

Canada's first home-grown, international ballet star spends eight hours every weekday at rehearsal. "My life isn't exciting. It's not profitable. It's just mine," she once told a writer from *Maclean's*. She added: "When you're good—really good—at one thing, I suppose it does mean you're maladjusted for a lot of other things." She had to give up skating and skiing—they are too dangerous. She is on tour about eight months every year, which makes it very difficult to sustain personal relationships outside the company. Of course her life includes jet-setting, and glittering social affairs where she meets the rich and famous, but she wouldn't much enjoy these things even if she weren't dead tired so much of the time. In spite of her dizzying rise to stardom, Karen Kain has retained an appealing simplicity.

Born in Hamilton, Ontario, she entered the National Ballet School at 11, and just barely made it into the corps de ballet at 17, having starved herself before the audition to get her weight down. She became a principal dancer a year later.

Her career received a boost when guest artist Rudolf Nureyev picked her as his partner in *Swan Lake* and as Princess Aurora in *The Sleeping Beauty.*

Other triumphs followed: critical acclaim at her New York debut in *Giselle;* two medals at the Second International Ballet Competition in Moscow; an open invitation to dance with the Royal Ballet in London; works created especially for her by famed French choreographer Roland Petit. [HS-1979]

[Karen Kain retired in 1996. In the citation for the Governor General's Performing Arts Award she received in 1997, she was declared "one of the great prima ballerinas of the age." She danced virtually all the great classic roles, choreographers created works specifically for her, and she performed with most of the world's major dance companies. She has also been the subject of numerous television shows and documentaries, and has written her autobiography, *Movement*

right: Karen Kain in Don Juan, *1974*

Never Lies. As well as holding several honorary degrees and awards, Karen Kain was named Companion of the Order of Canada in 1991. Eds.]

KATE REID

Generally regarded as the finest actress ever developed in Canada, Kate Reid has had a prestigious acting career spanning more than three decades; she has appeared in over one thousand roles, on stage, radio, and television.

Born in London, England, on 4 November 1930, Daphne Kate Reid was the only daughter of Colonel Walter C. and Helen Reid. Kate's family emigrated to Oakville, Ontario, when Kate was only three-and-a-half. As a child, Kate attended Havergal College, an exclusive private girls' school in Toronto. She did not enjoy the experience, and so in her late teens, while recovering from a skiing accident which kept her out of school, she entered a drama course at Toronto's Royal Conservatory of Music. Thus it has been said that her acting career began quite by accident.

She continued her study of drama at the University of Toronto, and by the age of 18 had played several roles for Ontario summer-stock companies. By the time she was 26, Kate had performed in more than 50 theatrical roles. She went to New York City to study under a famous drama coach. The energy and exuberance with which she attacked her roles caused her reputation as an actress to spread quickly. In 1958, while living in London, England, she received rave reviews for her portrayal of Catherine Ashland in *The Stepmother*. In 1959 she began a six-year association with the Ontario Stratford Festival.

Kate has lent her talents to performing such roles as Martha in the Broadway production of *Who's Afraid of Virginia Woolf,* Nellie in a CBC production of *Nellie McClung,* and Mrs. Warren in the George Bernard Shaw play *Mrs. Warren's Profession,* at the Shaw Festival at Niagara-on-the-Lake in 1977.

Kate Reid's ability to portray characters of immense emotional dimension has won renown in Canada and abroad. Her honours include a Tony nomination for her portrayal of Caitlin Thomas in the Broadway production of *Dylan;* an honorary doctor of letters degree from Toronto's York University; and, for her "great contribution to the dramatic arts in Canada," the Order of Canada in 1974. [HS-1982]

[Kate Reid continued to pursue her acting career until her death in 1993. Eds.]

DORA MAVOR MOORE

Dora Mavor Moore was responsible, perhaps more than anyone else, for the existence and growth of professional theatre in Canada. Known as the "godmother of Canadian theatre," she was unquestionably its most fiercely dedicated grande dame. The list of her accomplishments and associations reads like a who's who of Canadian theatrical arts and artists.

She was the first Canadian to enrol in the Royal Academy of Dramatic Art in London, England, and was one of the few Canadians to star at the Old Vic, playing Viola in *Twelfth Night.*

In 1946, she founded the New Play Society, a non-profit theatrical workshop and drama school that produced dozens of original Canadian plays, among them the first such play to be booked into the Royal Alexandra Theatre in Toronto. The New Play Society also produced *Spring Thaw,* the annual topical revue that holds the Canadian theatrical long-run record. Dora Mavor Moore was one of the people instrumental in launching the Shakespearean Festival in Stratford, Ontario. It is difficult to name a project or talent in Canadian theatre that was not somehow associated with this fiery and energetic woman.

Famous for her eighty-hour work weeks and her aversion to profit, Dora Mavor Moore was also known for her unflinching belief that theatre was for people. "I hate like billy-oh the whole idea of charging even $2.50 for a theatre seat," she once said. "Theatre is for the masses." [HS-1976]

[Dora Mavor Moore died in 1979. Toronto's annual theatre awards are named in her honour. Eds.]

Marriage and motherhood need not be a hindrance but rather an inspiration to industrial or professional work.
—Emily Murphy, 1932

By the time most girls reach their teens, fairy tales (where princesses are invariably very young and beautiful) and countless ads, movies, and magazines have already well taught them that their fates depend on a frantic race with time. They must catch him before they reach the age of 25, or risk losing all.
—Louise Delude, 1978

right: Lucy Maud Montgomery

In the 20th century, women have produced some of the landmark events in Canadian publishing. However, from 1936 to 1996 only 25% of the Governor General's awards for literature were given to women. Despite this, the late 20th century stars of Canadian literature are almost all women. Many of them are among the most prolific and most widely known contemporary writers in the world.

LUCY MAUD MONTGOMERY

Lucy Maud, author of the famous *Anne of Green Gables* series, wrote to a longtime correspondent, "Biography is a *screaming farce.* No man or woman was *ever* truly depicted." In deference to that sentiment the following quotes allow her to introduce herself:

"What a blessing it is that we can so dream into life the things we desire!"

"For the past four days I've been scrubbing and whitewashing and digging out old corners and I feel as if all the dust I've stirred up and swept out and washed off has got into my soul and settled there and will remain there forever, making it hopelessly black and grimy and unwholesome."

"I used to feel woefully discouraged at times over those icy little rejection slips. But I kept on. Whatever gifts the gods had denied me they had at least dowered me with stick-to-it-iveness."

"I write fast, having 'thought out' plot and dialogue while I go about my household work."

"I am a petite person with very delicate features; my photos, at least the 'head and bust' ones, represent me usually as a strapping, personage with quite a large pronounced face."

"So you wish 'married women everywhere were real companions for their husbands.' So do I—as heartily as I wish that married men everywhere were real companions for their wives."

"I had to go out to tea and attend garden parties galore and I was generally bored to death, especially when people thought themselves bound to say something about my book."

The liberation of women will not be complete until a female writer can get up on a stage and read poetry, dead drunk...and stagger... and still be considered as loveable as Dylan Thomas.
—Margaret Atwood, 1979

How different my two aunts are. One lives in sound, the other in stone. Obasan's language remains deeply underground but Aunt Emily, B.A., M.A., is a word warrior. She's a crusader, a little old grey-haired Mighty Mouse, a Bachelor of Advanced Activists and General Practitioner of Just Causes.
—Joy Kogawa, from *Obasan*, 1981

"There's a hundred of me...Some of the 'me's' are good, some not. It's better than being just two or three, I think—more exciting, more interesting." [HS-1977]

MARTHA OSTENSO

Martha Ostenso was one of the first Canadian writers to deal resolutely and honestly with what it means to live on the prairies. Before 1925, novelists had brushed across the West with a wash of moralistic optimism. The romances of Nellie McClung and Arthur Stringer, to name two of the first generation of prairie writers, were cozy hideaways where winter blizzards and human greed were incidental—if they existed at all— and where good always prospered in the end.

Ostenso's world was more sullen and less sure. In *Wild Geese,* her first and most praised novel, she wrote about the conflict between Caleb Gare, a northern Manitoba pioneer, and Judith, his stormy daughter. Ravenous for wealth, Caleb had sold his soul for his farm. In Ostenso's words he was "a spiritual counterpart of the land, as harsh, as demanding, as tyrannical as the very soil from which he drew his existence."

Himself enslaved by the prairie, he in turn oppressed his wife and children.

Only Judith broke loose. No milksop romantic heroine, she throbbed with vigour; hers was "a great, defiant body, her chest high and broad as a boy's; her hair...wild-locked and black." Unlike her father, who lived for his cultivated fields, Judith burned with the untamed energy and fertility of the woods. The life she chose for herself was not her father's compulsive self-denial, but "a magnificent seeking through solitude—an endless quest," which is symbolized by the call of wild geese.

Born in Norway, Ostenso grew up in western Canada and the United States. At 18, she spent a summer teaching school in northern Manitoba. Here she said, *Wild Geese* was "waiting to be put into words. Here was human nature stark, unattired by the conventions of a smoother, softer life. A thousand stories are there, still to be written."

After the success of *Wild Geese* she left Canada for New York and Minnesota. Her other published work includes 11 novels, and many short stories and poems. She died in Seattle in 1963 at the age of 63. [HS-1978]

GABRIELLE ROY

Gabrielle Roy's writing verges on the religious, as one commentator noted: "... it affirms over and over again the value of all, even seemingly insignificant, lives. No character of Roy's, no matter how oppressed, how inarticulate, remains unable to perceive a meaning in life that, for moments at least, transfigures his daily drudgery."

Mlle Roy experienced poverty growing up in St Boniface, a French-speaking Winnipeg suburb, but never anything like what she discovered during the Second World War in St Henri, the poorest district of Montreal. "I had never seen such indigence as there was in St Henri. I never thought that what I started writing would turn into a novel. But little by little it did, as the bitter thought came to me that the war was a kind of salvation for the people living there."

This novel, *Bonheur d'occasion (The Tin Flute)*, was an outstanding event in Canadian literature. In 1947

above: Gabrielle Roy

We don't have an Iliad *or a* Song of Roland, *but we have our tales and legends....if only you knew everything that was in them.*
—Antonine Maillet, 1972

left: Martha Ostenso

it became a Literary Guild choice in the United States, winner of the Governor General's Award for fiction in Canada, and of the Prix Fémina in France—the first Canadian work to win a major French award. In 1947 Mlle Roy became the first woman appointed to the Royal Society of Canada.

Throughout her adult life she called her beloved Quebec home. Included in her impressive list of books, all written in French, is *Rue Deschambault, (Street of Riches),* a volume of imaginative stories based on her past which won her a second Governor General's Award in 1955. She won a third Governor General's Award in 1978 for her final novel *Ces enfants de ma vie (Children of My Heart).*

Biographer Phyllis Grosskurth writes:

"Her characters tend to be simple folks used as archetypes of all our endeavors to find happiness and wrest some sense out of chaos. Such happiness and understanding as they find is always fleeting, often paradoxical, usually late. Certain themes recur: a central mother figure, maternity, the passage of generations, the indestructible beauty and power of nature, the chicken-and-egg cycle of time. Her narratives are simple, straightforward, uncomplex, and celebrate the virtues of courage, loyalty, endurance and spiritual generosity." [HS-1979]

[A film based on *The Tin Flute* was released in 1983. Gabrielle Roy's autobiography *La Détresse et l'enchantement (Enchantment and Sorrow)* was published in 1984, a year after her death. Eds.]

ANNE HÉBERT

There was a strong expectation that French Canadian girls growing up in the 1930s would either marry and have children, or enter a convent. Anne Hébert did neither. She became a writer recognized in both Canada and France, where she spent much of her time.

Born into a cultured Quebec City family, Anne showed an early interest in writing. "I was privileged because my father was a writer and he encouraged me all along," she says. "In my family writing was considered a perfectly normal occupation for a woman. It was in the outside world that I encountered obstacles."

Unable to find a publisher for *Le Torrent,* a collection of short stories, Anne Hébert had the book printed at her own expense. Today it is considered a landmark of French Canadian literature.

Official recognition came in 1960 when she won the Governor General's Award for Poetry, and became a member of the Royal Society of Canada. Northrop Frye, the dean of Canadian critics, wrote the preface to a bilingual edition of her key poem, *The Tomb of the Kings.* Parisian critic André Rousseaux called her "one of the greatest contemporary poets in the French language."

Lately, Anne Hébert has turned to writing novels, but she says "all art at a certain level becomes poetry." Her first novel, *Les Chambres de Bois,* won three literary awards. *Kamouraska* won a coveted prize in France and was made into a film starring Genevieve Bujold. *Les Enfants du Sabbat,* a story of witchcraft in a Quebec convent during the nineteen-forties, was published in 1975.

Anne Hébert radiates a serene, girlish beauty that contrasts with the passion and stark violence of her writing. Her heroines are women who break out of a stultifying environment as they struggle towards freedom and life. They echo Anne Hébert's own transcen-

below: Anne Hébert

dence of the restrictions on women's aspirations, and, at a different level, the awakening of Quebec after the Duplessis years. [HS-1978]

[Anne Hébert's work is known around the world, having been translated into several languages. She won numerous national and international prizes, including three Governor General's Awards. Her last novel, *Am I Disturbing You?,* published six months before her death in January 2000, was a finalist for the 1999 Giller Prize. Upon her death she was paid tribute by both the Governor General and the Prime Minister, who declared her, respectively: "one of the most important writers of our time" and "among the most prominent figures in modern literature." Eds.]

JANE RULE

Jane Rule was 15 when she identified with Stephen Gordon, the heroine of the classic lesbian novel, *The Well of Loneliness,* who stated: "I shall never be a great writer because of my maimed and insufferable body." Now it is clear Rule has overcome the curse she feared, for she is fast being recognized as an important Canadian writer.

In the beginning of her writing career she had difficulty being published because her novels centred on lesbians who were successful at love and life. Twenty-two American publishers rejected *The Desert of the Heart* before Macmillan Company took it on in 1964. Rule has countered the "heartbreak-and-booze" tradition in lesbian fiction and in her own life, having lived happily with her mate, Helen Sontoff, for the last 20 years. She says, "Love is the terrible secret people are suspected of unless they're married, then one always suspects they don't."

Praise for her novels has come from such diverse writers as Joyce Carol Oates, Faith Baldwin, Marian Engel, and Margaret Laurence, who, in a *Globe and Mail* review of *Theme For Diverse Instruments,* described her as "one of the best writers we have, [whose] work compares very well indeed with the best fiction being written anywhere."

Rule has published novels, short stories, and social and literary criticism. She has been active in the women's movement; is interested in all the arts; has a record company called Rulebook Records; and has a flock of foster children from Greece to Vietnam. She retired from the English Department at the University of British Columbia several years ago to devote herself to her writing, moving to Galiano Island where she now resides. [HS-1978]

[Since 1978 Jane Rule has continued to publish. She remains a committed social activist and an important figure in the gay and lesbian community. In 1998 she was inducted into the Order of British Columbia. Eds.]

In my desire to be free I have overturned centuries of dogma, ideas, attitudes with a why?
—Dorothy Cox, 1975

left: Jane Rule

right: Alice Munro

ANTONINE MAILLET

Winner of the Prix Goncourt, France's most prestigious literary prize, Antonine Maillet is l'Acadie's foremost author. *Pélagie la charrette,* her prize-winning novel, tells of the expulsion of the French settlers from New Brunswick and Nova Scotia. The hero of the novel, Pélagie, helps her companions to leave, and becomes a leader of the movement to return to Acadia.

Antonine Maillet was born in Bouctouche, New Brunswick. After attending local schools, she studied at the Universities of Moncton and Montreal. She also studied oral literature in France before taking a doctorate at Laval. Her thesis topic, "Rabelais and the Folk Traditions of Acadia," reflects her deep interest in the literary traditions of her native land. She worked at Radio-Canada, and taught at several Canadian universities, including Laval.

Madame Maillet, who published her first novel in 1958, has an impressive string of writing awards. In addition to the Prix Goncourt, she has won the Governor General's Award for *Don L'Orignal,* the Prix Champlain for *Pointe-aux-Coques,* and the Prix des Volcans for *Mariagélas.* Perhaps the work best known across the country is *La Sagouine.* La Sagouine is a "poor woman, not a feeble woman." She is a cleaning lady, a woman who has seen all of life, and who comments on what she sees. She has captured the attention of her audiences. Written in the popular speech of the region, the poverty and daily struggle in *La Sagouine* reflect the struggle, yet also the humour, of Acadia.

Through the character, Antonine Maillet is not afraid to comment on anything. She discusses war, lotteries, the new year, Christmas, religion, and the separation of body and soul—all facts of life that are worthy of her attention. La Sagouine's struggle with census forms underlines the identity struggle of the Acadian. She is not from Quebec, and she is no French Canadian; she's Acadian, does not speak English, yet she lives on the North American continent. How can one define one's self when one's nationality is not recognized and given legitimacy? La Sagouine gives us all cause to reflect. [HS-1981]

I think the earth desperately needs women's creativity and many voices right now to help challenge and undo the deeply destructive patterns of patriarchy...[I] think that personal spiritual work, both individually and collectively...is essential to releasing our creative woman energy to its full potential, so that we can work together effectively to transform the world.—Di Brandt, 1995

[Antonine Maillet has continued to be a prolific writer of novels, plays, adaptations and translations. She is the recipient of 20 honorary doctorates, is a Companion of the Order of Canada, an Officier des Arts et des Lettres de France, and an Officier de l'Ordre national du Québec. Eds.]

ALICE MUNRO

One of our foremost contemporary writers, Alice Munro was born in the small town of Wingham, Ontario. She attended the University of Western Ontario for two years, then settled into suburban domesticity, first in Vancouver, where her first two daughters were born, then in Victoria, where the family opened a bookstore in 1963. A third daughter was born three years later. Munro returned to the University of Western Ontario as a writer in residence in 1974.

Munro started writing at an early age and she kept it up throughout the years of raising her family. She feels that being a housewife helped her because she was able to develop her art without pressure to earn a living.

Dance of the Happy Shades, a collection of stories, won the Governor General's Award in 1968, and *Lives of Girls and Women* was winner of the Canadian Booksellers' Association International Book Year Award in 1972. Dramatized versions of several of her works have been seen on CBC television.

Eileen, the narrator of her story "Memorial," says: "I do not believe things are there to be worked through....Illness and accidents. They ought to be respected, not explained. Words are shameful....Silence the only possible thing."

Yet in her writing Alice Munro attempts the impossible: to express hitherto unnamed states of consciousness, as she delves into seemingly ordinary lives with uncanny perception. Most of her central characters are intelligent, sensitive women who chafe at the restrictions and narrow horizons of small-town life. Personality is revealed through illuminating incidents, visual detail, and most of all, a masterful use of dialogue. Thoughts are laid bare, motives are scrutinized, family relationships are dissected, yet through it all Munro manages to convey the complexity and essential mystery of all human beings. [HS-1978]

[Since Herstory profiled Alice Munro, she has been acknowledged one of the world's greatest short story writers. Her work has been translated into thirteen languages. She is the recipient of numerous national and international honours, including the National Book Critics Circle Prize, the Giller Prize, the Canada-Australia Literary Prize, the Los Angeles-based Lannan Literary Award, and three Governor General's Awards. She is the first winner of the Marian Engel Award. In 1995 she won the W.H. Smith Award, given to the best book in any category published in the UK. In 1997 she was the first Canadian to receive the PEN/Malamud Award for Excellence in Short Fiction, and in 2001 she received another U.S. honour: the Rea Award for lifetime achievement. Eds.]

MARGARET LAURENCE

Margaret Laurence has created some of the strongest characterizations of women in Canadian literature. Through each novel runs a common theme of survival—women who struggle with the contradictions in their own lives.

Margaret Laurence writes about women because: "I'm a novelist and I'm a woman. I write about what I know." The novel, as Laurence says, is not a social statement but it "tries to say 'Look, here is the woman, in this situation and this is how she feels. Draw your own conclusions, but for heaven's sake, know this is how she feels.'"

Her career has included many impressive achievements. In 1964 three of her novels were published simultaneously in the United States—an extraordinary feat in the literary world. *Rachel, Rachel,* a sensitive film about a lonely schoolteacher in a small town, was made from the novel *A Jest of God.* Laurence was the first head of the Writers' Union of Canada.

Although the character of Stacey in *The Fire Dwellers* had been "there for a long time," the decision to write about her came with doubts: "Who on earth, I asked myself when I began writing this novel, is going to be interested in reading about a middle-aged housewife, mother of four? Then I thought; the hell with it—some of my best friends are middle-aged housewives; I'm one myself...and I was fed up with the current fictional portraits of women of my genera-

Some of us have suspected for a long time that a good deal of the teaching of the world regarding women has come under the general heading of "dope."
—Nellie McClung, 1915

There ought to be a different category for women who are writers and who need grants for housekeepers. Right now they won't give money for this. Male writers can get grants to take leave from their jobs, women can't. But housework is work.
—Margaret Laurence, 1974

left: Margaret Laurence

right: Joy Kogawa

tion—middle-aged mums either being presented as glossy magazine types, perfect, everloving and incontestably contented or else as sinister and spiritually cannibalistic monsters."

Laurence wrote *The Stone Angel* while raising her family. She considers her fifth and last novel, *The Diviners,* built around a woman who has a strong sense of herself as a person and a writer—to be her best. Whether this will prove to be so or not, it has firmly established her as one of Canada's finest writers. [HS-1975]

[Margaret Laurence died at her home in Lakefield, Ontario, in 1987. She has been the subject of numerous works of criticism, biography and documentary. Her writing has been adapted for radio, television and stage and translated into many languages. She was awarded the Order of Canada and honorary degrees by over a dozen Canadian universities. Until her death, she continued to promote the causes she believed in. Her memoir, *Dance on the Earth,* was published posthumously in 1988. Eds.]

JOY KOGAWA

The publication of *Obasan* in 1981 forced many Canadians to acknowledge the injustice suffered by Japanese-Canadians during World War II. Drawing on her own experience, Joy Kogawa created a sensitive, perceptive, and historically accurate picture of the effect of the internments. The characters in the novel reveal all the frustration, bitterness, and sense of helpless futility that come from such an experience. The confiscation of all their properties, their banishment, the ostracism from society because of their physical appearance, caused untold physical and psychological damage to Japanese-Canadians. Joy writes about this sense of alienation with a gentleness simmering with anger.

Joy Kogawa was born in Vancouver in 1935, the daughter of Gordon Goichi and Lois Nakayama. In 1942 she and her family were relocated to an internment camp in Slocan, British Columbia. Joy remained there until 1945, when she moved to Coaldale,

It makes me wild with rage to be described as a "female novelist." You never hear people referring to male novels and gentlemen novelists. I'm a novelist and I'm a woman. I write about what I know.
—Margaret Laurence, 1973

Alberta. After World War II the Canadian government gave the internees the option of either moving to Japan, which to most was a foreign country, or settling east of the Rocky Mountains. Joy's family chose to remain in Canada.

Joy lived in Coaldale until 1953. In 1957 she moved to Vancouver, where she married David Kogawa. In 1968 she divorced and moved with her two children to Ottawa, where she worked as a freelance writer and as a staff writer in the Office of the Prime Minister.

For *Obasan,* she received the Books in Canada First Novel Award in 1982, the 1983 American Book Award of the Before Columbus Foundation, and the Canadian Authors' Association 1982 Book of the Year Award. [HS-1986]

[Dividing her time between Vancouver and Toronto, Joy Kogawa is still well-known for her poetry, novels, and activism in the Japanese-Canadian redress movement. Her publications include: *Itsuka,* the sequel to *Obasan* (1992); *The Rain Ascends* (1995); and *Song of Lilith,* a book of poems with artwork by Lilian Broca (2001). Eds.]

MYRNA KOSTASH

All of Baba's Children, the nonfiction best-seller for which Myrna Kostash is best known, came "...from a complex of experiences I've had in the new left, the counterculture and the women's movement, as well as the experience of having been born and raised an ethnic." When *All of Baba's Children* was published in 1977, one reviewer wrote: "...she strips away the tinsel glamour of romanticism to reveal the often stark reality of the Ukrainian-Canadian experience." Another describes it as "...moving...powerful...bitter...irritating...."

Myrna estimates that 90% of her writing is about things that disturb her. Her comments on the women's movement, radical perspectives on ethnicity, and western regionalism and its discontent have appeared in *Maclean's, Saturday Night,* and *Chatelaine.*

A steady diet of heavy topics "...is absolutely joyful work...in discovering one understands something at last, that there are people around that share that same perspective and that one doesn't have to roll over and play dead. You can be useful, productive and creative as well as critical. All of these things coming together is a very joyful experience."

The attention and direction of a mentor at the beginning of her career helped. "This process is described in other professions of women, where in a patriarchal system, a powerful male figure will coach you along. Robert Fulford of *Saturday Night* gave me that confidence."

She peaked rapidly as a magazine writer in Toronto but soon "...discovered that there was a growing conflict between what I wanted to do as a writer and a thinker and what magazines would support. It was fine in 1975 to be a feminist because that was International Women's Year. But boy all that stuff got dropped in 1976. You have to make your choice between surviving in this machinery and churning out real fluff pieces and getting alienated from your labor or sticking to your guns and discovering that there's no market. That's why I turned to books."

She moved west. She discovered room for innovation. She got away "from the horrible fear of turning

into another Toronto hack..." and she wrote *All of Baba's Children.* [HS-1981]

[Myrna Kostash still makes Edmonton her home where she continues her career as a writer of articles, books, and documentaries including: *No Kidding: Inside the Worlds of Teenage Girls* (1987); *Bloodlines: A Journey into Eastern Europe* (1993); and *The Next Canada: In Search of Our Future Nation* (2000).

It's interesting to note that women are among Canada's best writers, and that the pioneer writers, such as Susanna Moodie, were all women.
—June Callwood, 1976

left: Myrna Kostash

right: Margaret Atwood

MARGARET ATWOOD

It seems to me that the proper path for a woman writer is not an all-out manning (or womaning) of the barricades, however much she may agree with many of the aims of the [women's] movement. The proper path is to become a better writer.
—Margaret Atwood, 1976

"The only important thing about being a writer is what you write." What Margaret Atwood has written and continues to write makes her one of Canada's most acclaimed writers. She has published two novels *(The Edible Woman* and *Surfacing)* and several volumes of poetry, including *The Circle Game,* for which she won the Governor General's Award in 1967. She has also completed a survey of Canadian literature, *Survival: A Thematic Guide to Canadian Literature.*

Margaret Atwood strongly believes in developing our Canadian artistic identity. She has travelled to Ontario schools and colleges giving readings and speaking on this topic. It was as a result of questions from students and teachers regarding Canadian literature that she wrote *Survival,* published in 1972. In it she points out two of the most prevalent themes in Canadian literature—victims and survival.

She is a strong supporter of Canadian writers. This support has included being a board member and an editor for the House of Anansi, a small Canadian publisher which has often taken the risk of publishing new writers' work.

She has come face to face with those who do not really think a woman is serious when she says she is a writer. What is important is that Margaret Atwood takes herself seriously and refuses to deny her talents. She writes mainly about women and her works portray women with whom female readers can really identify.

A lady is someone whose name is published three times: when she's born, when she gets married, when she dies. I didn't see why I should have to deal with that shit.
—Margaret Atwood, 1975

She feels close to other women writers and has high expectations of them. She now feels supported by other women. This is in contrast to her college days when she often felt other women were hostile towards her ambitions. This change shows that women's changing view of themselves and other women can lead to support for, rather than a denial of, each others' talents. [HS-1977]

[Margaret Atwood has been widely acclaimed as one of the world's foremost authors. Since 1977, she has published numerous novels, collections of poetry, short stories, essays, and works of criticism. She has received many awards and honours including:

Companion of the Order of Canada (1981); another Governor General's Award (1986) for *The Handmaid's Tale;* the Giller Prize (1997) for *Alias Grace;* and the Booker Prize (2000) for *The Blind Assassin.* Eds.]

CAROL SHIELDS

Unlike most Canadian writers, Carol Shields is not identified with a particular region. The characters, events, and scenes in her novels are found in every part of Canada; her poetry tells of human experience. Carol's novels focus upon the people who inhabit what might be called the inner suburbs.

Carol always wanted to write. As a youngster growing up in the Chicago area, she published poems in school and local papers. When she was 25, she sold a story to the CBC, and her career was truly launched. Since that first CBC story, she has published several collections of poetry and, in 1976, her first novel, *Small Ceremonies.* Her range also extends to more academic writing; she wrote her master of arts thesis on Susanna Moodie [see p. 210] for the University of Ottawa.

Carol feels that women tend to write about human relationships. She bases this judgment on both her own experience and her study of other writers. She also wholeheartedly seconds Virginia Woolf's famous dictum that a woman who writes needs five hundred pounds a year and a room of her own. Carol has a room which she uses only for writing, not for mending clothes or any of the other countless tasks a woman with a family is heir to.

To satisfy social instincts and to justify what she calls her work ethic, Carol has taught writing classes at the University of Manitoba. One of her classes was for people who are part of the workforce, but who wish to develop their writing skills. She enjoys teaching as it helps her to develop her own ideas about her craft.

Carol says that the first novel published brings the greatest pleasure and after that the rewards lie in becoming a better writer. She has been called a writer of "genuine sensitivity, with a generous, quick-witted style." Her future development as a writer can only bring pleasure to her readers in all parts of the country. [HS-1982]

[Carol Shields certainly gained the attention of Canada's readers after she first caught *Herstory's* eye in 1982. She was the author of numerous novels, short stories, plays, and poems. In 1995 *The Stone Diaries* won both the Pulitzer Prize and the Governor General's Award, and in 1998 she was not only made an officer of the Order of Canada, but *Larry's Party* won the Orange Prize and the National Book Critics Circle Award. Winnipeg honoured her with the "Carol Shields Book Award." Despite her battle with breast cancer, she published four books after 2000, including: an anthology, *Dropped Threads;* a biography of Jane Austen; and a novel, *Unless.* Carol Shields died on 16 July 2003. Eds.]

left: Carol Shields

The surprise in the women's Lib cracker box is liking women better, from which flows liking the self more.
—June Callwood, 1973

Cut off from the world of affairs and from a history of their own, women may have turned instinctively to the present moment and to the immediate concern of what it means to be a woman.—Carol Shields, 1978

The woman writer in Canada...exists in a society that, though it may turn certain individual writers into revered cult objects, has little respect for writing as profession, and not much respect for women either.
—Margaret Atwood, 1976

Another group of Canadian women writers is emerging as we begin a new millenium. First Nations women and women of colour are asserting their right to tell their own stories.

WEST COAST WOMEN & WORDS

West Coast Women & Words is a Vancouver-based organization whose mandate is to support and encourage women writers, publishers, teachers, and others who communicate through the written word. It is sustained by government funding, membership dues, and a lot of energy and enthusiasm.

This grassroots feminist organization emerged from the Women & Words conference held in Vancouver in July 1983. Innovative and sometimes controversial, the event was attended by 750 women who went on to establish Women & Words groups across Canada. An anthology, *Women and Words/Les femmes et les mots*, worked on simultaneously with the conference, was published in 1985. *In the Feminine*, the proceedings of the 1983 conference, included contributions from Margaret Atwood and Marian Engel, among others.

People think that women of colour who write have only been around since [Alice Walker and Toni Morrison] were on the cover of Newsweek.... *But we have been here longer than that.*
—Barbara Smith, 1988

West Coast Women & Words has produced plays, the national bilingual Women's Peace Write campaign, historical research, seminars, workshops, radio programs, and in 1985 founded West Word Summer School/Retreat for Women, now an annual event. The group's most successful project, West Word, has offered courses in poetry, fiction, playwriting, fiction/theory, speculative fiction, and creative documentary. Ann Decter describes the intensity of this unforgettable event: "West Word was not just about writing. It was about feminist writers across country knowing we are not working alone, although many of us are working in isolation....About collaboration, communication, verification and strength in numbers. And it was about living, for two invaluable weeks, in a world guided by feminist consciousness." [HS-1990]

SISTER VISION PRESS

Women Aboriginal and racial minority writers have difficulty getting their work accepted by mainstream Canadian publishers. Often, they are told the market to which they would appeal is too small because Canadian readers would not identify with their work.

Cultural critic Marlene Nourbese Philip has pointed out that this response rests upon twin false assumptions, first, that Canadian publishing is market driven, and second, that people only read literature by writers of their own ethnic or racial background. The former is simply false, the latter racist: "The reason why African, Asian and Native writers have difficulty getting published has little to do with the audience and markets and much to do with racism and power: power to exercise that racism by deciding which books ought and ought not to be published, reviewed and critiqued."

Unfortunately, women of colour have not found feminist presses much more hospitable. Rather than wait for existing publishers to change their practices, in 1985 Makeda Silvera and Stephanie Martin founded Sister Vision Press, the first and still the only Canadian publishing house devoted exclusively to the work of

right: Freda Ahenakew, author and academic devoted to the preservation of Native languages and culture

I n our media-saturated lives, we are continually bombarded with visual images. It is vitally important that women's perspective forms part of our increasingly visual world.

ALANIS OBOMSAWIN

Alanis Obomsawin is a 46-year-old Abaneki woman from the Odanak Reserve in Quebec. She is a singer, storyteller and filmmaker. While these words may describe what she does, they cannot convey the great depth, respect and caring which she brings to her work.

As a singer and storyteller she has travelled to schools, summer camps, museums, art centres, folk festivals, and retirement homes, sharing the songs and legends of native people. Her main interest is children and their education, and she has visited native communities across the country, in order to sing and play with them. She believes her people's custom of telling stories and songs to young children is a very important one. It has played an integral part in her own life. "Many stories were told and most of them were about

top left: Anne Anderson, author of over 100 Cree-language publications, including children's books, cookbooks, and an authoritative Cree-English dictionary

Indian women have been invisible to white historians who have given Indian girls very few heroines with whom they can identify. These historians have overlooked the long period between Pocahontas and Buffy Sainte-Marie.
—Sherrill Cheda, 1973

women of colour. Their mandate is to discover and develop writing by Black women, First Nations women, Asian women, and women of mixed racial heritage.

The impetus for Sister Vision Press arose not simply from a desire to broaden publishing opportunities for women of colour, but also "out of a need for autonomy, our need to determine the context and style of our work and to control the words and images that are produced about us." Through its books, Sister Vision Press is able to explore the intersection of oppressions based on race and sex: "Our books challenge sexism and heterosexism in our respective communities, and racism, bias and prejudice in Euro-Centric communities."

Since its inception, Sister Vision Press has published oral history, theory, and research, fiction, poetry, and writing for children and young people. Some of its authors have long been established, others are just emerging. With this breadth of focus, Sister Vision "has served as a forum for many women who are writing in isolation," achieving its goal of not simply publishing, but of acting "as a cultural and political literary force." [HS-1996]

bottom left: Alanis Obomsawin

animals because the best friends of our people were animals....When I slept, that was the best time because I had all my dreams, all my animals, a life of my own. I guess they formed my own beliefs and way of expressing myself."

It was through her work as an entertainer that Alanis was asked to work with the National Film Board of Canada as a consultant. Since 1967 she has worked with the film board as writer, director, and producer. Throughout the years she has made many educational materials, such as *Mother of Many Children,* a one-hour documentary about native women. Her film strips about Indian life have been used all over the world.

Her main concern is to help native people communicate without outside interference. Using her power to help others characterizes her work and her art. "If you have power—power of any kind—and you keep it for your own pleasure, to me, that has no value. But it's important that if you have it, you use it for the people." [HS-1981]

[In 1983 Alanis Obomsawin was made a member of the Order of Canada. She has directed over 20 films and has received numerous honours and awards in recognition of her commitment to social justice. She received the 2001 Governor General's Award in Visual and Media Arts for her "longstanding career and significant contribution to Canadian filmmaking." Eds.]

My films are always about human relationships. To me, the core...is about people and their inability to connect—people who love each other very much, but somehow have difficulty expressing that love.
—Norma Bailey, 1991

WOMEN & FILM: THE NFB'S STUDIO D

In 1974 the National Film Board of Canada (NFB) founded Studio D to provide a forum for women filmmakers. Studio D grew out of the Challenge for Change program, which for a decade between 1965 and 1974 produced films designed to help citizens affect decision-making processes. Studio D has male filmmakers as well, but its main objective remains bringing women's perspectives to the films it produces—perspectives that are often lacking in the media of our culture. Studio D films and filmmakers have won national and international awards while continuing to focus on their original mandate of producing films for women, about women, by women.

Studio D productions have been well received by audiences, and many of their titles will be familiar. *Not a Love Story* (1981), a film about pornography, attracted nation-wide attention; *If You Love This Planet* (1982) is an Academy Award-winning film about the consequences of nuclear war as described by Dr. Helen Caldicott; *Speaking Our Peace* (1984) argues that women's peacemaking skills must be applied to global politics to avert nuclear confrontation; *Behind the Veil* (1985), a film about Roman Catholic nuns, includes scenes from an entirely enclosed order, the Trappists, that could have been filmed only by an all-female crew; *DES, An Uncertain*

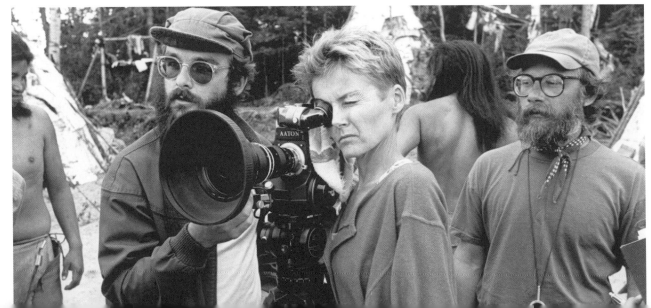

right: Filmmaker Norma Bailey, producer of Daughters of the Country *series for the National Film Board of Canada, and of the feature film* Bordertown Café.

Legacy attracted a large audience when shown on the CBC English television network in 1985; *Abortion: Stories From North and South* (1985) ranges from Northern Ireland to South America and challenges the viewer to face the reality of the continuing practice of abortion, sanctioned or unsanctioned.

At the beginning of their second decade Studio D issued this statement: "We profoundly believe in the films we make. The objectivity we practise is that of not letting one's own set of vested interests interfere with another person's telling of her own truth. But we do not believe there is value, at this time, in the kind of 'objectivity' that pretends detachment when dealing with matters of life and death, of justice, truth and human well-being." [HS-1987]

[In 1986, Studio D executive producer Kathleen Shannon received the Order of Canada "for her contribution to the women's movement through the Studio." Her successors, Rina Fraticelli and Ginny Stikeman, developed New Initiatives in Film, to address under-representation of Aboriginal women and women of colour. In 1993 Studio D earned its first Genie with the release of the widely successful *Forbidden Love*—the first major film on Canadian lesbian culture. After 22 years and over 125 films Studio D was shut down in 1996, due to budget cuts. However women continue to have a voice at the NFB, producing nearly half of its English films since 1990. Eds.]

WTN—WOMEN'S TELEVISION NETWORK

"TV advertisers will pay a premium for shows that attract large numbers of women between the ages of 18 and 49, based on the assumption that they make the majority of purchases and buying decisions," notes commentator Ron Weiskind. That fact alone should ensure programming that realistically portrays women. Yet a recent American survey found that women were in only one-third of all prime-time roles and only one-quarter of roles in children's shows. Moreover, the majority of those roles go to white actresses under the age of 35. Women are also under-represented behind the camera. In Canadian broadcasting, women make up only 1% of senior management in the private sector and 17% at the CBC.

Enter Women's Television Network (WTN), Canada's first channel devoted to programming by, for, and about women. The idea of establishing a women's network had been considered since 1989. Studies had shown that women are unique in the way they "learn, communicate, and interact." Polls indicated that a majority of Canadian women would support more information-based shows that directly related to their lives—beyond simply cooking and gardening. WTN suggests women "have the right to watch our stories, hear our issues discussed and have opportunities to author our own images."

Their licence was granted by the CRTC on 6 June 1994, and it was immediately evident that WTN would do business differently. All senior positions, from that of president and CEO, to those of vice-presidents of programming, marketing, and engineering and operations, as well as 98% of staff positions, are held by women. Their commitment and professionalism is evident when one considers they had only six months between being granted their licence and going on air 1 January 1995. When they started, they "didn't have a paper clip." The senior management had well-established careers elsewhere, but everyone "viewed [WTN] as a chance you only get once in a lifetime, a tremendous opportunity."

Above all, their mandate expresses an appreciation of the diversity of women's experiences: no single age, ethnic group, or philosophy dominates. Independent Canadian producers created a quarter of programming in the first year. Additionally, a portion of revenues is earmarked for The Foundation, established "to administer research grants, scholarships, and apprentice positions to enhance the roles women have in television production, management and programming."

Those hoping to see a positive role model for women on screen and off now have a channel they can turn to. [HS-1996]

[Women's Television Network was sold in 2002 and renamed W Network. Eds.]

wtn

Expanding Horizons

We sometimes forget the power we actually have.
—Barbara Barde, 1992

Today, a new generation of Canadian women musicians, singers, and songwriters are internationally celebrated. They, and we, owe a debt to those independent artists who led the way.

above: Kate and Anna McGarrigle

Do we dare take responsibility for our own lives and our own futures as individuals and not just as women? Do we dare fly and take the consequences?
—Marylu Antonelli, 1975

KATE AND ANNA McGARRIGLE

What do you do when you grow up in a close family that regards music as much a part of daily life as sleeping and eating? The chances are that you will gather like-minded friends around you as you grow older, and simply keep up the old tradition. That is precisely what Kate and Anna McGarrigle have done, except that in the process they have also become two of Canada's best-known singer-composers.

Their richly harmonized arrangements are popular not only in Canada; in 1976 they completed two European tours, one North American tour, and had their first album, *Kate and Anna McGarrigle*, proclaimed second-best album of the year by *The New York Times*. Their second album, *Dancer with Bruised Knees,* was released early in 1977, and promises to be even more successful.

The McGarrigles grew up in the village of St Sauveur des Monts, Quebec, and later moved to Montreal. A continuing favourite pastime was performing together and with friends, occasionally writing songs themselves. Their fame might have ended with Kate McGarrigle singing on minor folk circuits, had she not sent one of Anna's songs, "Heart like a Wheel," to Linda Ronstadt. The song was a hit, and three years later Maria Muldaur bought two more of the sisters' songs. Within the next year, they were contracted to record *Kate and Anna McGarrigle.*

Success has not drastically changed Kate and Anna. Their music continues to reflect their own personal, relaxed style, and their own experience of French Canada. [HS-1979]

[Since *Herstory* first noted them, Kate and Anna McGarrigle have released more albums and entrenched their international reputation. While performing and recording worldwide, they have also composed music for movie, television, and stage productions, and have themselves been the subjects of numerous documentaries and specials. In 1994, they were awarded the Order of Canada. The family's musical tradition is being continued by Kate's children, Rufus and Martha Wainwright. Eds.]

BUFFY SAINTE-MARIE

Buffy Sainte-Marie is an internationally acclaimed singer, songwriter, and recording artist. She is Cree, a descendant of Chiefs Pay-e-Pot and Starblanket, and was born in the Qu'Appelle Valley of southeastern Saskatchewan.

Music became important to Buffy at an early age. She was adopted by a non-Indian family and raised in a small New England town where, "they didn't believe in Indians. They thought we were all dead, had been stuffed and put in museums." Her childhood was lonely and scarred by violence. "Music saved my life by being a friend when I really needed one."

appearances on *Sesame Street* that Buffy hopes to effect the most change. To millions of young viewers, Buffy is a thoroughly contemporary person who just happens to be an Indian.

"I want to get across the fact that Indian people still exist...that we have feelings and families, that we fall in love and have babies like everybody else, that we have language, mathematics, law, government and more to say than How and Ugh." [HS-1979]

[Buffy Sainte-Marie appeared for five years on *Sesame Street* with her son Dakota Wolfchild Starblanket. In 1982 her song "Up Where We Belong," for the film *An Officer and A Gentleman,* won an Academy Award. In 1993 she helped establish a new Juno Awards category "for music of aboriginal Canada." Buffy continues to draw crowds on the international concert circuit, and also performs regularly on reserves across North America. In the United States, she was given the Award for Lifetime Musical Achievement by First Americans in the Arts. The award has since been named after her. Eds.]

left: Buffy Sainte-Marie

...in the music business, what matters is not being male or female, but whether people will listen to your music.
—Sylvia Tyson, 1975

Buffy began singing her songs on the coffee house circuit of the 1960s, for five dollars a night. At that time she was known as a folksinger with a message: her song "The Universal Soldier" became the anthem of the anti-war movement; songs like "Now That the Buffalo's Gone" and "My Country 'tis of Thy People You're Dying" set her apart from other protest singers by focusing for the first time on the plight of the North American Indian.

In the 12 years since then, Buffy and her music have undergone a transformation. She describes her recent music as "pow-wow rock"—a combination of funky rock and haunting Indian chants and rhythms which is uniquely hers.

Her goal is to bridge the gap between Native people and the rest of the world. To this end, she founded and financed the Nihewan Foundation for the education of Indian professionals, and is active in the Native North American Women's Association, and the American Indian Movement. But it is through her

JONI MITCHELL

Joni Mitchell was first exposed to folk music in 1962 at Saskatoon's Louis Riel Coffeehouse. Inspired by the performances, she bought a baritone ukulele and an instruction book and practised until she had mastered various folk songs. The following year, while studying at the Alberta College of Art, she decided to actively pursue her talent in music.

Today Joni is known for her ever evolving styles in a long and diverse career as a musician. She refuses to jeopardize the creativity of her music by catering to one particular audience. Her 17 collections range from folk to jazz to pop. "I have to keep my spirit high...my creativity flowing. I've learned not to be afraid of failure—because out of the ashes of failure may come a great idea." The longevity of her career has justified her refusal to make commercial success her sole criterion. She is not afraid to take chances. "My records sell steadily over a long period of time, more like books....I

What do Indian people need? We need a sense of our own joy, our own beauty, our own dignity, our own life and laughter.
—Buffy Sainte-Marie, 1978

think I lost a few people with the more jazzy projects but gained others who couldn't get into my previous work."

Joni is also an accomplished artist. Her work has been displayed at shows in New York, London, and Japan. These vibrant pieces show that her diversity in music also extends to her art. Joni enjoys her dual talents. She explains, "When I get writer's block I don't panic—I just pick up a brush." She believes that her childhood on the prairies has strongly influenced her work as an artist and as a musician:

"My creative drive is based on a series of powerful images. The royal blue moment of morning, the fury of a hailstorm that I watched in wonder as it completely devastated a friend's father who watched his crop, all his work, torn and shredded. The train rolling around the curve at Maidstone, with the sun flashing in deep pink from the elevators across the road. That is all part of me. I am a flatlander." [HS-1992]

[Joni Mitchell has produced over 20 albums, and continues to influence generations of artists and fans alike. In 2000 the Mendel Art Gallery in her hometown, Saskatoon, hosted the first retrospective of her artwork. Eds.]

What we call reality is a certain relationship between sensation and memories which surround us at the same time.
—Joni Mitchell, 1990

LILLIAN ALLEN

Lillian Allen grew up in Spanish Town, Jamaica. Since 1969, she has played a central role in creating a black cultural presence in Canada. Lillian is one of Canada's foremost dub poets. Dub "is a poetry particular to black culture," says Allen, "which...hovers in a realm somewhere between poetry and music....[It] is often based upon a reggae beat....The beat, the rhythm, then, is an inseparable part of dub poetry." Dub, as a living cultural expression, is Lillian's chosen art form to capture the ferment of the black power, feminist, and peace movements in Canada.

Raised in a formal British school system. Lillian soon learned the importance of language in maintaining imperialism and oppression. "I was conscious of the tension between how you expressed yourself at home and how you were supposed to express yourself at school. It was assumed that if you wanted to make something of yourself and get ahead, you had to leave your culture and language behind."

But Lillian refused to do that, leaving behind her country to carry on her cultural and political work. During the late 1970s, Lillian travelled across Canada

right: Joni Mitchell

with Clifton Joseph performing their poetry. "Dub validates the lives and aspirations of those ignored and excluded from the dominant culture," she proclaims. "It articulates a just vision of the future. It carries a spirit of celebration, empowerment and joy."

Although dub poetry has gained international recognition, the League of Canadian Poets refused membership to the three leading dub poets in Canada in 1984. Lillian Allen was one of those poets. Supporters argued that dub is "outside the confines of 'print-bound' culture and cannot be assessed by traditional academic standards, nor by values of white, middle-class academics. It must therefore be approached as its own unique genre and appreciated in terms of its own tradition and culture." The League was still unaccommodating.

Lillian has self-published several books of poetry. *Rhythm an' Hard Times* (1982) has sold over 8,000 copies. Her debut album, *Revolutionary Tea Party,* won the Juno Award for best Reggae/Calypso recording of 1986.

Lillian Allen is committed to the use of art in community education, organizing, and community development. [HS-1989]

[Lillian Allen was made a member of the League of Canadian Poets in 1986. She won a second Juno for *Conditions Critical* (1988), and Landmark Album of the Past 20 Years, by *Ms.* magazine in 1991 for *Revolutionary Tea Party.* She is a playwright and a filmmaker and professor of creative writing at the Ontario College of Art and Design. Lillian is a recognized authority, activist, and consultant on issues of diversity and culture. Eds.]

CONNIE KALDOR

In Connie Kaldor's song, "Wanderlust," she says, "Every once in a while in a woman's life she has to pack her bags and hit the trail." For a uniquely talented singer and performer, the road can become a demanding way of life. For a writer of songs that are touching, humorous, and often gritty, it can be a source of inspiration: "I have to mix the writing with going out and finding things, experiencing things, and seeing things....there are so many stories out there—untold stories that will make great songs." She says song writing is "like falling in love." But like true love, it requires hard work and dedication: "I have trouble disciplining myself to write, because of all the various pressures."

The pressures began to mount when Kaldor turned to music on a full-time basis in 1978. From her home in Regina, her first wanderings led her to Edmonton. There she began to chafe against her own limitations as a solo performer and those imposed on her by business concerns. She felt a move to Vancouver was necessary if her career was to develop. Working with a band and collaborating with other performers has encouraged change and growth in her music. Her kinship to the prairies remains strong, however—she planted wheat in her Vancouver garden.

Much of her material reflects a wandering spirit. In "God Made Mamas to Cry," she sympathizes with the

top left: Lillian Allen

To write is powerful medicine, magic, weaponry and love. To write poetry is the ultimate in that power. It is a sweet and yielding power, as well as being an incisive and bludgeoning one.
—Maxine Tynes, 1986

left: Connie Kaldor

mothers of "wandering children who just forget to write." But often her characters are dreaming of the freedom of the road. The hard-grained drifter in "Sheep Creek" breathes in the Rocky Mountain air "if only in my [his] dreams," and a Husky truck stop waitress watches through a frosted windowpane for a "Bird On the Wing." Her sympathy with women runs like a connecting thread throughout, without binding her to any feminist stereotype. "One of These Days" deals unapologetically with loneliness; a young girl is the victim in a conflict between her parents in "Caught In the Crossfire"; "Get Back the Night" reclaims lost territory in a powerful way; "Jerks" laughs heartily at male chauvinist Neanderthals. With typical humour she says: "After all, I'm a woman—I've been practising all my life. I started as a young girl and worked my way up." [HS-1987]

[Now living in Montreal with her husband, singer Paul Campagne of Hart Rouge, and their two children, Connie Kaldor has nine albums and a 1989 Juno Award to her credit. In 1997 she signed a U.S. record deal and, touring internationally, continues to be known for her theatrical and entertaining live shows. Eds.]

I believe that music is really powerful— it can lift spirits, heal people, and make you feel great.
—Connie Kaldor, 1982

right: Loreena McKennitt

LOREENA McKENNITT

Loreena McKennitt explores traditional and contemporary Celtic themes with her haunting vocals and the Celtic harp. She travels often to England and Scotland "to track down the music not only in a historical sense but to find the many instances where it still exists in a very living and informal way, often in a pub over a pint with a fiddle, whistle or guitar."

Although she was born into an Irish-Canadian family in Morden, Manitoba, Loreena was not exposed to Celtic music until she moved to Winnipeg in 1976. She discovered the music at folk sessions and coffee houses and soon began listening to recordings of a Celtic artist from Brittany. "It was Alan Stivell's recording of the celtic harp that I was instinctively drawn to, the imagery evoked by the harp, whistle, cello and sounds of the ocean which swept me to a time past and pulled at my primitive heartstrings." She purchased a Celtic harp in the early 1980s and commenced her exploration of the music. "I maintain that music chose me more than me it."

She began by playing on the streets of Toronto. "I love the social context of busking....It was the whole function of music in older cultures. The bards provided a voice to the voiceless." She sold tickets for her first concert while busking at the St. Lawrence market.

Enjoying the creative control that accompanies managing her own career, she says that, although she has been approached by every major company, "my value system is such that signing with a major company isn't the end all deal." She has built her career with self-determination and creativity. She explains "I'm very much at the helm of the ship." [HS-1992]

[Shortly after this profile was published, Loreena McKennitt signed an unusually advantageous and rights-retaining deal with a major label. She has sold over 12 million records worldwide, received two Juno awards and composed for theatre and film. Her scores of gold, platinum, and multiplatinum records attest to her international popularity. Loreena McKennitt has steered her own course with staggering success. Eds.]

JANE SIBERRY

Jane Siberry's innovative music reflects her unique perspective: "I decide on a concept when I feel a physical sensation...anything that doesn't move falls by the wayside."

In 1987 Warner Bros. offered her a worldwide recording contract with complete creative control. Critics have praised her since her first European appearances in 1988. Her success is rooted in her ability to trust in herself. Lenny Waronker, president of Warner Brothers, says "She's gifted with her own musical identity."

She does not limit herself to following only one path. After her first year of university she switched from the music program to the science program. Her first love remained music but she chose the sciences because of her "curiosity about the world." In typical fashion, her 1989 album *Bound by the Beauty* covers a range of themes from nature to trains and hockey.

Jane chooses her lyrics carefully:

"When I work on the lyrics for the melodic hooks that people will be particularly attracted to or repeat in

their heads, I try to make sure that it is not negative, because I think it's dangerous to say something negative over and over again. It affects people on the subconscious level...it doesn't mean the lyrics have to be happy but not frivolously negative....People have to be especially careful of what they send out because it will have a resonance."

Jane considers herself fortunate in her career. "If you don't love what you do, you fade away." [HS-1991]

[Jane Siberry has produced more than a dozen albums and branched into film and video. In 1996 she founded her own label SHEEBA, devoted to the distribution of "all things Siberry." She continues to be an innovator with a devoted following of fans and critics alike. Eds.]

K.D. LANG

"Singing is everything to me and all the rest of the stuff, all the controversy, all the adversity, all the work...it means nothing compared to the singing." k.d. lang has always pursued her art in a uniquely personal way. From her hometown of Consort, Alberta, lang began as something of a novelty act. Her frenetic "cow-punk" stage show and claims to be the reincarnation of Patsy Cline, attracted curiosity and eventually praise for her talent. Despite three Grammy Awards, numerous Junos and Canadian Country Music Association Awards, lang has remained outside the traditional country music establishment. Her public declaration of homosexuality and outspoken support of vegetarianism often placed her in conflict with a characteristically conservative country music audience. However, her undeniable ability and dedication to her craft have earned a respect which makes her a valuable role model.

As *Chatelaine's* woman of the year in 1988, and Canadian Academy of Recording Arts and Sciences' artist of the decade in 1991, lang's considerable talents have legitimized her individuality. Says Margaret Atwood, "You can't defy convention, you can't counter tradition. Unless, of course, you are very good. k.d. lang is very good."

An unconventional approach to both career and

left: Jane Siberry

Everyone is always telling you that you need exotic things to make you happy, but if you can make the things around you exotic to yourself, then you have a never-ending resource of pleasure.
—Jane Siberry, 1989

All this could look like a hard act to follow, but you can never really plan anything. You can't plan how much a rose is going to grow, and people aren't any different.
—k.d. lang, 1992

top right: Needleworkers, Port Colborne, 1909

personal life has allowed lang to explore various musical styles and artistic mediums. "My parents brought me up with no limitations. They supported my self-confidence and never said 'Only boys can do that'....I did whatever I wanted to." Indeed, k.d. lang has earned respect for her character as well as her talent: "We admire k.d. for her voice and because there is nothing phony about her....I think k.d. represents the freedom we all wish we had," writes biographer William Robertson.

She is a woman who has found success on her own terms. Her honesty and integrity appeal to fans in a profound way. One woman wrote of recovering from severe depression following a child's death: "k.d.'s sense of fun, her total abandonment to the music and the sheer beauty of her voice reached into the depths of my grief and pulled me back out with a feeling of incredible joy. If everyone were as 'real' as Kathy Dawn, life would be a 'real' joy." [HS-1994]

[In 1995 k.d. received the BRIT award for Best International Female Artist. Three years later, she was voted #33 of 100 Greatest Women of Rock and Roll and also received the Michael Callen Medal of Achievement from GLAMA for furthering and nurturing gay and lesbian music. She is an international celebrity with a "mantel-full" of awards, who continues to stretch her range as an actor in film and television. Eds.]

Quilters are nice people to know; in quilting one develops qualities that tend to carry over into other spheres of one's life—precision, patience, gaiety, whimsy and a sense of orderliness.
—Mary Conroy, 1982

The point is, if you've got the goods, you'll make it. If you're a woman, you'll probably go through more grief and more heartache along the way, but they can't stop you.
—Rita Letendre, 1975

Once again, *Herstory* comes full circle. Women's history ebbs and flows, but we can hope each time to gain new ground. *Herstory* is proud to reclaim the artistry of women's traditions and celebrate the excellence of women's artistic achievement.

ART OR CRAFT?

"Men work in the outside world and women adorn the home." Feminist Art Historians Rozsika Parker and Griselda Pollock pointed out in their landmark 1981 book *Old Mistresses* that this attitude, which became entrenched in the Victorian era, has long influenced our perceptions of the art world.

Painting and sculpture, considered "high art," also have the status of professional work created for public audiences and galleries. The overwhelming majority of artists whose work we place in this category are men. Their names are familiar to us; they are thought of as "great" artists—the Old Masters.

In contrast are the "lesser arts," usually domestic crafts made for the family. Historical examples of this work are frequently anonymous or, if they are signed, little is known about the artist.

Women, looking after their homes and families by making necessary and practical items, have often done so with such skill and design that art galleries have finally started appreciating the technical prowess and aesthetic sophistication of their work.

For many women who continue this work for enjoyment and family, the "crafts" are still a combination of the domestic and the creative—art for the home. [HS-2000]

right: k.d. lang

PITSEOLAK ASHOONA

Pitseolak Ashoona, whose name means "sea pigeon," started drawing when James Houston came to Cape Dorset, asked for drawings and encouraged the Inuit to send their work south. She had her first one-woman exhibition of prints and drawings in 1971. The story of Pitseolak, and also of how Cape Dorset became an internationally recognized artists' colony, is told through recorded interviews with author Dorothy Eber in Eber's book *Pitseolak—Pictures Out Of My Life.*

Pitseolak says about herself: "I have lost the time when I was born but I am old now—my sons say maybe I am 70. [I draw] the things I have never seen, monsters and spirits, the old ways and things we did long ago before there were many white men.

"I know I have had an unusual life, being born in a skin tent and living to hear on the radio that two men have landed on the moon. To make prints is not easy. You must think first and this is hard to do. But I am happy doing the prints. After my husband died I felt very alone and unwanted; making prints is what has

made me happiest since he died. I am going to keep on doing them until they tell me to stop. If no one tells me to stop, I shall make them as long as I am well. If I can, I'll make them even after I'm dead." [HS-1974]

[Pitseolak Ashoona produced over 7,000 drawings and 250 prints in her 20-year career. She became a member of the Royal Canadian Academy in 1974 and the Order of Canada in 1977. She died in 1983. Eds.]

JESSIE OONARK

When Jessie Oonark died in March of 1985 Canada lost one of its most respected artists. Equally eloquent on paper or cloth, Oonark was considered by critics to be among the most talented Inuit artists. Her wall hangings have been presented to visiting dignitaries, including the Queen and Pope John Paul II. A four by six metre hanging of Oonark's is on display in the National Arts Centre, her prints are exhibited in major galleries and museums throughout North America, and she illustrated several books.

above: Pitseolak Ashoona

I think being a feminist means one likes being a woman and wants to make a statement that it's a good thing to be a woman.... Every woman must decide she's a person and stand up for herself.
—Anne Szumigalski, 1985

If we lose concern for literature, art, history and philosophy, our civilization has suffered the ultimate defeat.
—Mary Quayle Innis,
Leading Ladies, Canada, 1639-1967, 1978

left: Quilters with handmade quilt, New Brunswick

right: Mary Pratt

Jessie Oonark won many awards, was a member of the Royal Canadian Academy and an honorary member of the Canadian Crafts Council.

Jessie married and raised a family before gaining an international reputation. She passed on her love of art: three of her eight children—Janet Kigusiuq, William Noah, and Nancy Pukingrnak—are also well-known Baker Lake artists.

Oonark's art covers a range of Inuit culture, spirit life, the close human relationship with it, and Inuit village life. She has employed many of the techniques of clothing construction used by earlier women of the north. This talented Inuit woman preserved the artistic and spiritual ways of her people. [HS-1986]

MARY PRATT

The still-life paintings of Mary Pratt reflect light like the sun on water, and in the meeting of light and substance the mundane becomes magic. Creating images of everyday things she loves has shed new light on her role as a Newfoundland homemaker as well. Before 1969, raising her four children and supporting her husband Christopher's art career had taken precedence. With the completion of *Supper Table,* which records the dining room table before the remnants of a meal are cleared away, she turned a corner and began to celebrate domestic life by painting it.

"The things that turn me on to paint are the things I really like. Seeing the groceries come in for instance. Or cooking....I'm getting supper, and suddenly I look at the cod fillet spread out on tinfoil and I think 'that's gorgeous, that's absolutely beautiful.'" Food and its wrappings are common themes: *Baked Apples in Tinfoil* (1969), *Salmon On Saran* (1974), *Eggs In An Egg Crate* (1975), *Steamed Pudding* (1977), and *Christmas Turkey* (1980). Her gleaming surfaces conceal content and reveal form. Pratt captures her transitory subjects by photographing them and then working from the slides.

Alex Colville, with whom she studied at Mount Allison University, suggests: "Her use of photography implies a faithfulness to optically perceived reality...thus an acceptance of the physically existing world...." But a fine line exists between the precision of execution which celebrates a subject, and the intense scrutiny which condemns it. *Service Station* (1978), which Pratt terms a "female statement about a male world," portrays the butchered and bloody hindquarters of a moose hoisted behind a tow truck:

"I have quite strong feelings about the women's movement without really being a part of it...I have a lot to thank it for, but not the origin of the work, not the impetus to paint. I do think it's important for a woman to work within her own frame of reference, and not feel it is inferior to feel the way a woman feels. The minute you try to adopt the mannerisms and attitudes of men, it all breaks down....

"It's a happy woman who can say, 'I paint what I like' and it's nice to have people like it...the least anyone should do is pursue an activity or job they like. It's a shame anyone has to be miserable." [HS-1987]

[Mary Pratt continues to live and work in Newfoundland. She has built a national reputation and her art can be found in public and private collections across the country. In 1995 her work was the subject of a nationally touring retrospective. Eds.]

I always knew I was an artist, but in the South African context it wasn't permissible to be that self-indulgent. Once I became politically aware, then there were things I had to do rather than "mess" around with art. I think if I lived there now, I might feel differently. Art can be as valid a statement as anything else.
—Ann Newdigate Mills, 1989, tapestry artist, on her life before immigrating to Canada.

DAPHNE ODJIG

There was a time in artist Odjig's life when to find work she pretended to be part French and English, rather than an Odawa Indian: "I hated this lie, but I was desperate." Sometimes she would use the English translation of her name, Fisher. Now, at sixty-five, a life-long artistic exploration which has brought her honour among her own people and international fame has also given her back to herself.

She signs her work with her mother's family name, Odjig, as her grandfather did on the tombstones he carved at the Wikwemikong Reserve on Manitoulin Island [see pp. 40, 43] where she grew up. Sketching with him for hours, she learned to draw the world she saw in her imagination. She feels that the development of this inner vision is especially important for natives because of their unique cultural background and cultural expression: "Only when you discover yourself can you be secure."

Her art reflects traditional Indian life and folklore as well as European influences, notably that of Picasso. In an early phase, pen and ink drawings captured the vanishing culture of the relocated Chemahawin people in northern Manitoba. Her move to Winnipeg in 1967 marked the beginning of a period of intense energy and political activity. Here she opened the first native art gallery and encouraged others. Her work was increasingly in demand. Using acrylics she developed a style combining the legends of her people with a sophisticated social awareness. In 1975, she settled in British Columbia, where her creative energies were renewed and vision crystallized. The result was the highly acclaimed *The Indian in Transition,* an 8' x 27' mural in which she documents native history, while expressing her dismay at the destruction of cultural values and her commitment to their preservation. Ultimately, it is a hopeful vision: "...bitterness is of no use to an artist."

Today, on the shores of Lake Shushwap, Odjig listens to the voices in the wind and enriches our lives by painting her dreams: "Sometimes I sit there and I think about our natives and I feel sad but I brush it off, and I go in and start to paint again. I'm an optimist. That's an Indian characteristic. I feel the Indians will be proud again." [HS-1987]

[Daphne Odjig has had solo exhibitions around the world and is the recipient of several honours, including the Order of Canada (1987). A monograph of her work, *Odjig: The Art of Daphne Odjig, 1960-2000,* was published in 2001. Now in her eighties and in poor health, she still hopes to get back to painting. Eds.]

DOROTHY KNOWLES

"Since I started to paint I've felt driven to paint one painting after another." These are the words of Dorothy Knowles, who has been acclaimed by respected critics as the best landscape painter in Canada.

It was not until she was 22 years old and taking a night school art class that Dorothy recognized she possessed talent. As she says, "It was just there; it just seemed natural." From that point on, her career as an artist became increasingly vital, finally achieving an international reputation.

In 1951 she married William Perehudoff, also an artist; they made their home in Saskatoon. Many of her works are the product of the quiet and beautiful surroundings of Emma Lake, Saskatchewan, where Dorothy has spent many hours at the family cabin,

The parent is the one who should preach to the younger ones in order to keep the language, the culture in the Indian world. To teach them about the history of the Indian people in their native tongue, we must, as a united group, try to retain and to practise our own culture which will take us a long, long way.
—Helen Fineday, Sweetgrass Reserve

left: Daphne Odjig

right: "The Pool" by Dorothy Knowles

and where she and her husband have attended the influential artists' workshops.

Dorothy's paintings have been exhibited throughout North America at various galleries, including the Waddington Galleries in Montreal, where she is displayed along with such notable artists as Jack Bush, Kenneth Noland, and Jules Olitski. It has been the rule that her exhibits have sold out, many paintings being purchased prior to framing. This success is paralleled by the honour bestowed upon Dorothy in 1977, when her work was selected to be shown in the Hirschorn Museum in Washington, DC, in an exhibit entitled "Fourteen Canadians: A Critic's Choice." [HS-1979]

[At the age of 75, Dorothy Knowles continues to paint "one painting after another," and critics and audiences still agree that she is one of the finest landscape painters in Canada. Eds.]

[She] spoke of women's history, how our scholars are going back looking for it and how we have been denied our own reflection.... And she used the word "herstory" to illustrate the new language that we need....Everything comes together...
—Dorothy Inglis, 1988

ANGELIQUE MERASTY

below: Birch bark biter Angelique Merasty

Traditionally, the Woodland Cree Indians gathered together once or twice a year. One of the pastimes of the women was to see who could create the most beautiful birch bark biting. Sarah Ballantyne, Angelique's mother, was considered to be the champion of this art form, and she passed on her skills to her daughter in the traditional way.

A true artist, Angelique sees her art form in her mind. She uses no tools of any kind other than her teeth. The birch bark must be soft and supple, free of black flecks and knots, and contain just the right amount of moisture. A good piece of bark can have up to ten layers, only half of which may be suitable for creations. Angelique folds the piece of bark crosswise to make a rectangle, then again to make a triangle. Then she bites out her pattern, using mainly her eye teeth, producing shading by varying the pressure of her teeth. She may remove and refold the bark but the patterns will usually be symmetrical, depicting flowers, insects, and birds, forms which reflect Angelique's close relationship to nature.

Angelique has no daughter to pass her craft on to, and she comments that the young women around her don't seem to be interested in learning the art of birch bark biting. Her unique art form might well cease to exist when she is unable to continue. [HS-1985]

[A video, *Wismag: A story about the ancient art of birch bark biting*, showing Angelique working with a young birch bark biter, was released in 1993 by Filmwest Associates. Angelique died in 1996. Her works have been exhibited nationally and internationally and many have been preserved in the ethnology collections of Canadian museums. Eds.]

RESEARCHING WOMEN

On page 97 of this book is a photograph titled "Society of Independent Spinsters, University of Alberta, 1908." From simply looking at the image, by gazing into these women's faces, it is hard to divine their story. Was this an ironically defiant club of like-minded free spirits, or a serious support group formed on behalf of these "unfortunate" singles? These women may have written a thorough description of the group, its history and foundation, its aims and its membership. But more likely not. This club may have kept minutes, but they will doubtless have been lost or destroyed long ago. There may be, at best, some brief record in the U of A archives, a scribbled note perhaps, or some passing reference in a forgotten letter. Maybe there is another photograph with names handwritten on the back to jog a distant memory. However, it is highly unlikely that any formal history of this group remains. This single image sums up neatly the inherent obstacles encountered when one attempts to write historically about women.

It is a game of inferences, speculation, lost memory, and lost lives. What we have learned in pursuing these stories is that women's history is fundamentally a chronicle of absence. With few notable exceptions, women are not talked about; their experiences are not recorded; their names are not even attached to their own photographs. And indeed, their names are sometimes not even their own. Women are often mentioned only as the "wife of" or "mother of" some more historically significant figure.

When a researcher wants to learn about women of the past it is not a simple matter of going to the library. Unlike other topics, there will not be an abundance of published sources. The main source of information is still unpublished material—the gleanings of various public and private archives, local history rooms, and museums. These invaluable institutions house the artifacts and evidence that women have left behind—their letters, diaries, notes, and drawings. The development of women's history as a discipline and the rich resources of the Internet now mean that easily accessible sources are more prevalent than ever. But the field of women's history is still wide open. There is much to be done to reclaim the buried fragments of women's experience. Researching even relatively contemporary women requires the patience and deductive reasoning of an archeologist. Those who want to research women's histories need to be resourceful.

Some words of advice from those of us who have been doing this difficult and rewarding work for a number of years: Archives are still the best, and most under-used, resource. When you go to an archive, draw on the expertise of the resident archivists. Tell them that you are looking for materials on women—any materials on women; women in agriculture, women at work, women in the arts. Think of every possible angle. Ask if there are finding aids to the collection that focus on women. Ask if the archive holds any major collections of women's papers. Look in the subject index under "women." You might well find papers, minute books, or annual reports created by women's groups. Look at those papers, gather the names of women who look interesting, note dates and look in newspapers and other periodicals of the day to see what you can find. Read reports and articles written by women. You will discover what was important to them at the time. Read women's magazines from the 19th and early 20th centuries. You may discover an interesting woman. When you find one woman, you may find another, who will lead you to yet another and so on. Researching women is detective work. It takes time, patience, and imagination, but it is worth the effort.

Let this approach to women's history colour your view of your own world. Read current newspapers and magazines with an eye for stories about interesting women. Read between the lines of more traditional histories, where women seem to hide in the gaps and silences. This is especially true of women of colour.

Always be sceptical of traditional accounts of how things were done. Remember that men may have declared the wars and mostly fought in them, but women were usually there picking up the pieces as best they could. Their stories are just as "heroic" as the men's. And finally, an invaluable resource is the oral history of our elders—people who can remember the stories and wisdom passed on over generations. Talk to other people, especially other women. Let them know you are interested in hearing about the women they know of. Start with your own families, especially your mothers, aunts, and grandmothers. Learn your own history from the women's point of view.

This approach to history is radical, subversive, and, sadly, still revolutionary. In this century, academic history has undergone several transformations. It has broadened its scope of research and interest to include non-western cultures and races, to consider society and culture as well as politics and economics, and, through publications like *Herstory*, to consider and record the lives of women. Much work has been done since 1972. Archives have been scoured, photographs examined, letters and diaries combed. The "dregs of history" have been squeezed to see what remaining drops of knowledge and insight they can impart. When it comes to women's history, there are now far more formal historical records, more books, more documents and documentary than ever before. But much has been irretrievably lost. Schoolchildren are still taught the exploits of explorers and "Fathers of Confederation," while we have forgotten the names of the women who helped make the development of Canada possible.

However, we do know enough to know that women's lives have been important. And that is why history, and researching women's history in particular, matters. It makes a difference what is recorded, who is named. To discover, unearth, reclaim, and, above all, tell the story cobbled together from scraps of letters, from faded and blurry photographs is essential work. Unless we create institutions, disciplines, media, and people with the interest to record these stories, they are lost and we lose our own past and ourselves along with it. History tells us where we have been, who we are, and what the future may hold. To glimpse the lives of those who have gone before us, those who have lived ordinary lives, as well as those who have achieved extraordinary accomplishments, is to know something of ourselves and our potential. History is a vision of possibility as much as it is memory of the past. By expanding history, by exploring herstory, we broaden our own horizons.

THE *HERSTORY* COLLECTIVE

1974 *(above)—adults, l to r,* Erin Shoemaker, Colleen Pollreis, Beth Foster, June Bantjes, Gwen Morrison-Gray, and collective children

1975—Beth Foster, Gwen Morrison-Gray, Colleen Pollreis, Erin Shoemaker, Muriel Wiens

1976—Beth Foster, Erin Shoemaker, Pam Baxter, Joanne Fink Blythe, Muriel Wiens, Candace Savage, Dorothy Hudec

1977—Pam Baxter, Joanne Fink Blythe, Dorothy Hudec, Candace Savage, Muriel Wiens

1978—Pam Baxter, Anne Benedict, Joanne Fink Blythe, Jennifer Evans, Dorothy Hudec, Apolonja Kojder, Lenore Rodgers, Candace Savage, Anne Skarsgard, Erin Shoemaker, Vera-Marie Wolfe

1979—Jennifer Evans, Dorothy Hudec, Apolonja Kojder, Lenore Rodgers, Sue Sanders, Candace Savage, Anne Skarsgard, Erin Shoemaker, Vera-Marie Wolfe

1980—Katherine Arbuthnott, Noella Leydon (Nelson), Kathy Morpurgo, Karen Murdock, Colleen Odegard, Sam Stewart, Georgina Taylor, Patty Williams

1981 *(below)—back, l to r:* Katherine Arbuthnott, Joanne Blythe, Georgina Taylor, *front, l to r:* Kathy Morpurgo, Sam Stewart, Patty Williams, Noella Leydon (Nelson), *absent:* Glenis Joyce

1982—Joanne Blythe, Julienne Colbow, Thirza Jones, Noella Leydon (Nelson), Lisa Lough, Kathy Morpurgo, Deb Newlyn, Patty Williams

1983—Moreen Blair, Mary Gilliland, Lisa Lough, Shirley Martin (Perkins), Patty Williams

1984—Moreen Blair, Mary Gilliland, Lisa Lough, Shirley Martin (Perkins), Patty Williams

1985—Moreen Blair, Mary Gilliland, Lisa Lough, Raymonde Martel, Shirley Martin (Perkins), Patty Williams

1986—Dianne Brydon, Miriam Caplan, Mary Gilliland, Shirley Martin (Perkins), Barbara Roberts, Patty Williams, Gail Youngberg (McConnell)

1987 *(below)—back, l to r:* Mary Gilliland, Patty Williams, Shirley Martin, *front, l to r:* Miriam Caplan, Gail Youngberg (McConnell), Nancy Cochrane, Dianne Brydon

1988—Dianne Brydon, Miriam Caplan, Nancy Cochrane, Joan Ellsworth, Mary Gilliland, Jane Haddad, Shirley Martin, Patty Williams, Gail Youngberg (McConnell)

1989 *(below)—front, l to r:* Shirley Martin, Dianne Brydon, Gail Youngberg (McConnell), Jane Haddad; *back, l to r:* Patty Williams, Nancy Cochrane, Mary Gilliland, Joan Ellsworth

1990—Anna-Marie Boquist, Dianne Brydon, Nancy Cochrane, Mary Gilliland, Myrna Lamontagne, Shirley Martin, Patty Williams, Gail Youngberg (McConnell)

1991—Anna-Marie Boquist, Dianne Brydon, Mary Gilliland, Myrna Lamontagne Shirley Martin, Jill Webber (Hrabinsky), Patty Williams, Gail Youngberg (McConnell)

1992—Anna-Marie Boquist, Dianne Brydon, Mary Gilliland, Regine Haensel, Shirley Martin, Kate Sutherland, Jill Webber (Hrabinsky), Patty Williams, Gail Youngberg

1993—Cheryl Avery, Anna-Marie Boquist, Dianne Brydon, Mary Gilliland, Shirley Martin, Kate Sutherland, Jill Webber (Hrabinsky), Patty Williams, Gail Youngberg

1994-1996 *(above)—back, l to r:* Gail Youngberg, Mary Gilliland, Patty Williams, Elizabeth Diamond, *front, l to r:* Cheryl Avery, Mona Holmlund, *absent:* Jill Webber Hrabinsky, Shirley Martin, Kate Sutherland

1997—Cheryl Avery, Elizabeth Diamond, Mary Gilliland, Mona Holmlund, Jill Webber Hrabinsky, Shirley Martin, Patty Williams, Gail Youngberg

1998—Cheryl Avery, Elizabeth Diamond, Mary Gilliland, Terry Harley, Deanna Herman, Mona Holmlund, Shirley Martin, Patty Williams, Gail Youngberg

1999-2000—Cheryl Avery, Mary Gilliland, Terry Harley, Deanna Herman, Mona Holmlund, Shirley Martin, Patty Williams, Gail Youngberg

2001—Cheryl Avery, Mary Gilliland, Terry Harley, Deanna Herman, Mona Holmlund, Shirley Martin, Patty Williams, Shelley Woloshyn, Gail Youngberg

2002-2003 *(below)—back l to r:* Shirley Martin, Patty Williams, Shelley Woloshyn, Karen Millard, Mary Gilliland, *front l to r:* Roma Kail, Deanna Herman, Cheryl Avery, Terry Harley

ACKNOWLEDGEMENTS

We are very grateful for the friendship of the women of the Saskatoon Women's Calendar Collective 1994-2002 who supported and encouraged us throughout this project: Cheryl Avery, Elizabeth Diamond, Mary Gilliland, Terry Harley, Deanna Herman, Shirley Martin, Patty Williams, and Shelley Woloshyn. Above and beyond the call of duty, Cheryl offered expert and invaluable navigation of the *Herstory* archives and a herculean effort to secure and organize the photographs. On very short notice, Mary, Terry, and Patty willingly sacrificed their time to review the manuscript and see it through to publication. Without the effort, dedication, and expertise of these four women this book would not have been possible.

We would like to acknowledge our debt to the other women of the *Herstory* Collective since its inception, whose work is here commemorated: June Bantjes, Beth Foster, Gwen Morrison-Gray, Colleen Pollreis, Erin Shoemaker, Pam Baxter, Joanne (Fink) Blythe, Muriel Wiens, Candace Savage, Dorothy Hudec, Anne Benedict, Jennifer Evans, Apolonja Kojder, Lenore Rodgers, Anne Skarsgard, Vera-Marie Wolfe, Sue Sanders, Katherine Arbuthnott, Noella Leydon (Nelson), Kathy Morpurgo, Karen Murdock, Colleen Odegard, Sam Stewart, Georgina Taylor, Glenis Joyce, Julienne Colbow, Thirza Jones, Lisa Lough, Deb Newlyn, Moreen Blair, Shirley (Perkins) Martin, Raymonde Martel, Dianne Brydon, Miriam Caplan, Barbara Roberts, Nancy Cochrane, Joan Ellsworth, Anna-Marie Boquist, Myrna Lamontagne, Jill Webber Hrabinsky, Regine Haensel, Jane Haddad, Elizabeth Diamond, Deanna Herman, and Kate Sutherland.

There are many other individuals, not formally part of the Collective, whose help has been invaluable. Barbara Bowie generously stepped in with moral and practical support when it was most needed. Sian Gardner made work possible when time was short. Our publisher since 1985, Coteau Books of Regina, has stood by us during this long process. In particular Duncan Campbell, shared our vision of what a book like this could be. Above all we have to acknowledge the tremendous patience with which those closest to us have endured the slow progress of this project. It was interrupted numerous times for personal and professional reasons and we are humbled by their abiding confidence. Chief among those to whom we extend our gratitude are our families and friends. An exemplar of their support was Gail's husband John McConnell, who, throughout his lengthy illness, continued to offer advice and encouragement.

Finally we acknowledge with deep appreciation the support of the Government of Canada through the Canadian Studies Program, Canadian Heritage. The opinions herein do not necessarily reflect the views of the Government of Canada.

FURTHER READING

Herstory articles are composed from first person interviews, oral histories, and both published and unpublished sources. Here is a select bibliography of some of the published sources used for the articles reprinted in this anthology. The original *Herstory* calendars containing these articles and their specific sources are available at some libraries in Canada, or from Coteau Books (coteau@coteaubooks.com or 1-800-440-4471).

Ainley, Marianne Gosztonyi (ed.). *Despite the Odds: Essays on Canadian Women and Science.* Montreal: Véhicule Press, 1990.

Allen, Max (ed.). *Ideas That Matter: The Worlds of Jane Jacobs.* Owen Sound, ON: Ginger Press, 1997.

Anderson, Margaret (ed.). *Mother Was Not a Person.* Montreal: Black Rose Books, 1972.

Armstrong, Pat and Hugh Armstrong. *The Double Ghetto: Canadian Women and Their Segregated Work.* Toronto: McClelland and Stewart, 1986.

Bacchi, Carol Lee. *Liberation Deferred? The Ideas of English-Canadian Suffragists, 1877-1918.* Toronto: Univ. of Toronto Press, 1983.

Backhouse, Constance. *Petticoats and Prejudice: Women and the Law in Nineteenth-Century Canada.* Toronto: Women's Press, 1991.

Bannerman, Jean. *Leading Ladies of Canada.* Galt, ON: Highland Press, 1967.

Bassett, Isabel. *The Parlour Rebellion: Profiles in the Struggle for Women's Rights.* Toronto: McClelland and Stewart, 1975.

Beavan, Emily Shaw. *Sketches and Tales Illustrative of Life in the Backwoods of New Brunswick, North America, Gleaned from Actual Observation and Experience During a Residence of Seven Years in that Interesting Colony.* London: Routledge, 1845.

Bertley, Leo. W. *Canada and Its People of African Descent.* Quebec: Bilongo Publishers, 1977.

Braithwaite, Rella and Tessa Benn-Ireland. *Some Black Women: Profiles of Black Women in Canada.* Toronto: Sister Vision Press, 1993.

Brennan, T. Ann. *The Real Klondike Kate.* Fredericton, NB: Goose Lane Editions, 1990.

Bristow, Peggy, et al. *We're Rooted Here and They Can't Pull Us Up.* Toronto: Univ. of Toronto Press, 1994.

Brown, Rosemary. *Being Brown: A Very Public Life.* Toronto: Random House, 1989.

Bruce, Jean. *Back the Attack! Canadian Women During the Second World War—At Home and Abroad.* Toronto: Macmillan, 1985.

Cameron, Agnes Deans. *The New North.* New York & London: D. Appleton & Co., 1910.

Campbell, Kim. *Time and Chance: The Political Memoirs of Canada's First Woman Minister.* Toronto: Doubleday Canada Ltd, 1996.

The Canadian Encyclopedia. Edmonton: Hurtig, 1988.

The Canadian Who's Who. III, 1938-1939. Toronto: Trans-Canada Press, 1939.

Canadian Woman Studies

Casgrain, Thérèse. *A Woman in a Man's World.* Toronto: McClelland and Stewart, 1972.

Cleverdon, Catherine. *The Woman Suffrage Movement in Canada.* Toronto: Univ. of Toronto Press, 1974.

Cochrane, Jean, et al. (eds.). *Women in Canadian Life: Sports.* Toronto: Fitzhenry & Whiteside, 1977.

Conrad, Margaret, et al. (eds.). *No Place Like Home: Diaries and Letters of Nova Scotia Women, 1771-1938.* Halifax: Formac, 1988.

Cook, Ramsey and Wendy Mitchinson (eds.). *The Proper Sphere: Women's Place in Canadian Society.* Toronto, Oxford Univ. Press, 1976.

Corrective Collective. *Never Done: Three Centuries of Women's Work in Canada.* Toronto: Canadian Women's Educational Press, 1974.

Crean, Susan. *Newsworthy: The Lives of Media Women.* Toronto: Stoddart, 1985.

Crnkovich, Mary (ed.). *"Gossip": A Spoken History of Women in the North.* Ottawa: Canadian Arctic Resources Committee, 1990.

Cruikshank, Julie. *Life Lived Like a Story: Life Stories of Three Yukon Native Elders.* Vancouver: Univ. of British Columbia Press, 1990.

Danylewycz, Marta. *Taking the Veil: An Alternative to Marriage, Motherhood, and Spinsterhood in Quebec, 1840-1920.* Toronto: McClelland and Stewart, 1987.

Dickason, Olive. *Canada's First Nations: A History of Founding Peoples from Earliest Times.* Toronto: McClelland and Stewart, 1992.

Dictionary of Canadian Biography

Dood, Dianne and Deborah Gorham (eds.). *Caring and Curing: Historical Perspectives on Women and Healing in Canada.* Ottawa: Univ. of Ottawa Press, 1994.

Duley, Margot. *Where Once Our Mothers Stood We Stand.* Charlottetown: gynergy books, 1993.

Duncan, Sara Jeannette. *A Social Departure.* New York: D. Appleton & Co., 1890.

Drummond, Julia (ed.). *Women of Canada: Their Life and Work.* National Council of Women of Canada, 1900.

Ellis, Miriam Green. *Down North.* Miriam Green Ellis Collection, Cameron Library, Univ. of Alberta, Edmonton.

Fife, Connie (ed.). *The Colour of Resistance: A Contemporary Collection of Writing by Aboriginal Women.* Toronto: Sister Vision Press, 1993.

Finlayson, Judith. *Against the Current: Canadian Women Talk About Fifty Years of Life on the Job.* Toronto: Doubleday Canada Ltd, 1995.

Fitts, Sr Mary Pauline. *Hands to the Needy: Mother d'Youville, Apostle to the Poor.* Garden City, NY: Doubleday & Co., 1950.

Fitzgerald, Maureen, et al. (eds.). *Still Ain't Satisfied: Canadian Feminism Today.* Toronto: Women's Press, 1982.

French, Doris. *High Button Boot Straps.* Toronto: Ryerson Press, 1968.

Frideres, James (ed.). *Native Peoples in Canada: Contemporary Conflicts.* Scarborough, ON: Prentice Hall Canada Inc., 1993.

Gould, Jan. *Women of British Columbia.* Vancouver: Hancock House, 1975.

Gillet, Margaret, *We Walked Very Warily: A History of Women at McGill.* Montreal: Eden Press, 1981.

Griffith, N.E.S. *The Splendid Vision: Centennial History of the National Council of Women of Canada 1893-1993.* Ottawa: Carleton Univ. Press, 1993.

Hacker, Carlotta. *The Indomitable Lady Doctors.* Toronto: Clarke, Irwin and Co., 1974.

Hallet, Mary and Marilyn Davis. *Firing the Heather: The Life and Times of Nellie McClung.* Saskatoon: Fifth House, 1993.

Hayden, Joyce. *Yukon's Women of Power: Political Pioneers in a Northern Canadian Colony.* Whitehorse: Windwalker Press, 1999.

Healy, W.J. *Women of Red River.* Winnipeg: Women's Canadian Club, 1923.

Herrington, W.S. *Heroines of Canadian History.* Toronto: Briggs, 1903.

Hill, Lawrence. *Trials and Triumphs: The Story of African Canadians.* Toronto: Umbrella Press, 1993.

Horsby, Jim. *Black Islanders: Prince Edward Island's Historical Black Community.* Charlottetown: Institute of Island Studies, 1991.

Hubbard, Mrs Leonidas. *A Woman's Way Through Unknown Labrador: An Account of the Exploration of the Nascaupee and George Rivers.* London: J. Murphy, 1908.

Hungry Wolf, Beverly. *The Ways of My Grandmothers.* New York: William Morrow and Company, Inc., 1980.

Howel, Reet (ed.). *Her Story in Sport: A Historical Anthology of Women in Sports.* New York: Leisure Press, 1982.

Innis, Mary Quayle (ed.). *The Clear Spirit: Twenty Canadian Women and Their Times.* Toronto: Univ. of Toronto Press, 1966.

Jackell, Susan. *A Flannel Shirt and Liberty: British Emigrant Gentlewomen in the Canadian West, 1880-1914.* Vancouver: Univ. of British Columbia Press, 1982.

Johnston, Jean. *Wilderness Women.* Toronto, Peter Martin Associates, 1973.

Kealy, Linda (ed.). *A Not Unreasonable Claim: Women and Reform in Canada 1880's-1920's.* Toronto: Canadian Women's Educational Press, 1979.

_____ and Joan Sangster (eds.). *Beyond the Vote: Canadian Women and Politics.* Toronto: Univ. of Toronto Press, 1989.

Kinear, Mary (ed.). *First Days, Fighting Days: Women in Manitoba History.* Regina: Canadian Plains Research Centre, 1987.

King, Dennis. *The Grey Nuns and the Red River Settlement.* We Built Canada Series. Agincourt: Book Society of Canada Ltd, 1980.

Kivi, K. Linda. *Canadian Women Making Music.* Toronto: Green Dragon Press, 1992.

Kostash, M., et al. *Her Own Woman: Profiles of Ten Canadian Women.* Toronto: Macmillan, 1975.

Lang, Marjory. *Women Who Made the News: Female Journalists in Canada.* Montreal: McGill-Queen's Univ. Press, 1999.

Latham, Barbara and Cathy Kess (eds.). *In Her Own Right: Selected Essays on Women's History in B.C.* Victoria: Camosun College, 1980.

Legacy: A History of Saskatchewan Homemaker's Clubs and Women's Institutes 1911-1988. Saskatoon: Saskatchewan Women's Institutes, 1988.

Light, Beth and Veronica Strong-Boag. *True Daughters of the North: Canadian Women's History: An Annotated Bibliography.* Toronto: Ontario Institute for Studies in Education, 1980.

_____ and Joy Parr. *Canadian Women on the Move 1867-1920.* Toronto: New Hogtown Press, 1983.

_____ and Ruth Roach Pierson (eds.). *No Easy Road: Women in Canada 1920's to 1960's.*

Documents in Canadian Women's History. Toronto: New Hogtown Press, 1990.

Livesay, Dorothy (ed.). *Forty Women Poets of Canada.* Montreal: Ingluvin Publications, 1971.

Long, Wendy. *Celebrating Excellence: Canadian Women Athletes.* Vancouver: Polestar, 1995.

Luckyj, Natalie. *Visions and Victories: 10 Canadian Women Artists 1914-1945.* London, ON: London Regional Art Gallery, 1983.

Lugrin, N. de Bertrand. *Pioneer Women of Vancouver Island 1843-1866.* John Housie (ed.). Victoria: Women's Canadian Club of Victoria, 1928.

MacEwan, Grant. *...And Mighty Women, Too: Stories of Notable Western Canadian Women.* Saskatoon: Western Producer Prairie Books, 1975.

MacLeod, Enid Johnson. *Petticoat Doctors: The First Forty Years of Women in Medicine at Dalhousie University.* Lawrencetown Beach, NS: Pottersfield Press, 1990.

Makeda, Silvera (ed.). *The Other Woman: Women of Colour in Contemporary Canadian Literature.* Toronto: Sister Vision Press, 1995.

Manitoba Clubs of the Canadian Federation of University Women. *Extraordinary Ordinary Women: Manitoba Women and Their Stories.* Winnipeg, 2000.

Manning, Ella. *Igloo for the Night.* Toronto: Univ. of Toronto Press, 1946.

_____. *A Summer on Hudson Bay.* London: Hodder & Stoughton, 1949.

McClung, M.G. *Women in Canadian Literature.* Toronto: Fitzhenry & Whiteside Ltd, 1977.

McClung, Nellie. *In Times Like These.* (Veronica Strong-Boag, ed.). Toronto: Univ. of Toronto Press, 1972.

McDonald, David. *For the Record: Canada's Greatest Women Athletes.* Rexdale: Mesa Assoc., 1981.

McGahan, Elizabeth. *Whispers from the Past: Selections from the Writings of New Brunswick Women.* Fredericton: Goose Lane Editions, 1986.

McLaren, Angus and Arlene Tigar McLaren. *The Bedroom and the State: The Changing Practices and Politics of Contraception and Abortion in Canada 1880-1980.* Toronto: McClelland and Stewart, 1986.

McLaughlin, Audrey. *A Woman's Place: My Life and Politics.* Toronto: Macfarlane Walter & Ross, 1992.

McMullin, Lorraine (ed.). *Re(Dis)covering Our Foremothers: Nineteenth Century Canadian Women Writers.* Ottawa: Univ. of Ottawa Press, 1990.

McMurchy, Marjorie. *Women of To-day and To-morrow.* Women's Department, Canadian Reconstruction Association, 1919.

Merritt, Susan E. *Her Story: Women from Canada's Past.* St Catherines, ON: Vanwell Publishing, 1993.

Miller, Christine and Patricia Chchryk (eds.). *Women of the First Nations: Power, Wisdom, Strength.* Winnipeg: Univ. of Manitoba Press, 1996.

Morgan, Henry J. *Types of Canadian Women.* Toronto: Briggs, 1903.

_____. *Canadian Men and Women of the Time.* Toronto: William Briggs, 1912.

Murphy, Claire Rudolf and Jane G. Haigh. *Gold Rush Women.* Anchorage: AlaskaNorthwest Books, 1997.

National Council of Women of Canada. *Women of Canada: Their Life and Work.* Ottawa: National Council of Women, 1900.

Nelson, Mariah Burton. *Are We Winning Yet? How Women Are Changing Sports and Sports Are Changing Women.* New York: Random House, 1991.

Nicholson, G.W.L. *Canada's Nursing Sisters.* Toronto: Samuel Stevens, Hakkert and Company, 1975.

Norcross, E. Blanche. *Pioneers Every One: Canadian Women of Achievement.* Don Mills: Burns and MacEachern Ltd, 1979.

Panabaker, Janet. *Inventing Women: Profiles of Women Inventors.* Waterloo: The Women Inventors Project, 1991.

Pederson, Diana. *Changing Women, Changing History: A Bibliography of the History of Women in Canada.* Ottawa: Carleton Univ. Press, 1996.

Prentice, Alison, et al. (eds.). *Canadian Women: A History.* Toronto: Harcourt Brace Canada, 1996.

_____ and Susan Mann Trofimenkoff. *The Neglected Majority: Essays in Canadian Women's History.* Toronto: McClelland and Stewart, 1985.

Rasmussen, Linda, et al. (eds.). *A Harvest Yet to Reap: A History of Prairie Women.* Toronto: Canadian Women's Educational Press, 1976.

Render, Shirley. *No Place For a Lady: The Story of Canadian Women Pilots, 1928-1992.* Winnipeg: Portage and Main Press, 1992.

Richards, Janet Radcliffe. *The Sceptical Feminist.* London: Penguin Books, 1980.

Robertson, Heather. *Salt of the Earth: The Story of the Homesteaders in Western Canada.* Toronto: James Lorimer and Company, 1974.

Rosenberg, Stuart. *The Jewish Community in Canada: A History.* Toronto: McClelland and Stewart, 1970.

Royal Society of Canada. *Claiming the Future: The Inspiring Lives of Twelve Canadian Women Scientists and Scholars.* Markham, ON: Pembroke Publishers, 1991.

Sadlier, Rosemary. *Leading the Way: Black Women in Canada.* Toronto: Umbrella Press, 1994.

Sangster, Joan. *Dreams of Equality: Women on the Canadian Left, 1920-1950.* Toronto: McClelland and Stewart, 1989.

Savage, Candace. *Our Nell: A Scrapbook Biography of Nellie McClung.* Saskatoon: Western Producer Prairie Books, 1979.

_____. *Foremothers: Personalities and Issues from the History of Women in Saskatchewan.* Regina: Project of the coordinator for the status of women, 1970.

Schaffer, Mary. *Old Indian Trails.* Toronto: William Briggs, 1911.

Scheier, Libby, et al. (eds.). *Language in Her Eye: Views on Writing and Gender by English Canadian Women Writers.* Toronto: Coach House Press, 1990.

Smith, Cyndi. *Off the Beaten Track: Women Adventurers and Mountaineers in Western Canada.* Jasper, AB; Coyote Books, 1989.

Speaking Together: Canada's Native Women. Ottawa: Secretary of State, 1975.

Speare, Jean E. (ed.). *The Days of Augusta.* (Mary Augusta Tappage) Vancouver: J.J.Douglas Ltd, 1973.

Spender, Dale. *Nattering on the Net: Women, Power and Cyberspace.* Toronto: Garamond Press, 1995.

Staton, Pat and Beth Light. *Speak With Their Own Voices.* Toronto: Federation of Women Teachers' Associations of Ontario, 1987.

Stephenson, Marylee (ed.). *Women in Canada.* Toronto: New Press, 1973.

Strong-Boag, Veronica and Anita-Clair Fellman (eds.). *Rethinking Canada: The Promise of Canadian Women's History.* Toronto: Copp Clark Pitman, 1991.

_____. *The New Day Recalled: Lives of Girls and Women in English Canada 1919-1939.* Toronto: Penguin Books, 1988.

Thomas, Clara. *All My Sisters: Essays on the Work of Canadian Women Writers.* Ottawa: Tecumseh Press, 1987.

Timmins, Leslie (ed.). *Listening to the Thunder: Advocates Talk About the Battered Women's Movement.* Vancouver: Women's Research Centre, 1995.

Tippett, Maria. *By a Lady: Celebrating Three Centuries of Art by Canadian Women.* Toronto: Viking/Penguin, 1992.

Tulloch, Elspeth. *We, the Undersigned: A Historical Overview of New Brunswick Women's Political and Legal Status 1784-1984.* Moncton: New Brunswick Advisory Council on the Status of Women, 1985.

Van Kirk, Sylvia. *"Many Tender Ties": Women in Fur-Trade Society in Western Canada, 1670-1870.* Winnipeg: Watson & Dwyer, 1980.

Visser, Margaret. *The Way We Are.* Toronto: Harper Collins, 1994.

Wiebe, Nettie. *Weaving New Ways: Farm Women Organizing.* Saskatoon: National Farmer's Union, 1987.

Williams, Patricia. "Celebrating Herstory: 25 Years of Women's History in the Community." *Saskatchewan History.* 50, #2, Fall 1998, 28-30.

Winks, Robin W. *The Blacks in Canada: A History.* Montreal: McGill-Queen's Univ. Press, 1971.

The Women's Book Committee. *Jin Guo: Voices of Chinese Canadian Women.* Toronto: Women's Press, 1992.

Yaccato, Joanne Thomas. *Balancing Act.* Scarborough: Prentice-Hall, 1994.

Zaremba, Eve. *Privilege of Sex: A Century of Canadian Women.* Toronto: House of Anansi Press, 1974.

SELECTED INTERNET RESOURCES

Here are some web-based resources that we have found useful. Each of these sites has links to other useful sites. The addresses are correct as of press time; if you experience problems with any of these sites, try using a search engine, such as Google, to locate the organization.

Canadian Archival Information Network. A project of Canadian archives, this site is an entrance into the rich holdings of major Canadian archives. *www.cain-rcia.ca/cain_e.htm*

Canadian Women's Studies On-Line. A large site from the University of Toronto; the resources page is particularly useful. *www.utoronto.ca/womens/resrces.htm*

The Fawcett Library. An excellent library and archives devoted to women's history; mainly about British women, but includes Empire/Commonwealth, as well as other parts of the world. *www.thewomenslibrary.ac.uk*

The Genesis Project. Project from Britain that has links to websites relevant to women and women's history around the world, including Canadian sites. *www.genesis.ac.uk*

The *Herstory* website. This website features an exhibit created in 1995. *http://library.usask/ca/herstory*

Nellie Langford Rowell Women's Studies Library at York University. This site has information, as well as a links page. *www.yorku.ca/nlrowell/*

National Library of Canada, Celebrating Women's Achievements. The site features short biographies and photographs of women who were firsts in a number of areas. *www.nlc-bnc.ca/women/index-e.html*

INDEX

PHOTOGRAPH CREDITS

p. viii Alice and Mary Hagar and children, courtesy Yukon Archives, Claude Tidd Collection, #7504 [*Herstory 2003*].

p. 2 Univ. of Saskatchewan Archives, Saskatoon Women's Calendar Collective fonds [*Herstory 1999*]

p. 2 Snake People Woman, courtesy University of Saskatchewan Archives, Institute for Northern Studies fonds, INS 561/NMC J5530 [*Herstory 1995*].

p.3 Gudrid, illustration by Patricia Wilson Johnston, first published in Jean Johnston, *Wilderness Women*. Toronto: Peter Wilson & Associates, 1973 [*Herstory 1978*].

p. 3 Woman of Nootka Sound, illustration by J. Webber, first published in James Cook, *A Voyage to the Pacific Ocean*. London: W. and A. Strathan, 1784 [*Herstory 1987*].

p. 4 Micmac Woman (Christianne Paul Morris), courtesy New Brunswick Museum [*Herstory 1987*].

p. 4 Marie Guyart de l'Incarnation sculpture, artist unknown. First published in Mary Quayle Innis (ed.), *The Clear Spirit*. Toronto: University of Toronto Press, 1967 [*Herstory 1978*].

p. 5 Marguerite Bourgeoys, courtesy National Archives of Canada PA-023401 [*Herstory 1977*].

p. 5 Ojibway Woman and Child, first published in H.Y. Hind, *Narrative of the Canadian Red River Exploring Expedition of 1857, and of the Assiniboine and Saskatchewan Exploring Expedition of 1858*. London: Longman, Green, Longman & Roberts, 1860 [*Herstory 1985*].

p. 6 Map showing area of Kirke land holdings in Newfoundland; from W.G. Handcock, *An Historical Geography of the Origins of English Settlement in Newfoundland: A Study of the Migration Process*. PHD thesis, Univ. of Birmingham, 1979 [*Herstory 1990*].

p. 7 Habitante in Her Summer Dress, originally published in John Lambert, *Travels through Lower Canada, and the United States of North America, in the Years 1806, 1807, and 1808*. London: Richard Phillips, 1810 [*Herstory 1992*].

p. 8 O-ma-ma-ma sketch, artist unknown, courtesy Saskatoon Public Library Local History Room [*Herstory 1982*].

p. 9 Laura Secord, illustration by C.W. Jefferys, courtesy National Archives of Canada, C-7025 [*Herstory 1996*].

p. 10 "An Eskimo Woman," artwork by Angelica Kauffman, courtesy National Archives of Canada, C-95201 [*Herstory 1989*].

p. 11 "Mary March," artwork by Henrietta, Lady Hamilton, courtesy National Archives of Canada, C-87698 [*Herstory 1985*].

p. 12 Marie Marguerite d'Youville, first published in H.J. Morgan, *Types of Canadian Women*. Toronto: William Briggs, 1903 [*Herstory 1976*].

p. 12 Grey Nuns visiting harvesters, courtesy Archives of Manitoba, Stovel Advocate Collection 283, no. N10202. [*Herstory 2000*]

p. 13 ...Élisabeth Bruyère, courtesy Archives of the Congregation of the Sisters of Charity [*Herstory 1991*].

p. 13 "The Seignory of Beauharnois," artwork by Katherine Jane Ellice, courtesy National Archives of Canada, C-13370 [*Herstory 1985*].

p. 14 Thanadelthur, illustration by Cathryn Miller [*Herstory 1977*].

p. 15 Natawista, courtesy Glenbow Archives, NA-5014-1 [*Herstory 1995*].

p. 16 Josette Legacé Work, courtesy British Columbia Archives, A-01825 [*Herstory 1999*].

p. 17 Women on Wharf, courtesy Vancouver Public Library, #1869 [*Herstory 1980*].

p. 17 Jane Howse Livingston, courtesy Glenbow Archives, NA-14-94-3 [*Herstory 1987*].

p. 18 Pages from first edition of the Bible printed in Cree syllabics. London: British and Foreign Bible Society, 1861 [*Herstory 1988*].

p. 19 Christine Dumas Pilon, photographer Omer Ranger, ca 1918 [*Herstory 1987*].

p. 20 Elizabeth Scott Matheson, *Saskatchewan History*, vol. XIII, no. 2, spring 1960, p. 42 [*Herstory 1975*].

p. 20 Mary Amirault, courtesy Wilfred Amirault [*Herstory 1979*].

p. 21 Ella Margaret Strang, courtesy National Archives of Canada, C-57069 [*Herstory 1975*].

p. 21 Mary Augusta Tappage, courtesy National Film Board of Canada [*Herstory 1994*].

p. 22 Janet Weir, courtesy Jean Miller [*Herstory 1994*].

p. 23 Katherine Ryan, courtesy Katherine Ryan McKernan, first published in Ann Brennan, *The Real Klondike Kate*. Fredericton: Goose Lane Editions, 1990 [*Herstory 1994*].

p. 23 Catherine Schubert, courtesy British Columbia Archives [*Herstory 1979*].

p. 24 Mina Hubbard, first published in Mina Hubbard, *A Woman's Way Through Unknown Labrador*. London: J. Murphy, 1908 [*Herstory 1979*].

p. 25 Agnes Deans Cameron, first published in Agnes Deans Cameron, *The New North: Being Some Account of a Woman's Journey Through Canada to the Arctic*. New York: D. Appleton & Co., 1910 [*Herstory 1976*].

p. 25 Miriam Green Ellis, courtesy Univ. of Alberta Archives, MG Ellis Collection [*Herstory 1976*].

p. 26 Ella Manning, photograph by Canapress Photo Service [*Herstory 1986*].

p. 26 Mary Jobe and Bess MacCarthy, courtesy Whyte Museum of the Canadian Rockies Archives, NA66-1928 [*Herstory 1998*].

p. 27 Mary Schaffer, first published in Mary Schaffer, *Old Indian Trails*. Toronto: William Briggs, 1911 [*Herstory 1979*].

p. 28 Sylvia Stark, courtesy British Columbia Archives [*Herstory 1979*].

p. 28 "Portrait of a Negro Slave, 1786," artwork by François Malepart de Beaucourt, courtesy McCord Museum of Canadian History, M12067 [*Herstory 1998*].

p. 29 Mattie Mayes, courtesy Saskatchewan Archives Board, R-A7691 [*Herstory 1994*].

p. 30 "Mrs Brown boiling the spuds," courtesy Provincial Archives of Alberta, B.576 [*Herstory 2000*].

p. 30 "Waiting for the boat," courtesy Provincial Archives of Alberta, A11.455 [*Herstory 1991*].

p. 31 "In the lee of a Red River cart," courtesy Saskatoon Public Library Local History Room, LH907 [*Herstory 1999*].

p. 31 Sod Hut, courtesy Saskatoon Public Library Local History Room, LH2157 [*Herstory 1985*].

p. 31 Sarah Dodds Peardon, courtesy Jean Miller [*Herstory 1993*].

p. 32 Stoneboat, courtesy Saskatchewan Archives Board, R-B7330 [*Herstory 1981*].

p. 32 "Mrs Joe Mayo washing clothes," courtesy Provincial Archives of Alberta, A4985 [*Herstory 1991*].

p. 33 Alalia Fancy Stevens, Nova Scotia, courtesy Thelma Pepper [*Herstory 1988*].

p. 33 Margaret Scott, courtesy Mabel Taylor [*Herstory 1980*].

p. 34 Moto Suzuki, photograph by Robert Minden. First published in Daphne Marlatt (ed.), *Steveston Recollected*. Victoria: Provincial Archives of British Columbia, 1975 [*Herstory 1978*].

p. 34 Women cleaning salmon, photograph by Rex Weyler, courtesy British Columbia Archives. First published in Daphne Marlatt (ed.), *Steveston Recollected*. Victoria: Provincial Archives of British Columbia, 1975 [*Herstory 1979*].

p. 34 Doukhobor women ploughing, courtesy Saskatchewan Archives Board, A4071 [*Herstory 1979*].

p. 35 Anahareo, courtesy Ontario Department of Natural Resources [*Herstory 1977*].

p. 36 Madeleine Gould, courtesy Madeleine Gould [*Herstory 1995*].

p. 36 Demar Halkett Hastings, courtesy John McConnell [*Herstory 1989*].

p. 37 Taktu, courtesy Univ. of Saskatchewan Archives, Institute for Northern Studies fonds, INS 167 [*Herstory 1995*].

p. 37 Ada Muskego, courtesy Saskatchewan Indian Cultural College [*Herstory 1979*].

p. 38 Violet McNaughton, courtesy Saskatchewan Archives Board, T.R. Melville Ness collection, S-MN-B 1785 [*Herstory 1974*].

p. 40 Iroquois Woman, first published in George Heriot, *Travels Through the Canadas, ... To Which is Subjoined a Comparative View of the Manners and Customs of Several of the Indian Nations of North and South America*. London: Richard Phillips, 1807 [*Herstory 1992*].

p. 40 Mrs Wolf Child and her daughter, courtesy Provincial Archives of Alberta, A5643 [*Herstory 1992*].

p. 41 Poyettak, Kakikagiu and Aknalua, first published in John Ross, *Narrative of a Second Voyage in Search of a North-West Passage, and of a Residence in the Arctic Regions During the Years 1829, 1830, 1831, 1832, 1833*. London: A.W. Webster, 1835 [*Herstory 1999*].

p. 42 "Québecoise," drawing by C.W. Jefferys, courtesy National Archives of Canada, C-6563 [*Herstory 1994*].

p. 42 York Factory, courtesy National Archives of Canada, C-8609 [*Herstory 1985*].

p. 43 Unidentified Métis woman, courtesy National Archives of Canada, PA-68270.

p. 44 Canadian Women's Christian Temperance Union convention, 1946, courtesy Saskatoon Public Library Local History Room, PH 89-251 [*Herstory 1986*].

p. 45 *The Champion,* courtesy British Columbia Archives, D-07573 [*Herstory 1999*].

p. 45 "Sinking Fast, No Regrets," cartoon from the *Grain Growers' Guide,* 29 November 1916, courtesy Saskatchewan Archives Board, slide 127 [*Herstory 1980*].

p. 46 Graphic by Cathryn Miller [*Herstory 1977*]

p. 46 Laura McCully, first published in John Garvin (ed.), *Canadian Poets.* Toronto: McClelland & Stewart, 1926 [*Herstory 1977*].

p. 47 Illustration by Ricardo, first published in *The Canadian Magazine,* July 1930 [*Herstory 1995*].

p. 47 "The Door Steadily Opens," cartoon from the *Grain Growers' Guide,* 21 September 1910 [*Herstory 1974*].

p. 48 Presentation of petition by Political Equality League for Enfranchisement of Women, 23 December 1915, courtesy Archives of Manitoba, Events 173/3 (N2484) [*Herstory 1979*].

p. 49 "19 April 1916" (Murphy, Jamieson and McClung), courtesy City of Edmonton Archives, EA-10-2070 [*Herstory 1977*].

p. 50 Alice Jamieson, courtesy Glenbow Archives, NA-2315-1 [*Herstory 1990*].

p. 51 Sarah Ramsland, courtesy Leonore Andrews [*Herstory 1978*].

p. 51 Roberta MacAdams campaign poster, courtesy Glenbow Archives, NA-1404-3 [*Herstory 1980*].

p. 51 Dorise Nielsen campaign pamphlet, courtesy Saskatchewan Archives Board, pamphlet collection G-96.1, United Progressive Movement [*Herstory 1974*].

p. 52 Agnes Macphail, courtesy Univ. of Saskatchewan Archives, Saskatoon Women's Calendar Collective fonds.

p. 53 Maquette for the "Famous Five" sculpture, photograph by Mark Mennie, courtesy Famous 5 Foundation [*Herstory 2000*].

p. 53 Emily Murphy conducting juvenile court, courtesy City of Edmonton Archives, EA-10-2010.

p. 54 Nellie McClung, courtesy Univ. of Saskatchewan Archives, Saskatoon Women's Calendar Collective fonds [*Herstory 2000*].

p. 55 Henrietta Muir Edwards, courtesy Glenbow Archives, NA-2607-1 [*Herstory 2000*].

p. 55 Irene Parlby, courtesy Glenbow Archives, NA-273-1 [*Herstory 2000*].

p. 56 Louise McKinney, courtesy Univ. of Saskatchewan Archives, Saskatoon Women's Calendar Collective fonds.

p. 57 Charlotte Whitton, courtesy Diefenbaker Canada Centre.

p. 57 Florence McOrmond, courtesy Grant McOrmond [*Herstory 1986*].

p. 58 Cairine Wilson, courtesy National Archives of Canada C-8408 [*Herstory 1996*].

p. 59 Thérèse Casgrain, ca 1940s, photograph by La Rose, courtesy National Archives of Canada, PA-178194 [*Herstory 1974*].

p. 59 Thérèse Casgrain, 1967, courtesy National Archives of Canada PA-127292 [*Herstory 2000*].

p. 60 Louise Lucas, illustration by H. Hutton, courtesy Western Development Museum (Saskatoon) [*Herstory 1975*].

p. 61 Ellen Fairclough, courtesy Diefenbaker Canada Centre.

p. 63 Flora MacDonald, courtesy Flora MacDonald [*Herstory 2000*].

p. 64 Flora MacDonald, courtesy Diefenbaker Canada Centre.

p. 65 Cap à l'Aigle, Québec, photograph by William James Topley, courtesy National Archives of Canada, C-17814 [*Herstory 2000*].

p. 66 Irene Murdoch, photograph by W. Petrigo, *Network of Saskatchewan Women Newsletter* [*Herstory 1975*].

p. 67 Alberta church women, courtesy Provincial Archives of Alberta, B9533 [*Herstory 1991*].

p. 68 Ethel Ewaysecan, courtesy Poundmaker Historical Centre [*Herstory 1998*].

p. 69 Rosemary Brown, courtesy Rosemary Brown [*Herstory 2000*].

p. 70 52% Solution, courtesy *Western Star,* [Corner Brook, NF] [*Herstory 1989*].

p. 71 Nellie Cournoyea, courtesy Nellie Cournoyea [*Herstory 1994*].

p. 72 Mary Simon, photo by Andrews-Newton Ltd [*Herstory 1988*].

p. 72 Ethel Blondin-Andrew, courtesy Ethel Blondin-Andrew [*Herstory 1992*].

p. 73 Rosemarie Kuptana, courtesy William Belsey, photographer [*Herstory 1995*].

p. 74 Delia Opekokew, courtesy Delia Opekokew [*Herstory 1996*].

p. 75 Elizabeth Pauline MacCallum, courtesy National Archives of Canada, PA-112766 [*Herstory 1993*].

p. 76 Louise Fréchette, courtesy Louise Fréchette and the United Nations photo archives [*Herstory 1995*].

p. 77 Bertha Wilson, courtesy Bertha Wilson [*Herstory 2000*].

p. 78 Louise Arbour, photograph by V. Tony Hauser, courtesy International Criminal Tribunal for the former Yugoslavia, and Louise Arbour [*Herstory 1999*].

p. 79 Kim Campbell, courtesy *The StarPhoenix* [Saskatoon] [*Herstory 2000*].

p. 80 Women in front of YWCA, Toronto, ca 1913, courtesy National Archives of Canada, PA-126710.

p. 82 Mary Sheffield, courtesy Donna Strawson, Fred Victor Mission, Toronto [*Herstory 1994*].

p. 83 Lutie DesBrisay, first published in H.P. Wood, *They Blazed the Trail.* [*Herstory 1980*].

p. 84 Agnes Machar, first published in H.J. Morgan, *Types of Canadian Women.* Toronto: William Briggs, 1903 [*Herstory 1989*].

p. 84 Lady Edgar, first published in H.J. Morgan, *Types of Canadian Women*. Toronto: William Briggs, 1903 [*Herstory 1996*].

p. 85 Mary Ann Shadd Cary, courtesy National Archives of Canada, C-29977 [*Herstory 1975*].

p. 85 Margret Benedictsson, courtesy University of Manitoba Archives, Icelandic Collection [*Herstory 1996*].

p. 86 Joséphine Dandurand, first published in H.J. Morgan, *Types of Canadian Women*. Toronto: William Briggs, 1903 [*Herstory 1988*].

p. 87 Marie Lacoste Gérin-Lajoie, first published in National Council of Women, *Women of Canada: Their Life and Work*. Ottawa: National Council of Women, 1900 [*Herstory 1989*].

p. 88 "Le Travail," courtesy National Archives of Canada, C-108134 [*Herstory 1987*].

p. 89 "Everybody's Doing It," first published in the *National Council of Women Yearbook, 1915-1916* [*Herstory 1982*].

p. 89 Anna Leonowens, courtesy Nova Scotia Archives and Records Management, [*Herstory 1980*].

p. 90 The Holman sisters, courtesy Jean Miller [*Herstory 1999*].

p. 90 Lady Aberdeen, first published in National Council of Women, *Women of Canada: Their Life and Work*. Ottawa: National Council of Women, 1900 [*Herstory 1985*].

p. 91 Four VON district nurses, 1898, first published in J.M. Gibbon, *The Victorian Order of Nurses for Canada, Fiftieth Anniversary, 1897-1947*. Ottawa: VON Canada, 1947 [*Herstory 1988*].

p. 91 VON district nurse, 1922, courtesy British Columbia Archives, file 149 BC Organizations, catalogue # 69898, negative D-6359 [*Herstory 1992*].

p. 92 Adelaide Hoodless, [*Herstory 1977*].

p. 93 Federated Women's Institutes of Canada, courtesy City of Edmonton Archives, 662448 [*Herstory 1999*].

p. 93 Helen Macmurchy, courtesy Univ. of Toronto Archives, Department of Graduate Records, A73-0026/293 (67) 000 [*Herstory 1994*].

p. 94 "The Face of Poverty," courtesy City of Toronto Archives, James Collection, no. 676 [*Herstory 1995*].

p. 95 Annie Gale, courtesy Glenbow Archives, NA-2393-3 [*Herstory 1996*].

p. 95 Cherry pickers, courtesy Phyllis Davidson [*Herstory 1988*].

p. 96 Weaving at a loom, courtesy National Archives of Canada, PA-040744 [*Herstory 1975*].

p. 96 Violet McNaughton, Zoe Haight, and Erma Stocking, courtesy Saskatchewan Archives Board, R-A8490 [*Herstory 1987*].

p. 97 Society of Independent Spinsters, courtesy Univ. of Alberta Archives, Ethel Anderson Collection [*Herstory 1981*].

p. 98 Adelaide Plumptre, courtesy City of Toronto Archives, SC349 #7 [*Herstory 1991*].

p. 99 Savella Stechishin, courtesy *The StarPhoenix,* [Saskatoon] Saskatchewan Archives Board S-SP-B5438 (1).

p. 99 Mary Anna Wigley, courtesy British Columbia Archives, Arthur Wigley file, HP 59197 [*Herstory 1991*].

p. 100 Women's Labour League, ca 1925, courtesy Archives of Manitoba [*Herstory 1980*].

p. 101 Elizabeth Bagshaw, courtesy the *Hamilton Spectator* [*Herstory 1979*].

p. 102 Dorothea Palmer, courtesy *Maclean's* magazine [*Herstory 1976*].

p. 102 Babes and nurses, courtesy Archives of Manitoba, Foote Collection [*Herstory 1981*].

p. 103 Mary Panagoosho Cousins, courtesy National Film Board of Canada [*Herstory 1974*].

p. 103 Well Baby Clinic, courtesy Provincial Archives of Alberta, A-11763 [*Herstory 1993*].

p. 104 Mothers' Council Demonstration, courtesy Glenbow Archives, NA-3634-10 [*Herstory 1993*].

p. 104 Winnifred Stewart, courtesy *Edmonton Journal* and Provincial Archives of Alberta J-5037.

p. 105 Carrie Best, courtesy Black Cultural Centre for Nova Scotia [*Herstory 1995*].

p. 106 Mary Helen Moonen, courtesy *Wetaskiwin Times* and the City of Wetaskiwin Archives [*Herstory 1992*].

p. 106 Laure Gaudreault, first published in E.B. Allaire, *Profils féminins*. Québec: Editions Garneau, 1967 [*Herstory 1977*].

p. 107 Federation of Women Teachers' Associations of Ontario, courtesy FWTAO [*Herstory 1995*].

p. 108 Immigrant Women of Saskatchewan, courtesy Nayda Veeman [*Herstory 1990*].

p. 109 Mrs Hoy Kam Gee and Mrs Jou Lee, courtesy National Archives of Canada, PA-124939 [*Herstory 2001*].

p. 110 Leone Pippard, courtesy Leone Pippard [*Herstory 1992*].

p. 111 Mary Jo Leddy, courtesy Mary Jo Leddy [*Herstory 1989*].

p. 112 Kathie Storrie, courtesy Kathie Storrie [*Herstory 1981*].

p. 113 Norma Baumel Joseph, courtesy Norma Baumel Joseph [*Herstory 1992*].

p. 114 Yvonne Peters, courtesy Yvonne Peters.

p. 115 Shirley Turcotte, courtesy National Film Board of Canada [*Herstory 1990*].

p. 116 Peggy Mason, courtesy Department of External Affairs [*Herstory 1992*].

p. 117 The Life Quilt for Breast Cancer, photograph by Robert Coates, courtesy Judy Reimer [*Herstory 1999*].

p. 117 Flora Mike, courtesy Univ. of Saskatchewan Archives, Saskatoon Women's Calendar Collective fonds [*Herstory 1999*].

p. 118 December 6th Women's Grove Memorial, Manitoba, courtesy Sally Papso [*Herstory 1998*].

p. 119 Heidi Rathjen, courtesy Heidi Rathjen [*Herstory 1999*].

p. 120 Interval House illustration by Candace Savage [*Herstory 1979*].

p. 120 Veronica Strong-Boag, [*Herstory 1992*].

p. 121 Jane Jacobs, courtesy Jane Jacobs.

p. 122 Toronto Black Women's Collective, courtesy National Film Board [*Herstory 1994*].

p. 123 Women's prison, 1895, courtesy National Archives of Canada, PA-27437 [*Herstory 1975*].

p. 123 Joan Lavallee, courtesy Univ. of Saskatchewan Archives, Saskatoon Women's Calendar Collective fonds [*Herstory 1995*].

p. 124 Mary Ellen Turpel-Lafond, courtesy Federation of Saskatchewan Indian Nations.

p. 125 "Listening to the radio," courtesy Glenbow Archives, NA-1319-1 [*Herstory 1996*].

p. 125 Major appliances, courtesy Saskatchewan Archives Board Ag.12.II.80 [*Herstory 1990*].

p. 126 Carol Lees, courtesy Carol Lees [*Herstory 1995*].

p. 126 Home Economics students, 1950, courtesy British Columbia Archives HP74146 [*Herstory 1993*].

p. 127 Erna Seeghal sewing, courtesy National Archives of Canada, PA-127040 [*Herstory 1999*].

p. 128 Mount Allison graduates, courtesy Mount Allison Univ. Archives, acc. 000 540 [*Herstory 1994*].

p. 130 Elsie Hall, courtesy Univ. of Saskatchewan College of Law [*Herstory 1993*].

p. 130 Mary Electa Adams, courtesy Mount Allison Univ. Archives, acc. 000 021 [*Herstory 1993*].

p. 131 Nisbet School, courtesy Provincial Archives of Alberta, H530 [*Herstory 1991*].

p. 132 Georgina McGill, courtesy Saskatoon Public Library Local History Room, LH 2692 [*Herstory 1988*].

p. 132 Mary McAlpine, courtesy Univ. of New Brunswick Archives [*Herstory 1997*].

p. 133 Emily Stowe, courtesy Univ. of Saskatchewan Archives, Saskatoon Women's Calendar Collective fonds [*Herstory 1974*].

p. 133 Quaker women, courtesy Univ. of Saskatchewan Archives, Saskatoon Women's Calendar Collective fonds [*Herstory 1977*].

p. 134 Augusta Stowe-Gullen, courtesy Univ. of Saskatchewan Archives, Saskatoon Women's Calendar Collective fonds [*Herstory 1974*].

p. 134 Elizabeth Smith-Shortt, first published in Carlotta Hacker, *The Indomitable Lady Doctors.* Toronto: Clarke, Irwin & Co., 1974 [*Herstory 1980*].

p. 135 A Girl from Canada, courtesy National Archives of Canada, C-63256 [*Herstory 1988*].

p. 136 Canada's Call to Women, courtesy Glenbow Archives [*Herstory 1996*].

p. 137 Immigrants for Domestic Service, courtesy National Archives of Canada, C-009652 [*Herstory 1975*].

p. 139 Telephone operators' picnic, courtesy City of Vancouver Archives, CVA-17-90 [*Herstory 1993*].

p. 140 Telephone operators, courtesy City of Vancouver Archives, CVA-17-44 [*Herstory 1992*].

p. 140 Clara Brett Martin, first published in H.J. Morgan, *Types of Canadian Women.* Toronto: William Briggs, 1903 [*Herstory 1979*].

p. 141 Kit Coleman, first published in H.J. Morgan, *Types of Canadian Women.* Toronto: William Briggs, 1903 [*Herstory 1976*].

p. 141 Edith Berkeley, courtesy Mary Needler Arai [*Herstory 1988*].

p. 142 Carrie Derick, courtesy National Archives of Canada, C-68506 [*Herstory 1976*].

p. 143 Jennie Smillie Robertson, courtesy Univ. of Toronto Archives [*Herstory 1987*].

p. 143 Women's College Hospital, first published in *History of Women's College Hospital,* 1974 [*Herstory 1977*].

p. 144 Alice Wilson, courtesy Geological Survey of Canada [*Herstory 1974*].

p. 144 Ethel Mary Cartwright, courtesy Univ. of Saskatchewan Archives, A-3222 [*Herstory 1994*].

p. 145 Black women graduates, courtesy National Film Board of Canada [*Herstory 1991*].

p. 146 "Wings for the Ladies," first published in *Canadian Aviation Magazine,* 1943 [*Herstory 1974*].

p. 146 Grace Hutchison and Nellie Carson, courtesy Saskatchewan Archives Board, A-9579 [*Herstory 1985*].

p. 147 "Lady aviator," courtesy Provincial Archives of Alberta, A. Blyth Collection, BL15 [*Herstory 1992*].

p. 148 Mona Harragin, courtesy Glenbow Archives, NA-2677-1 [*Herstory 1988*].

p. 149 Lydia Gruchy, Univ. of Saskatchewan Archives, Saskatoon Women's Calendar Collective fonds, courtesy Lydia Gruchy [*Herstory 1976*].

p. 150 Illustration by Sylvia Regnier [*Herstory 1981*].

p. 151 Lunch room, 1916, courtesy National Archives of Canada, PA-24439 [*Herstory 1975*].

p. 151 WWI munitions worker, first published in *Women in the Production of Munitions in Canada*. Ottawa: Imperial Munitions Board Canada, 1916 [*Herstory 1991*].

p. 152 WWI munitions factory, courtesy National Archives of Canada, PA-24627 [*Herstory 1985*].

p. 152 Shop stewards, 1942, courtesy North Vancouver Museum and Archives, 8073 [*Herstory 1995*].

p. 153 Three factory women, courtesy National Archives of Canada [*Herstory 1982*].

p. 153 "The Newest Creation," first published in the *National Council of Women Yearbook, 1917-1918* [*Herstory 1981*].

p. 153 "Canada Calls" recruiting poster, courtesy Desmond Morton [*Herstory 1994*].

p. 154 CWAC, courtesy National Archives of Canada, PA-141007 [*Herstory 1994*].

p. 154 Olive Carroll, courtesy Olive Carroll Roeckner [*Herstory 1996*].

p. 155 Kathleen Jeffs, courtesy Canadian Dietetic Association [*Herstory 1980*].

p. 155 Victory bonds poster, courtesy National Archives of Canada, C-91844 [*Herstory 1994*].

p. 155 Warrior's Day parade, courtesy City of Toronto Archives, James Collection, no. 727 [*Herstory 1995*].

p. 156 Mary Doyle, courtesy National Archives of Canada, C-124548 [*Herstory 1986*].

p. 156 Toronto transit conductor, courtesy National Archives of Canada, PA-54029 [*Herstory 1999*].

p. 157 Luise Herzberg, courtesy Paul Herzberg [*Herstory 1996*].

p. 158 Nellie Andrews, courtesy Victoria Univ. / United Church of Canada Archives [*Herstory 1989*].

p. 159 Mary "Bonnie" Baker, courtesy Saskatchewan Sports Hall of Fame [*Herstory 1991*].

p. 160 Henrietta Goplen, courtesy Henrietta Goplen [*Herstory 1991*].

p. 161 Women RCMP, photograph by Don Healy, courtesy *The Leader-Post* [Regina] [*Herstory 1979*].

p. 162 Deanna Brasseur, courtesy Deanna Brasseur [*Herstory 1993*].

p. 163 Christine Silverberg, courtesy Calgary Police Service [*Herstory 2000*].

p. 164 Antoinette Morteas, courtesy Peggy Smith [*Herstory 1986*].

p. 164 Women workers, courtesy National Archives of Canada, PA-24363 [*Herstory 1975*].

p. 165 Regina Women's Construction Co-op, courtesy Regina Women's Construction Co-op [*Herstory 2001*].

p. 166 First Ascent, courtesy National Archives of Canada, PA-99822 [*Herstory 1982*].

p. 168 Mattie Gunterman, courtesy Vancouver Public Library, #2215 [*Herstory 1976*].

p. 169 Hannah Maynard composite, courtesy British Columbia Archives, 92057 [*Herstory 1985*].

p. 170 "Farmerettes," courtesy Archives of Manitoba, Jessop Collection 199, N3230 [*Herstory 1996*].

p. 171 Cora Hind, courtesy Univ. of Saskatchewan Archives, Saskatoon Women's Calendar Collective fonds [*Herstory 1974*].

p. 172 Maude Abbott, first published in Carlotta Hacker, *The Indomitable Lady Doctors*. Toronto: Clarke, Irwin & Co., 1974 [*Herstory 1978*].

p. 172 Georgina Pope, first published in H.J. Morgan, *Types of Canadian Women*. Toronto: William Briggs, 1903 [*Herstory 1978*].

p. 173 Ethel Johns, courtesy Univ. of British Columbia Archives, M. Street fonds [*Herstory 1980*].

p. 174 Maud Leonora Menten, courtesy Univ. of Toronto Archives, Department of Graduate Records file, A73-0026/318 (11a) [*Herstory 1991*].

p. 175 Frances McGill, courtesy Saskatchewan Archives Board, R-A 12654 [*Herstory 1987*].

p. 176 World champion woman steer roper, courtesy Saskatoon Public Library Local History Room, LH 2868 [*Herstory 1974*].

p. 176 Edmonton Grads, courtesy Univ. of Saskatchewan Archives, Saskatoon Women's Calendar Collective fonds [*Herstory 1975*].

p. 177 Fannie Rosenfeld, courtesy National Archives of Canada [*Herstory 1979*].

p. 177, 1928 Olympic relay team, courtesy National Archives of Canada, PA-150984 [*Herstory 1999*].

p. 178 Ethel Catherwood, courtesy Saskatoon Public Library Local History Room, LH 3473 [*Herstory 1974*].

p. 178 Hockey team, courtesy Archives of Ontario, Duncan Dunoran Photograph Collection, C 128-1-4-0-12 (I0002412) [*Herstory 1996*].

p. 179 Dorothea Mitchell, courtesy Mitchell Press Ltd [*Herstory 1978*].

p. 179 "Fastest fingers," Alexandra Studio, 1928 [*Herstory 1987*].

p. 180 Mary Pickford, courtesy National Archives of Canada, PA 67269 [*Herstory 1996*].

p. 181 Olive Ross, courtesy Provincial Archives of Alberta, 70.447/7c [*Herstory 1991*].

p. 181 Nursing sisters, WWI [*Herstory 1999*].

p. 182 Plucking chickens, first published in *Multiculturalism,* vol. 11, no. 4 [*Herstory 1981*].

p. 182 Molly Lamb Bobak, courtesy National Archives of Canada, 113771 [*Herstory 1996*].

p. 183 A family of scientists, courtesy Marianne Gosztonyi Ainley [*Herstory 1988*].

p. 183 Alice Vibert Douglas, courtesy Queen's Univ. Archives [*Herstory 1990*].

p. 184 Margaret Newton, courtesy Univ. of Saskatchewan Archives [*Herstory 1987*].

p. 184 Elsie Gregory MacGill, courtesy National Archives of Canada, PA-139429 [*Herstory 1989*].

p. 185 Elinor Black, courtesy Fred Black [*Herstory 1995*].

p. 186 Sylvia Fedoruk, courtesy Univ. of Saskatchewan [*Herstory 1988*].

p. 187 Mabel Timlin, courtesy Univ. of Saskatchewan Archives, [*Herstory 1976*].

p. 188 Lily Inglis, courtesy *The Kingston Whig Standard* [*Herstory 1988*].

p. 188 Helen Creighton, Univ. of Saskatchewan Archives, Saskatoon Women's Calendar Collective fonds, courtesy Helen Creighton [*Herstory 1976*].

p. 189 Eleanor Milne, photograph by Michel Proux, courtesy George Wilkes [*Herstory 1991*].

p. 190 Jean Sutherland Boggs, first published in *Communique* [*Herstory 1978*].

p. 190 Mary Scorer, courtesy Aleine Fiddler [*Herstory 1990*].

p. 191 Sheila Fischman, photograph by Donald Winkler, courtesy Sheila Fischman [*Herstory 1988*].

p. 192 Diane Thornton Dupuy, courtesy Diane Thornton Dupuy [*Herstory 1994*].

p. 193 Janina Fialkowska, courtesy Janina Fialkowska and Harry Oesterle [*Herstory 1992*].

p. 194 Lynn Johnston, photograph by Ed Eng Photography, courtesy Lynn Johnston.

p. 195 Marie-Louise Gay, courtesy Marie-Louise Gay [*Herstory 1989*].

p. 196 Pauline Jewett, photograph by Vivian Frankel [*Herstory 1976*].

p. 197 Ellen Bruce, photograph by Angela Wheelock [*Herstory 1990*].

p. 198 Joan Donaldson, courtesy CBC Newsworld [*Herstory 1993*].

p. 199 May Ebbitt Cutler, courtesy *Maclean's* magazine [*Herstory 1978*].

p. 199 Wendy Clay, courtesy Office of the Surgeon-General [*Herstory 1996*].

p. 200 Denise Verreault, courtesy Denise Verreault [*Herstory 1991*].

p. 201 Roberta Bondar, courtesy Roberta Bondar [*Herstory 1989*].

p. 202 Vicki Keith, courtesy Vicki Keith [*Herstory 1993*].

p. 203 Joan Oliver, courtesy Glenbow Archives, NA-4868-246 [*Herstory 2003*].

p. 204 Silken Laumann, courtesy Melanie Mcvittie, Sylvia Hamilton and Silken Laumann [*Herstory 1994*].

p. 205 Sylvie Fréchette, photograph by Claude Denis, courtesy Sylvie Fréchette [*Herstory 1995*].

p. 206 Denise Martin, courtesy Denise Martin [*Herstory 1999*].

p. 206 Catriona LeMay Doan, courtesy *The StarPhoenix* [Saskatoon] [*Herstory 2000*].

p. 207 Olympic curling team, photograph by Brian Schlosser, courtesy *The Leader-Post* [Regina] [*Herstory 2000*].

p. 208 Ursuline orchestra, courtesy Archives des Ursulines de Québec [*Herstory 1995*].

p. 210 Susanna Moodie, first published in H.J. Morgan, *Types of Canadian Women.* Toronto: William Briggs, 1903 [*Herstory 1975*].

p. 211 Rosanna Leprohon, first published in H.J. Morgan, *Types of Canadian Women.* Toronto: William Briggs, 1903 [*Herstory 1987*].

p. 212 Emma Albani, courtesy National Archives of Canada, PA-127289.

p. 212 Maud Allan, courtesy Victoria and Albert Theatre Museum, Gabrielle Enthoven Collection [*Herstory 1990*].

p. 213 Charlotte Morrison, first published in H.J. Morgan, *Types of Canadian Women.* Toronto: William Briggs, 1903 [*Herstory 1976*].

p. 214 Two women with camera, courtesy National Archives of Canada PA-12938 [*Herstory 1992*].

p. 214 Pauline Johnson, courtesy National Archives of Canada, C-146693.

p. 215 Koo-Tucktuck, courtesy British Museum, MM002071 [*Herstory 1996*].

p. 215 Self-portrait, Frances Johnston, courtesy David Mandeville [*Herstory 1982*].

p. 216 Mary Dignam, first published in *Women of Canada, Their Life and Work. Ottawa: National Council of Women, 1900* [*Herstory 1977*].

p. 217 Frances Loring and Florence Wyle, first published in Rebecca Sisler, *The Girls.* Toronto: Clarke, Irwin & Co., 1972 [*Herstory 1975*].

p. 218 Mary Wrinch artwork, courtesy National Gallery of Canada [*Herstory 1977*].

p. 218 "Market Among the Ruins of Ypres," artwork by Mary Riter Hamilton, courtesy National Archives of Canada, C-132012 [*Herstory 1989*].

p. 219 Emily Carr, first published in Emily Carr, *Growing Pains: The Autobiography of Emily Carr.* Toronto: Oxford Univ. Press, 1946 [*Herstory 1974*].

p. 220 Maud Lewis, courtesy Bob Brooks Photography [*Herstory 1999*].

p. 221 Paraskeva Clark, courtesy

National Film Board of Canada, S-1949 [*Herstory 1991*].

p. 221 "Girl on a Hill," artwork by Prudence Heward, 1928, courtesy National Gallery of Canada, no. 3678.

p. 222 Celia Franca in *Giselle,* 1956, courtesy National Archives of Canada, PA-153948.

p. 223 Violet Archer, courtesy Univ. of Alberta Archives.

p. 223 Portia White, courtesy Nova Scotia Archives and Records Management [*Herstory 1978*].

p. 224 Karen Kain in *Don Juan,* 1974, courtesy National Archives of Canada, PA-133984.

p. 226 Lucy Maud Montgomery, courtesy National Archives of Canada, C-011299 [*Herstory 1977*].

p. 227 Martha Ostenso, first published in Kunitz, *Twentieth Century Authors.* New York: Wilson, 1942 [*Herstory 1978*].

p. 227 Gabrielle Roy, first published in Gabrielle Roy, *Ces enfants de ma vie.* Ottawa: Editions Internationales Alain Stanké, 1977 [*Herstory 1979*].

p. 228 Anne Hébert, courtesy National Film Board of Canada [*Herstory 1978*].

p. 229 Jane Rule, photograph by Betty Fairbank [*Herstory 1978*].

p. 230 Alice Munro, courtesy John Reeves, photographer [*Herstory 1978*].

p. 231 Margaret Laurence, photograph by Beverly Rockett [*Herstory 1975*].

p. 232 Joy Kogawa, courtesy Joy Kogawa [*Herstory 1986*].

p. 233 Myrna Kotash, courtesy Univ. of Regina Archives.

p. 234 Margaret Atwood, courtesy W.E. Toye [*Herstory 1977*].

p. 235 Carol Shields, [*Herstory 1982*].

p. 236 Freda Ahenakew, courtesy Univ. of Saskatchewan Archives.

p. 237 Anne Anderson, courtesy *Edmonton Journal.*

p. 237 Alanis Obomsawin, courtesy Secretary of State [*Herstory 1981*].

p. 238 Norma Bailey, courtesy National Film Board of Canada, S-19232 [*Herstory 1993*].

p. 239 WTN logo, Univ. of Saskatchewan Archives, Saskatoon Women's Calendar Collective fonds, courtesy WTN [*Herstory 1994*].

p. 240 Kate and Anna McGarrigle

p. 241 Buffy Sainte-Marie, courtesy Michelle Vignesse [*Herstory 1979*].

p. 242 Joni Mitchell, photograph by Larry Klein, courtesy Myrtle Anderson [*Herstory 1992*].
p. 243 Lillian Allen, courtesy Rafy [*Herstory 1989*].

p. 243 Connie Kaldor, courtesy Suzanne Campagne and Connie Kaldor.

p. 244 Loreena McKennitt, courtesy Loreena McKennitt [*Herstory 1992*].

p. 245 Jane Siberry, courtesy Jane Siberry [*Herstory 1991*].

p. 246 Needleworkers, courtesy Port Colborne Historical and Marine Museum [*Herstory 1989*].

p. 246 k.d. lang, courtesy Caryn Weiss, *Visages* [*Herstory 1994*].

p. 247 Pitseolak, courtesy Dorothy Eber [*Herstory 1980*].

p. 247 Quilters, courtesy National Archives of Canada, PA-44890 [*Herstory 2000*].

p. 248 Mary Pratt, courtesy John Reeves [*Herstory 1987*].

p. 249 Daphne Odjig, courtesy Daphne Odjig [*Herstory 1987*].

p. 250 "The Pool," artwork by Dorothy Knowles, courtesy Dorothy Knowles and the Mendel Art Gallery [*Herstory 1979*].

p. 250 Angelique Merasty, photograph by Frank Fieber [*Herstory 1985*].

ABOUT THE EDITORS

A writer, editor, teacher, and activist who helped shape the women's movement in Saskatchewan, GAIL YOUNGBERG grew up in Kirkland Lake, Ontario. She attended the University of Toronto, and moved to Saskatoon with her husband in 1964. She joined the Saskatoon Women's Calendar Collective in 1986, focusing on Native issues, family violence, and pay equity. Gail died in December 2000.

A native of Saskatoon, MONA HOLMLUND has worked as a video producer, lecturer, researcher, and writer. Her work is focused on women's history, gender, and representation, including *Women Together: Portraits of Love, Commitment, and Life* (1999). Mona joined the *Herstory* Collective in 1992. She currently lives in Cambridge, England, where she is completing a PHD in cultural history.